Cusanus

Cusanus

THE LEGACY OF
LEARNED IGNORANCE

edited by Peter J. Casarella

The Catholic University of America Press
Washington, D.C.

The paper used in this publication meets the minimum requirements
of American National Standards for Information Science—Permanence of Paper for Printed Library Materials, ANSI Z39.48-1984.
∞

LIBRARY OF CONGRESS CATALOGING-IN-PUBLICATION DATA

Cusanus : the legacy of learned ignorance / edited by
Peter J. Casarella.

     p. cm.

    Includes bibliographical references and indexes.

    ISBN 13: 978-0-8132-1426-9 (alk. paper)

    ISBN 10: 0-8132-1426-2 (alk. paper)

    1. Nicholas, of Cusa, Cardinal, 1401–1464.   I. Casarella,
Peter J.   II. Title.

BX4705.N58C77 2006

230′.2′092—dc22

                  2005000801

❧ Contents

Acknowledgments

As the outcome of an academic conference, the publication of this volume owes not a little to the organizations that sponsored that event. These include the American Cusanus Society, the Lutheran Theological Seminary at Gettysburg, Long Island University, C. W. Post Campus, and the Lumen Christi Institute. The Catholic University of America, Washington, D.C., was the site of the conference, and the editor would like to thank the following sponsors from this institution: the School of Theology and Religious Studies, the School of Philosophy, the Center for Medieval and Byzantine Studies, the Council for Research in Values and Philosophy, and the Columbus School of Law.

A special word of thanks goes to two outstanding research assistants, Meredith Rice and James Lee, for their assistance with the editing of the manuscript. David McGonagle, Theresa Walker, and the staff at the Catholic University of America Press were both gracious and helpful in the editing process. Finally, I would like to thank the contributors, without whose efforts neither the symposium in Washington nor this volume would have been conceivable.

Preface

It is my privilege as president of the American Cusanus Society to write a brief preface to this excellent collection of studies on Nicholas of Cusa (1401–64) and his philosophical, theological, political, ecclesiological, mathematical, and cosmological ideas. These studies by leading Cusanus scholars from many countries grew out of a sixth-centennial symposium to celebrate Cusanus's birth, which was held at the Catholic University of America in 2001 under the title of "Nicholas of Cusa: 1401–2001."

A philosopher, theologian, canon lawyer, mathematician, church-statesman, and cardinal, Cusanus was one of the most original and important thinkers of the fifteenth century. Seriously concerned about the nature of God, the relationship between the infinite and the finite, and other fundamental philosophical, theological, and scientific problems, he was at the same time deeply involved in the practical, legal, and political problems of his day, such as the Council of Basel (1435–37), the imperial diets of Nuremberg (1438), Mainz (1439), Frankfurt am Main (1400 and 1442), and again Nuremberg (1443), the legation journey to Germany and the Low Countries (1451–52), and the reform of the monasteries and the clergy of South Tyrol, Orvieto, and Rome. In his *Nikolaus Cusanus* (1964), which is as a whole critical of Cusanus, Karl Jaspers acknowledged: "[Cusanus] is the only one of the great philosophers to have led a busy life in the world from an early age to the day of his death."

In the studies collected here, the reader is invited to examine and ponder many of Cusanus's main ideas and concepts in various fields. Who is not intrigued by such concepts and ideas discussed in this book as "coincidence theology," "God as the *facies facierum* (exemplar of all faces)," "'comparative' or 'graded' infallibility," "perspective," "imperial humanism," "a finite infinity," and "a predecessor of Einstein's theory of relativity"? In the aftermath of the attacks on the World Trade Center and the Pentagon on September 11, 2001, and the recent war in Iraq, we are keenly aware not only of the sufferings of the victims and their families and the impact of terrorism, but also of the basic, underlying problems of religious tolerance and intolerance and of interreligious harmony and conflict. After the fall of Constantinople in 1453, Cusanus was, as is discussed in this book, certainly one of those who proposed a serious study of the Qur'an and advocated discussions with the Muslims.

Those perennial and current problems that occupied and engaged Cusanus's mind are studied and discussed by the authors of the chapters in this book. As Karsten Harries indicates, Paolo dal Pozzo Toscanelli (1397–1482), Italian humanist, mathematician, astronomer, geographer, and Cusanus's close friend from his Paduan days to his deathbed in Todi, is believed to have assisted Christopher Columbus (1451–1506), who instead of reaching his goal, "the Indies," which included Cipangu (Japan) and Cathay (China), described in detail by Marco Polo (1254?–1324) in his *Travels,* discovered America on his famous voyages. I would like to think that, if he were alive, Cusanus, who was familiar with Marco Polo's *Travels,* would be delighted to learn that the serious studies of his ideas and his influence could be produced as a book in the New World in commemoration of his sixth centenary.

On behalf of the American Cusanus Society, I wish to express our gratitude to the Catholic University of America for its willingness to hold the symposium in 2001 on its campus. With great sincerity, I wish to thank the members of the organizing committee (Gerald Christianson, Elizabeth Brient, Donald Duclow, and Thomas Izbicki) and its chair, Peter Casarella, for their arduous work in preparation for the conference. As the chair himself put it recently, we can now "see the fruits of our long labors for the 2001 celebration" in this important book.

MORIMICHI WATANABE
American Cusanus Society
Long Island University

⚭ Introduction
Peter J. Casarella

Nicholas of Cusa: 1401–2001

As Morimichi Watanabe has already indicated, the contributors to this volume all participated in a conference in October 2001 at the Catholic University of America to mark the sixth centenary of the birth of Nicholas of Cusa. The previous May some of the participants had also attended a gathering in Nicholas's birthplace. Following the precedent already set at the symposium in Bernkastel-Kues, the participants in the Washington conference discussed "Nicholas of Cusa: 1401–2001."[1] Although the two events were separated in time and place, serious effort was made in each case to link the one whom Klaus Kremer named "one of the greatest Germans of the fifteenth century" with the present.[2]

In fact, the six-hundredth jubilee for Cusanus studies witnessed commemorative events and academic conferences throughout the globe.[3] In its anticipation, members of the American Cusanus Society and others went to the Waseda University in Tokyo October 6–8, 2000. The proceedings from that conference were published in 2002.[4] Looking back, one appreciates more than ever these sage words from the preface of that book: "The location and the timing of the conference [at Waseda University], which took place one year before the chronological anniversary, fulfilled the old proverb: Light comes from the East."[5] Surveying the events of the

1. Cf. *600 Jahre Nikolaus von Kues 1401–2001,* ed. Helmut Gestrich, Klaus Kremer (Trier: Paulinus, 2003). This volume commemorates a weeklong celebration of Cusanus in his birthplace and includes remarks prepared for the occasion by the president of the Federal Republic of Germany as well as Pope John Paul II.

2. Klaus Kremer, *Nicholas of Cusa (1401–1464): One of the Greatest Germans of the 15th Century* (Trier: Paulinus, 2002).

3. Cf. Peter Casarella, "Reflections on the End of a Cusanus Jubilee Year," *American Cusanus Society Newsletter* 19, no. 1 (June 2002): 3–7.

4. *Nicholas of Cusa: A Medieval Thinker for the Modern Age,* ed. Kazuhiko Yamaki (Richmond, Surrey: Curzon Press, 2002).

5. Ibid., viii.

recent jubilee year, one can certainly agree that its sun rose in Tokyo but also that its radiance was felt in Menaggio (Italy), Bernkastel-Kues (Germany), Deventer (the Netherlands), Brixen-Bressanone (South Tyrol), Buenos Aires (Argentina), Coimbra (Portugal), Salamanca (Spain), Tours (France), and Olomouc (Czech Republic).[6] During the jubilee year the sun literally never set on the world of Cusanus scholarship. The jubilee was impressive in both the sudden upsurge of scholarly activity and the diversity of its multiple epicenters. Interest in Cusanus's life and thought had never been restricted to his native Germany, but previous generations of scholars scarcely knew on this scale either the breadth or the global scope of their task.

The Essays in This Volume

The essays do not represent a single, monolithic approach to the thought of Nicholas of Cusa but encompass rather four closely intertwined and overlapping kinds of research. One approach is to focus on the ancient and medieval tradition of which Nicholas saw himself to be a part. A second mode of inquiry looks at particular ideas or texts of Cusanus in their own right. A third method treats the figure and thought of Cusanus in terms of his relationship to other thinkers of the fifteenth century. Finally, a fourth perspective opens the door to a contemporary retrieval of Cusanus's thought. Only a few of the essays can be placed into one category alone, and some do not fit very well into any of the categories. The diverse voices of the volume are nonetheless all attuned to the multifaceted but still not discordant legacy of the thinker of the fifteenth century.

The volume opens with a consideration of a sermon of Nicholas of Cusa on the Lord's Prayer. Nancy Hudson introduces the text, which was translated from Nicholas's own Moselle-Franconian dialect by Frank Tobin. Although this quintessentially Cusan text has never before been published in a complete English translation, its inclusion here has as much to do with its philosophical and theological acuity as its (for Cusanus at least)

---

6. Cf. *American Cusanus Society Newsletter* 19, no. 1 (June 2002): 9–10. For a list of currently published proceedings from the 2001 events, see the suggestions for further reading at the end of this volume.

altogether unique vernacular form. As Hudson rightly notes, this sermon is in the first instance homiletic and practical in character, and Tobin's lucid translation sheds considerable light on how Cusanus used this medium to communicate his theory of learned ignorance to a nonphilosophical audience. The homiletic character of the text of 1441 does not prevent Cusanus from introducing themes that also appeared in his recently completed *De docta ignorantia* ("On Learned Ignorance," 1440), e.g., the notion of a wholly transcendent divine unity grounded in the Trinitarian union and manifest *mutatis mutandis* in the created world, the communal offer of divine forgiveness and spiritual bread mediated in and through the body of Christ, and a theology of naming that includes the distinctively Cusan strategy of articulating abstract thoughts by breaking linguistic compounds into their literal, semantic components. The sermon thus testifies to the legacy of learned ignorance in both form and content.

The second contribution, written by Bernard McGinn, deals with Nicholas of Cusa's contribution to the *via negativa* or apophatic tradition of Western mysticism. Although it is presented as an interpretation of Nicholas's treatise *De visione Dei* ("On the Vision of God"), McGinn also places Nicholas's project in the context of certain trends in the Christian Neoplatonic tradition of speculative theology. McGinn begins with the Biblical background to the question of whether God can be seen and then turns, inter alia, to Clement of Alexandria ("the first real encounter in the Christian tradition between Platonic mysticism and Christian spiritual teaching"), Plotinus, and Meister Eckhart.

One surprising conclusion of his essay is the discovery of a para-liturgical beginning to Cusanus's treatment of the icon in *De visione Dei*. Nicholas states that the omnivoyance and infinity of Christ's gaze begins to be revealed only when each brother following the icon in procession asks the other about its meaning. Seeing God takes on a semiotic character. Voices from the past are written into a text pregnant with liturgical and meditative meaning, which, however, admonishes that the invisible God of faith is quite distant from the way we normally look at things. Perhaps for the first time in the history of Christian mysticism, McGinn asserts, Cusanus was able to provide an account that integrated divine invisibility, the face-to-face vision promised in Scripture, and divinization understood as filiation.

Jasper Hopkins's essay on Nicholas of Cusa's relationship to Anselm of Canterbury contains a salutary admonition against reading Cusanus's texts solely through the lens of the present. Hopkins is highly critical of these who wish to see Nicholas's thought as a template or forerunner for post-Kantian styles of philosophizing and theologizing. While resonances with the post-Kantian heritage are clear (and acknowledged by Hopkins), he claims that the more urgent task for Cusanus research today is the sober assessment of Cusanus's differences from and relation to his immediate past. In this regard, Hopkins avers that Nicholas not only made use of St. Anselm's writings, but he sought to expand and supplement some of the ideas of Anselm that he incorporated into his own thought. This act of supplementing leads Cusanus to speak of God in an unusual way, for example, "God is the Being of being and the Not-being of not-being." In these paradoxical formulations, Hopkins maintains, "Anselm's thought becomes *aufgehoben:* it becomes subsumed, elevated, and transformed." Ironically employing a term famous for its Hegelian coinage, Hopkins thus illustrates the radical creativity imbedded in Cusanus's medieval heritage. For Hopkins one need not be proto-modern in order to break with timeworn traditions.

The next two essays introduce Cusanus's philosophy of God and of God's image in the human person, respectively. Louis Dupré's survey of the question of pantheism from Eckhart to Cusanus looks not only at historical relationships but also at the religious content of each thinker's thought. He claims that Cusanus in most essentials followed Eckhart's metaphysics, although he articulated the critical distinction between creator and creation more precisely than his Dominican predecessor. In Dupré's estimation Eckhart gets into trouble with ecclesiastical authorities for using language of Thomist vintage in new and daring ways. By contrast, Nicholas's theological genius lies in his avoidance of that set of technical terms and forging of his own language of transcendence, one that implies a reciprocal relationship of God to creation not wholly unlike contemporary process thought.

Wilhelm Dupré then takes up Cusanus's idea of the human person as the living image of God. Nicholas, he argues, builds upon a richly Trinitarian heritage of biblical, patristic, and medieval theology to focus on the image as experienced in ordinary existence. The awareness of being a *liv-*

ing image, he states, forces us to confront the meaning of human existence. On the most theoretical level, the image symbolizes the always imperfect assimilation of divine creativity in the finite configurations of the
world. Practically speaking, the image is itself a self-reflexive experiment,
an "autopoetic process" whereby "the mind becomes aware of God as it
discovers its true nature." Dupré also introduces the notion of the "affective" significance of the image. In real life images are never reproduced in
a purely mechanical way. The dynamics of understanding and creating
artifacts discloses an experience of beauty and as such offers a foretaste
of what Cusanus calls "the sweet unity of every delectable thing." The
yearning for beauty is present at the core of human existence. Learned ignorance prohibits a premature fulfillment of the striving, but "the divine
seed" implanted by God in our intellectual natures can mature without
limit in daily life.

Karsten Harries breaks new ground with his essay on Cusanus's possible relationship to the Renaissance theorist Leon Battista Alberti. The essay makes a strong case for the direct influence of Alberti's thinking on
the philosophy of Nicholas of Cusa even though Harries readily admits
that the evidence is entirely circumstantial as far as textual documentation
goes. But the scope of Harries's article is not just historical. Like Alberti,
Cusanus embraces a perspective construction, revalorizes the role of
sense perception, and favors a mathematical ordering of nature. Harries
also isolates an aesthetic bond between the two figures of the quattrocento. Following the Platonic admonition that beauty itself is what lets us
see, Cusanus insists (in the carbuncle metaphor of *De li non aliud* ["On the
Not Other"]) that the "substantial light" of an object can be seen more
clearly "in the glow of brighter splendor." For Cusanus beauty beckons
the viewer not only to more closely inspect individuals but to respond, in
Harries's words, to what lies outside "the house our reason built."

Whereas Harries lays the groundwork for a Cusan philosophical aesthetic, Walter Andreas Euler considers a specific work of art in relation to
Nicholas's remarkable syntheses of non-Christian religions, *De pace fidei*
("On the Peace of Faith") and *Cribratio alkorani* ("The Sifting of the
Qur'an"). Euler begins with the thesis put forward by the German art historian Wolfgang Speyer that a previously unattributed Italian painting depicts a dialogue between the founders of the three monotheistic religions:

Jesus, Moses, and Mohammed. The image, if properly identified and dated by Speyer, would then serve as a pictorial unfolding of some principles of dialogue found in Cusanus's two major attempts at a theology of religions.

Euler then turns to the image of Islam in the Cusan writings and uncovers both the conventional and the novel elements contained therein. First, although Cusanus adopts many of the purely polemical medieval teachings regarding Islam, his method of "sifting" through the text is thoroughly his own and still valuable for contemporary reflection. Second, the very notion that Islam contains a seed of truth and therefore contributes to an adequate understanding of the human path to God is developed in the *Cribratio alkorani* in precisely the same context in which Cusanus is making a defense of his Christological universalism. In other words, for Cusanus the consideration of truth *within* the Qur'an is enhanced rather than negated by a consideration of Christ as a cosmic mediator of salvation. If one is looking for a critical standard for modern interreligious dialogue, Cusanus's program is no doubt deficient. On the other hand, Euler lays the foundation for grasping how Cusanus's theology of religions can be viewed as a relatively synthetic whole.

Not nearly enough attention has been paid to Cusanus's role in the history of art, and what exists looks almost exclusively at the brief mention in *De visione Dei* of a self-portrait by the Flemish artist Rogier van der Weyden as well as the various links between Cusanus's theory of perspective and that of Italian humanists.[7] For that reason, we include in this volume a "brief report" by Il Kim that examines the conclusions of the first part of Euler's essay. Kim, who responded to Euler's presentation at the 2001 conference, subsequently traveled to the Franciscan convent in Sassoferrato that houses the painting discovered by Speyer.

---

7. See, for example, Clifton Olds, "Aspect and Perspective in Renaissance Thought: Nicholas of Cusa and Jan van Eyck," in *Nicholas of Cusa on Christ and the Church: Essays in Memory of Chandler McCuskey Brooks for the American Cusanus Society,* ed. Gerald Christianson and Thomas M. Izbicki (Leiden: E. J. Brill, 1996), 251–65; Graziella Vescovini, "Nicolas of Cusa, Alberti and the Architectonics of the Mind," in *Nexus II: Architecture and Mathematics,* ed. Kim Williams (Fucecchio: Edizioni dell'Erba, 1998), 159–71; Gerhard Wolf, "Nicolaus Cusanus 'liest' Leon Battista Alberti: Alter Deus und Narziß (1453)," in *Porträt,* ed. Rudolf Preimesberger, Hannah Baader, and Nicola Suthor (Berlin: Reimer, 1999), 201–9, and note 31 below.

The painting in question, it now appears, was repainted at a later date. The Mannerist style and use of oil on canvas point to a dating in the sixteenth century or even later. Furthermore, the three haloed figures thought by Speyer to be patterned on the dialogue of *De pace fidei* are shown by Kim to represent St. Luke, Moses, and Christ. The painting gives a unique perspective on the lawgiver from the Old Testament, but not the one attributed to it by Speyer. The figures reinforce the Franciscan order's renunciation of material wealth and indictment of the scandalous wealth of the Borgia Pope at the end of the fifteenth century, Alexander VI. Critical research based upon direct observation thus calls into question Speyer's generous attempt to trace the influence of Cusanus's ideal of interreligious harmony. Kim's careful analysis serves as an edifying lesson in how art historians and Cusanus scholars can test their ideas in mutual dialogue.

Cusanus occupied himself on a daily basis with affairs of the Church, and not just as a preacher. He was trained as a canon lawyer and pursued a wide variety of canonical and legal issues. As a philosopher, theologian, preacher, *and* canonist, Cusanus had a view of the Church that was central to his intellectual heritage. Thomas Prügl's exploration of Cusanus's concept of infallibility bears out a hitherto unrecognized connection between his philosophy and his ecclesiology. The concept of infallibility as it has developed since the nineteenth century has focused on the authority granted to the bishop of Rome. Cusanus, however, constructs a theory of the infallibility of the Church as such. Prügl makes a convincing argument that infallibility as an ecclesiological concept is just as important to Cusanus's thought as the notions of consent, representation, and reception, all of which are widely discussed in current Cusanus scholarship. To be sure, after Cusanus broke with the conciliarists at the Council of Basel and sided with the pro-papalist party that supported Pope Eugene IV, he modified his ideas about infallibility. Even his mature concept of ecclesial infallibility, however, possesses a range of meanings that look to the Church's sacramentality and is found in a context that highlights the saving activity of Christ. As a papalist, Cusanus remains skeptical about a view of infallibility constructed on purely human terms and still heeds the need for consent and reception in the Church.

The next two essays treat Nicholas of Cusa as a political thinker. Cary

Nederman's essay compares Cusanus's political theory with that of his humanist contemporary Aeneas Sylvius Piccolomini (Pope Pius II). Cusanus and Piccolomini represent two distinct alternatives to the civic republicanism of the fifteenth century. Whereas standard portraits of these two staunch defenders of "the old idea of universal Empire" highlight their resistance to the emerging autonomy of the nation-state, Nederman demonstrates that both thinkers, and especially Cusanus in his strong preference for political consent, acknowledge the conventional origins of imperial jurisdiction. Nederman labels the new theory "imperial humanism." It conforms to neither the strict imperialism of the Middle Ages (e.g., Dante) nor the incipient voluntarism and individualism of the modern age (e.g., John Locke, Thomas Hobbes). If Nederman's analysis here is correct, it appears that even in the realm of political structures the thinker of learned ignorance has bequeathed an unexpectedly creative vision and, at least in Nederman's estimation, a surprisingly resilient heritage.

Continuing with the theme of political thought, Paul Sigmund then considers the current debate regarding the relationship between medieval and modern constitutionalism. Sigmund's work on this particular question extends back to his 1963 Harvard dissertation, which was published as *Nicholas of Cusa and Medieval Political Thought*.[8] For the 2001 conference Sigmund identifies those elements of Cusanus's political thought that represent a break with the medieval tradition and those that remain firmly rooted in medieval political thought. This careful assessment of the exact sense of "constitutionalism" in the *De concordantia catholica* ("The Catholic Concordance") leads to a *via media* between Brian Tierney and Francis Oakley, on the one hand, and the critics of the continuity thesis (including, especially, Cary Nederman) on the other. An especially innovative aspect of Sigmund's proposal is the consideration of George Lawson's *Politica sacra et civilis* (1660) as a kind of way station between the still medieval metaphysics of hierarchy in the constitutionalism of Nicholas of Cusa and the definitively modern and individualist contract theory of John Locke.

Elizabeth Brient's essay returns to the theme of perspective already developed by Louis Dupré and Karsten Harries but treats it from the stand-

8. Paul E. Sigmund, *Nicholas of Cusa and Medieval Political Thought* (Cambridge, Mass.: Harvard University Press, 1963).

point of mathematics. She identifies three distinct mathematical analogies in Cusanus's works and explores their significance for his thought as a whole. First, from the example of counting, one can induce the sense in which the superlative is always the implicit measure of the comparative. Second, by considering rival hypotheses of an infinitely extended divided line, one comes to an awareness of the infinite as the *essence* of the finite. Third, by examining the metaphor of an *n*-sided polygon inscribed into a circle, one can illustrate how the infinite is the goal and perfection of the finite. At first glance it seems that Cusanus is positing the mathematical asymptote as the final limit-concept on human knowledge of God. In fact, Brient argues, the inscribed polygon considered as an aspect of learned ignorance figures mathematically the hypostatic union of divinity and humanity in Jesus Christ. The Cusan synthesis thus embraces even sacred geometry.

The concluding essay by Regine Kather reprises the theme of perspective while also pointing to a radically new understanding of Cusanus's contribution to science. Kather's essay extends the theme of science into the era of quantum physics. To be sure, much separates Cusanus from modern science in both theory and practice, and Kather is quick to highlight the methodological gulf. For example, Nicholas's hypothesis of the relativity of the earth's motion without any experimental confirmation disqualifies him as scientifically credible in the eyes of some scientists today. Kather nonetheless documents how Cusanus's conjectures regarding the relativity of motion are based on the more comprehensive theory of perspective found in *De visione Dei*. Cusanus anticipates a well-known trajectory in the history of modern science, that is, the path that leads from the overcoming of the closed Ptolemaic world of the ancients by Nicholas Copernicus and Galileo Galilei to the positing of infinite worlds by Giordano Bruno. This was in fact the path that originally brought the Neokantians and Ernst Cassirer to the study of Cusanus. Without these developments the specific achievement of a mathematical construction of nature in Newtonian mechanics and Kantian philosophy would be unthinkable.

The connection between Cusanus and Albert Einstein, Kather argues, is both more tenuous and more profound than the Kantian one. Einstein posits (if only later to reject the hypothesis in light of an experimental confirmation to the contrary) the speed of light as an absolute measure of things. To that degree his philosophy seems to counter Cusanus's central intuition that there is an infinite disproportion to the measurable world. The bond between Cusanus and Einstein, Kather posits, is rather a spiritual one. Einstein's sense of awe at nature and its inherent order, what he termed a *kosmische Religiosität,* is not far from Nicholas's search for the divine being as the "immaterial center of the universe." Separated by centuries and by vastly different conceptions of God and the world, Cusanus and Einstein both counter the modern legacy whereby the Copernican revolution of the human mind is the last word on man's position in the cosmos. In this way, Cusanus and Einstein are both promoters of the not so modern but all the more timely philosophical ideal that nature is far more than physical concepts can reveal.

Claiming the Legacy: A Comparison of Two Jubilees

There is a distinct scholarly advantage to celebrating the jubilees of famous thinkers in a regular way. By charting these trajectories, one can take stock of the changing nature of research. How did scholarship on Cusanus develop in the period leading up to the jubilee of 2001? The year 1964 is a fitting reference point, for it was the year in which scholars marked the fifth centenary of Cusanus's death. That year academic conferences were also held in Bernkastel-Kues and Brixen-Bressanone, Cusanus's German birthplace and episcopal see in South Tyrol, respectively.[9] The Institut für Cusanus-Forschung had been established only four years earlier but was already under the direction of the renowned Catholic theologian and Cusanus scholar Rudolf Haubst. (Not until 1980 was it moved to its present location in Trier.) The jubilee events of 1964 took place while the Second Vatican Council was in session, and some speakers compared Cusanus's project to build a bridge between Church and world to parallel efforts underway among the bishops in Rome.[10] The scholar-

9. In addition, the April 1964 meeting of the Asociación Española de Filosofía Medieval was dedicated to the topic. These proceedings were published as *Nicolás de Cusa en el V centenario de su muerte, 1464–1964* (Madrid: Instituto Luís Vives de Filosofía, 1967).

10. During the congress of 1964, the sitting Bishop of Brixen-Bressanone, Monsignor Josef Gargitter, actually referred to Cusanus as a "Brückenbauer zwischen Welt und

ship in 1964 on Cusanus had a somewhat different orientation than today. In 1964, for example, Ernst Cassirer's interpretation of Cusanus was still a focal point. His highly influential interpretation of Cusanus in *The Individual and the Cosmos in Renaissance Philosophy* had been published thirty-seven years earlier, although the English translation was then only one year old.[11]

The volume of essays from the 1964 conference in Brixen was edited by the Paduan philosopher Giovanni Santinello. The title itself, *Nicolò Cusano agli inizi del mondo moderno (Nicholas Cusanus at the Origins of the Modern Age),* highlights the strong interest in the question of the modern age and particularly its genesis.[12] Much as in the recent jubilee year, there were papers in Brixen on particular ideas in Cusanus's thought (e.g., Rudolf Haubst on evolution, Paul Sigmund on equality, and Morimichi Watanabe on tolerance) as well as papers on his place in the history of philosophy, theology, political thought, and the history of the Church. Questions about Cusanus's complex relation to Platonism abounded, and the plenary address by F. Edward Cranz dealt with Cusanus's transmutation of Platonism in comparison to Luther's.[13] On the other hand, Paul Oskar Kristeller in his contribution to the published volume strengthened the case for close connections between Cusanus and Renaissance Platonism. Kristeller's essay treated a recently discovered manuscript containing a Latin translation of Gemisthos Plethon's *De fato* with a preface dedicated to the Cardinal from Kues. Raymond Klibansky, a founder of the mod-

---

Kirche." *Nicolò Cusano agli inizi del mondo moderno. Atti del Congreso internazionale in occasione del V centenario della morte di Nicolò Cusano,* ed. Giovanni Santinello (Florence: G. C. Sansoni Editore, 1970), 4.

11. Ernst Cassirer, *Individuum und Kosmos in der Philosophie der Renaissance* (Lepizig/ Berlin: B. G. Teubner, 1927) [ET: *The Individual and the Cosmos in Renaisssance Philosophy* (New York: Harper and Row, 1963)].

12. Hans Blumenberg is listed as a participant at the Brixen conference but did not contribute to the proceedings. His much discussed interpretation of the genesis of modernity (including the pivotal roles of Cusanus and Giordano Bruno at its epochal threshold) in *Die copernikanische Wende* (Frankfurt: Suhrkamp, 1965) and *Die Legitimität der Neuzeit* (Frankfurt: Suhrkamp, 1966, rev. ed., 1988) appeared shortly after this date.

13. Cranz's scholarship had a great influence on American Cusanus scholars. This seminal essay and several posthumously published pieces are now available in F. Edward Cranz, *Nicholas of Cusa and the Renaissance,* ed. Thomas Izbicki and Gerald Christianson (Aldershot: Ashgate, 2000).

ern edition of Cusanus's works, gave an inaugural speech in his capacity as president of the Canadian Society for the History and Philosophy of Science, in which he highlighted the interest in North America in "the originality of Cusanus's conception of the world."[14] The Georgetown philosopher Thomas McTighe likewise treated Nicholas of Cusa's theory of science and its metaphysical background. He emphasized how Cusanus effectively destroyed scholastic ontology and thereby paved the way for modern science. Hans-Georg Gadamer also acknowledged the tension between Cusanus's thought and the dominant patterns of the Christian Middle Ages but paid even greater attention to his Neoplatonically inspired theology of the Word and Cusanus's place in modern German philosophy. Gadamer, for example, highlighted the Neokantian revival of the nineteenth and twentieth centuries (from Hermann Cohen to Cassirer) and the pivotal role that the rediscovery of Cusanus's thought played in that movement.

There is a surprising continuity of themes between *Nicolò Cusano agli inizi del mondo moderno* and the more recent endeavors in Washington, Bernkastel-Kues, Tokyo, and elsewhere. Many of the basic approaches and themes still followed today were clearly present in 1964. For example, in both Brixen and Washington there was a single presentation dedicated to Cusanus and Islam. The essay on this topic from 1964 was written by Georges Anawati, O.P., a noted expert on Muslim philosophy, theology, and mysticism. It begins with these still timely words: "Islam is of the order of the day not only from a political point of view where incidences of public unrest that marked diverse countries of the Near East have nearly created great international crises but also from a religious and cultural point of view since we see the Second Vatican Council making an official overture to an Islamic-Christian dialogue."[15] Anawati applauds the modern, irenic spirit of *De pace fidei* but also notes how certain key apologetic motifs in the *Cribratio alkorani,* for example, the fallacious insistence that Mohammed was actually an adherent to the heretical Christian sect known as Nestorians, fall outside the bounds of modern critical scholarship on the origins of Islam. In Anawati's judgment, the *Cribratio* fails to

14. *Nicolò Cusano agli inizi del mondo moderno,* 15.
15. Georges C. Anawati, "Nicolas de Cues et le problème de l'Islam," in *Nicolò Cusano agli inizi del mondo moderno,* 141.

live up the contemporary standard of showing an absolute respect for the opinion of one's interlocutor, a principle that he himself had defended in the third session of the Second Vatican Council.[16] Cusanus, according to this line of interpretation, is actually neither a purely medieval nor a wholly modern thinker. He seems rather to straddle the epochal categories of medieval and modern, and on this particular point most of the authors from the 2001 conference were in general agreement.

But the differences of perspective between 1964 and 2001 are just as striking. In the wake of Cassirer (but not always in complete agreement with him), the conference participants in 1964 discussed whether Cusanus should be categorized as a Neoplatonic thinker and whether he served as a forerunner of modern social and scientific developments. Many of the papers from 1964 were oriented toward the idea that Cusanus's thought was an original synthesis of ancient, medieval, and Renaissance sources whose principal function was to pave the way for modernity. By contrast, some of the presentations given in 2001 represented an outright backlash against the "forerunner" approach. A second difference concerns the issue of spirituality. In 1964 none of the sermons was available in the present critical edition, making it rather difficult to offer a comprehensive account of Cusanus's spirituality. There is but one paper on spirituality in the volume from 1964, and typically for that period this essay deals with the spirituality of the Brothers of the Common Life.[17]

In 2001, by contrast, most of the presenters took it for granted that Cusanus had been claimed as a proto-modern figure, although some chose to challenge the thesis altogether.[18] With respect to Nicholas's role in modern science, the focus in 2001 was not so much on modernity's origins as on its manifold mature expressions. In Regine Kather's essay in the present volume, for example, Cusanus's importance for science extends

16. Ibid., 173, N. 32.

17. Gerd Heinz-Mohr, "Bemerkungen zur Spiritualität der Brüder vom gemeinsamen Leben," in *Nicolò Cusano agli inizi del mondo moderno*, 471–85. The question of whether Cusanus studied with the Brothers of the Common Life is not settled by Heinz-Mohr and has been the subject of protracted debate in the intervening period. See, for example, the essays by Martin Hoenen and Nikolaus Staubach in *Conflict and Reconciliation: Perspectives on Nicholas of Cusa*, ed. Inigo Bocken (Leiden: Brill, 2004).

18. See, for example, the essay by Jasper Hopkins in this volume as well as the discussion (in the essays by Sigmund and Nederman) of the debate regarding the continuity and discontinuity between medieval and modern constitutionalism.

clear up to Einstein and is not limited to or even based upon his distancing of himself from scholastic categories. Like Karsten Harries she finds that Cusanus's timeliness for the third millennium lies equally in the aesthetic and spiritual core of his pre-Copernican cosmology. In fact, there is a spiritual depth to all of Cusanus's thought that was slighted by some of the presentations in 1964 but became the focus of several of our sessions in 2001. In this volume, this new orientation can be found in the contributions on Cusanus's sermon on the Lord's Prayer and the treatment of infallibility as a characteristic of the church as a whole. Moreover, there was nothing in 1964 comparable to Bernard McGinn's brilliant treatment of the place of Cusanus's apophatic mysticism in the history of Christian spirituality and liturgical practices. New topics arose in 2001. In contrast to 1964, the contributors to the present volume pay attention to perspectival knowing, apophatic mysticism, liturgy, aesthetics, and the visual arts.

Can one isolate a distinguishing feature of Cusanus scholarship from the proceedings of 2001? The very concept of modernity has matured considerably. It is *not* the case that the participants in the 2001 conference were trying to claim Cusanus as a "postmodern" thinker. Several authors continued to address Cusanus's relevance to typically modern questions such as individualism, human creativity, freedom, and the evolution of a consensual theory of constitutional rights, and others rejected the modern classification in the first place. Nonetheless, the positing of modernity as an inherently ambiguous category, so widely discussed in the academy today but not prominent in the proceedings of 1964, has also changed Cusanus scholarship at the beginning of the third millenium.[19] In 2001 it is no longer possible to herald Cusanus as a forerunner of the modern age without also making him at least complicit by association in the genesis of modernity's myopias. By the same token, the overcoming of modernity's excesses—whether such excess is posited in the anthropocentric eclipse of

---

19. There are exceptions. For example, in 1964 Eusebio Colomer sought to identify Cusanus's "intermediate place between classical and modern thought." Eusebio Colomer, "Modernidad y tradición en la metafisica del conocimiento de Nicolas de Cusa," *Nicolò Cusano, 273.* Gadamer also renders a balanced judgment when he claims that Cusanus stood "at the threshold of modernity" and "drew from the new feeling of life." According to Gadamer, Cusanus still managed to bring "to light an ontological truth that surpasses the most exaggerated expressions of the modern age *(die äußerste Zuspitzung der Moderne)." Nicolò Cusano agli inizi del mondo moderno,* 48.

a sense of meaning and wonder in the world or a positivistic separation of the Pope's juridical authority from the need for consent and reception in the Church as a whole—is also in view in many of the essays that follow.

The Present Legacy of Learned Ignorance

De docta ignorantia was the first truly philosophical and the most programmatic work of Nicholas of Cusa. He inherited the concept of learned ignorance from a rich philosophical and literary tradition of Christian, Jewish, and Muslim authors, most notably, St. Augustine, Dionysius the Areopagite, Moses Maimonides, Algazali, and Petrarch.[20] One can also demonstrate that the Cusan concept of learned ignorance not only has been received positively into a wide variety of contemporary philosophical schools but was interpreted variously even within his own century.[21] More recent scholarship has begun to explore the question of how Cusanus's program for a philosophy of learned ignorance was interpreted in subsequent centuries, and especially by philosophers and theologians of the modern period.[22]

In light of such a complex history, is it even possible to speak six hundred years after Cusanus's birth of a single legacy of learned ignorance? The answer must be negative, for distinct legacies were claimed in Washington and throughout the world in 2001. But the very fact of a more thoroughly globalized scholarship on Cusanus already attests to a new interpretative horizon. Cusanus is no longer seen simply as a forerunner of modern German philosophy. It is not that one cannot extract a national

---

20. One recent attempt can be found in Hans G. Senger, "Nichtwissen als Wissensform: Ignoranzkompensation von Petrarca bis Erasmus," in *Nicolaus Cusanus zwischen Deutschland und Italien. Beiträge eines deutsch-italienischen Symposiums in der Villa Vigoni*, ed. Martin Thurner (Berlin: Akademie Verlag, 2002), 633–53.

21. See, for example, Ernst Cassirer, "Cusanus in Italy," in Cassirer, *The Individual and the Cosmos*, 46–72, and Raymond Klibansky, "Anhang: Zur Geschichte der Überlieferung der *Docta ignorantia* des Nikolaus von Kues," in Nikolaus von Kues, *Die belehrte Unwissenheit*, Buch III, ed. Hans Gerhard Senger, Schriften des Nikolaus von Kues in deutscher Übersetzung, Heft 15c (Hamburg: Felix Meiner, 1977), 205–36.

22. See, for example, Stephan Meier-Oeser, *Die Präsenz des Vergessenen. Zur Rezeption der Philosophie des Nicolaus Cusanus vom 15. bis zum 18. Jahrhundert* (Münster: Aschendorff, 1989), and Hubert Benz, *Individualität und Subjektivität: Interpretationstendenzen in der Cusanus-Forschung und das Selbstverständnis des Nikolaus von Kues* (Münster: Aschendorff, 1999).

heritage as a distinguishing feature of Cusan identity, for he himself expatiates on his German style as a source of both inelegance of Latin expression and a "very clear judgment without dissimulation."[23] In other words, in claiming Cusanus as a paradigm for a globalizing culture, there is little need to devaluing Nicholas's German identity or real sense of rootedness in the Mosel River valley.

At the same time, Cusan thought arose out of a quasi-nomadic existence imposed on an extraordinary individual by political and ecclesiastical forces outside of his personal control. In this respect Nicholas of Cusa deserves to be likened as much to the *idiota* (layman) of his dialogues of 1450 as to the "professional" philosophers and theologians of the fifteenth century. Long before ascending to the rank of a Roman cardinal, Cusanus was always on the move. Much of his thinking can also be characterized as itinerant. The borders that Cusanus encountered in the waning days of the *imperium* may have been more fluid than at any time after the establishment of modern nation-states. In any case, the fact that Cusanus moved between different regional identities, languages, and even conceptions of God is much more at the foreground of the contemporary scholarship than it was in 1964.[24]

Cusanus was a loyal son of the Mosel and staunch defender of both the institutional Church and a Christian empire. He is not so much a universalizing *citoyen du monde* as a highly introspective cartographer of uncharted spaces. Cusanus is like the metaphorical mapmaker in the *Compendium*. He surveys the truth in a moving image, for the mapmaker sees himself in a certain sense as the creator of the traversable world. Cusan philosophy is thus the result of taking in the sense data from a wide variety of experiences and places and then looking deep into the heart of the matter for the concealed "place" where God and humanity are united.[25] What kind of place is this cartographic world? The very notion of "place" for Cusanus is neither a purely interior nor a merely exterior one. The figural map is ultimately a symbolic reality, whose locality, Nicholas reminds

23. *De concordantia catholica*, h XIV (1938), 2, pp. 2–3.

24. See Martin Thurner, "'tedesco di nazione ma non di costumi'? 'Nicolaus Cusanus zwischen Deutschland und Italien' im Spiegel der Forschung," in *Nicolaus Cusanus zwischen Deutschland und Italien*, 11–24.

25. Nicholas of Cusa, *Compendium*, ch. 8 in h XI/3 (1964), 22ff., p. 17ff.

us, bears a considerable likeness to an infinite sphere lacking both measurable circumference and a definable center. The reality of divine presence in the new map of the world is above all a matter of "intensive" infinity.[26]

At the beginning of the third millennium, Nicholas's project of learned
ignorance continues to involve a healthy dose of skepticism about the
real. Cusanus questions each finite perspective by drawing upon the idea
of an infinite horizon, but he does not aim to reduce the reality of truth to
a merely perspectival showing. He is confident that truth is worth pursuing and that the pursuit itself adds nobility to human existence. Learned
ignorance has its shortfalls. In its pursuit one cannot either ignore the
modifier *(docta)* or pretend to have penetrated the depths of the substan-
tive *(ignorantia)*.[27] The search for learned ignorance involves the real assimilation of wisdom and the frank admission of limit. The Cusan hunt
for truth traverses boundaries of many sorts, and in each case the individual crossing matters in its own right. Each traversal opens up a new window to the limitless presence of the infinite in the finite. Cusanus highlights and valorizes alterity without broaching cultural relativism.

In thought and action the man of the fifteenth century displayed a remarkable resolve to immerse himself in new experiments, to reconsider
new conjectures, and to restore life to calcified institutions. His indefatiga-
ble (but not always irenic) return to new attempts reflects a deeply spiritual outlook. The essays in this volume hardly represent a single approach
to Cusan spirituality, yet a thread may still be discernible in the labyrinth.
Cusanus saw in the very fragility of human *ars* the embodiment of the divine in the world. The analogy is particularly emphasized in the dialogue
Idiota de mente ("The Layman on the Mind") but can also be considered an
overarching Cusan theme. As Clyde Lee Miller, himself a participant in
the 2001 conference, writes:

---

26. Cf. Elizabeth Brient, *The Immanence of the Infinite: Hans Blumenberg and the Threshold
to Modernity* (Washington, D.C.: The Catholic University of America Press, 2002), 212–13.

27. Cf. Peter Casarella, "Nicholas of Cusa (1401–1464), On Learned Ignorance: Byzantine Light en route to a Distant Shore," in *The Classics of Western Philosophy*, ed. Jorge J. E.
Gracia, Gregory M. Reichberg, and Bernard N. Schumacher (Oxford: Basil Blackwell,
2003), 184.

The divine Mind is the eternal and infinite Art/Artisan, the One who creates our universe and stands as Exemplar for all human making and artistry. As image of the Divine, the human mind will reflect this creative power in its own productive activity.[28]

In 1964 the artist imagery was used to emphasize human freedom and man's quasi-divine capacity to recreate the entire world in his own image. Today that optimistic refrain has not so much been silenced as placed in a new light.

The Cusan image of the human person as a *Deus humanatus* (in Hopkins's translation, "God manqué") is just as expressive as before but bears a new connotation. In our rapidly globalizing culture, the art of human knowing is considered increasingly to be of a highly limited and deeply fragmented sort. We are surrounded by hourly reminders of the unparalleled ease with which we can communicate, relocate, and produce, but the conjectural quality of our grasp of the whole is underscored by the fact of constantly expanding horizons. The "modern" Cusan impulse to reconstruct nature mathematically has been eclipsed by the very technology it engendered. A laptop or computer screen is no portal to the infinite if the seeker of wisdom is rendered "worldless" in the process.[29] Today the urgent plea for the kind of religious tolerance envisioned by Nicholas may sound hollow not because it needs to be purified of its distinctively Christian content but because it must face a level of global fear and mistrust not unlike that of 1453.[30]

Several of the essays in this volume note the Cusan combination of the perspective construction with a vision of beauty. This aesthetic turn in Cusanus scholarship suggests that the category of beauty itself may beckon us to a new sense of wonder. This development represents another important new direction in Cusanus scholarship.[31] Cusanus was not interested in promoting a merely "aesthetic" reintegration with the world, for he

28. Clyde Lee Miller, *Reading Cusanus: Metaphor and Dialectic in a Conjectural Universe* (Washington, D.C.: The Catholic University of America Press, 2003), 117.

29. The notion of modern worldlessness, which is drawn from the writings of Hannah Arendt, is analyzed brilliantly in Brient, *The Immanence of the Infinite,* 74–93.

30. Cf. Peter Casarella, "Cardinal Nicholas of Cusa: An Introduction," *Communio: International Catholic Review* 28 (Winter 2001): 843–47.

31. An important, although still relatively unknown, study is Giovanni Santinello, *Pensiero di Nicolò Cusano nella sua prospetttiva estetica* (Padua: Liviana editrice, 1958).

weaves together faith and beauty. Accordingly, the positive content of Christian faith bears unlimited wisdom for philosophy, especially for those thinkers who are prone to confusing the artistry of the human mind with that of its infinite ground. Cusanus claimed that the human image participates in the divine archetype but cannot approximate its inexhaustible creativity. As Louis Dupré notes in his essay, the notion of "growing" into the image is what ultimately distinguishes Cusanus's proposal from that of pantheism. The Cusan philosopher rightfully praises the human capacity to recreate nature so long as one recognizes even more clearly the human *incapacity* to create lasting spiritual meaning simply by the exercise of individual volition. For Cusanus the limit imposed by this openly theological construct is not so much a privation of one's humanity as a thoroughly positive endowment. In a global culture with increasingly fewer limits, learned ignorance remains a path for limitless discovery of a finite self.

Abbreviations

h   Nicolai de Cusa Opera omnia iussu et auctoritate Academiae
Litterarum Heidelbergensis. Leipzig-Hamburg: Meiner, 1932–.
For example, h I, N. 121, p. 78 refers to volume I, paragraph 121,
page 78.

MFCG   Mitteilungen und Forschungsbeiträge der Cusanus-Gesellschaft,
1961–.

p   Nicolai Cusae Cardinalis Opera, Paris ed. (1514), ed. Jacques
Lefèvre d'Etaples. Reprinted by Frankfurt/Main: Minerva, 1962.

PG   Patrologia Graeca, ed. J.-P. Migne (Paris).

PL   Patrologia Latina, ed. J.-P. Migne (Paris).

Introduction by Nancy Hudson
annotated translation by Frank Tobin

I. NICHOLAS OF CUSA'S SERMON ON THE *Pater Noster*

The text of the sermon on the *Pater noster* (the "Our Father") is based on a homily given by Nicholas of Cusa on January 1, 1441, in Augsburg. The transcription and dissemination of the sermon was done at the request of the bishop of Augsburg, Cardinal Peter von Schaumberg.

Seven manuscripts of the sermon in his native Mosel-Franconian dialect and one incomplete early Latin translation are extant. Although the written version remains in the form of a sermon, it incorporates many of the philosophical concerns with which he was preoccupied, including those of *De docta ignorantia*. Certainly the Neoplatonic movement of a divine source flowing out in theophany, return, and final theosis underlies the structure of the sermon. However, there is evidence that his philosophical preoccupation is only a means for explaining the *Pater noster* rather than an end in itself. That is, the sermon remains a sermon, speaking *to the audience* rather than *about God*. In the first paragraph his explanation of the prayer as a teaching tool that acts as sustenance for "each and every person in this visible world" suggests that the philosophy clearly serves the prayer rather than vice versa. Cusanus has not given us a theological description of God, a hymn to God's greatness, or a speculative treatise. The sermon on the *Pater noster* is, quite simply, a homily on how to live one's life.

An analysis of the sermon reveals a clear, detailed, and even artistic structure. The introduction catches our attention by impressing on us that the words of the prayer are divine words. Then Nicholas of Cusa justifies why he presumes to interpret God's own words. Although no one is able completely to understand Christ's teaching, the grace of God has given some clearer insight, just as some are better able to gaze at the sun. Finally, he outlines the four points into which he has divided the phrases of the *Pater noster*: (1) God as universal source, (2) the flowing out, (3) the return, and (4) the final goal of divine union. Before taking up these four points, he again reassures us that the prayer is perfect, with not a single word out of place.

Cusanus's method consists of a dissection of the prayer not merely into sentences, but into phrases and discrete words, where even conjunctions are invested with sometimes surprising meaning. His initial severing of "Our Father" from "who art in the heavens, hallowed be thy name" has the effect of transforming the entire sentence from an address to and a description of God into an invitation to know an immanent God who gives us our very being. The basis of this contention is not mere causality but theophany, for, as he states, "ten are from one and have nothing from themselves."[1] Accordingly, "we are nothing of ourselves." Because "a father is a natural, first, and highest source and is alone a beginning of us all," God's oneness is the source of the being of all things.

This line of thinking is further supported by his interpretation of "in the heavens." "Heavens" does not describe some otherworldly location but "those natures with understanding." In addition to locating the divine in human rationality, Cusanus here employs the notion of human being as microcosm ("The highest creatures . . . have in their power the lowest, just as the mobile, living nature of trees has in it the lowest elements."). This raises a possible discrepancy between where one finds knowledge of God (i.e., in the intellect) and the notion of theophany. While he previously called God "the Father in whom all things are," here he sets up an apparent opposition between "all natures beneath humankind," whose "common mother" is the earth, and "heavenly, spiritual natures."

Perhaps the answer is found later in his comments about Christ having taught us to pray that the will of God be done "as in heaven, so also on earth." Because the earthly realm is where human desires hold sway, "the sensual, fleshly nature must be turned toward the intelligent nature and remain united with it in obedience." Cusanus is not pitting intellect

---

1. This passage builds upon Nicholas's view that "one" is not just a single unit but an enfolding of all numbers. See the essay by Elizabeth Brient in this volume for more on his use of mathematical analogies.

against flesh but offering pastoral advice to people living in an imperfect world.

Nicholas finds Trinitarian significance in the phrase "Thy will be done." Accordingly, "Thy" refers to the Father, "be done" to the Son, and "will" to the Holy Spirit, as all things flow out from the Father. Moreover, the conjunctive phrase "so also" indicates the microcosmic element in human nature, for there is a composition of spiritual elements joining it to heaven and corporeal elements connecting it to earth.

In his understanding of the phrase "Thy kingdom come to us," Cusanus suggests that, while we look forward to "the peaceful, immortal kingdom," it is not a merely a future state. Since "God alone is everything that is able to exist," individual existence itself is a participation in the kingdom of God. The kingdom is "union in God" and therefore a partially realized destiny. This notion is further supported in his interpretation of the phrase "Thy will be done as in heaven, so also on earth." The notion that all things flow out from God and "that all things are everything that they are from one threefold God" is again based not upon mere causality but upon divine immanence.

Correspondingly, sin is division or separation from God. He writes: "[Y]ou should turn away from this world toward God. . . . [Y]ou find on this earth many things: stars, animals, trees, etc. Then you see that these things are dissimilar. . . . [A]ll things are separated and divided." God is immanent in all earthly things, but to the extent that they are divided, he is not to be found there. Perhaps the metaphor of a living mirror that Cusanus uses in *De visione Dei* is useful to understand what is meant here: a reflection of something owes its existence to what it reflects, but one does not turn to the reflection to know the reflected object truly.[2]

Like the other parts of his sermon, Cusanus's discussion of the phrase "our daily bread give us today" is given a depth that goes beyond its immediate meaning. It is much more than a simple appeal for physical sustenance. It does, however, refer to living the practical, daily life of a Christian. We are to pray for union with God mediated through Jesus Christ (the bread of life).

The conjunction "and" between the two phrases "Our daily bread give us today" and "forgive us our guilt" does much more than join two inde-

2. See *De visione Dei,* ch. 4, N. 13; ch. 8, N. 32; ch. 12, N. 49; ch. 15, N. 67.

pendent imperatives. For Nicholas, it implies that forgiveness is possible for us only in union with Christ in this heavenly bread. In this same passage, Cusanus singles out the word "our" for special notice regarding the unity of the Christian church. We are to think of ourselves as members of a Christian community rather than as individuals. In asking for "our" daily bread, we acknowledge that no supernatural gifts are given to us except insofar as we are members of the faithful. And in begging for forgiveness of "our" guilt, we recognize that forgiveness takes place only in the union of the church, where one prays for the removal not only of one's own guilt. Rather, *all* pray that *all* may be forgiven. The word "our" also reminds us of our obligation to be unselfish and generous toward others. In asking for "our" daily bread, Nicholas admonishes, we admit that it is not exclusively ours but must be shared with the needy. Refusal to do so signifies that we have acquired and possess these things unjustly.

The multifaceted universality of the sermon is distinctive. Because "all intelligible wisdom is hidden in the simple words of Christ's teaching," Nicholas's meditations encompass all existence, from the workings of the Trinity to the lowest elements of the physical world. His main theme is the progression of all things' flowing out from their source and their circling back to this source as their final goal. The sermon's form and the introduction's as well coincide with the circular motion that is their content. Likewise, the preacher/author anticipates our final goal by mentioning it in the opening paragraph and then completes the circle in the course of the sermon. Also, there is a global aspect to what Nicholas expects of his audience. He guides them up to the heights of refined thought on the divine aspects of language, the Trinity, and the relation of creatures to God and then descends to the practical, moral requirements of everyday life: that we must share our material possessions with the less fortunate, and that—as is clearly assumed in reciting the *Pater noster*—we can expect God to forgive us only if we have forgiven the offenses of our fellow humans.

Cusanus's general approach can be summed up by his words: "In his wisdom Christ is given to us in his teaching. For in the teaching of the master lies the performing of the skill; and so we find Christ in his teaching. And the teachings of the holy *Pater noster* in which Christ dwells prove this to us." The Lord's Prayer is not a message to God or even a model for other messages. It is, rather, a gift given to us; it is where we find Christ himself and thus union with God. The *Pater noster* is the teaching of Christ, the very dwelling place of God.

Vernacular Sermon on the *Pater Noster*[3]

1   In his humblest humanity Jesus was true God, and his words and teaching were thus [divine] as well. And so the *Pater noster,* in the simplicity of its words, embraces the highest teaching and wisdom. For just as divinity lay hidden in the humanity of Christ, so also all intelligible wisdom is hidden in the simple words of Christ's teaching, which no one in this world can completely comprehend, so that each and every person might have in this world incorruptible food in the hidden wisdom of God under the words and sensible signs, as the Christian person awaits the eternal food of the highest intellectual life [that lies] completely open without any signs or mediation of feeble sensuality.[4] That is why one person, in accordance with the grace of God, can have a clearer and higher insight into the words of the *Pater noster* than another, just as one person has sharper eyes than another for gazing at the sun. And although everyone in his simplicity is able to have his own particular satisfying sweetness in this prayer, God has nevertheless given to one person an advantage over another person, each to his own benefit. And for this reason one person teaches another, and they desire to learn from each other.

2   This is my understanding of the *Pater noster* at this time, and I have confidence that such understanding will be increased and clarified in me from day to day, as I also desire to know from God that in you a prayer[5] proceeds from desire and the desiring will proceeds from hope. For what a person does not hope for, a person does not desire. But hope follows faith and understanding. No one hopes for something that he does not be-

---

3. Translated from *Sermo* XXIV in h 16, 1, *Sermones* I (1430–1441), ed. Rudolf Haubst et al. (Hamburg: Felix Meiner, 1991), 384–431.

4. Nicholas seems to use the words *sensuality* (here: *synlicheit*) or *sensual* in a generally Platonic sense. It refers to all sense perception but may also imply a negative evaluation, both in its relationship to the more highly valued intellectual life and as a moral danger threatening to drag down the soul.

5. As is the case with the Latin *oratio* and *orare,* but less so in the case of the English "prayer," the word group Nicholas chooses for prayer and praying (here: *bede*) always implies a begging or asking for something.

lieve or know. For this reason the highest [kind of] prayer must have the highest desire, hope, and faith. And that is what you should resolve to seek in the *Pater noster.*

3   <<Now our understanding is inclined toward knowing the truth, and therefore you find what you should believe in the truth: in God and in creatures. And when you have found the faith of truth,[6] through which you are illumined as to where a human's being[7] in its perfection can come, then you hope to come there. And when you find that such perfection is good, then you desire it, and you ask [for it] after you understand it, and you hope that you can come to it.>>[8] Thus it is that our understanding—inclined toward the truth—finds illumination in the *Pater noster* for knowing in an unwavering faith what the truth is.

First of all, concerning the beginning and source of all things; [then] concerning the flowing out of all things from God; [then] concerning the way[9] of the flowing back again of all things and concerning the final end.

4   The source—that is, the divine nature—is [contained] in the words "Our Father, who art in the heavens, hallowed be thy name. Thy kingdom come to us." The flowing out [is contained] in the words "Thy will be done as in heaven, so also on earth." The powerful way [is contained] in the words "Our daily bread give us today and forgive us our guilt as we do to our debtors. Lead us not into temptation." The final end [is contained] in the words: "But deliver us from evil. Amen."

6. That is, faith or belief in the truth.

7. I have generally translated *wesen* with "being." In the Latin version the editors usually translate it with *essentia*.

8. The lines enclosed by the angle brackets are found in only one part of the stemma and are based mainly on a manuscript sent by Nicholas to the monks at Tegernsee. They are found in the margin of this manuscript, and the editors consider them to have been added by Nicholas himself. In what follows we distinguish between interpolations mandated by English usage and based upon the critical edition of the text (square brackets) and those that represent textual emendations initiated by the editors of the critical edition (angle brackets).

9. Because Nicholas is playing with the word *mittel,* it is difficult to find an English equivalent. *Mittel* indicates a middle between our origin and final end on the one hand and both the agency of Christ and the instrumentality of our forgiving others on the other (cf. immediately below and sections n. 27ff.), which are necessary to our final end. I have chosen "way" as a translation for *mittel.*

5   The source is revealed to us in faith in the words "Our Father," in hope of understanding in the words "Hallowed be thy name," [and] in the desire of good in the words "Thy kingdom come to us." The flowing out of creatures is revealed to us in its order in the words "Thy will be done as in heaven, so also on earth." The way of conducting ourselves demands a powerful food and removal of the obstacle, a signpost and a protection. Without these four points no one can live well. The first point is in the words "Our daily bread give us today," the second in the words "Forgive us our guilt," the third in the words "As we forgive our debtors," [and] the fourth in the words "Lead us not into temptation." The final end of our journey toward the good is contained in the words "But deliver us from evil. Amen."

6   Nature, grace, and glory, and everything that a person desires to know, to the extent possible for us on this earth at the level at which the professors with the highest understanding can comprehend it, [all this] is to be found in this holy prayer, in which there is nothing superfluous, nothing lacking, nothing too difficult, nothing too easy, nothing too long, nothing too short, nothing without cause and proper order, where the first thing must be first and the last last. For the phrase "Our Father who art in the heavens" can suffer no [other] before it. And the phrase "Hallowed be thy name" proceeds from the first [phrase], and the third [proceeds] from the two that precede it. The phrase "Thy will be done" proceeds from those that precede it. And so it goes all the way to the end, each [phrase] in its place. This most sacred prayer I interpret briefly as follows.

7]"Our Father"

A father is a natural, first, and highest source and is alone a beginning of us all. The word "our" indicates this, for "our" is not one thing; rather, "our" is many. But many have one source, as the number instructs us.[10] Ten or twenty is more than one and is many. But that ten are ten or twenty are twenty—that they have from one. Ten is nothing other than one ten times. And so if there were no one, there could be no ten. And thus ten are from one and have nothing from themselves; rather, what they are

10. Nicholas distinguishes here between the meaning and the grammatical form of *noster* to make his point. *Noster* in its meaning implies a plurality or many. Because it modifies a noun in the singular *(pater),* its grammatical form is singular in number.

is from one, and in them is nothing other than one. Hence we are all, however many of us there be, from one. And we are nothing from ourselves. And what we are we are in the Father without whom we cannot be. And thus we have from the words "Our Father" how all creatures are from one Father and in one. After this follows:

8]"Thou art."

Here we note: because the Father is, he is the being of all things.[11] For all things are from him and in him. And thus God is everything that is in each thing that is. Then follows:

9]"In the heavens."

By heavens I mean the highest creatures. Hence these simple words teach me how God the Father is in all things. For he is "in the heavens." The highest creatures are those natures with understanding. They have in their power the lowest, just as the mobile, living nature of trees has in it the lowest elements.[12] And the life of the senses of animals contains within it mobile life. For this reason both the animal and the tree grow and get bigger. Rational nature includes sensual nature, as in [the case of] the human being. And intelligent heavenly nature includes within it the rational, as in the [case of the] angels. And therefore there is one God, the Father, in whom all things are, in the heavens. Thus he is in all [things] and is one God, Father, in many heavens. And there are many heavenly natures[13] in which one God, the Father, is undivided and unmixed.

10   From this you note that this earth of sensuality is far off from knowledge of God. For he is in the heavens of the highest understanding. And he is found there with the eyes of intelligent natures that we too have in our souls. For he is the highest spiritual nature, which our sensual and

---

11. In expressing the idea of God as the being of all things, Nicholas may well have in mind Exodus 3:14 *(ego sum qui sum)* and the long history of its interpretation by Christian thinkers. More specifically, he may be thinking of Meister Eckhart's repeated elaborations on this verse occurring in both his Latin and his vernacular works. See, for example, *Predigt 52 (Die deutsche Werke* [Stuttgart: W. Kohlhammer, 1958–], vol. 3, 486–506) or *Expositio libri Exodi (Die lateinische Werke* [Stuttgart: W. Kohlhammer, 1958–], vol. 2, 1–227), especially nn. 14–22.

12. Cf. *De docta ignorantia*, II, 13; nn. 175–180.

13. Cf. Thomas Aquinas, *De spiritualibus creaturis*, resp. et ad 4.

bodily eyes cannot behold. And thus note that God the Father is the being of all things![14] And he is in each [thing], as he is in all [things], and [is] in no thing in a different way. But he is comprehensible and recognizable in the heavens of intelligent natures.

11]"Hallowed be thy name."

A name is a characterization. By means of names, we have differentiating knowledge. And the better the name indicates that which it names, the more right and true it is. Hence a true name is an actual likeness of the thing named and is like a comprehensible word that flows out from the power of the intellect and is a likeness of the intellect. Thus the name of God the Father is the highest word like unto the intellectual nature of the Father.[15] And because the name is the one most like the Father and is the highest name that cannot be more true, more right, or more like, the name cannot be less than the Father. Otherwise, if it were less, it would be able to be more than it is. And then it would not be the highest, most true name. But because it is like the Father, it is like God, as the Father. But God the Father is the sole source of all things, as mentioned above. Therefore the name which is like the Father has to be the same sole God who is the Father, although the name is not the Father but [rather] the name of the Father which, because it is from the Father, we can name as his highest likeness the Son—in likeness of the sensual birth by which the son is from the father. But just as no son on this earth is so like his father—he could certainly be more like [him]—so it is that no thing can ever be so like another thing that it could not be more like it. For the highest and truest likeness is exclusively the Son of the Father or the name. Therefore, all likeness on this earth is mixed with unlikeness. And the name of God the Father is not to be found on this earth in any like things without a greater unlikeness.

---

14. Though puzzled by the editors' decision to employ an exclamation point this one time in the sermon, we have followed them in doing so.

15. In this section Nicholas makes repeated use of the noun *glichnijs,* which encompass the meanings "likeness," "similarity," "sameness," and "equality," and the adjective *g(e)lich,* which encompasses the meanings "like," "similar," "same," and "equal.". In themselves the words do not distinguish between these possible meanings. I have decided to stick to "likeness" and "like" throughout in order to reproduce Nicholas's consistent use of terms. For one elaboration of this thought on the Trinity, see *De pace fidei,* ch. 7.

12   Now since God cannot be known otherwise than in his name, so it is that we hope we can come to the point that we know him beyond our understanding, in that God the Father illumines us in his name so that we might sanctify it.[16] For when we sanctify his name, that comes from the light given us by the Father in which we see his name above all names (Phil. 2:9). When we see his name there [in heaven], then we will sanctify it above everything that is holy, true, and just. For we shall see that the name is the true name and the just name, the highest likeness and the "mirror of wisdom" in which alone God the Father can be seen and known, and all that which is named in heaven and on earth has no true name without defect and dissimilarity except in this name. And so no thing can be known in truth except in this name.

13   Christ taught us so to pray that the name be sanctified through us. In this is contained the unfathomable teaching of coming to the knowledge of God, which we cannot achieve on our own but rather by the grace of God which sanctified us, so that we can sanctify the name of the knowledge of God above all knowledge. If our understanding sanctifies God's name alone and does not find or seek pleasure or rest in any other thing, then a person has what he has asked God for in the words "Hallowed be thy name."

14   "Thy kingdom come to us."

A country is a union; a kingdom [is] a union in a king. God's kingdom is a union in God. The divine kingdom is the divine and highest union which cannot be greater. The union of the Father and Son, who is utterly like the Father, is the highest union. Union comes forth from one thing and its equal, just as division [comes forth] from dissimilarity. Hence from one thing and that which is utterly similar comes forth the highest union. The highest union, which cannot be greater, must be God. For everything that exists, that is able to be, is God. And what is not God is able to be other than it is through God. But God alone is everything that is able to exist. Hence the highest union is God whom we call the Holy Spirit, who comes

---

16. In the original this pronoun *(in)* can refer either to God the Father or to his name. In the Latin version it has been interpreted as referring to God the Father *(eum)*, even though the verse being explained is "Sanctified be thy name." I have chosen to refer it to God's name.

forth from one and its like, that is, from the Father and the Son. And so you note that the Father's kingdom is the highest union, the Holy Spirit.

15   And therefore, when a person is raised up into the knowledge of God in his name and has seen that God alone is the most desirable and highest good, he then finds that God is the kingdom of all bliss and the love of all lovableness, and that only in this kingdom is there holy, everlasting peace and union, and that outside this kingdom all love is transitory, mixed with suffering, and all peace is unstable, mixed with discord, and that all friendship and union are fragile. Hence we should pray with great longing that this kingdom come to us in which nothing can be lacking to us but we shall be eternally blessed.

16   We ask that this "kingdom come." By this we understand that we should believe, though we are creatures and live on this earth in much want—and must remain creatures, that the peaceful immortal kingdom may come to us. And thus we are taught by Christ that we have the capacity to be "children of God" and that God's kingdom can come to us as an eternal inheritance, and that we have in us an immortality to which God's kingdom can come.

We are also taught that our highest hope should be to possess the kingdom of eternal joy. And by praying for the kingdom we are taught that God can give us this kingdom through grace and that we have no right to demand it. For on our own we are "children of anger" (Eph. 2:3) and of discord and of sin, that is, of separation. For *sin (sunde)* comes from *to separate (sundern),* that is, to divide. Hence on our own we are not born for the kingdom of peace and union, but only through grace. But because Christ teaches us to beg God for it, we understand that God wants to be begged for it and that he does not want to deny us his grace for it.

Because, however, you are taught to say "Thy kingdom come to us," you thereby note that God's kingdom is in the future, after this transitory time; and that this kingdom of the world which now exists, in which we now are, is incapable of grasping the kingdom of God, and that you should have patience in this world and await with great longing God's kingdom after this world; and in your kingdom, in which you now are, strive to make yourself so lovable to God and to unite yourself [with him] that God's kingdom may be able to come to you.

17   But by asking that his kingdom come to us, you note thereby that you come to God's kingdom not otherwise than by God's kingdom coming to you, just as our body does not otherwise come to life except by the life of the soul coming to it.

Now you have the first part of the holy *"Pater noster"* very briefly, and you well understand from what I have said that the teaching of Christ cannot be fully understood.

18   Now note from these three phrases that I have thus interpreted for you how you should turn away from this world toward God. First of all, you find on this earth many things: stars, animals, trees, etc. Then you see that these many things are dissimilar. A star is not like an animal, an animal not like a tree, and that nothing is like anything else. Then you see that all things are separated and divided: the stars there up above, the earth here below, fish in the water, birds in the air. And each is divided from the others.

These three things any person easily notices on this earth: many, dissimilar, and separated. And out of many comes dissimilar, and out of them both comes separated. Now if you want to come to God, note the origin of many: it is one. Because many are united in one as in their source, turn away from many to one. Then you can say: "Our Father, you are in the heavens."

Then note where unlike is like: that is, in God's Son. And so turn away from unlike and unjust and toward like and just. Then you are turning toward God's Son and may well pray "Hallowed be thy name."

Then note where all division and separation is united; that is, in the true peace which is the Holy Spirit. Therefore turn away from all separation of sin[17] that divides you and God and neighbor—whether in anger or hate—to a union of love and peace. Then you can well pray "Thy kingdom come to us." And the paths are necessary for you and are also sufficient if you follow the teaching.

19]"Thy will be done as in heaven, so also on earth."

---

17. Here Nicholas plays on his derivation of *sin* from "to separate" *(sunderung der sunden).*

In these words we are taught that all things flow out from God according to God's will, and that all things have no other cause of their being than God's will that heaven is heaven and earth is earth and human being is human being. That is for no other reason than that God wills it thus. Therefore, in the word "let it be done,"[18] together with the will, all things flow out from the Father into their being. This is nothing else but [the fact] that all things are everything that they are from one threefold God: from the Father in his Word, that is, the Son; with his will, that is, the Holy Spirit. Therefore, note that in the three words "Thy will be done"[19] all things are signified in their flowing out: from God the Father in the word "thy," from God the Son in the word "be done," from God the Holy Spirit in the word "will." And just as the three words signify the Holy Trinity and in the three words the Holy Trinity is meant, so also does each and every thing that exists have an image of God and the Holy Trinity in it through which image the thing is; for no thing is anything except insofar as and to the extent that it is an image of God.

O man, note the small words "Thy will be done," which indicate for you the flowing out of all things in the Holy Trinity. For if you want to know how man became man you are taught here, so that you know that there is no other cause than that this became the will of God the Father. The same is true of all things. There follows:

20]"As in heaven, so also on earth."

From this you notice the order of all things. For all things that God created are named here according in their order: heaven, earth, and along with them a "so also." Note here a highest heavenly nature, which is spiritual, and a lowest earthly nature, which is corporeal, and a middle nature united out of both, which is heavenly and earthly, namely, human nature, which has the heavenly, angelic nature above it, and under it it has earthly nature, that is, all the natures of the elements.

From this you notice how all natures beneath humankind have no common ground with the heavenly, spiritual natures, and that, therefore, God, who is in heaven, is not clearly known through them. For they are out of the earth. It is their common mother. And out of it the other ele-

18. The Latin word is, of course, a single word, namely, *fiat*.
19. That is, *fiat voluntas tua*.

ments are raised up. And out of the elements stones and mobile natures and those having sense perception are raised up. And because this nature is earthly from its mother, it is subordinate to heavenly nature.

21   But heavenly nature is spiritual and more like God and hence more noble. For in an intelligent nature we find a spiritual being, intellect, and will. This being is directed toward eternity and immortality; the intellect is directed toward truth; the will to the good. Thus you find that the heavenly, spiritual nature is a radiant reflection of God and the Holy Trinity— a radiant reflection of God the Father, who is eternal in his immortality; a radiant reflection of the Son in the intellect, the truth which shines in the intellect [and] through which the intellect has the brightness of wisdom for truth; a radiant reflection of the Holy Spirit in the will, which from the light of the Holy Spirit desires nothing but what is good. Hence the will desires nothing but the good. For the good flows forth from the Holy Spirit, and [the will] has its desire for the good from the flowing out of the Holy Spirit, just as the intellect is inclined to nothing else than to truth from the flowing out of God's Son.

22   Now it is the case that human nature, united out of a heavenly and an earthly nature, finds in the spirit of its soul the heavenly inclination to immortality, truth, and the good above itself, to God. And in its earthly, sensual nature there is an inclination beneath it toward the transitory, false, seeming good, so that these laws are dissimilar and against each other (Rom. 7:21–25).

23   Therefore, Christ teaches us to pray that the will of God "be done on earth as in heaven," that the sensual, fleshly nature might turn toward the intelligent [nature] and remain united with it in obedience. This is for this reason: because then a person is completely above himself in the heaven of his intellect, where God dwells, [and] walks in peace. And because we are asking for this we are acknowledging that, left to ourselves, we are of a feeble nature and, without God's grace, cannot withstand the flesh and sensuality. And our earthly nature cannot receive the heavenly law through which it becomes a sharer in divine eternity without God's grace, which God is certainly eager to give us if we ask with devotion "Thy will be done as in heaven, so also on earth"; as this and many other important teachings are revealed to us in the words of Jesus Christ.

24]"Our daily bread give us today."

Earlier we prayed that our earthly nature might become obedient to [our] spiritual, heavenly nature. Now because such a thing cannot happen because of the weakness of [our] nature unless we have a kind of food that nourishes us daily and unceasingly, thus it is that Christ teaches us to pray to God for the food of life, through which we might be fed to have the power to defend ourselves against death and weakness. Now because two natures are united in us—a heavenly and an earthly one, we pray for the bread necessary for both natures: for heavenly bread in which is heavenly immortal life, above all independence of all creatures, as the evangelist Matthew writes (Mt. 6:11), and for the bread for all necessities which today in this sensual life can come to us.

25 Earlier we understood that the intelligent, spiritual nature is fed immortally with the truth and the Word of God, that is, with the eternal Son of God, who is wisdom. Therefore, we ask that the Word become food for our human nature. Now food must be united with that which is being fed. Otherwise, it isn't food. Therefore, we ask that truth, or God's Word, be united with our nature, be given to us. For this is the bread in which we can have immortal life. And our bread is of our nature. Therefore, we ask that God give us our bread—that is, Jesus Christ—into our heart of life as a food of life. And our bread is given us as a food of life if we receive Jesus in our heart with complete faith as a food of life. For then our life unites itself in our own human nature in Christ, in whom our nature is united immortally with the divine life. And thus we are then fed in our bread that God has given us.

26 Now note how the words "our daily bread" reveal to you, first of all, that such is our bread and then that it is necessary for us for life, and that we should have hope that we shall be fed with it, and that this cannot happen except with God's grace, and that God wants to be asked for it with devotion and love, and then he shall give it. The words of the prayer indicate all this to us. From this note what is required for a person to be able to have life. For it is necessary that he have Christ, who is the heavenly bread. But Christ belongs to no one except through the belief that he is "the bread of life," and through hope and love and in a gift of God rich in grace. Note here: Since Christ is the food of life, Christ makes up for all

that is lacking in us, just as food takes care of our need. And hence Christ is the food of all foods, in complete perfection, to relieve all weaknesses. And so, whatever is lacking in us, whether it be in our being, in justice, wisdom, or truth, and in peace, love, or goodness, we shall find it all in that bread.

<<Then we direct our desire to that bread, and our faith and hope and love are increased; thus it is that God gives us this bread every day, and this is the most sublime, holiest sacrament that we should long for and re-ceive in this prayer with great love and devotion as the most sublime gift of God.>>[20]

27]Now you well understand that a person cannot come to the eternal, immortal possession or attainment of the highest good otherwise than in Christ Jesus in whom all our weaknesses are made good, but rather that in him we all become perfect and in him rise from death and shall be unit-ed with life. For he is "the living bread" (Jn. 6:41 and 51) that is beyond all substance or independent existence of all creatures. And in him all crea-tures are in their highest perfection. And he is what preceded and [is] the crown of God's entire creation, and all the works of God rest in him. And [he] is the beginning of the flowing out of all creatures and the way[21] for [their] flowing back again and the final goal of all perfection. For human nature unites in itself all natures, heavenly and earthly, and it is united in Christ, the Son of God. Thus is Christ the final goal of all perfection. For he "alone is the highest" above all heavenly and earthly natures.

28   From this you note that he is not the kind of food that turns into our nature, as bodily food does, for he alone is the highest. Rather, he is a food of life that unites us in itself and makes us alive in his life, just as your soul is a food of natural life for your body and all your members. The soul does not turn itself into the body and take upon itself corporeal nature. Rather, the soul unites in itself your body and all your members. In this union the body lives in the life of the soul. Here note that all crea-tures that come to eternal life are like members of the body of Christ in which the life of Christ is in such a way that in them nothing else lives but

20. See note 8.
21. See note 9.

Christ (1 Cor. 6:15 and 12:12–27). And this is nothing else but that rational creatures are united in one body which is united in the life of Christ.

29   Now observe carefully. If you want Christ to live in you, then you must be united in him; just as, if your finger might wish that your soul live in it, so your finger has to be united with the body and through the body with the soul. For if you separate your finger from the soul by cutting the finger off the body, you separate it from life. And thus you see that you must be united with Christ if you are to live. But this union with Christ cannot take place unless you are united in the body of Christ, which is the holy congregation of the Christian church.

And that is why you pray "Our daily bread give us today." By saying "our" you acknowledge that you are united with the congregation. By saying "bread" you acknowledge a living food of many united in him [Christ]. By saying "give us today" you acknowledge that the food is not given to one who is separated but to many united. Therefore, note from the teaching of Christ that faith and the sacrament and all the virtues cannot help you attain life unless you are a member of the body of the faithful of Christ in one union.

30   You should also note that you are taught "to pray without ceasing" every day (1 Th. 5:17). For just as the infusion of your soul is always necessary for the members of your body if your members are to live, so is this heavenly bread always necessary for your soul. And this you note well from the word "daily" and from the word "today." For if this bread is necessary daily, and if we pray that this bread that we have need of daily be given to us today, then we are also acknowledging, since it is necessary for us every day, that we should pray for it every day.[22] Christ teaches us that we should ask for this bread. Because during the time of this sensual life we, as well-traveled wayfarers [heading] for eternal life, need this food without which we, as such travelers, cannot live in time, Christ teaches us that we should ask for this bread.

31   Now notice that Christ is our bread as we make our way toward him; and [he] is given to us in his being, in his wisdom, and in his goodness, ac-

---

22. Here we deviate from the punctuation of the original in the critical edition.

cording to what we are capable of receiving in this time of mutability. For our eyes of the flesh in this sensual world <<cannot see>>[23] Christ, who is immortal and since his resurrection [is] invisible to mortal eyes because of his most agile and incomprehensible spiritual splendor. Because of this nature, Christ is a spiritual food for our soul. So it is that Christ under the form of bread is given to us on this journey, where we cannot see him with sensual eyes but [only] with the eyes of faith. And so Christ is truly in this sacrament under the form of bread. And everything that the senses thereby see, touch, taste, smell, or grasp is not the true body of Christ, but rather the true signs or sacraments of the body which is there and is seen only with the understanding of faith.[24] That is the most sublime gift of God given to us wayfarers as our food until we come out of this world of sensuality to the heavens of understanding where we shall see Christ not hidden under the sacraments and not by faith, but [rather] in truth "as he is" (1 Jn. 3:1).

32   We ask for this bread and should receive it with total faith, the greatest possible hope, and the greatest amount of love. We should truly receive Christ under this sacrament in the belief that he completely and truly is [there] under each form of bread in all sacraments, just as our soul is invisibly [but] truly and completely [there] in all our members and in each one of them, and just as one face [is] in many eyes that see it and one word [is] in many ears that hear it and one skill [is] in many masters who can perform it and one truth [is] in many intellects that note it. And just as our soul does not grow when we are small and become bigger, but only the body [grows], so also Christ is not bigger under the form of a larger or smaller bread, or under many or fewer sacraments. We should also hope that we shall come from faith to the truth and should thus receive Christ with great love, so that we may be united with him in love as our good and salvation.

In his wisdom Christ is given to us in his teaching. For in the teaching of the master lies the performing of the skill; and so we find Christ in his teaching. And the teachings of the holy *Pater noster* in which Christ dwells

---

23. The bracketed words are not in the manuscripts. I here follow the editors, who find them necessary for rendering this sentence intelligible.

24. Cf. *De pace fidei*, Ch. 18.

prove this to us. For the teaching of Christ is full of all wisdom, full of all virtue, and cannot be improved upon, just like its master.

33][25]   Now in these words "Our daily bread give us today" note: Since we are wayfarers, Jesus teaches us that we should not be full of cares, for God will provide for our needs in this life, from day to day,[26] until we go from here. Therefore, we should not strive to gather up greedily many things, as though we were not wayfarers but rather inhabitants of this earth, or as though God did not know what needs we have or were not able to provide in time.

We are also taught that we should not ask more from God than for daily necessary bread. For, otherwise, he will not answer our prayers. And if more than what we need should come to us, it does not come to us from God for our own sake but for the necessity of your giving to the poor and needy; so that you might realize, when you ask God for "our daily bread," that such bread that God gives is not yours alone, but is "ours," [namely, belongs to] those who need it after you. But if you do not share with the needy the left-over bread that remains after covering your needs, then that is a sign that you have acquired the bread unjustly and greedily and that you possess it unjustly and that you are unworthy of God who has determined to give what is necessary to you and to everyone. In this you, like an "unfaithful servant" (Mt. 25:21ff.), are withholding their share from the poor children of God against his will.

34   In this and in other teachings of Christ in this holy *Pater noster* and in the holy gospels, God gives us Christ, who is "the way, the truth, and the life" (Jn. 14:6). God also gives us food for our journey in the life of Christ by feeding us on our journey. For we find there what we need for our journey. If our conduct is flawed because of pride, we find food in the humble conduct of Christ. If we want to seek it and adopt it, then this need is made good and the flaw of pride is gone. If we mirror our life in the life of Christ, then we see what we are lacking and what we should do. If we want to make our way to Christ in eternal life, then we should exert ourselves in this life to walk as Christ walked. And for the sake of

---

25. A paragraph number was added here that is lacking in the critical edition.
26. Cf. Mt. 6:25–34 and Exod. 16.

our salvation we should not despise the path that Christ, God and man, walked "for the sake of our salvation" in [his] humanity in which he is like us.

35   But if you cannot keep completely to this path, it is nevertheless necessary that you follow the path with such effort that you can reach the end, where Christ is. But if you leave the path and turn your back on it, then you are off the path of life, on the path of death, and will not come to Christ. Here note how you are fed on your journey from the works of the journey of Christ. But if you neither ask for nor receive this food, then the "living bread" will be lacking to you. And that is what you can note from the words written above.

36]"And forgive us our guilt"

Christ teaches us that we should ask God for forgiveness for our guilt. In this we note that all of us because of our nature are burdened with guilt. Since according to the teaching of Christ everyone should pray thus, everyone also acknowledges being guilty. And this guilt is ours because it is our nature. Hence it is common to each and every one, and God is neither the source nor cause of our guilt. For it is ours. That is why we ask for forgiveness. From this note that God alone forgives the guilt that we have incurred against him if we devoutly ask him. Here learn that you should believe that God can justify the sinner and forgive his guilt. And no guilt, great or small, is excluded. Note that God's power is his mercy, and through his gracious mercy he makes an unjust person into a just person, just as through his omnipotence he makes something out of nothing: out of a dead person a living person, out of one nature a different one, out of water wine, according to his will. For his will is his power, and he can do anything he wants, and it has to happen. Note also that no one should despair of God's mercy but [one] should unswervingly harbor the hope that God will forgive him. For Christ teaches you to pray for forgiveness of guilt. If you were not able to be forgiven, Christ would not have taught you to hope for forgiveness of guilt and ask for it.

37   You should also note that this petition begins with an "and." For it says "And forgive us." This "and" joins this petition to the previous one: "Our daily bread give us today *and* forgive us our guilt." For forgiveness

of guilt cannot come about for us without this bread, but with union in this heavenly bread we can ask for forgiveness of guilt. For we have as our own a guilt-laden and sinful nature that has only been cleansed in Christ. And so the grace cleansing us of sin cannot approach our nature except through Christ, who makes good and gives compensation for all our weaknesses if we are united to him in his body, so that the quittance[27] of our redemption can then be made out. Since Christ, in whom we in our nature have all done enough, is united to us with his merits we are then justly heard by God—but not otherwise, because of the incapacity of our nature.

38   Note also that you pray "Forgive us *our* guilt." For whoever is separated from others and intends to pray for himself and not for others cannot say "Forgive us." And therefore he achieves nothing. For we learn here that forgiveness of sins takes place in the unanimity of the holy congregation of the Christian church, outside of which church faith in Christ can help no one to be redeemed from his guilt.

39]"As we forgive our debtors"

In this holy *Pater noster,* in which everything that is necessary for us is summarized for instruction, we find nothing else that we should do than in this phrase. Here it says "As we forgive our debtors." And so all the laws of Christ that we should carry out are contained here: forgive. Christ teaches us that God does not forgive us otherwise than as "we forgive." Note here that the law of Christ is that "you do to others as you want done to you." The words "Forgive us our guilt as we forgive our debtors" indicate this. But if you ask God to forgive you and you do not forgive, you are denying [forgiveness] to yourself. Your "debtor" is God's creature, just as you are. And God wants him to be freed by you, just as much as it seems to you that it is good for you that God do for you what you don't want to do for your debtor. How are you then worthy to receive the good of forgiveness if you are not good [enough] to do it?

---

27. The word in the original is *quitancie,* which the editors enclose in quotation marks. The English word is somewhat rare in modern usage but related to "acquittal." Here the term derives from medieval Latin, and is the origin of the modern German *Quittung.* It signifies the discharging of a debt or a document evidencing such a discharge.

40   Note what a reasonable and clear law that is, which everyone must approve of and understand. Whoever asks God to forgive him and does not forgive and thinks that his prayer will be answered thinks that God is not God, and that injustice [is] justice, and that evil is good. But whoever believes, as Christ teaches us, that God forgives as we forgive has a right belief in God—that he is the just, best God. And this person can reckon with this hope from his own actions of forgiving that God will forgive him and he can lovingly ask for it. From this note, man, that here a single path is opened for you through which you can know whether you are being heard by God and are a child of God. This [path] is that you see and note from your [own] action whether you do to others as you would have done to you; that is, whether you forgive your debtors honestly and bring them nothing but love. Then without a doubt you can have full confidence that you have achieved from God pardon for all your sins and are a child of eternal life. For you are not failing to fulfill any law because in loving your neighbor, which is revealed in [your] actions in the forgiveness of guilt, is the fulfillment of all laws.

41]"Lead us not into temptation"

Here we are taught that, although we have fulfilled the law and gained forgiveness of our sins, we still are not sure that we will persevere and not fall into guilt by being led into temptation. Temptation begins when we are free of sin; and we ought to believe that we can be protected by God, that we shall persevere and shall not fall, and to hope that we shall attain it and ask devoutly of God: "Lead us not into temptation," as though we wanted to say: "Lord, no deception under the form of good in its seductiveness has the power to lead me astray unless you do it; that is, that you determine it in this [sense] that all things happen through your permitting them or wanting them. So we ask you, do not remove the hand of your protection against evil temptation. Then I cannot fall. Otherwise, by removing your protection you lead me into temptation, just as the sun by setting gives us night in which we do not see."

42   Note also how we fall back into sin when we are led by a temptation of [something] seeming to be good which is presented to us in sensuality by this visible world or in reason by an evil spirit who tries to lead the understanding away from truth. And if we do not beseech God to preserve

and protect us, we are led astray and come into temptation and accept it as good. Thus we have fallen away from God, who is the highest good, into deceiving, seeming good. We have no other way against this than, according to the teaching of Christ, to ask God in every temptation that we not be led astray, according to the words of this holy prayer.[28]

43]"But deliver us from evil"

Here in these final words we have [it] from Christ's teaching that in this world we cannot be without evil temptation. For we are where evil is. So we ask for deliverance. In this we acknowledge that there is another kingdom where there is no evil but only the highest, true, and unmixed good; and that our deliverance from evil is deliverance from this sensual, knavish, deceiving world. And we long for the glory of the eternal good, in which alone we can be delivered from all evils. For outside the highest glory there is no place for the pure, everlasting, constant good. We ask for that deliverance.

In this we believe and acknowledge that, although we are now in the life of the sensual world and cannot leave it except through death, after this sensual death we can have an existence in a constant eternal good, and we hope to arrive there. And we ask with great love, and we desire to arrive there, although this cannot be without sensual death. And because of this in this prayer our sensuality is drawn into the spirituality of our understanding, and the will of God "as in heaven" of our understanding is on this sensual earth. For the whole human being has directed itself totally beyond itself into God, desiring to be separated and delivered from this temporal evil life, so that in eternity it can be with God, who is "the good." Hence, "God" is named from the good.

44   Note here: Whoever would not like to die this sensual death in order to come to God and prays for deliverance from evil, such a person gains nothing, because he is praying against his heart. And whoever prefers this evil world to God remains separated from God and the good and is for eternity in evil from which he can never be delivered. And therefore, this is the prayer of a person who bears a right, immaculate, and undiluted love of God. For he puts God before his temporal existence and every-

---

28. That is, as this holy prayer bids us do.

thing that is created and is not God. He asks for deliverance from this frail, transitory life so that he can be with his most beloved good, without which good he does not care to live. For he understands that he does not live except in union with God, whither his love leads him and where he is through love alone, although he is still held captive in this sensual world and in his fleshly temple. The person prays devoutly for deliverance whose life is such suffering because of the love that he bears for God. [So great is the suffering] that it seems to him that he is held captive in a miserable, murky, filthy prison; and if he were to leave, that he would be coming to the constant, good, and highest joy, to his most beloved whom alone he desires.

45   This person, therefore, is in God's love and has arrived there according to the articles of the holy *Pater noster.* And [what] he finds especially to belong to God—above all phrases—[is] liberation from evil, which is the bestowing of eternal life. For eternal life is nothing else but the highest that we can desire—and we can desire nothing but good—that is, God himself. This person says, "O Lord, because you have forgiven me my guilt through heavenly bread, 'do not lead me into temptation!' Do not let me remain long in this deceiving world in which I cannot be without temptation or remain unseduced without your protection, 'but deliver me,' Lord, 'from all evil!' For that is your inheritance,[29] far removed from all evil, to which you have called me in your Son Jesus."

46   Note here: If you want to know what eternal joy is that no one can comprehend because of its magnitude, then you will find that eternal joy cannot be better, more concisely, or more clearly understood by us than as Christ teaches us here. For joy is deliverance from evil. Do you want to know what hell is? Christ teaches you that hell is an eternal captivity in evil. Deliverance from evil is the highest joy; not to be delivered or captivity in evil is the greatest sadness and punishment. The highest heavenly joy is to be eternally in that good that is God, separated from evil. The greatest hellish or infernal suffering is to be separated from that good which is God.

A kingdom that is nothing else but good or God is called the kingdom

---

29. That is, what you have promised that we shall inherit.

of heaven. That is the highest kingdom. The kingdom where there is nothing but malice and evil is hell. For hell is under or beneath and is hell in its division, discord, upheaval, and ignorance, darkness. This is why the princes of hell are called "princes of darkness" or devils. But the kingdom of the heavens is concord, peace, love, wisdom, everything good and brightness. This is why the Prince, whom we ask to deliver us from hell and all evil, is called Deliverer from all evil. Amen.

Bernard McGinn

2. SEEING AND NOT SEEING

Nicholas of Cusa's *De visione Dei* in the History
of Western Mysticism

In Exodus 33:20 God tells Moses, "You cannot see my face, for no one will see my face and live." But in Genesis 32:30 Jacob names the place where he wrestled with a divine adversary "Phanuel," claiming "I have seen God face-to-face and my soul has been saved."[1] Similarly, after his vision of "the Lord sitting on a high and lofty throne" in the Temple, Isaiah announces, "with my own eyes I have seen the King, the Lord of hosts" (Is. 6:5); but in Deutero-Isaiah 45:15 we find the proclamation: "Truly, you are a hidden God, the Savior God of Israel."[2]

Equally contradictory texts about whether or not God can be seen in this life, and, if he can be, how that vision is to be understood, are found in the New Testament. Some passages announce that God will be seen by the justified, the most famous being the beatitude, "Blessed are the pure of heart for they shall see God" (Mt. 5:8), a text that does not make it altogether clear whether this vision will be in the here or hereafter.[3] 1 Timothy 6:16, however, speaks of God, "dwelling in unattainable light" as He whom "no one sees or can see." The prologue to John's Gospel announces that "No one has ever seen God; the Only-Begotten Son of God, who is in the Father's bosom, has revealed him."[4] The Johannine emphasis on the Son as the only one who sees the Father and can therefore re-

1. Cf. Exodus 24:10 and Numbers 12:8.

2. On seeing God in the Hebrew Bible and early Jewish texts, see Friedrich Nötscher, *"Das Angesicht Gottes schauen" nach biblischer und babylonischer Auffassung* (Darmstadt: Wissenschaftliche Buchgesellschaft, 1969); and Elliot R. Wolfson, *Through a Speculum That Shines: Vision and Imagination in Medieval Jewish Mysticism* (Princeton: Princeton University Press, 1994), ch. 1.

3. See also Hebrews 12:14.

4. John 1:18. See also John. 6:46, 1 John 4:12, and Matthew 11:27.

veal him is also evident in the passage in chapter 14 where Philip asks Jesus, "Show us the Father," and Jesus responds, "Who sees me, sees the Father. How can you say, 'Show us the Father'?" (Jn. 14:8–11). Finally, texts in both the Pauline and Johannine letters stress the eschatological character of the vision of God. 1 Corinthians 13:12 is powerful in its contrasts: "We see now mysteriously through a mirror, but then face-to-face; now I know in part; then I will know as I am known."[5] This reappearance of the Old Testament theme of "face-to-face vision" *(visio facialis)* was to be of considerable significance in the Christian mystical tradition. Finally, 1 John 3:2 also stresses the eschatological character of the vision of God, adding an important reference to filiation: "Beloved, now we are God's sons and it has not yet been revealed what we shall be; but we know that when he has appeared, we will be like him, because we will see him as he is."

Faced with these conflicting texts, one might expect the history of Christian thought to show a Hamlet-like hesitation—"To see or not to see, that is the question." Rather, there has been well-nigh universal agreement that the vision of God in heaven, however understood, is the goal of human life. A broad stream of Christian thought and practice, especially among the mystics, also held that some kind of seeing of God is possible in this life as preparation for and foretaste of what is to come. Precisely why early Christians found the notion of "seeing God" usually unproblematic may reflect their cultural location in a society that privileged the visual in so many ways. This is certainly the case with regard to Platonic philosophical spirituality that placed seeing God *(theōria theou)* as the ultimate human fulfillment.[6]

Seeing God in Christian Tradition

The brief autobiographical fragment that the converted philosopher Justin narrates at the beginning of his *Dialogue with Trypho* (c. 160) gives

---

5. See 2 Corinthians 3:18.

6. For an introduction to both Platonic and Christian *theōria/contemplatio*, see the lengthy multi-author article "Contemplation," in the *Dictionnaire de spiritualité* (Paris: Aubier, 1937–94), vol. 2:1643–2193 (cc. 1716–62 by René Arnou deal with contemplation in ancient philosophy).

us a window on this encounter. Justin speaks of his restless intellectual journey through the schools of Stoics, Peripatetics, and Pythagoreans, until he finally begins to make progress in "the contemplation of ideas" under the guidance of the Platonists. "I expected quite soon," he says, "to look upon God, for this is the goal of Plato's philosophy."[7] But a wise old man convinced him that while the Platonists were right about the goal, they could not really show him the way to that end. The mind *(nous)* begotten by God can, indeed, come to see its Unbegotten Creator, but only as a gift given by the Holy Spirit in reward for a virtuous life, not as an innate capacity of its nature.[8]

No brief paper could hope to give an adequate treatment of the history of the theme of *visio Dei* in Christian thought and mysticism. Even classic books, such as those of K. E. Kirk and Vladimir Lossky,[9] or the recent massive work of Christian Trottmann on scholastic disputes on the *visio beatifica*,[10] provide only a part of the story. Nevertheless, the problematics of "seeing God" are central to Christian mysticism, and they also provide us with a vantage point to consider Nicholas of Cusa's contribution to the mystical tradition. In the 1450s the Cardinal became involved in the medieval debate on the relation of love and knowledge in the path to union with God. After briefly setting forth his views in several letters of 1452 and 1453,[11] Cusanus realized that a more adequate solution to the

7. *Iustini Martyris. Dialogus cum Tryphone,* ed. Miroslav Marcovich (Berlin: Walter de Gruyter, 1997), ch. 2.6 (p. 73).

8. *Dialogus* 4.1 (pp. 76–77). Edward Baert, "Le thème de la vision de Dieu chez S. Justin, Clement d'Alexandrie et S. Grégoire de Nysse," *Freiburger Zeitschrift für Philosophie und Theologie* 12 (1965): 439–97, provides an introduction to the role of vision in Justin and Clement, discussing this passage on 440–55.

9. K. E. Kirk, *The Vision of God: The Christian Doctrine of the "Summum Bonum"* (London: Longmans and Green, 1932); and Vladimir Lossky, *The Vision of God* (London: Faith Press, 1963).

10. Christian Trottmann, *La vision béatifique. Des disputes scolastiques à sa définition par Benoît XII* (Rome: École française de Rome, 1995).

11. These letters can be found in Edmond Vansteenberghe, *Autour de la docte ignorance. Une controverse sur la théologie mystique au XVe siècle,* Beiträge zur Geschichte der Philosophie des Mittelalters, Band XIV, heft 2–4 (Münster: Aschendorff, 1915), 107–62. The key text is the letter Cusanus sent to Caspar Aindorffer and the monks of the Benedictine house at Tegernsee in September 14, 1453, which is No. 5 (pp. 113–17). For a summary of the controversy, see Alois Maria Haas, *Deum Mistice Videre . . . in Caligine Coincidencie. Zum Verhältnis Nikolaus von Kues zur Mystik* (Basel and Frankfurt: Helbing, 1989), 11–31.

issue demanded a broader perspective, one based on an investigation of what it means to see God. The result was his central mystical text, the *De visione Dei,* or *De icona,* as he sometimes called it, composed in late 1453.[12]

Cusanus had few predecessors in composing a distinct treatise on the problem of seeing God in this life.[13] In that sense his *De visione* was a novel work, however much it was influenced by the rich range of sources typical of his wide reading. How important seeing God was for Cusanus can be judged from his many other considerations of the problematics of seeing and not-seeing God. Major treatments can be found in two treatises of 1445, the *De quaerendo Deum* ("On Seeking God") and the *De filiatione* ("On Being a Son of God"), as well as in the *De beryllo* ("On [Intellectual] Eyeglasses") of 1458, and the late *De apice theoriae* ("On the Summit of Contemplation") of 1464.[14] If Cusanus's decision to compose a treatise on the topic of seeing God was unusual, the centrality of the theme of *visio Dei* in his writings and in the mystical tradition at large was not.

In order to get some grasp of the Cardinal's contribution, it may be helpful to take a brief, though obviously incomplete, look at some aspects of the history of the problem of seeing and not-seeing God in the history of Christianity. Clement of Alexandria is a good starting point, because it is with the Alexandrian catechist of the late second century that we get

---

12. In the Sept. 14, 1453, letter (Vansteenberghe, 116), Cusanus says that the *De visione Dei* was originally intended to be a chapter in his *Complementum theologicum.* The critical edition of the *De visione Dei* in the Heidelberg Academy's monumental *Nicolai de Cusa Opera Omnia* (Leipzig-Hamburg, 1932–) was not available at the time of this writing. In its absence I will cite and translate from the edition given in Jasper Hopkins, *Nicholas of Cusa's Dialectical Mysticism: Text, Translation, and Interpretive Study of the De Visione Dei* (Minneapolis, Minn.: Banning Press, 1985). I will, however, use the numbering system for sections to be employed in the critical text and followed by H. Lawrence Bond in his translation of the treatise in *Nicholas of Cusa: Selected Spiritual Writings,* Classics of Western Spirituality (New York: Paulist Press, 1997), 235–89. All translations are my own unless otherwise noted. The text is now available in h VI (2000).

13. There were, of course, a number of scholastic treatises that dealt with the beatific vision. Some of these considered how this ultimate seeing related to possible vision on earth. This issue will not be pursued here.

14. A full understanding of Cusa's treatment of *visio Dei,* and his role in the Christian mystical tradition, would demand a treatment of these and other texts. One important issue in such a study would be to determine to what extent Cusanus may have changed his position, as H. Lawrence Bond argues he does, in the *De apice theoriae* (see Bond's "Introduction," *Nicholas of Cusa,* 60–70). I detect less difference between the two treatises.

the first real encounter between Platonic philosophical mysticism and Christian spiritual teaching. Clement introduces, if in an unsystematic way, three of the essential themes of Christian mysticism that form the basis for Cusa's discussion almost thirteen centuries later: (1) the attempt to understand the scriptural vision of God in terms of Platonic *theōria;* (2) the exploration of the relation between seeing God and divinization; and (3) the use of categories taken from Hellenistic philosophy to express biblical teaching about God's invisibility and unknowability.[15] Clement's thought, especially as found in his *Stromateis,* raises, for the first time in Christian theology, the fundamental *aporia* with which Cusanus wrestled: how can the utterly invisible God become visible in a divinizing vision that is the goal of Christian faith? We need not argue that Cusanus's answer in the *De visione* was directly influenced by Clement in order to claim that the issues that emerged for the first time in the Alexandrian were those that Cardinal Nicholas saw as essential for the correct understanding of what it means to see God.

With Clement and his contemporaries Theophilus and Irenaeus we witness a concerted effort on the part of the leaders of nascent Orthodox Christianity to vindicate the goal of seeing God for their own understanding of belief in Jesus against the varieties of Gnostic Christianity.[16] In constructing his case, Clement uses the term *theōria* some eighty-five times, linking it with the true *gnōsis* (saving knowledge) that he sought to defend against Valentinian understandings of the word. For him, biblical texts on the eschatological vision of God (e.g., Mt. 5:8, 1 Cor. 12:13) demonstrate that *theōria* is the fruit and goal of true *gnōsis*. In book 7 of his *Stromateis,* for example, he says that gnostic souls "keep always moving to higher and higher regions, until they no longer greet the divine vision in or by means of mirrors [1 Cor. 12:13], but with loving hearts feast forever on the uncloying, never-ending sight. . . . This is the apprehending vision of the pure of heart [Mt. 5:8]."[17] While the final goal of such *theōria* is in heaven,

15. For an introduction to Clement's mysticism, see Bernard McGinn, *The Foundations of Mysticism: Origins to the Fifth Century* (New York: Crossroad, 1991), 101–8.

16. For a consideration of *theōria* in Clement, see Baert, "La thème de la vision," 460–80; and P. T. Camelot, *Foi et gnose. Introduction à l'étude de la connaissance mystique chez Clément d'Alexandrie* (Paris: Vrin, 1945), ch. 4.

17. Clement of Alexandria, *Stromateis* 7.3.13 (Otto Stählin edition in *Griechischer Christlicher Schriftsteller* series [GCS], Vol. 3:10.10–16). Clement cites Matthew 5:8 eighteen

it begins in this life and progresses through "mystic stages" (*tas prokopas tas mystikas: Strom.* 7.10.57) that involve both contemplation and action.[18] Their aim is divinization. (Clement introduced the verb *theopoiein* ["to be made like God"] into Christianity.) In his *Protrepticus* we find him using the famous formula, which first occurs in his contemporary Irenaeus: "the Logos of God became man so that you may learn from man how man may become God."[19]

Clement was the first to privilege seeing God as the hope of all Christians, and he played a role in emphasizing deification as the telos of the taking on of flesh by the Word. Clement was also important for his efforts to demonstrate that the biblical God was no less "unknowable," at least to human forms of knowledge, than the apophatic transcendent principle that contemporary Middle Platonist philosophers were exploring with such subtle insights.[20] In the second book of the *Stromateis,* he follows the lead of Philo in identifying Moses as the model philosopher and mystic. "Moses, convinced that God will never be known to human wisdom, says, 'Reveal yourself to me' (Ex. 33:13), and finds himself forced to enter 'into the darkness' where the voice of God was present; in other words, into the unapproachable, imageless, intellectual concepts relating to ultimate reality."[21] In discussing the reason why the apostles insisted on veiling the mysteries of faith in *Stromateis* 5, Clement cites both Plato's Letter 2, as well as various Pauline texts (e.g., 1 Cor. 2:6–7 and 3:1–3), to demonstrate

---

times—far more than any second-century Christian author before him (e.g., Justin does not use the text at all, and Irenaeus cites it only three times). See *Biblia Patristica. Index des citations et allusions bibliques dans la littérature patristique, Vol. 1: Des origines à Clément d'Alexandrie et Tertullien* (Paris: CNRS, 1975), 232–33. Clement also quotes 1 Cor. 13:12 fourteen times.

18. See, e.g., *Strom.* 2.10.46 (GCS 2:137.14–16), and 7.16.102 (GCS 3:72.7–8).

19. Clement, *Protrepticus* 1.8 (GCS 1:9.9–11).

20. On Clement's role as the father of Christian apophaticism, see Deirdre Carabine, *The Unknown God: Negative Theology in the Platonic Tradition, Plato to Eriugena* (Louvain: Peeters, 1995), 226–33; and Raoul Mortley, *From Word to Silence, vol. 2: The Way of Negation, Christian and Greek* (Bonn: Peter Hanstein, 1986), ch. 2. Both Mortley and Carabine show that while some negative terminology is found in Justin, Clement is "the first Christian to advocate a method of negative thinking, a mode of thought calculated to take the mind to the transcendent wholeness" (Mortley, 44).

21. Clement, *Stromateis* 2.2.6 (GCS 2:116). I have used the translation of John Ferguson, *Clement of Alexandria: Stromateis Books 1–3,* Fathers of the Church (Washington: The Catholic University of America Press, 1991), 160.

the necessity for not putting in writing the higher knowledge that he describes as "the meat that is mystic contemplation; for this is the flesh and blood of the Word, that is, the comprehension of the divine power and essence."[22] Following Johannine teaching, Clement emphasizes that our only access to knowledge of the divine essence is through the Incarnate Word.

Clement of Alexandria never explicitly analyzed the problematics of just how the invisible God comes to be seen. Nor, despite his frequent use of biblical texts about seeing God, did his student, Origen. A better sense of the issues that Cusanus confronted in taking up the aporia of seeing what cannot be seen can be found in Neoplatonic mystics, both those directly utilized by the Cardinal and others who had a role in providing insights that were passed on to him through tradition, both pagan and Christian.

Cusanus did not have direct contact with the texts of Plotinus; but, as Werner Beierwaltes has shown, there are fascinating analogies between the two thinkers, especially when they discuss the intellectual vision of the First Principle.[23] A transcendent First cannot be seen, but if that First is also immanent in all things, it must somehow be present in the very act of seeing. Plotinus explored this issue in two remarkable treatments of how *Nous,* or Pure Intelligence, can be said to see the invisible One, or Good.

In *Ennead* V.5.7–10, he begins from an analysis of physical seeing as requiring both an object of sight and a medium in which to see, moving upward to the comparable dynamic in how *Nous* sees objects, to finally explore the mysterious inner light that grounds vision both in us and in the Intellect insofar as it is directed towards the First Principle, which cannot be seen at all.[24] Plotinus struggles to describe how this inner light does not

---

22. *Stromateis* 5.10.65 (GCS 2:369–70), where Clement cites Plato, Ep. 2 (312D and 314BC). *Stromateis* V.10–12 gives the heart of Clement's apophatic teaching. In the *Paedagogus* 1.7.57 (GCS 1:124) Clement identifies the Word with the "face of God" seen by Jacob (Gen. 32:29).

23. Werner Beierwaltes, *Visio facialis—Sehen ins Angesicht. Zur Coincidenz des endlichen und unendlichen Blicks bei Cusanus,* Phil.-hist. Klasse. Sitzungsberichte Jahrgang 1988, Heft 1 (Munich: Bayerische Akademie der Wissenschaften, 1988), 34–38, and 40–43.

24. *Enneads* V.5.7–10, as found in *Plotinus,* with an English translation by A. H. Armstrong, 7 vols., Loeb Classical Library (Cambridge: Harvard University Press, 1966–88),

come or go but rather "appears or does not appear," "within and yet not within," staying "in nothing" *(menei hoti en oudeni).* If *Nous* were able to remain in the "absolute nowhere" *(holōs mēdamou)* where this light dwells, "it would always behold him, or rather not behold him, but be one with him." The mystery of the "placelessness" of "the First, which is the Principle," is as much a source of wonder for Plotinus as it later will be for Cusanus in the *De visione.* "It is really a wonder how he is present without having come, and how, though he is nowhere, there is nowhere where he is not."[25]

The second passage, found in *Ennead* VI.7.35–36, discusses how soul, when it becomes *Nous* and sees the "god, at once lets everything go."[26] This act of "true contemplation" *(tēs ontōs theas)* fuses see-er and seen. "By the continuity of his contemplation," Plotinus says, "he no longer sees a sight, but mingles his seeing with what he contemplates, so what was seen before has now become sight in him, and he forgets all other objects of contemplation."[27] Plotinus equates this with what he calls the second power of *Nous,* that is, the pre-intellective vision of "Intellect in love *(Nous Erōn),* when it goes out of its mind 'drunk with nectar.'" He concludes, "Intellect always has its thinking and always its not thinking, but looking at that god in another way."[28]

Late antique Christian authors also took up the issue of how we can be said to see God, both in this life and in the next. Augustine devoted much

---

5:174–87. Armstrong uses the third *editio minor* of Henry and Schwyzer with a few changes.

25. *Ennead* V.5.8 (1–25) (Armstrong 5:178–81).

26. On this text, see Pierre Hadot, "Structure et thèmes du Traité 38 (VI, 7) du Plotin," *Aufstieg und Niedergang der römischen Welt. Teil II. Principat. Band 36: Philosophie, Wissenschaft, Technik. 2 Teilband: Philosophie,* ed. Wolfgang Haase (Berlin: Walter de Gruyter, 1987), 624–76.

27. *Ennead* VI.7.35 (7–17) (Armstrong 7:194–95).

28. *Ennead* VI.7.35 (20–31) (Armstrong 7:196–97). Proclus refers to this passage in his *In Parmenidem* VII 142A3–4. See *Proclus. Commentaire sur Le Parménide de Platon. Traduction de Guillaume de Moerbeke,* 2 vols., ed. Carlos Steel (Leuven: University Press, 1985), 2:511.75–81. This work was known to Cusanus. See Karl Bormann, *Cusanus-Texte. Marginalien III. 2. Proclus Latinus. Die Exzerpte und Randnoten des Nikolaus von Kues zu den lateinischen Übersetzungen des Proclus-Schriften. 2.2 Expositio in Parmenidem Platonis,* Abhandlungen der Heidelberger Akademie der Wissenschaften, Phil-hist. Klasse, Jahrgang 1986, 3 Abh. (Heidelberg: Carl Winter-Universität Verlag, 1986), 149–50, with Cusanus's marginal note.

attention to the scriptural texts about seeing and not-seeing God,[29] as well as to the underlying theoretical issues.[30] His insistence that the intellectual vision of God is the essence of beatitude was of great weight in the later Latin theological tradition. Cusanus knew and cited many of Augustine's treatments.[31] Nevertheless, the Cardinal's solution to the problem of how we can see the invisible God in this life was based on a version of Neoplatonic dialectical thinking not found in Augustine.

In the case of thinkers such as Dionysius, John Scottus Eriugena, and Meister Eckhart, who form the "great tradition" of Latin dialectical Neoplatonism, the situation is different. Cusanus also knew these thinkers intimately, and he found in them significant resources for his thought in general, and for his understanding of the *visio Dei* in particular. Dionysius's *De mystica theologia* is a key text for Nicholas of Cusa, especially because of the way in which it emphasizes the absolute invisibility of God.[32] Moses, the archetypal mystic, cannot contemplate the God who cannot be seen, but only the place where he dwells.[33] He must break free of all that can be perceived by the eyes of the body and of the mind, "away from what sees and is seen, and plunge into the truly mysterious darkness of unknowing" in order to be "supremely united to the Wholly Unknown by an inactivity of all knowing."[34] This removal of all knowing and all see-

29. Augustine's discussions of how to understand the various appearances of the Persons of the Trinity described in Scripture can be found in the *Enarrationes in Psalmos* 138.8 (PL 37:1788–90), *In Iohannis evangelium* III,17 (PL 35:1403), and especially *De Trinitate* II–IV (PL 42:845–912).

30. Among Augustine's many discussions about seeing God, consult *Confessiones* VII, IX, and XIII; *De Trinitate* IX–XIV; *De genesi ad litteram* XII; and Epp. 147–148. In addition, a number of places in the *Enarrationes in Psalmos* treat *visio Dei* (e.g., *Ennar.* 97.3, 121.8, 125.9, and 149.4).

31. On the relation between Augustine and Nicholas of Cusa, see F. Edward Cranz, "St. Augustine and Nicholas of Cusa in the Tradition of Western Christian Thought," *Speculum* 28 (1953): 297–316.

32. On Dionysius and Cusanus, see Werner Beierwaltes, "Der verborgene Gott. Cusanus und Dionysius," in Beierwaltes, *Platonismus und Christentum* (Frankfurt: Klostermann, 1998), 130–71; and William J. Hoye, "Die Vereinigung mit dem gänzlich Unerkannten nach Bonaventura, Nikolaus von Kues und Thomas von Aquin," in *Die Dionysius-Rezeption im Mittelalter,* ed. Tzotcho Boiadjiev, Georgi Kapriev, and Andreas Speer (Turnhout: Brepols, 2000), 477–504.

33. Dionysius the Areopagite, *The Mystical Theology,* ch. 1 (*Patrologia Graeca* 3: 1000D).

34. Ibid., ch. 1 (1001A).

ing, however, leads to a paradoxical higher vision that Dionysius describes as seeing "above being that darkness concealed from all the light among beings."[35] Dionysius, however, does not engage in any extended analysis of this "not-seeing seeing," nor does he explicitly relate it to the other fundamental mysteries of Christian faith, as Cusanus does.

The influence of Eriugena on the thought of Nicholas of Cusa has been greatly illuminated by recent scholarship.[36] The Irishman's dialectical Neoplatonism displays a fundamental affinity with Cusanus's view of *visio Dei* in the way in which it identifies God's seeing with his creative action: "God's seeing is the creation of the entire universe, for it is not one thing for him to see and another to make, but his seeing is his will and his will is his working."[37] In exegeting John 1:18, Eriugena, like Dionysius, presents a strong case for God's absolute invisibility.[38] Citing both Dionysius and Augustine, he concludes: "If anyone says he has seen him, namely God, he has not seen him, but rather something made by him. For he is altogether invisible, 'who is better known by not-knowing,' and 'ignorance of whom is true wisdom.'"[39] What we do not find in Eriugena, though, is a

35. Ibid., ch. 2 (1025B). For other texts on this higher seeing, which Dionysius often buttresses by quoting 1 Tim. 6:16, consult *Epistle 5* (1073A); *The Celestial Hierarchy* 4.3 (180C); and *The Divine Names* 4.11 (708D).

36. See Werner Beierwaltes, "Cusanus and Eriugena," *Dionysius* 13 (1989): 115–52, especially 126–30 on *visio absoluta*.

37. Iohannes Scottus Eriugena, *Periphyseon 3* (*Patrologia Latina* 122: 704B): "Visio dei totius uniuersitatis est conditio. Non enim aliud est ei uidere et aliud facere, sed uisio illius uoluntas eius est et uoluntas operatio." For other texts on the *visio Dei*, see, e.g., *Peri. 3* (676C–77A).

38. *Commentarius in Evangelium Iohannis* I.xxv (in Jean Scot, *Commentáire sur L'Évangile de Jean*, ed. Édouard Jeauneau [Paris: Editions de Cerf, 1972], 114–26). See also the Irishman's discussion of CH 4.3 in his *Expositiones in Ierarchiam Coelestem* IV.3 (in *Iohannis Scoti Eriugenae: Expositiones in Ierarchiam Coelestem,* ed. Jeanne Barbet [Turnhout: Brepols, 1975], 74–79), and his teaching in *Peri.* V about the final *reditus* in which even the saved never pass beyond the seeing of *theophaniae theophaniarum* (e.g., 998B–1001A). On the contrast between Eriugena, who denies a vision of the divine essence, even in heaven, and standard medieval theology on this issue, see Dominic J. O'Meara, "Eriugena and Aquinas on the Beatific Vision," in *Eriugena Redivivus. Zur Wirkungsgeschichte seines Denkens im Mittelalter und im Übergang zur Neuzeit,* ed. Werner Beierwaltes (Heidelberg: Carl Winter, 1987), 214–36.

39. Eriugena, *Commentarius* I, xxv.95–99 (pp. 124–26): "Hinc est quod Dionysius ait: 'Et si quis eum—deum uidelicet—uidisse dixerit, non eum uidit, sed aliquid ab eo factum.' Ipse enim est omnino inuisibilis est, 'qui melius nesciendo scitur,' et 'cuius ignorantia uera est sapientia.'" The first and third quotations are from Dionysius, *Epistula 1* (1065A); the central quote is from Augustine, *De ordine* II.xvi.44 (PL 32:1015).

treatment of the way in which human seeing both reveals and conceals the divine *visio absoluta*. This aspect of the Neoplatonic dialectics of vision, however, was available to Cusanus in Meister Eckhart.

Eckhart's mystical thought centers on the birth of the Word in the soul out of the *grunt,* the fused identity of God and human.[40] This is the Dominican's reworking of the ancient Christian theme of divinization understood as filiation—our becoming God by realizing our essential oneness in the Word who became flesh.[41] "Whatever God the Father gave to his Only-Begotten Son in human nature," said Eckhart, "he gave all this to me. I except nothing, neither union, nor sanctity; but he gave the whole to me, just as he did to him."[42] Eckhart was suspicious of claims for direct visionary contact with God widespread in his era, poking fun at those who wished to see God with the same eyes they used to look at a cow. His sermons, theological commentaries, and treatises contain a number of discussions of the meaning of *visio Dei,* both here and in the world to come.[43] Eckhart, like Dionysius and Eriugena, held that in reality God

40. On Eckhart's mysticism of birth out of the ground, see Bernard McGinn, *Meister Eckhart's Mystical Thought: The Man from Whom God Hid Nothing* (New York: Crossroad, 2001), especially ch. 3.

41. Dietmar Mieth in "Gottesschau und Gottesgeburt. Zwei Typen christlicher Gotteserfahrung in der Tradition," *Freiburger Zeitschrift für Philosophie und Theologie* 27 (1980): 204–23, distinguishes two ideal types of mysticism, vision of God and divine birth. Whatever the validity of this broad distinction, it seems that both forms are combined in Cusanus. See Niklaus Largier, "The Space of the Word: Birth and Vision in Eckhart and Cusanus" (unpublished).

42. Meister Eckhart, German sermon (hereafter Pr.) 5A, as found in *Meister Eckhart. Die deutschen und lateinischen Werke* (Stuttgart-Berlin: Kohlhammer, 1936–), DW 1:77.10–13 hereafter abbreviated DW for the German works, and LW for the Latin writings. This passage was condemned as heretical in art. 11 of the bull "In agro dominico."

43. In the Latin works, see, for example, the treatment of Gen. 32:28 (*In Gen.* nn. 296–97); and the discussion of Ex. 20:21, and 33:13–23 (*In Ex.* nn. 235–38, and nn. 271–81). Is. 45:15 was a favorite Eckhart scriptural text, which he cites eight times. Also important is the treatment of Jn. 1:18 (*In Io.* nn. 187–98 in LW 3:156–67). Eckhart's exegesis of Jn. 14:8 (*Domine, ostende nobis patrem et sufficit nobis),* one of the most important passages in his John commentary (*In Io.* nn. 546–76 in LW 3:477–506), centers on how union with the Father "suffices," not on how God is seen. Eckhart also has a few discussions of a related theme, one of the burning theological issues of the day, i.e., whether the *beatitudo* of heaven consisted primarily in knowing or in loving (see, e.g., Prr. 7, 19, 37, 43, 52, 60, 70, 83). There are important treatments of *visio Dei* in a number of the Middle High German sermons, e.g., Prr. 3, 9, 15, 23, 32, 36, 45, 57 (on creatures as mirrors; cf. DW 2:600–602), 59 (on face-

cannot be seen, or, if he is said to be seen, he must be seen as Absolute Nothingness. His *Predigt* (German sermon) 71, interpreting Acts 9:8 ("Saul rose from the ground and opening his eyes saw nothing"), is a good example of this visionary apophasis.[44] Perhaps the most important link between Eckhart and Cusanus on *visio Dei*, however, concerns the mutuality of the gaze. Eckhart's dialectical view of fused-identity—"God's ground is the soul's ground, and the soul's ground is God's ground"—led him to preach that insofar as we can be said to see God, this cannot be other than God seeing himself. He expresses this ocular identity in *Predigt* 12: "The eye in which I see God is the same eye in which God sees me. My eye and God's eye are one eye and one seeing, one knowing, and one loving."[45] The mutuality of *visio* suggested by Paul's text in 1 Corinthians on face-to-face vision was not exactly a new theme in Christian mysticism, having been richly developed by William of St. Thierry in the twelfth century.[46] What is new with Eckhart was understanding this as a form of fused identity, that is, there is only one eye and one act of seeing. This was the view advanced by Cusanus when he said: "The being of a creature is equally your seeing and your being seen."[47]

The desire to see the invisible God found in Scripture, expounded and clarified through materials taken from Greek speculation on *theōria theou*, had been a part of Christian mysticism from the second century. Despite the centrality of this visionary trajectory, however, and notwithstanding

---

to-face vision; cf. DW 2:636), 73, and 83. The most important sermons on seeing God are the group Prr. 69–72 (DW 3:159–254), commenting on scriptural texts on vision (Jn. 16:16, Acts 9:8, and Mt. 5:1).

44. Pr. 71 (DW 3:211–31).

45. Pr. 12 (DW 1:201.5–8). See also Pr. 76 (DW 3:310–12), as well as Pr. 86 on face-to-face vision (DW 3:487–88). The same teaching is also found in the Latin works; see, e.g., *Liber Parabolorum Genesis* n. 219 (LW 1:697–98), a discussion of Israel's face-to-face vision of God; and *Expositio sancti Evangelii secundum Iohannem* n. 107 (LW 3:91–93). Eckhart's teaching often uses the example of the union of the eye and its object in physical seeing (see, e.g., Pr. 48 [DW 2:416–17]).

46. On William of St. Thierry's view of face-to-face vision, especially as found in his *Meditativae Orationes* 3, 8, and 10, see Bernard McGinn, *The Growth of Mysticism: Gregory the Great through the Twelfth Century* (New York: Crossroad, 1994), 247, 261–64. William as a possible source for Cusanus has been noted by Donald F. Duclow, "Mystical Theology and Intellect in Nicholas of Cusa," *American Catholic Philosophical Quarterly* 64 (1990): 121.

47. *De visione Dei* 10.40 (Hopkins, 164): "Esse creaturae est videre tuum pariter et videri."

the analyses of *visio Dei* found in a number of mystics, systematic treatments of seeing God, especially those that did not compromise the utter invisibility of the divine nature, were few. When Nicholas of Cusa entered the late medieval debate over the relation of love and knowledge to mystical union, he took it as an opportunity to rethink *theologia mystica* from the vantage of *visio Dei.* The result remains among his most significant contributions to the history of thought.

Cusanus on Seeing and Not-Seeing God

Cusanus's *De visione Dei* has been often analyzed.[48] Fortunately, the treatise is a true classic, so, like Augustine's *Confessions,* the *De visione* resists closure or any final interpretation. Part of the richness of the treatise rests in its mystagogical character. Cusanus loved to employ "similitudes"—mathematical, geometrical, mechanical examples—to illustrate his teaching; but the *De visione* is different in the way in which it integrates the fundamental exercises of seeing, hearing, and speaking into a praxis designed to lead his monastic audience, by experience *(experimentaliter),* into what he calls "ready access to mystical theology" *(facilitas mysticae theologiae).* Just how far each practitioner of his method will be able to advance in this *facilitas* is not up to any outsider to judge, as the Cardinal emphasizes in chapter 17 with his remarks on his own practice:

Trusting in your infinite goodness, I tried to undergo a rapture so that I might see You who are invisible and the unrevealable vision revealed. How far I got, You

---

48. Literature on the *De visione Dei* is large. Along with the studies of Haas, Beierwaltes, and Duclow already noted, I have profited especially from Louis Dupré, "The Mystical Theology of Nicholas of Cusa's *De visione dei*"; and Clyde Lee Miller, "God's Presence: Some Cusan Proposals," in *Nicholas of Cusa on Christ and the Church,* ed. Gerald Christianson and Thomas M. Izbicki (Leiden: Brill, 1996), 205–20, and 241–49. See also the brilliant analysis of Michel de Certeau, "The Gaze of Nicholas of Cusa," *Diacritics: A Review of Contemporary Criticism* 3 (1987): 2–38. I also recommend H. Lawrence Bond, "The 'Icon' and the 'Iconic Text' in Nicholas of Cusa's *De Visione Dei,*" in *Nicholas of Cusa and His Age: Intellect and Spirituality,* ed. Thomas M. Izbicki and Christopher M. Bellitto (Leiden: Brill, 2002), 177–97. For a general summary of Cusa's mysticism focused on the *De visione Dei,* see Werner Beierwaltes, "Mystische Element im Denken des Cusanus," in *Deutsche Mystik im abendländische Zusammenhang. Neu erschlossene Texte, neue methodische Ansätze, neue theoretische Konzepte,* ed. Walter Haug and Wolfram Schneider-Lastin (Tübingen: Niemeyer, 2000), 425–48.

know, not I. And your grace, by which You assure me that You are incomprehensible, is sufficient for me [2 Cor. 12:9]; and by it You raise up a firm hope that under your guidance I may come to ultimate delight in You.[49]

In the preface, Cusanus begins his mystical handbook by creating a paraliturgy around the *icona,* the image of the omnivoyant face of Christ, probably of the Veronica, or "Suffering Christ" type, which he sent to the Tegernsee monks.[50] Michel de Certeau has provided a penetrating analysis of the dynamics of the gaze set forth by Cusanus in the *praxis devotionis* described in the preface.[51] As in the normal monastic liturgy, this ritual commences with a procession by the community.[52] Each monk first stands observing the icon's atemporal gaze seemingly directed to him alone. Then, each moves from his original location to the opposite side, in amazement at the "change of the unchangeable gaze" that introduces temporality and mutability into the experience. The crucial part of the experiment, however, is the transition from the visual realm to the audible, the speaking and hearing that form the believing community—that is, faith is what enables us to begin to move beyond the perspectival as particular toward a more universal viewpoint. The simultaneous omnivoyance, or infinity, of Christ's gaze begins to be revealed only when each brother asks the other as they meet coming from opposite directions whether the icon's gaze has moved simultaneously with him too. As de

49. *De visione Dei* 17.79 (Hopkins, 214): "Conatus sum me subicere raptui, confisus de infinita bonitate tua, ut viderem te invisibilem et visionem revelatam irrevelabilem. Quo autem perveni tu scis; ego autem nescio. Et sufficit mihi gratia tua, qua me certum reddis te incomprehensibilem esse, et erigis in spem firmam, quod ad fruitionem tui te duce perveniam."

50. For comments on the possible identity of the *icona* and further literature, see Bond, "The 'Icon' and the 'Iconic Text,'" 180–83.

51. De Certeau, "The Gaze of Nicholas of Cusa," especially 11–21.

52. De Certeau, "'The Gaze,'" 14, speaks of Cusa's exercise as a "mathematical liturgy," but the processional aspect indicates that it is no less monastic. The question of the relation between Cusa's new liturgy with its accompanying *lectio divina* and *meditatio/oratio* and the ordinary practice of the Benedictine life is complicated and deserves more work. For one analysis, see Mark Führer, "The Consolation of Contemplation in Nicholas of Cusa's *De visione dei,*" *Nicholas of Cusa on Christ and the Church,* 221–40, who argues for a closer relation of the text to traditional monastic practice than seems evident to me, though I agree with his claim that Cusanus sought "a revitalization of mental prayer" (p. 224). The relation between the *De visione Dei* and meditative and contemplative practices is also taken up in Bond, "The 'Icon' and the 'Iconic Text.'"

Certeau notes, willingness to share wonder and to believe one's brother expressed in the implied question, "You too?" is at the root of Cusanus's mystagogical exercise.[53] As the Cardinal puts it, echoing the famous formula of *fides quaerens intellectum,* "He will believe him, and unless he believed, he would not grasp that it is possible."[54]

It is only on the basis of such asking, hearing, and believing that we, that is, each member of the community of faith, begin to grasp with amazement (not rational understanding) the experience of being seen by an infinite and omnipresent gaze. Since in God there is no difference between seeing and speaking ("O Lord, your gaze speaks, for your speaking is not other than your seeing," as chapter 10 puts it),[55] we can also understand that what we have learned about God's seeing is true of how he addresses us. This realization is effected through a second "experiment," one of meditative prayer on the meaning of the liturgical praxis introduced in the preface. During the course of this extended *oratio/meditatio* that comprises the remainder of the treatise, Cusanus introduces other similitudes to help advance his argument (e.g., clock and mirror), and also encourages other practices (e.g., praying the Our Father in chapter 8), but he continues to return to the master symbol of the *icona.*[56]

The first three chapters of the *De visione* form an introduction, laying down the premises for what will follow. They are meant to be read and studied, whereas the remainder of the work is an exercise that is meant to be put to practice. This is evident from the way in which in these first three chapters Cusanus speaks in his own voice as teacher, but beginning in chapter 4, he asks the *frater contemplator* to gaze once again upon the *icona dei* so that "a contemplation *(speculatio)* will arise in you, and you will be stirred up and speak."[57] With few exceptions, the rest of the trea-

53. De Certeau, "The Gaze," 14–23, on the stages of the exercise, especially p. 20 on the dialogue, "You too?" "Yes."

54. *De visione Dei* Pref. 3 (Hopkins, 116): ". . . credet ei; et nisi crederet, non caperet hoc possibile." There is a reminiscence here of the famous text of Is. 7:14: "Nisi crederetis, non intelligetis," but with a typically Cusan twist.

55. *De visione Dei* 10.38 (Hopkins, 160): "Et occurrit mihi, Domine, quod visus tuus loquatur; nam non est aliud loqui tuum quam videre tuum" (trans. H. Lawrence Bond).

56. For subsequent references to the visual exercise of the *icona,* see *De visione Dei* 1.5, 4.9, 5.13, 6.17 and 19, 9.32 and 35, 10.38, 15.61 and 64, and 22.94.

57. *De visione Dei* 4.9 (Hopkins, 124): "Et quia visus eiconae te aeque undique respicit et non deserit quocumque pergas, in te excitabitur speculatio, provocaberisque et dices: . . ."

tise is in the form of a prayer, not in Cusa's own voice, but in the voice of the brother speaking for Cusanus (though Cusanus is actually speaking for the brother). Thus, the *ego* of the author and the *tu* of the addressed are here fused through their shared calling out to the divine *Tu* in mystagogic prayer. The shifting perspectives of the *De visione* function on many levels, for, as H. Lawrence Bond has noted, the text is both an iconography, or explanation of the meaning of the image, and "an icon, picturing by its own form, with words or other symbols, so as to signify, convey, and transpose the reader from one state of awareness or experience to another."[58]

The originality of Cusanus's verbal-audial transpositions becomes evident from a comparison with a work that Cusanus knew well. In the *Confessions* Augustine had created a new kind of mystical text, in which he made his confession, that is, gave his testimony, to God in his own voice, while God responded to him in the words of Scripture that the bishop himself quoted so liberally throughout the book (about a third of the total text). Although Cusanus uses scriptural citations fairly often, he does not employ the Bible as the "other voice" as Augustine did. Is God then silent in the *De visione?* Yes, in the sense that the appeal to silence is an essential part of Cusanus's message;[59] but, from another perspective, God's speaking is as omnipresent as his gaze—and just as immanent. If seeing God is the same as being seen by him (and vice versa) and God's seeing is his speaking, then the outpoured prayer of the *contemplator* speaking for and with Cusanus is itself God's hidden Word continuously breaking forth in human voice. Thus, the content of Cusanus's message of what it means to see God—a seeing that is being-seen and a speaking that is hearing oneself being-spoken—is already inscribed in the dynamics of the text's voices.[60]

The rest of the *De visione* falls into three sections. In Section I (chapters 4–16) there is an extended analysis of what *visio Dei,* understood as both God's own seeing and our vision of him, might mean. Central to this part

58. Bond, "The 'Icon' and the 'Iconic Text,'" 184.

59. See, e.g., *De visione Dei* 6.21 and 7.25 (Hopkins, 138, 144). On silence in the *De visione,* see Günter Stachel, "Schweigen vor Gott. Bemerkungen zur mystischen Theologie der Schrift *De visione Dei,*" MFCG 14 (1980): 167–81.

60. On this form of "reverse dialectic" of the divine presence-in-absence, see Miller, "God's Presence: Some Cusan Proposals," 244–45; and Beierwaltes, *"Visio Facialis,"* 18–19.

are the themes of *visio facialis,* the *murus paradisi* ("wall of paradise" or *murus coincidentiae* ["wall of coincidence"]), and God as *infinitas absoluta* ("absolute infinity"). The essential conclusion, as Bond well puts it, is that "Our seeing is a being seen. God is never the object of our sight; God is the eternal subject of seeing."[61] The brief Section II (chapters 17–18) shows why a proper understanding of seeing God reveals that God is a loving Trinity. Finally, Section III (chapters 19–25) demonstrates that our only access to vision of the *unitrinus deus* is through the filiation, or sonship, bestowed on us by the union of the divine and human natures in Jesus.[62] It is obviously impossible in a brief compass to follow the details of the Cardinal's development of all these themes, but a consideration of some key elements in light of the trajectory of thought sketched above will help show how Cusanus was able to provide, perhaps for the first time in the history of Christian mysticism, an account that integrated divine invisibility, the face-to-face vision promised in Scripture, and divinization understood as filiation.

As the reader proceeds through the pyrotechnics of Cusanus's experiments with thought and language in the first section, it is often difficult not to lose the way—to become mystified about how one chapter relates to another.[63] The structure of the argument is not linear but prismatic, in the sense that different facets of the problematic of seeing the unseeable are held up to our mental gaze in such varied ways that their very profusion helps deepen the amazement that is essential to the mystagogic exercise. In order to prevent dazzlement from becoming mere confusion, however, it is useful to look at this first long section in the light of its conclusion in chapter 16 before we proceed through it in order. In this conclusion to Section I, Nicholas of Cusa summarizes his dialectics of vision by affirming that the more we comprehend that God is incomprehensible, the more we attain the goal of our own infinite desire.[64] The *contemplator* who recognizes this can thus say, "I see you, O Lord my God, in a

61. Bond, "The 'Icon' and the 'Iconic Text,'" 192.

62. Many of these essential themes of the *De visione* can also be found in the *De filiatione* 1.52–54 and 3.62–71 (h IV 1:39–42, 46–52).

63. Bond, "The 'Icon' and the 'Iconic Text,'" 190, notes how each chapter can be considered as a separate meditation.

64. *De visione Dei* 16.69.

kind of mental rapture, because if sight is not satisfied with seeing, nor the hearing with hearing, then how much less the intellect by understanding."[65] The mental rapture that Cusanus speaks of here is not a loss of consciousness, or a new insight into *a* truth, but, to adopt the language of Bernard Lonergan, a kind of transcendental reverse insight—that is, an understanding that our drive toward total understanding can be understood only as the affirmation of the existence of an *incomprehensible* Truth that is both within us as infinite desire and outside us on the other side of what Cusanus calls "the wall of paradise."[66]

The operative identity that fuses our infinite desire with God's Absolute Infinity, described in this passage, is what Cusanus had been exploring since the early pages of the treatise. In chapter 5, for example, he says, "In seeing me, you who are the hidden God [Is. 45:15] give yourself to be seen by me. . . . To see you is not different from your seeing the one who sees you."[67] More daringly, in chapter 7 he roots the goal of our infinite desire in the actualization of the freedom God's creative gaze bestows on each of us as *contemplator:* "When I thus rest in the silence of contemplation, you, O Lord, respond in the depths of my heart and say, 'You be yours and I too will be yours.' . . . This rests in my power, not in yours, O Lord."[68] Lest some unwary Augustinian literalist conclude that this smacks of Pelagianism, Cusanus adds the plea, "But how will I be mine, if you do not teach me, Lord?"[69] From the perspective of the Cardinal's dialectical Neoplatonism, God's transcendent otherness is identical with his absolute immanence.

The intellect, as Cusanus concludes in chapter 16, is not satisfied by understanding something, because any act of understanding a thing by its nature is finite, not infinite. He also insists that intellect cannot be satisfied

---

65. *De visione Dei* 16.70 (Hopkins, 202): "Video te, domine deus meus, in raptu quodam mentali, quoniam si visus non satiatur visu nec auris auditu, tunc minus intellectus intellectu."

66. Bernard Lonergan, *Insight: A Study in Human Understanding* (New York: Longmans, 1957).

67. *De visione Dei* 5.13 (Hopkins, 130): "Videndo me das te a me videri, qui es deus absconditus. . . . Nec est aliud te videre quam quod tu videas videntem te."

68. Ibid., 7.25 (Hopkins, 144–46): "Et cum sic in silentio contemplationis quiesco, tu, domine, intra praecordia mea respondes dicens: 'Sis tu tuus et ego ero tuus.' . . . Per me igitur stat, non per te, domine."

69. Ibid., 7.26: "Quomodo autem ero mei ipsius nisi tu, domine, docueris me?"

by something intelligible of which it is totally ignorant. Rather, "only the intelligible which it knows to be so intelligible that it can never be fully understood can satisfy the intellect." He closes his summary with an appeal to a dialectical understanding of hunger and satiation probably based on Eckhart. Our never-ending desire for God is like a hunger that can be satisfied only by a meal, "which, although continually eaten, can never be fully consumed, because being infinite, it is not diminished by being eaten."[70]

The multiple facets of Nicholas of Cusa's argument in chapters 4–16 make ample use of what H. Lawrence Bond has called the "coincident theology" that the Cardinal had developed in his *De docta ignorantia*,[71] but the *De visione* extends this into the further dimension that Cusanus, following Dionysius, calls "mystical theology."[72] If coincident theology expresses the space where the cataphatic and apophatic approaches to God fuse into the paradoxical unity of the coincidence of opposites, then mystical theology, as found on the other side of the "wall of paradise," represents a kind of hyper-space, a dimension beyond any realm of language. Mystical theology is a "black hole" into which even coincidences of opposites vanish in order to be transformed in ways that cannot be conceptualized, though they can be said to be "seen" in a not-seeing seeing.

The relation between coincident theology as developed in the *De docta ignorantia* and the mystical theology set forth in the *De visione dei* will emerge more clearly from a brief commentary on the three sections of the Cardinal's great mystical treatise. On the basis of the three theological premises Cusanus puts forth in the introduction (chapters 1–3),[73] the con-

70. Ibid., 16.70 (Hopkins, 204): "sed solum ille cibus qui ad eum pervenit et licet continue deglutiatur, tamen numquam ad plenum potest deglutiari, quoniam talis est quod deglutiendo non imminuitur, quia infinitus" (trans. Bond). The passage from Eckhart is found in his *Sermones et Lectiones super Ecclesiastici* nn. 42–43 (LW 2:271–72). See Donald F. Duclow, "The Hungers of Hadewijch and Eckhart," *Journal of Religion* 80 (2000): 421–41.

71. Bond, "Introduction," *Nicholas of Cusa. Selected Spiritual Writings*, 26–36. Bond characterizes coincident theology as follows: "Because we start with God as absolute maximum in whom maximum and minimum coincide, and because we know God through God's coincident work in Christ, Cusanus says, we can, in consequence, see God as the enfolder and unfolder of all reality, and we can see the world in its unity and particularity operating 'coincidentally'" (36).

72. On the difference between the two, see Haas, "Deum mistice videre," 13–15; and Dupré, "The Mystical Theology of Nicholas of Cusa's *De visione dei*," 205.

73. These three premises are: (1) whatever can be affirmed of the omnivoyant gaze of

templation of *visio facialis Dei* found in Section I (chapters 4–16) begins with two chapters in which the prayer of the *frater contemplator* explores the identity of the divine gaze with the other affirmations made about God in positive theology. God's seeing, Cusanus argues, is the same as his love, his existence, his maximum goodness, indeed, his Absolute Maximality itself *(absoluta maximitas)*.[74] As the exercise of meditating on the mutuality of the gaze extends itself to the affirmation of the identity of see-er and seen in chapter 5, the contemplative also experiences the gaze as the biblical tasting and seeking of God, as well as God's having mercy and working all things from within.

These considerations set up the investigation of the *facies Dei* that commences in chapters 6 and 7.[75] Here Cusanus's coincident theology appears explicitly, but in a form of negative theology based on Scripture and thematized by Dionysius. "Your gaze, Lord, is your face," says Cusanus, transferring the eschatological vision of the face of God promised in 1 Corinthians 13:12 into the face that gazes upon each of us here and now. God is the *facies facierum,* the exemplar of all faces (or what we might call "modes of attention"). Therefore, every face that looks toward the divine face sees itself, that is, it sees its own transcendent truth in the Exemplar.[76] This form of seeing is one that cannot be conceived by the mind (it has no *conceptus*); it can only be experienced in darkness and unknowing since it takes place "under a veil and in a mystery," in "a secret and hidden silence."[77] The fruit of this *visio facialis,* as explained in chapter 7, is found through realizing our freedom to love God in learned ignorance and the cloud of unknowing.[78]

After this, Cusanus returns to the positive pole of his theology, introducing a new exercise, praying the Our Father, and a new series of vi-

---

the *icona dei* is eminently true of the absolute uncontracted gaze of God (ch. 2); (2) God's *visus absolutus* embraces all modes of seeing as the *contractio contractionum* (ch. 3); and (3) as the *absoluta ratio,* God enfolds the *rationes* of all things, and therefore in him there is no real distinction of his attributes.

74. *De visione Dei* 4.10–12.

75. Miller, "God's Presence: Some Cusan Proposals," 243–47, rightly notes the shift from the investigation of the mutuality of the gaze to the mutuality of the face beginning in chapter 6.

76. *De visione Dei* 6.18–20.

77. Ibid., 6.21.

78. Ibid., 7.23–26.

sual similitudes—the book, the eye, the mirror, and the infinite ocular sphere—to further his exploration.[79] Positive theology and coincident theology, however, once again are put in doubt by the limit situations expressed in negative theology. This is evident from how chapter 9 begins, for the first time, to explore two new ways of using limits to go beyond them—the language of *infinitas* and the image of the *murus paradisi*.[80] All contracted forms of existence are found in God, the Absolute Form and "essence of essences," in a simple and infinite way.[81] Thus motion and rest, and all opposites are found in "a face absolute from these conditions, because it exists above all standing and motion, in simplest and most Absolute Infinity."[82] This is the coincidence of opposites, the cloud above reason, where "impossibility coincides with necessity." Cusanus calls it the wall of paradise whose gate is guarded by reason. "It is on the other side of the coincidence of contradictories," he says, "that You will be able to be seen, and nowhere on this side."[83] God both embraces the coincidence of opposites and also goes beyond it.[84]

The Cardinal continues the exploration of the *murus paradisi* in chapter 10 with a series of comments on the coincidences of seeing and being seen, hearing and being heard, earlier and later, now and then, and the like, that are found at the entrance of paradise. "But You, my God, who are Absolute Eternity, exist and speak beyond the now and then."[85] In chapter 11 he explores many different aspects of the Cusan dialectic of enfolding *(complicatio)* and unfolding *(explicatio)*, while chapter 12 exam-

---

79. Ibid., 8.29–30.

80. Much has been written on Cusanus's striking image of the *murus paradisi* or *murus coincidentiae*. See especially Rudolf Haubst, "Die erkenntnis-theoretische und mystische Bedeutung der 'Maurer der Koinzidenz,'" MFCG 18 (1989): 167–95; Walter Haug, "Die Maurer des Paradieses. Zur mystica theologia des Nicholas Cusanus in 'De visione Dei,'" *Theologische Zeitschrift* 45 (1989): 216–30; and Peter Casarella, "Neues zu den Quellen der cusanischen Mauer-Symbolik," MFCG 19 (1990): 273–86.

81. *De visione Dei* 9.33–34.

82. Ibid., 9.35.

83. Ibid., 9.36–37 (Hopkins, 160): "Et iste est murus paradisi in quo habitas, cuius portam custodit spiritus altissimus rationis, qui nisi vincatur, non patebit ingressus. Ultra coincidentiam contradictoriorum videri poteris et nequaquam citra" (trans. Bond).

84. See Werner Beierwaltes, "Deus Oppositio Oppositorum [Nicolaus Cusanus, *De visione dei* XIII]," *Salzburger Zeitschrift für Philosophie* 8 (1964): 179–81.

85. *De visione Dei* 10.42 (Hopkins, 166): "Tu vero, deus meus, ultra nunc et tunc existis et loqueris, qui es aeternitas absoluta."

ines the Eriugenian paradox of how God both creates and is created. This brings him once again to the seemingly unsurmountable barrier he now calls the *murus absurditatis*,[86] and to the first discussion of how it may be possible to "leap over *(transilire)* that wall of invisible vision where You are to be found."[87] As long as we think of the Creator as creating, we are on our side of the wall of paradise; when we conceive of the "Creatable Creator" *(creatorem creabilem)*, we are at the wall itself. "But when I see You as Absolute Infinity to whom neither the name of Creating Creator nor Creatable Creator applies, then I begin to gaze at You in an unveiled way and to enter into the garden of delights."[88]

The notion of Absolute Infinity introduced here, one which Cusanus analyzes in detail in chapter 13, has rightly been seen as central to his entire treatise.[89] The first part of this chapter is a dialectical argument similar to what Meister Eckhart set forth in his exploration of Divine Oneness as distinct indistinction.[90] Cusa's wall is the limit of all conceptual naming, but *infinitas* is not really a name—it is the recognition of a "necessary impossible." We cannot see, in the sense of understand, *how* "an end without end is an end," but we must assert *that* God as infinite essence is the end without end, namely the necessary end of all things.[91] Such an assertion goes beyond just affirming a coincidence of contradictories, because when we speak of God's absolute infinity we admit a coincidence of contradictories *without contradiction,* that is, "the opposition of opposites without opposition."[92] This is *docta ignorantia,* a seeing that is not seeing.

86. Ibid., 12.49.   87. Ibid., 12.47.

88. Ibid., 12.50 (Hopkins, 176): "Sed absolutam cum te video infinitatem, cui nec nomen creatoris creantis nec creatoris creabilis competit, tunc revelate te inspicere incipio et intrare ortum deliciarum."

89. See especially Beierwaltes, *"Visio Facialis,"* 23–28; and "Mystische Elemente," 429–33, 438. On the importance of chapter 13 as the denouement of the book, see Bond, "The 'Icon' and the 'Iconic Text,'" 190–92.

90. Eckhart, *Expositio Libri Sapientiae,* nn. 144–57 (LW 2:481–94). For a translation, see *Meister Eckhart Teacher and Preacher,* ed. and trans. Bernard McGinn (New York: Paulist Press, 1986), 166–71.

91. *De visione Dei* 13.53.

92. Ibid., 13.54. See Beierwaltes, "Deus Oppositio Oppositorum," 179–82, on the two related meanings of *oppositio oppositorum:* (1) "Nichts von Allem" as found in *De visione Dei* 13 and the *De non aliud* and (2) "Allem in Allem" as taught in the *De theologicis complementis* ("Complementary Theological Considerations"), 13 et al.

In the remaining three chapters of this long first part of the *De visione,* Cusanus goes on to show how infinity is the key that unlocks earlier aspects of his argument. It also provides a launching pad for other dialectical terms that he was to explore in his subsequent writings. God enfolds all things without the otherness that makes one thing different from another in the unfolded realm.[93] Divine infinity is "the absolute and infinite power to be," the *potentia absoluta* that he would later analyze in his *Trialogus de possest.*[94] Chapter 15 returns to the image of God as mirror, something already mentioned in chapters 4, 8, and 12, concluding that as the "living mirror of eternity," God acts in a way opposite to our mirrors that reflect the image of a form—"what one sees in this mirror of eternity is not an image, but what one sees is the truth of which one who sees is an image."[95] He also reprises the notion of face-to-face vision, once again locating it in our present existence rather than in heaven. The dialectical mutuality of face-to-face vision means that "according to the changing of my face your face is equally changed and unchanged."[96] That is to say, God's face changes insofar as his infinite goodness never abandons the truth of our changeable faces; but as Absolute Goodness God's face can never change.

The introduction of divine goodness and love at this point, further explored in chapter 16, forms a bridge to the treatment of the Trinity and the Incarnation in the remaining two sections of the *De visione.* It also serves as a foundation for the Cardinal's final analysis of the relation of love and knowledge. The identity of seeing and being seen is identical with the coincidence of loving and being loved, absolutely, that is, supra-coincidentally, in God, where Love (i.e., the Holy Spirit) enfolds both Filial and Paternal Love, and mediately in our face-to-face relation to God. "You offer yourself to any of us looking on You," says Cusa, "as though You receive being from us, and You conform yourself to us so that we will love You more the more You seem like us."[97] Therefore, if our self-love is

---

93. *De visione Dei* 14.   94. Ibid., 15.61–62.

95. Ibid., 15.63 (Hopkins, 194): "quia id quod videt in illo aeternitatis speculo non est figura sed veritas, cuius ipse videns est figura" (trans. Bond). For earlier discussions of the *speculum* motif, see 4.12, 8.30–31, and 12.48.

96. Ibid., 15.65.

97. Ibid., 15.65 (Hopkins, 198): "O inexplicabilis pietas, offers te intuenti te, quasi recipias ab eo esse; et conformes te ei, ut eo plus te diligat, quo appares magis similes ei" (trans. Bond).

true love, we are really loving God. In chapter 16, as noted above, Cusanus concludes this whole discussion by showing that the infinite nature of our love and desire for God is the root of the *docta ignorantia* that brings us to epektetic, i.e., perpetually progressive, union with God here and in eternity.

Some readers might have thought that Cusanus would have been satisfied with setting forth his case for the proper understanding of how the invisible God can be seen in chapters 4–16 of the *De visione dei*. For him, however, the treatment was incomplete. It is necessary, from the Cardinal's perspective, that face-to-face vision of the kind he has presented be grasped as realizable only by seeing the God who is Trinitarian love revealed to us in Jesus Christ. While the later chapters of the *De visione Dei* have been somewhat less studied than the earlier ones, they are no less vital to Cusanus's mysticism.[98] Although replete with details important for his theology of the Trinity and Christology, their role in his mystical *summa* can only be briefly summarized here.

Following books 8 and 9 of Augustine's *De Trinitate*,[99] Cusanus derives his theology of the *deus unitrinus* from the notion of God as infinitely lovable, that is, an absolute oneness of "loving love, lovable love, and the love that is the bond of loving love and lovable love." This same threefold love is also present in our own experience of contracted love.[100] The plurality that we see in God is an otherness that is really identity (not just a coincidence of opposites), and therefore it lies beyond the wall of coincidence that "shuts out the power of every intellect, although the eye looks beyond into paradise" to see the secret love and hidden treasure it cannot name.[101] This transcending eye is the eye of love. Following an important theme in the history of Christian mysticism, Cusanus held that while intellect had a necessary role to play in the path to God, love was the higher

98. This has been recognized by recent investigators, such as Louis Dupré, "The Mystical Theology of Cusanus' *De visione dei*," 217–20; and Donald Duclow, "Mystical Theology and Intellect in Nicholas of Cusa," 118–29.

99. The sources of Cusa's Trinitarian theology in the *De visione Dei* cannot be fully explored here, but they certainly include Augustine's *De Trinitate*. For more on the Trinity in Cusa's mysticism, see Bernard McGinn, "Unitrinum Seu Triunum: Nicholas of Cusa's Trinitarian Mysticism," in *Mystics: Presence and Aporia,* ed. Michael Kessler and Christian Sheppard (Chicago: University of Chicago Press, 2003), 90–117.

100. *De visione Dei* 17.71–72.

101. Ibid., 17.75.

power.[102] Therefore, both love and intellect are necessary, as he says in chapter 18 when he finally takes up the issue that had led the Tegernsee community to turn to him for help. Insofar as both intellect and love bear the image of the Trinity, both are needed for uniting us with God, though in different ways. We are not united to God insofar as he is *intelligens* ("understanding") and *amans* ("loving") in himself, because the divine way of understanding and loving is beyond us. But since God has planted in us infinite desire to know him and to love him, he has also become for us *deus intelligibilis* ("the God to be understood") and *deus amabilis* ("the God to be loved"). Hence, "the rational human nature can only be united to your intelligible and lovable divine nature [i.e., God immanent in us], and a person, in receiving you, . . . crosses over into a bond with you so close that it can be named 'filiation.'"[103]

The entry of filiation leads into the final section of the *De visione* (chapters 19–25) in which the Cardinal describes how such sonship, the maximum bond of union, is made available to humans in the person of Jesus Christ.[104] Cusa's Christology is an even larger topic than the Trinity, so here I must restrict myself to a few remarks on some crucial issues in these final chapters of the Cardinal's mystagogical manual.[105]

Cusanus roots the necessity for the Incarnation in the Trinity itself.

102. Although he does not use the expression, I think Cusanus would have agreed with the formula popular with the Cistercian and Victorine mystics—*amor ipse intellectus est,* "Love itself is a form of knowing." This is evident in *De visione Dei* 24.113 (Hopkins, 260), in which he says that Christ as Savior teaches us two things: the faith by which the intellect *approaches* God, and the love that actually *unites* us with God. Where Cusanus is original is in conceiving this loving knowledge in terms of his distinctive dialectical view of *docta ignorantia* as the seeing that is not seeing. For an overview of the role of love and knowledge in mystical union, see Bernard McGinn, "Love, Knowledge, and *Unio Mystica* in the Western Christian Tradition," in *Mystical Union in Judaism, Christianity, and Islam: An Ecumenical Dialogue,* ed. Moshe Idel and Bernard McGinn (New York: Continuum, 1996), 59–86.

103. *De visione Dei* 18.82 (Hopkins, 218): "Et sic video humanam rationalem naturam tuae divinae naturae intelligibili et amabili tantum unibilem et quod homo te deum receptibilem capiens, transit in nexum qui ob sui strictitudinem filiationis nomen sortiri potest" (trans. Bond). The fusion of knowing and loving in face-to-face vision, of course, means that it is in the act of understanding ourselves as capable of understanding that we see God as Absolute Intellect and in experiencing ourselves as lovers we see that God is Pure Love.

104. Cusanus's emphasis on love as *filiatio* does not mean a total exclusion of the language of bridal union of the soul with God (not specifically Christ), which is mentioned in *De visione Dei* 18.80 (Hopkins, 216), but this is not a significant theme for the cardinal.

105. For more on my view of Cusa's Christology, see Bernard McGinn, "*Maximum*

God the Father as loving God gives birth to the *deus amabilis,* that is, the Son, with whom he is indissolubly united through the act, or connecting bond, that is the Holy Spirit. The *deus amabilis* is both the divine reason enfolding all things and also the object of desire that makes possible our own union with God. In order to attain that union, we must accept in faith "that blessed Jesus, as human son, was most profoundly united to your Son and that the human son could not be united to you, God the Father, except by the mediation of your Son, the absolute mediator."[106] Thus, in gazing at the loving Jesus (as in the icon of the face of the suffering Christ), we see the Son of God and through him also the Father, because Jesus is a human son in such a way as to be Son of God.[107] Cusanus is so concerned with mediation and union between the human and divine natures and modes of filiation that he fails to emphasize, though he never denies, the hypostatic character of the union of God and man in the person of the Word, thus giving his presentation the quasi-Nestorian tone that some critics have noted.[108]

Because Jesus is both God and man, truth and image, infinite and finite, he is seen to be within the wall of paradise, not outside it.[109] Jesus is the Tree of Life planted in Paradise (Gen. 2:8) who provides the food of heaven—nothing other than the meal of insatiable satiation referred to in chapter 16.[110] Here Cusanus cites John 1:18 to buttress his insistence that Jesus alone makes the Father visible, grants humans true happiness, and leads us to divinizing union:

Contractum et Absolutum: The Motive for the Incarnation in Nicholas of Cusa and His Predecessors," in *Nicholas of Cusa and His Age: Intellect and Spirituality,* 151–75.

106. *De visione Dei* 19.85 (Hopkins, 222): "Et video Ihesum benedictum hominis filium filio tuo unitum altissime et quod filius hominis non potuit tibi deo patri uniri, nisi mediante filio tuo mediatore absoluto" (trans. Bond).

107. Ibid., 20.88.

108. For example, in *De visione Dei* 20.87 (Hopkins, 226) he speaks of union as taking place by "attractio naturae humanae ad divinam in altissimo gradu"; in 20.88 (Hopkins, 228) he even says, "sic video naturam tuam humanam in divina natura subsistentem." In only one passage (23.102; Hopkins, 248) does he use more Chalcedonian language: "Sed video te, domine Ihesu, super omnem intellectum unum suppositum, quia unus Christus es . . ." For the "Nestorian" tone of these chapters, see Dupré, "The Mystical Theology," 218–19; and Jasper Hopkins, "Interpretive Study," *Nicholas of Cusa's Dialectical Mysticism,* 31–35.

109. *De visione Dei* 20.89.   110. Ibid., 21.91–92.

Every happy spirit sees the invisible God, and in you, Jesus, is united to the unapproachable and immortal God [1 Tim. 6:16]. Thus in you the finite is united to the infinite and to what cannot be united, and the incomprehensible is seized by eternal fruition, which is the most joyful happiness, never to be exhausted.[111]

In our seeing Jesus, "the Word of God humanified and the human deified,"[112] and in our being one with Jesus in our shared human nature,[113] our seeing, like his, comes to embrace all modes of vision and understanding, from the lowest forms of sense knowledge to the divine comprehensive gaze itself.[114] The circle is now complete; the mystagogical exercise of the *De visione* has reached its term. What began with the observation of the image of Christ's omnivoyant gaze of love has allowed the *frater contemplator* to experience the *docta ignorantia* that Cusanus now identifies with mystical theology.[115]

Nicholas of Cusa's place in the history of Christian mysticism has perhaps not been fully appreciated. He lived toward the end of a period (c. 1300–1500) which witnessed both new forms of vernacular mysticism, often of a highly personal and deeply emotional character, and attempts to create a form of scholastic mysticism, that is, organized treatises and handbooks on the nature of mysticism for the use of confessors and spiritual guides. The *De visione Dei* fits into neither of these categories, though it does inculcate actual spiritual practices designed to lead to union, and it is a structured summary of *theologia mystica* that takes positions on some of the key issues under dispute at the time. What I have tried to show is that the Cardinal's treatise was larger than its times. In *De visione Dei* Cusanus not only rethought and reformulated the fundamentals of the dialectical Neoplatonic mysticism developed by Dionysius, Eriugena, and

111. Ibid., 21.93 (Hopkins, 236): "Videt omnis spiritus felix invisibilem deum, et unitur in te, Ihesu, inaccessibili et immortali deo. Et sic finitum in te unitur infinito et inunibili; et capitur incomprehensibilis fruitione aeterna, quae est felicitas gaudiossima numquam consumptibilis."

112. Ibid., 23.101.

113. Ibid., 21.93.

114. Cusanus analyzes Christ's various modes of seeing in considerable detail in chapters 22 and 24.

115. Bond, "Introduction," in *Nicholas of Cusa: Selected Spiritual Writings*, 34–35, points out that *docta ignorantia* includes two functions for Cusa: recognizing one's incapacity to know God; and reconciling human ignorance with God's self-disclosure in Christ.

Eckhart, but he also sought to bring coherence to issues about God's visible invisibility that were rooted in Scripture and had been present in Christian mysticism since its earliest encounters with Hellenic philosophy. Cusanus "coincidated" the opposing scriptural positions on seeing God into a new synthesis. However we judge his effort, it was more than a mere summary of what had gone before. It was a new creation.

Jasper Hopkins

3. NICHOLAS OF CUSA'S INTELLECTUAL RELATIONSHIP TO ANSELM OF CANTERBURY

During this sexcentenary of the birth of Nicholas of Cusa, there is an almost ineluctable temptation to super-accentuate Cusa's modernity—to recall approvingly, for example, that the Neokantian Ernst Cassirer not only designated Cusa "the first Modern thinker"[1] but also went on to interpret his epistemology as anticipating Kant's.[2] In this respect Cassirer was following his German predecessor Richard Falckenberg, who wrote: "It remains a pleasure to see, on the threshold of the Modern Age, the doctrine already advanced by Plotinus and Scotus Eriugena, received [by Cusanus] so forcefully that time, numbers, spatial figures, and all categories . . . are brought forth out of the creative power of the mind."[3] Others have proclaimed Nicholas to be a forerunner of Spinoza,[4] of Leibniz,[5] of Hegel,[6] and, indeed, of German Idealism generally.[7]

1. Ernst Cassirer, *Individuum und Kosmos in der Philosophie der Renaissance* (Leipzig: Teubner, 1927), 10.

2. Ernst Cassirer, *Das Erkenntnisproblem in der Philosophie und Wissenschaft der neueren Zeit,* vol. 1, 2nd ed. (Berlin: Verlag Bruno Cassirer, 1911), 35–36. See also, for example, Ekkehard Fräntzki, *Nikolaus von Kues und das Problem der absoluten Subjektivität* (Meisenheim: Hain, 1972), 51.

3. Richard Falckenberg, *Grundzüge der Philosophie des Nicolaus Cusanus mit besonderer Berücksichtigung der Lehre vom Erkennen* (Breslau: Koebner, 1880), 139.

4. Maurice de Gandillac, *La Philosophie de Nicolas de Cues* (Paris: Éditions Montaigne, 1942), 448.

5. Robert Zimmermann, "Der Cardinal Nicolaus Cusanus als Vorläufer Leibnitzens," in *Sitzungsberichte der philosophisch-historischen Classe der kaiserlichen Akademie der Wissenschaften,* 8 (Vienna, 1852), 306–38; Henry Bett, *Nicholas of Cusa* (London: Metheuen, 1932), 139.

6. Frederick Copleston, *A History of Philosophy,* vol. 3 (Westminster, Md.: Newman Press, 1953), 245. Edmond Vansteenberghe, *Le Cardinal Nicolas de Cues (1401–1464)* (Paris, 1920; reprint ed., Frankfurt am Main: Minerva, 1963), 282.

7. Heinrich Rombach, *Substanz, System, Struktur. Die Ontologie des Funktionalismus und*

Most of these interpretations are wildly exaggerated and result from an excessive degree of enthusiasm that leads interpreters to the point of raving. However, rather than our mimicking them by endeavoring to apprehend Nicholas's thought as a pre-mirroring of various philosophical frameworks of the seventeenth through the nineteenth centuries—frameworks through which Nicholas's own philosophical works are then retrospectively further interpreted and measured—we will do better to take a more sober approach. Such an approach will begin by seeking to understand Nicholas's ideas in terms of both their historical antecedents and their fifteenth-century context. Moreover, it will proceed to demarcate the *creative lines of difference* that arise from his adapting certain of these antecedent and fifteenth-century ideas to three of his own fundamental fifteenth-century tenets: (1) the doctrine of the infinite disproportion between the finite and the infinite, (2) the doctrine of learned ignorance, and (3) the doctrine of the coincidence of opposites. Thus, we should orient Nicholas's thought by comparing it, first, with that of his more recent predecessors such as Ramón Llull and Meister Eckhart; then we should look at such more distant figures as Thomas Aquinas and Albertus Magnus and, finally, at such remote figures as Augustine, Proclus, Aristotle, Plato, and Pythagoras. And in seeking out those of his fifteenth-century contemporaries who influenced him, we should not overlook Leon Battista Alberti and Jean Gerson, along with the Italian humanists. Only after having explored all of the foregoing influences on Nicholas ought we to take up the issue of what residue of his thought, if any, resurfaces in the modern philosophers Descartes, Spinoza, Leibniz, Kant, and Hegel—not to mention such contemporary thinkers as Paul Tillich and Martin Heidegger.

One antecedent thinker who is not much discussed in relation to Nicholas of Cusa is the eleventh- and twelfth-century philosopher-theologian Anselm of Canterbury. Not even Karl Jaspers' book that (as edited by Hannah Arendt) bears the title (in English) *Anselm and Nicholas of Cusa*[8] interrelates the two philosophers; rather, it simply expounds each one's pat-

---

der philosophische Hintergrund der modernen Wissenschaft (Munich: Alber, 1965), 1:150. But see also my article "Nicholas of Cusa (1401–1464): First Modern Philosopher?" in *Renaissance and Early Modern Philosophy,* ed. Peter A. French and Howard K. Wettstein, Midwest Studies in Philosophy, vol. 26 (Boston: Blackwell, 2002), 13–29.

8. Karl Jaspers, *Anselm and Nicholas of Cusa,* ed. Hannah Arendt and trans. into English

tern of thought separately and disconnectedly. Surely, it is high time, at this sexcentenary turn of history, to take a keener look at how Anselm's thinking influenced Nicholas's and at how Nicholas adapted Anselm's ideas to his own.

Preliminarily, let us note that Nicholas expressly refers to Anselm by name and endorsingly cites certain of his works. Hence, there can be no question about the fact that he was familiar with the small corpus of Anselm's writings and that he unhesitatingly appropriated a number of Anselm's teachings. But, likewise, there can be no doubt about the fact that, at times, he extended Anselm's ideas, so that his own use of Anselm's teachings goes further than Anselm himself would ever have approved. Moreover, at other times, Nicholas supplements these teachings, so that he supports Anselm's line of thought by adding further rationales—rationales that Anselm himself had not given but that he would, in all likelihood, in some cases have accepted. In any event, in our exploring the intellectual relationship between Anselm and Nicholas, it will *not* be a question simply of our discerning parallels in their thinking.[9] Instead,

---

by Ralph Manheim (New York: Harcourt Brace Jovanovich, 1974) [excerpted from vol. 2 of Jaspers' *Die grossen Philosophen*].

9. Nor will there arise the issue of our *heuristically* relating Nicholas's thoughts to such modern ideas as Hegel's conception of the Absolute or Kant's notion that the categories-of-thought legislate to reality. Hans G. Senger, for example, makes an intriguing distinction between (1) the question of Nicholas's historical influence on Kant and Hegel and (2) the question of its being permissible to view Nicholas, from the twentieth-century standpoint, as a prefigurer (in certain respects) of Kant and Hegel. See Hans Gerhard Senger, "Überlegungen zur Wirkungsgeschichte des Nikolaus von Kues," in *En kai plēthos. Einheit und Vielheit,* ed. Ludwig Hagemann and Reinhold Glei (Würzburg: Echter, 1993), 174–210, here at 209: "Dabei sollte dann aber keine Unklarheit darüber aufkommen, daß wir uns dann nicht mehr im Bereich direkter Wirkungsgeschichte des Nikolaus von Kues bewegen. Es müßte vielmehr stets bewußt bleiben, daß mit einer solchen Bezugsetzung eine Wirkungsgeschichte rekonstruiert wird, die historisch so nicht gegeben, sachlich aber erlaubt und fruchtbar sein kann für eine Einlassung auf beides, auf die Cusanische Philosophie von der Moderne aus und auf die transzendentale Philosophie der Subjektivität von ihrer fernen Herkunft her." ("In this regard, then, [viz., re Cusanus's views in relation to Hegel's notion of the Absolute and Kant's theory of knowledge] let there be no unclarity about the fact that we are no longer dealing with the question of Cusanus' direct historical influence. On the contrary, we must always remain conscious of the fact that with such a comparison (e.g., between Cusanus and Hegel) we are reconstructing a narrative of Cusanus' discernible historical influence—a narrative that cannot with historical accuracy be characterized in just that way. Yet, the narrative is permissible as being factually elucidating and as being fruitful for an entrance (1) into Cusan philosophy as seen from the viewpoint of

without ignoring the parallels, we will want to look at Nicholas's express endorsements, explicit extendings, and overt supplementings of Anselm's reasoning. And in doing so, we will see that he refers by name to Anselm's treatise *De conceptu virginali* ("On the Virgin Conception"),[10] as well as referring to *De similitudinibus* ("On Likenesses"),[11] the work that contains Anselm's sayings. Moreover, he alludes to Anselm's *Meditation* I, his *Proslogion* ("An Address"), his *De veritate* ("On Truth"), his *De casu diaboli* ("On the Fall of the Devil"), and his *Cur Deus homo* ("Why God Became a [God-]man").[12] There can be no serious doubt that Nicholas had read the entirety of Anselm's corpus and was not drawing his knowledge of Anselm's views merely from secondary sources.[13]

First Consideration: The Description of God

The primary tenet that Nicholas appropriates for himself is Anselm's twofold description of God, according to which God is both something than which a greater cannot be thought[14] and something greater than can be thought.[15] These *Proslogion* descriptions can, for Anselm, be correlated

---

Modern philosophy and (2) into the transcendental philosophy of subjectivity from the point of view of its distant origins."

10. Nicholas of Cusa, *Sermo* VI (6:6–10) and (13:5–9). Unless otherwise indicated, all citations from Cusanus follow the chapters, paragraphs, and line numbers in the Heidelberg Academy of Letters' series *Nicolai de Cusa Opera Omnia* (Hamburg: Meiner Verlag, 1932–present). All citations from Anselm are taken from *Sancti Anselmi Opera Omnia*, ed. F. S. Schmitt, 6 vols. (Edinburgh: Thomas Nelson and Sons, 1946–61; reprint ed., Stuttgart: Friedrich Frommann Press, 1968), which is hereafter cited as S.

11. Nicholas of Cusa, *Sermo* VI (28:5–11).

12. Nicholas of Cusa, *Sermo* III (9:17–21); *Sermo* XX (14:10–12); *Apologia doctae ignorantiae* ("A Defense of Learned Ignorance") 8; *De docta ignorantia* I, 12 (*Die Belehrte Unwissenheit*, ed. Paul Wilpert and Hans Gerhard Senger, Schriften des Nikolaus von Kues in deutscher Übersetzung, Heft 15, 3 vols. [Hamburg: Felix Meiner, 1994–99], 34:3–6); *Sermones* (Paris ed., 1514), vol. III, fol. 170ʳ, line 21; and *Sermo* III (6:1–7:7).

13. By contrast, note how Nicholas appropriates certain aspects of Aristotle's political theory from a secondary source, i.e., Marsilius of Padua's *Defensor Pacis*. See Cusanus's *De concordantia catholica*, Preface to Book III.

14. Anselm, *Proslogion* 2.

15. Ibid., 15. Regarding the first formula, see, e.g., the following works of Cusanus: *Apologia doctae ignorantiae* 8, *De apice theoriae* 12, *Sermo* XLI (9:16–19), and *Sermones*, p, fol. 156ʳ, line 29. Regarding the second formula, see, e.g., *De quaerendo Deum* 5 (49), *Idiota de sapientia* ("The Layman on Wisdom") II (28); *De non aliud* 4 (11), *De venatione sapientiae* 26

with his puzzling, in *Monologion* ("A Soliloquy") 65, over how it is that since God is incomprehensible and ineffable, the things concluded in the earlier chapters of the *Monologion* could rightly be understood of Him. In other words, Anselm broods over the way in which the incomprehensible God can at all be apprehended. In *Monologion* 65 Anselm suggests that such a God can be apprehended only through likenesses, not as He is in and of Himself. Similarly, Anselm's formula in *Proslogion* 15 to the effect that God is greater than can be conceived implies that God cannot be conceived as He is in and of Himself but can be conceived only through likenesses. In *Proslogion* 15 Anselm is distinguishing between *apprehending* God's attributes and *comprehending* God's attributes: we can do the former but never the latter.

Nicholas of Cusa, in reading the *Monologion* and the *Proslogion*, interprets Anselm's view by extending it further than Anselm himself had intended. For, on Nicholas's interpretation, Anselm taught that God as something greater than can be thought is inconceivable, thereby implying that God is unnameable—or, better, implying that God is nameable only symbolically.[16] Nicholas here interprets Anselm to suit his own purposes. That is, he makes Anselm's view accord with his own view that since there is no comparative relation between the finite and the infinite, all discourse about God must be, necessarily, utterly symbolical—and, thus, must be an instance of learned ignorance. To be sure, a quick reading of *Monologion* 65 might seem to confirm the belief that Anselm himself drew this very conclusion. However, in our effort to understand the *Monologion* and the *Proslogion*, we must take account, as well, of Anselm's *Reply to Gaunilo*. For in *Reply* 8 Anselm makes clear his belief that not all likenesses to God are symbolical but that, rather, some likenesses are truly comparative. Accordingly, we rightly think of God as without beginning and as without end, as unchangeable, as timeless, as not able not to exist, and so on. Hence, God can be named the Self-Existent One, the Im-

---

(77), *Sermo* XX (6:4–5); *Sermo* CCIV (4:1–3), and *Sermones*, Paris ed. (1514), vol. II, fol. 138^r, lines 8–7 from bottom and fol. 156^r, line 30.

16. Nicholas of Cusa, *Sermo* XX (6:4–11): "Nam hoc solum habemus per Anselmum, quod Deus est melius quam cogitari possit. Hoc autem melius est innominabile, si non est cogitabile. Quare non est optimus nomen Dei, sed superoptimus. Unde secundum hoc, quia potius scimus quid Deus non est quam quid est, Deus potius est innominabilis quam nominabilis."

mutable One, and so on. Although God does not exist in the way that creatures do, nonetheless, according to Anselm, His existence can to some extent be both conceived and named by us analogically and non-symbolically—even if through a glass, darkly.

Second Consideration: A priori Reasoning

Although Nicholas takes over Anselm's two *Proslogion* descriptions of God, he does not likewise make use of Anselm's *Proslogion* argument for the existence of God—Anselm's so-called ontological argument. Nevertheless, he nowhere objects to Anselm's argument, as does, for example, Thomas Aquinas; and he nowhere seeks to replace it by an empirical argument. Instead, like Anselm, he accepts the validity of a priori approaches that purport to assure us of God's existence. Nonetheless, he formulates an a priori existence-argument that differs from Anselm's. For although he agrees with Anselm that God cannot not-exist,[17] his argument to the conclusion that, 'necessarily, God exists' moves by way of recourse to the notion of *presupposition:*

Since every question about what is possible presupposes Possibility, doubt cannot be entertained about Possibility. For doubt does not pertain to Possibility. For whoever would question whether Possibility exists sees . . . [that] without Possibility no question could be posed about Possibility. . . . And so, it is evident that Possibility itself precedes all doubt that can be entertained. Therefore, nothing is more certain than is Possibility itself, since [any] doubt [about it] can only presuppose it, since nothing more sufficient or more perfect than it can be thought.[18]

Possibility itself, says Nicholas, is "That than which nothing can possibly be better."[19] And this is tantamount to his stating that Possibility itself is That-than-which-a-greater-cannot-be-thought, so that, conversely, That than which a greater cannot be thought, namely, God, must be, and be thought to be, Possibility itself. In the end, then, Nicholas, being motivated by Anselm, does not merely repeat Anselm's ontological line of reasoning but creatively extends it so as to formulate a new strategy for arriving at Anselm's conclusions about God's self-existence and about the

17. Nicholas of Cusa, *Sermo* CCIV (2:1–5 and 3:1–2).
18. Nicholas of Cusa, *De apice theoriae* 13:4–14.
19. Ibid., 12:6–7.

indubitability of that existence. As concerns our present purposes, it does not matter that Nicholas's strategy is no more sound than was Anselm's strategy in *Proslogion* 2 and 3.

Third Consideration: Eternal Truth

Nicholas also alludes to another of Anselm's formulae: Anselm's definition of "truth" as "rightness perceptible only to the mind."[20] No doubt, Nicholas was familiar with Anselm's argument in *Monologion* 18, repeated in *De veritate* 1, that Truth—subsequently identified as God—is without beginning and end. For it was always true in the past that something was going to exist; and it will always be true in the future that something has existed. Since these propositions are true, there is Truth, without which no proposition could be true. Thus, Truth itself is without beginning, since it never began to be true that something was going to exist; and Truth is without end, since it will never cease to be true that something has existed.

As for Nicholas, he does not repudiate this reasoning any more than he repudiates Anselm's purported proof of God's existence in *Proslogion* 2. Nonetheless, he does not repeat the argument but formulates a cognate one of his own:

Now, everyone sees that God is Necessity itself, which cannot not-exist. For if it is true that God exists, I know that there is truth. On the other hand, if it is true that God does not exist, I again know that there is truth. Likewise, if you say that it is true that there is truth and say also that it is true that there is no truth, then no matter which of these contradictory alternatives you assert, you in either case affirm that there is truth. Hence, the truth is that there is Absolute Necessity-of-being, which is Truth itself, through which exists whatever is.[21]

20. Nicholas of Cusa, *De docta ignorantia* I, 12 (34:3–6). What Nicholas actually says is: "The most devout Anselm compared the maximum Truth to infinite rectitude. Let me, following him, have recourse to the figure of rectitude, which I picture as a straight line."

21. Nicholas of Cusa, *Sermo* CCIV (3:1–11). "Sed quod Deus sit ipsa necessitas, quae non esse non possit, quisque videt. Nam si verum est hoc, quod ipse sit, habeo veritatem esse; si verum est ipsum non esse, habeo iterum veritatem esse. Sic si dixeris verum esse veritatem esse, et similiter dixeris verum esse veritatem non esse, semper, qualitercumque dixeris contradictorie, affirmas ipsam esse. Unde veritas esse absolutam essendi necessitatem, quae est ipsa veritas, per quam est omne id quod est." Anselm himself, and possibly also Nicholas, is influenced by Augustine's *De vera religione* 39.73 (PL 34:154–155) and *De libero arbitrio* II, 12.

So, like Anselm, Nicholas uses the consideration that there must be Truth, since certain propositions will always be true. And it seems to him reasonable to identify Truth with God. If we look even farther back into the history of theology, we may judge that both Anselm and Nicholas were influenced by Augustine's argument concerning Truth—an argument found in his *De libero arbitrio* ("On Free Choice of the Will"), Book II, chapter 12.

Fourth Consideration: Theory of Atonement

Yet, Anselm's influence is predominant and central as regards Nicholas's doctrine of the Atonement—a doctrine that, to a large extent, Nicholas draws directly from Anselm's *Cur Deus homo*. Let us dwell at length upon this influence. Nicholas follows Anselm in arguing that to sin is to dishonor God—something that a rational creature ought to refuse to do even if his refusal were to occasion the destruction of himself and of everything that is not God. Accordingly, in order for a man to make satisfaction for his sin, he must give to God something that was not already owed to God—something whose worth surpasses the worth of everything that is not God. Since no human being who is merely a human being can make such satisfaction, a God-man was required. For only a God-man would be of Adam's race, would be able, by resuming obedience, to pay to God the honor that is owed Him, and would be able to make compensation, or satisfaction, for the *lèse majesté* ("dishonoring of the sovereign's majesty"), a phrase used by Nicholas in Latin *(laesa maiestas).*[22]

Moreover, Nicholas quotes Anselm's *Cur Deus homo* with respect to Jesus' not having been compelled to die in spite of the fact that God the Father willed for Him to die and in spite of the fact that Jesus could not do otherwise than what the Father willed. Nicholas states—with Anselm, mentioning Anselm by name—that all necessity and impossibility are subject to God's will.[23] Thus, it was necessary for Jesus to die only because Jesus Himself, as God, *willed to die* in order to pay the debt-of-sin on man's behalf.

22. Nicholas of Cusa, *Sermo* I (17:14); *Sermo* III (7:3).
23. Nicholas of Cusa, *Sermo* XXXV (3:1–8). Cf. Anselm, *Cur Deus homo* II, 17. See also *Cur Deus homo* I, 9; II, 5; and II, 11.

However, Nicholas does substantially more than just to telescope the argument of the *Cur Deus homo*. He adds an additional rationale for why the person of the Son of God—and not one of the other two persons—became incarnate. In *Cur Deus homo* II, 9, Anselm gave four reasons why it was most fitting for the *Son* to assume a human nature and to become a man (i.e., a human being).[24] The most significant reason is seen to be the following somewhat contrived set of considerations. Man in sinning against God acted from an autonomous will—one that was not subject to the will of God. But only God's will ought to be autonomous. Hence, in sinning by an autonomous act of willing, Adam arrogated to himself a *false* likeness to God. In this way he sinned more specifically against the person of the Son, who is the *true* likeness of God. "Hence, the punishment or the remission of the guilt is more fittingly assigned to Him to whom the wrong is more specifically done." Consequently, it is more appropriate that the Son, who is more specifically wronged, be the one to make remission by performing a meritorious act on man's behalf.

By contrast with Anselm, Nicholas adds a fifth rationale, doing so in his first sermon:

> Justice decrees that he who has sinned make satisfaction and that he make satisfaction in accordance with his having sinned. Man sinned; let man make satisfaction. Man willed to be God. Therefore, he sinned as gravely as God is great. Hence, a God-man must make satisfaction. And because man willed to be as wise as God, and because the Son [of God] is the Wisdom of the Father, it was fitting that not the Father, not the Holy Spirit, but the Son of the Father make satisfaction after having been made a man.[25]

Nicholas's reasoning parallels Anselm's insofar as Nicholas views Adam and Eve as having sinned more specifically against the Son of God. But Nicholas's explanation of this point differs considerably from Anselm's.

In a somewhat different vein, Nicholas also holds with Anselm, whom he again names expressly, that if Eve alone had sinned and not Adam, then mankind would not have inherited original sin, because, as he says, not the mother but "the father is the initiator of generation and is the

---

24. See also Anselm, *De Incarnatione Verbi* 10.
25. Nicholas of Cusa, *Sermo* I (23:22–29).

original transmitter unto his posterity."[26] Thus, unlike in the case of Eve, had *Adam* alone sinned, his posterity would still have contracted the guilt of original sin. Nicholas is here implicitly accepting Anselm's explicit consideration, in *De conceptu virginali* 9, that if Eve alone had sinned prior to her conceiving and procreating, God could have created from Adam's rib another woman, through whom the human race could be propagated sinlessly. For although the whole human race was present potentially in Adam's procreative power, it was not thus present in Eve.[27]

Nicholas also quotes endorsingly Anselm's notion of original sin, for in *Sermo* VI he writes:

In *De conceptu virginali* Anselm says that original sin is the lack of original justice together with [the presence of] the obligation to have justice. Every sin is a privation of an opposing justice. Hence, original sin is the deprivation of original justice.[28]

Now, as both Anselm and Nicholas maintain: because Jesus was not propagated by the power of Adamic human nature but by the miraculous power of the Holy Spirit, He did not inherit original sin. Unlike Anselm, however, Nicholas grants that the Virgin Mary was herself born free of original sin.[29] By contrast, Anselm does ascribe to Mary original sin, but he supposes that prior to her conceiving of Jesus, she was cleansed by faith, so that at the moment of that conception she was "beautified with a purity than which a greater cannot be conceived, except for God's."[30] Nicholas cites this Anselmian passage;[31] and, thus, it is clear that in this respect he is influenced by Anselm's reasoning. In going beyond Anselm to embrace the doctrine of the immaculate conception of *Mary*, Nicholas is aware that Scripture does not teach this doctrine but that it accords with the observance of the Church in his own day. In accepting this observance, he once again supplements Anselm's teachings without countermanding anything that Anselm actually states.

26. Nicholas of Cusa, *Sermo* VI (7:17–18).
27. Ibid., (7:7–9). Anselm, *De conceptu virginali* 23.
28. Nicholas of Cusa, *Sermo* VI (6:6–10).
29. Nicholas of Cusa, *Sermo* IX (11:24–29 and 11:13–17).
30. Anselm, *De conceptu virginali* 18. Cf. *Cur Deus homo* II, 16.
31. Nicholas of Cusa, *Sermo* VI (13:5–9).

A still further supplementing comes when Nicholas adds yet another reason why the Incarnation was necessary for man's salvation. This consideration has to do with the removing of man's ignorance. Simply put, Nicholas's reasoning goes as follows. Adamic man directs toward *this* life his every desire. He does not know how to seek that which is against this world, even as the eye does not know how to seek that which is *heard* but desires only to see and to see well. He continues:

> But because man did not know that he has the capability to have another life, he was not able to desire another life. Therefore, man was from birth ignorant. But in order that man be made wise and attain the highest end, Wisdom put on human nature; and Christ, the Wisdom of God, was made God-and-man, our Wisdom, so that in Him we might experience desires for another world. And because our fallen nature could not be elevated unless those earthly desires in it were mortified, Christ, in whom there is fullness, fills all our defects.[32]

Finally, Nicholas accepts Anselm's view that the Son of God assumed a particular human nature—that is, not universal human nature. Accordingly, the Son of God became incarnate as *a man,* that is, as a human being; He did not become incarnate as *man,* in a universal sense. Thus, the translation of the title *Cur Deus homo* as "Why God Became Man" tends to mislead us about Anselm's view. For the title suggests that God assumed human nature as such, thereby becoming man as such. Certainly, there have been theologians who have held just such a doctrine. In the nineteenth century, for example, Ferdinand Christian Baur asserted that "Christ as man, as the God-man, is man in his universality, not a single individual, but the universal individual."[33] Sometimes such a view has been projected back onto Anselm. However, Anselm states unequivocally in *De Incarnatione Verbi* ("On the Incarnation of the Word") 11 that the Word of God assumed an individual human nature.

By way of comparison, certain statements by Nicholas of Cusa may tend to give the false impression that he himself propounds the thesis that the Son of God assumed human nature as such, so that Christ did not *par-*

---

32. Nicholas of Cusa, *Sermo* XXXV (4:9–22).

33. Ferdinand Christian Baur, *Die christliche Gnosis* (Tübingen, 1835; reprint ed., Darmstadt: Wissenschaftliche Buchgesellschaft, 1967), 715: "Christus als Mensch, als Gottmensch, ist der Mensch in seiner Allgemeinheit, nicht ein einzelnes Individuum, sondern das allgemeine Individuum."

take of human nature but, rather, in Christ there is present human nature per se, of which all other men partake. Consider, for example, the following Cusan statement:

Christ's humanity—as elevated unto the maximal degree, insofar as it is united to the divine nature—is the truest and most perfect humanity of all men. Therefore, the man who clings to Christ clings to his own humanity, so that he is one with Christ, even as Christ [is one] with God. Accordingly, each one who adheres to Christ and is united to Christ—not in and through something other than in and through his own humanity, which is also Christ's humanity—has satisfied the debt [of sin], is justified, is enlivened. For his humanity, which is one in him and in Christ, is united to God the Word.[34]

But what Nicholas writes in one place must be interpreted with the help of what he writes elsewhere. And when we look further, we recognize that Nicholas is not claiming that a believer's nature is numerically one and the same as Christ's human nature; nor is he claiming that Christ's human nature *is* the species human nature, rather than being a particular instantiation of the species. Indeed, Nicholas is teaching, as is also Anselm, that Christ's human nature is the perfection and the goal of human nature—in the sense that it is a perfect human nature, whereas the individualized human nature in every other human being (except for Mary)[35] is marred by sin. We discern Nicholas's view quite lucidly when he writes:

If you conceive that Christ has the humanity of all men [i.e., of all human beings] and that He is man neither in the full breadth of the human species nor beyond the human species but that He is the most perfect end-goal of the species, then you see clearly how it is that the nature of your humanity obtains in Christ all fullness. [For your human nature is] present in Christ much more intimately than in a brother, a son, or a father—being there, rather, in the most precious identity that is positable with a numerical difference still preserved.[36]

---

34. Nicholas of Cusa, *Sermo* XXII (38:4–14): "Christi humanitas in illam maximitatem elevata, ut divinae naturae unitur, est omnium hominum verissima atque perfectissima humanitas. Homo igitur, qui Christo adhaeret, ille suae propriae humanitati adhaeret, ut sit unus cum Christo, sicut Christus cum Deo. Propter hoc quisque Christo adhaerens et unitus non in alio, sed in sua humanitate, quae est et Christi, satisfecit debito, iustificatur, vivificatur, quia ipsa sua humanitas, quae est una in eo et Christo, Deo Verbo unita est."

35. Nicholas of Cusa, *Sermo* VIII (13 and 27). Unlike Anselm, Nicholas maintains that Mary never sinned and that she was never even able to sin.

36. Nicholas of Cusa, *Sermo* XXXV, 5:1–9: "Si concipis Christum omnium hominum

So my individual human nature is not numerically Christ's human nature; and Christ's individual human nature is not numerically my human nature. Instead, my human nature and Christ's human nature are one and the same in species—Christ's individual human nature being the highest perfection of that species. Thus, insofar as a believer participates in Christ's human nature, he participates in perfection without participating in it perfectly. Only Christ partakes perfectly of human nature,[37] without His human nature's becoming human nature per se.

But Nicholas extends Anselm's position regarding *assumptus homo* ("the man assumed"): he extends it by incorporating it into the triad of doctrines mentioned earlier: the doctrine of *nulla proportio* ("no comparative relation"), the doctrine of *docta ignorantia,* and the doctrine of *coincidentia oppositorum* ("the coincidence of opposites"). For example, in *De docta ignorantia* III, 7, he reasons that Jesus' humanity is both absolute and contracted, that it is both corruptible and incorruptible. This reasoning is confused; and Nicholas is unable to straighten it out, even as we are unable to straighten it out for him.[38] At other times, Nicholas's statements are not so much confused as they are imprecise, so that he himself can later correct them. For example, *De docta ignorantia* III, 12, he states: "Since the union of the natures of Jesus is maximal, it coincides with the Absolute Union, which is God." Hereby he seems to suggest that the hypostatic union of the two natures in Christ and the Absolute Union of the persons in God—a Union that he identifies as the Holy Spirit—are both maximal, and therefore infinite, so that they coincide. But if the hypostatic union is an infinite union, how does Christ's human nature, which is

---

humanitatem habere et ipsum esse hominem non in latitudine speciei humanae neque extra, sed ut terminum speciei perfectissimum, vides plane quomodo tua humanitatis natura—in ipso multo intimius quam in fratre, filio, aut patre, sed in pretiosiore identitate quae salva numerali differentia dabilis est—omnem plenitudinem assequitur" [punctuation modified by author].

37. Nicholas of Cusa, *Sermo* LIV (5:20–26): "Unde, licet omnes homines per participationem humanitatis sint homines, tamen in nullo homine participatur ipsa humanitas sicut in alio: in uno clarius, in alio obscurius, in solo Christo, uti est in veritate, in omnibus aliter cum casu a veritate puritatis et perfectionis." See also *Sermo* CXXII (13:16–26).

38. See the following: Jasper Hopkins, *Nicholas of Cusa on Learned Ignorance: A Translation and an Appraisal of De Docta Ignorantia* (Minneapolis, Minn.: Banning Press, 1981, 2nd ed., 1985), 37–40, and Hopkins, *A Miscellany on Nicholas of Cusa* (Minneapolis, Minn.: Banning Press, 1994), 281–82.

subsumed in His divine nature, remain finite rather than passing over into an identity with the divine nature, since at infinity all differences disappear? In *De visione Dei* 20 Nicholas clarifies his position by further specifying his earlier statement in *De docta ignorantia*—his earlier statement to the effect that the union-of-natures in Christ is a maximal union. For in *De visione Dei* 20 he writes: "The union of Jesus's human nature, *qua* human, to the divine nature is maximal, because it cannot be greater. But it is not maximal and infinite in an unqualified sense, as is the Divine [i.e., the Absolute] Union." Thus, "the human nature cannot pass over into essential union with the divine nature, even as the finite cannot be infinitely united to the Infinite." This clarification brings Nicholas's theory of Atonement into line with Anselm's and with orthodoxy.

Fifth Consideration: Faith and Reason

Like Anselm and Augustine, Nicholas himself frequently cites Isaiah 7:9 in the Old Latin version: "Unless you believe, you will not understand." Moreover, he once cites it, approvingly, in a context in which he mentions both Anselm and Augustine as having subscribed to this relationship between faith and reason.[39] Furthermore, both Nicholas and Anselm recognize that that watchword has limited application, since both agree with Augustine that in some respects understanding precedes faith.[40] For neither Nicholas nor Anselm applies Isaiah 7:9 to understanding *that God exists*, since both give reasons that serve to *ground* belief in God's existence; and both think that these reasons ought to be given to unbelievers. On the other hand, both apply Isaiah 7:9 to understanding *that God is triune.*[41] With regard to the doctrine of the Trinity both hold orthodox views and embrace the Athanasian Creed.[42] Nicholas accepts what Anselm says in *De Incarnatione Verbi* and in *De processione Spiritus Sancti* ("On the Procession of the Holy Spirit"), with one exception—an

39. Nicholas of Cusa, *Sermo* XIX (6:21–22). See also *Sermo* XXXII (3:22–24); *Sermo* XLI (13:21); *Sermo* CXXXV (6:18); and *De docta ignorantia* III, 11 (244:8–9).

40. Augustine, *Sermo* 43.7.9 (PL 38:257–258).

41. Nicholas of Cusa, *Sermo* XIX (6:13–22); Anselm, *De Incarnatione Verbi* 1 (S, II, 7:11–12).

42. See Jasper Hopkins, "Verständnis und Bedeutung des Dreieinen Gottes bei Nikolaus von Kues," MFCG 28 (2003): 135–64.

exception that relates, once again, to his doctrines of *nulla proportio* and *docta ignorantia*. Whereas Anselm unhesitatingly asserts that the numerically three persons of God are numerically one,[43] Nicholas asserts that God is *non-numerically* three and one.[44] In *De possest* ("On Actualized-Possibility") the discussant John remarks to Nicholas: "You say that God is three but not numerically three. Are not the three persons numerically three persons?" And Nicholas responds: "Not at all. For the number which you view when you say this, is a mathematical number and is derived from our mind; and the beginning of this number [three] is oneness. But with God, trinity does not exist from any other beginning; rather, it *is* the Beginning."[45] Accordingly, says Nicholas, "we do not give God the name 'one' or 'three' or call Him by any other name whatsoever; for He exceeds every concept of one and of three and of whatsoever nameable thing."[46] Hence, "as Infinite, God is neither trine nor one nor any of those things that can be spoken of."[47]

In spite of this difference between Nicholas and Anselm as regards the doctrine of the Trinity, Nicholas, for purposes of worship, continues to speak of God as one and as three. Moreover, he uses all of the same predi-

---

43. Anselm, *De Incarnatione Verbi* 2 (S II, 13:14–21). See also *De Incarnatione Verbi* 9 (S II, 23:18–24:1).

44. Nicholas of Cusa, *Apologia doctae ignorantiae* 24; *De visione Dei* 17 (Jasper Hopkins, *Nicholas of Cusa's Dialectical Mysticism: Text, Translation, and Interpretive Study of the De Visione Dei* [Minneapolis, Minn.: Banning Press, 1985], 77:12–78:19).

45. Nicholas of Cusa, *De possest* (Jasper Hopkins, *A Concise Introduction to the Philosophy of Nicholas of Cusa*, 3rd ed. [Minneapolis, Minn.: Banning Press, 1986], 46:1–6). See also *De possest* 45 and 50. According to Nicholas, although numerical trinity is not real in God, non-numerical trinity is really present in God, so that Nicholas is not a Modalist. See n. 47 below.

46. Nicholas of Cusa, *De possest* 41:4–7.

47. Nicholas of Cusa, *De pace fidei* 7 (21:1–2). God is really both three and one—but not in any sense that reason *(ratio)* can understand. It is true for intellect (intellectus) that in God trinity is oneness. As Infinite, God is not numerically triune. Albert Stöckl (in his *Geschichte der Philosophie des Mittelalters*, vol. 3 [Mainz, 1866; reprint ed., Darmstadt: Scientia Verlag, 1968], 50–51) is wrong when he claims that Nicholas's Trinitarianism borders on pure Modalism (p. 50) and "sinks back into Modalism" (p. 51). Cf. *De docta ignorantia* I, 10 (27) and *De coniecturis* ("On surmises") I, 9 (*Mutmassungen*, ed. Joseph Koch and Winfried Happ, Schriften des Nikolaus von Kues in deutscher Übersetzung, Heft 17, 2nd ed. [Hamburg: Felix Meiner, 1971], 40:1–2). Just as intellect is higher than is reason (so that Nicholas distinguishes rational number from intellectual number), so God excels the domain even of intellect. But He is more discerningly approached by way of intellect than of reason.

cations that are traditionally used of God. For example, in *De visione Dei* 17 he speaks of God as a trinity of Loving Love, Lovable Love, and the Union of both. These predicates are not only a reflection of Ramón Llull's *Art amativa* ("Art of Love") but also of Anselm's *Monologion* 49–61 and of Augustine's *De Trinitate* ("On the Trinity") IX, 5 and XV, 17.[48] But, once again, whereas Anselm conceives of God analogically as Love, Nicholas conceives of Him metaphorically as Love. This difference results once again from Nicholas's doctrine of *nulla proportio.* Yet, Nicholas adorns his view of God as Love in Anselmian garb, by speaking of God as "Love than which nothing more delightful, nothing better, can be thought."[49]

Sixth Consideration: Anselmian Parallels

In other respects, too, Nicholas stands in the Anselmian tradition, so that he agrees with particular points in Anselm's position, even though there is little or no reason to suppose that Anselm was the primary influence on him. We find, for example, that Nicholas accepts Anselm's view of sin and evil as nothing, as having no being.[50] And yet, this view was also Augustine's[51] and Ramón Llull's[52] and others', so that no primary influence from Anselm can be established. Nonetheless, Nicholas does comment, in another of his sermons, that "sin and evil, although not something according to fact are nevertheless known."[53] And the phrase "according to fact" *("secundum rem")* is reminiscent of Anselm's distinction in *De casu diaboli* 11 between *secundum rem* and *secundum formam loquendi,* so that for Anselm evil itself is not something according to fact but

---

48. See also Augustine's *De Trinitate* VIII, 8 and 10. Regarding Lull, see *Art amativa,* ed. Salvador Galmés (Palma de Mallorca: Institut d'Estudis Catalans de Barcelona, 1933), 305–7.

49. Nicholas of Cusa, *Sermones* (Paris ed., 1514), Vol. II, fol. 138ʳ, lines 10–9 from bottom.

50. Nicholas of Cusa, *Sermo* I (16:4).

51. See, e.g., Augustine, *In Joannis Evangelium* I.1.13 *(PL* 35:1385): "Peccatum nihil est."

52. See, e.g., Raymond Lull's *Liber de praedicatione,* ed. Abraham Flores, Distinctio II B: Centum Sermones. Sermo 31 (II.3) [= Vol. 4, p. 123, in *Raimundi Lulli Opera Latina* (Palma de Mallorca, 1963)].

53. Nicolas of Cusa, *Sermones* (Paris ed., 1514), Vol. II, fol. 170ʳ, line 21.

is something only in a manner of speaking.[54] Nicholas also follows Anselm in maintaining that, as compared with God, all created things are as nothing and do not exist. Anselm expresses this idea vividly in *Monologion* 28 and *Proslogion* 22. Nicholas repeats it in *De quaerendo Deum* and *De venatione sapientiae* ("On the Pursuit of Wisdom").[55] But this time Nicholas is also following Augustine[56] and Meister Eckhart,[57] as well as Anselm, so that no one can claim that Anselm's influence is distinct or predominant.

We find Nicholas standing in the Anselmian tradition in multiple other ways. For instance, he adheres to the view that there is but one Exemplar of creation,[58] namely, the Word of God, a view subscribed to by Anselm in *Monologion* 30–35. Moreover, both of these philosophers appeal to Boethius's observation that a point within a point is but a single point; and in this way they symbolize their belief that eternity within eternity is but a single eternity.[59] Likewise, both men are willing to speak—in an extended and Pickwickian sense—of the world as eternal, even though, speaking more strictly, they call it temporal.[60] Similarly, Nicholas maintains, and Anselm takes seriously, the doctrine that the world was created all at once, though Anselm is noncommittal about this doctrine[61] and though neither Anselm nor Nicholas subscribes to Augustine's notion of *rationes seminales* ("seminal reasons"or "seminal causes").

Summarizing Conclusion

At first glance, it seems to almost everyone as if Nicholas of Cusa could not be more unrelated to anyone in the history of philosophy and

---

54. Anselm, *De casu diaboli* 11 (S I, 250:21–24).

55. Nicholas of Cusa, *De quaerendo Deum* 3 (45) and *De venatione sapientiae* 38 (111).

56. See Augustine, *Enarrationes in Psalmos* 134.4 (PL 37:1741).

57. Eckhart, *Expositio libri sapientiae,* ed. Josef Koch, 1.14a (34). [*Die lateinischen Werke,* vol. 2 (Stuttgart: Kohlhammer, 1992)], 354.

58. Nicholas of Cusa, *Idiota de mente* 2 (67).

59. Anselm, *De Incarnatione Verbi* 15. Nicholas of Cusa, *Idiota de mente* 9 (118); *De ludo globi* ("The Bowling-Game") I (9:8–9); and *De docta ignorantia* I, 7 (21).

60. Anselm, *Proslogion* 20. Nicholas of Cusa, *De dato Patris luminum* ("On the Gift of the Father of Lights") 3 (106); *De ludo globi* I (17–18).

61. Anselm, *Cur Deus homo* I, 18 (S II, 76:27–77:15). Nicholas of Cusa, *De genesi* ("On the Genesis [of All Things])" 2 (159).

theology than he is to Anselm of Canterbury. After all, the three tenets that largely define Nicholas's "metaphysic of contraction" seem altogether remote from Anselm's scholasticism.[62] For Anselm has no use for the triad of notions (1) that there is an infinite disproportion between the Creator and His creatures, (2) that, therefore, finite minds can never positively know *what* God is, given the alleged ground (3) that He is the coincidence of opposites (i.e., is undifferentiated 'Being' itself, which, with respect to its quiddity [or "whatness"], can never be conceived by anyone except itself). Unlike Anselm, Nicholas teaches that only God knows *what* He is; man knows only *that* He is and that some symbols befit Him more than do others. This befittingness is known through revelation—in particular, through the life and the teachings of Christ and through the Scriptures, Old and New.

However, we have seen that the intellectual relationship between Nicholas and Anselm is in many respects closer than an initial assessment betrays. For Nicholas takes over Anselm's descriptions of God, agrees with his approaching the question of God's existence by constructing a priori arguments,[63] subscribes wholesale to Anselm's theory of Atonement, to his doctrine of Incarnation, to his definitions of "original sin," of "truth," and of "evil." Furthermore, he agrees with Anselm regarding the relationship between the two natures in Christ. And he agrees likewise regarding the relationship between a believer's human nature and Christ's human nature, in spite of his stating, hyperbolically, that a believer becomes transformed into Christ.[64] Similarly, he lends credence to many features of Anselm's doctrine of the Trinity, Anselm's conception of faith, Anselm's emphasis on Mary's greatest conceivable purity except for God's. Surprisingly, though, he says nothing about Anselm's theory of free choice. Not surprisingly, however, he also says nothing about Anselm's dispute with Roscelin, which was no longer germane because Anselm had settled it definitively.

So, all in all, Nicholas, making use of Anselm's writings, seeks to extend and to supplement those of Anselm's ideas that he incorporates into

---

62. Cf. Jasper Hopkins, *Nicholas of Cusa's Metaphysic of Contraction* (Minneapolis, Minn.: Banning Press, 1983).

63. Note also Anselm's a priori line of reasoning in *Monologion* 1–4.

64. Nicholas of Cusa, *Sermo* III (11:12).

his own metaphysics. Such extending and supplementing lead Nicholas to speak in paradoxical ways: God, he says, is unknowable because He is infinitely knowable;[65] God is the Being of being and the Not-being of not-being;[66] God can give Himself to me only if He also gives me to myself.[67] In such paradoxicality Anselm's thought becomes *aufgehoben:* it becomes subsumed, elevated, and transformed. If we can recognize this transformed residue, we will better be able to discern the truth that whatever degree of modernity Nicholas's philosophical-theology may possess, it is a modernity that never attempts to uproot itself from its rich historical heritage. Accordingly, in last analysis, Nicholas is metaphysically nearer to Anselm and to Augustine than he is to Spinoza and to Leibniz; and (although I have not raised the issue here but, rather, elsewhere) he is epistemologically nearer to Thomas Aquinas and to Albertus Magnus than he is to Kant.[68]

What is new and challenging about Nicholas's metaphysics is the amount of agnosticism that he finds to be compatible with faith. For if in this lifetime the human mind can never know *what* God is and must be content to know *that* He is and to conceive of Him metaphorically, then this viewpoint paves the way for Kant later to extend agnosticism even to the question of God's *existence.*[69] The upshot is that even as Nicholas en-

---

65. Nicholas of Cusa, *Sermones* (Paris ed., 1514), Vol. II, fol. 138ʳ, line 29. Cf. Anselm, *Proslogion* 16 (S I, 112:21–22): The Light in which God dwells (I Timothy 6:16) is inaccessible because it is too resplendent.

66. Nicholas of Cusa, *De li non aliud*, Proposition 5 (Jasper Hopkins, *Nicholas of Cusa on God as Not-other*, 3rd ed. [Minneapolis, Minn.: Banning Press, 1987], 115:4–5). Cf. Anselm's paradoxical-sounding expressions: The Supreme Being exists in every place and at every time—and in no place at no time (*Monologion* 22). The Supreme Being is Substance beyond substance (*Monologion* 26).

67. Nicholas of Cusa, *De visione Dei* 7 (26:13–14). Cf. Anselm, *Proslogion* 1 (S I, 99:10–11): "I was striving unto God but collided with myself."

68. J. Hopkins, *Nicholas of Cusa: Metaphysical Speculations*, vol. 2 (Minneapolis, Minn.: Banning Press, 2000), 121–44. Jasper Hopkins, *Nicholas of Cusa on Wisdom and Knowledge* (Minneapolis, Minn.: Banning Press, 1996), 3–84. See also Hopkins, "Nicholas of Cusa (1401–1464): First Modern Philosopher?" (n. 7 above).

69. Consistency requires Nicholas to maintain—as he does—that even during the future life in Heaven believers will not know (other than symbolically) what God is, for creatures will remain finite. However, Nicholas, in speaking of the believer's sonship with God, sometimes gives the impression of maintaining that resurrected believers will know, other than symbolically, what God in and of Himself is. Note, e.g., *De filiatione Dei* 70: "Therefore, sonship is the removal of all otherness and all difference and is the resolution of all

larged the domain of faith so that it no longer was largely underpinned by Anselm's method of *sola ratione* ("by reason alone"), so Kant extended Cusa's agnosticism. Thereby Kant enlarged Cusa's domain of faith, which he now understood to include a series of faith-like postulates that permit one to give a unified answer to the *metaphysical* question "For what may I hope?", to the *epistemological* question "What can I know?", and to the *moral* question "What ought I to do?"

------

things into one thing—a resolution that is also the imparting of one thing unto all other things. And this imparting is *theosis*. Now, God is one thing in which all things are present as one; He is also the imparting of oneness unto all things, so that all things are that which they are; and in the [aforementioned] intellectual intuition *being something one in which are all things* and *being all things in which there is something one* coincide. Accordingly, we are rightly deified when we are exalted to the point that in a oneness [of being] we are (1) a oneness in which are all things and (2) a oneness [which is] in all things." It would seem that in knowing all things in God, we would also know God's Essence. But Nicholas rejects this view. "Perhaps that which is often heard disturbs you: viz., that God is incomprehensible and that sonship—which is an apprehension of Truth, which is God—cannot be attained. You have adequately understood, I think, that truth as it exists in something other [than itself] can be comprehended as existing only in some way other [than the way it exists in itself]. But since these God-revealing modes are intellectual, then although God is not attained as He is, nevertheless He will be seen, in the pureness of our intellectual spirit, without any bedarkening sensory image. And this vision is clear to the intellect and is 'face to face'" (author's emphasis). *De filiatione Dei* 3 (62).

What sometimes confuses readers is that Nicholas elsewhere speaks of the future face-to-face vision of God as seeing God *as He is*. Yet, in such a context Nicholas is distinguishing between seeing (or knowing) God *as He is* (1 John 3:2) and seeing (or knowing) *what* God is. Note, for example, *Sermo* IV (32:26–28): "Hoc tene: Deum in via cognoscere possumus 'quod est', in patria 'sicut est', et numquam hic vel ibi 'quid est', quia incomprehensibilis." ("Hold to the following: In this lifetime we can know *that* God is; in Heaven we can know Him *as He is*; but neither here nor there can we know *what* He is, because He is incomprehensible.") This is confusing because most of the time when someone states that God can be known as He is, he means that God's Quiddity, or Whatness, can be known—non-symbolically.

Louis Dupré

4. THE QUESTION OF PANTHEISM
FROM ECKHART TO CUSANUS

The term "pantheism" did not exist before the eighteenth century. Giordano Bruno and Baruch de Spinoza, now often associated with the pantheist position, were called atheists. The term was coined by the Irish philosopher John Toland and received the meaning that came to define it from Gotthold E. Lessing's confession that, to him, God was *hen kai pan,* one and all. The first Vatican Council condemned the doctrine according to which *"una eademque [est] Dei et rerum omnium substantia"* (the substance of God and all things are one and the same).[1] This kind of pantheism is incompatible with a religious attitude, since all religion requires some distinction between the worshipper and the transcendent person or object of the worship. The term, then, has become restricted to philosophical systems that, *from a theist point of view,* fail to make an adequate distinction between transcendent and immanent being. A total absence of distinction seems to occur rarely, if ever. Even Bruno and Spinoza distinguish the *natura naturans* from the *natura naturata.*[2] But, in addition, theists require that the relation between the Absolute and all relative being be conceived as one of causal dependence, traditionally expressed in the notion of creation. The ninth-century John Scottus Eriugena was censured for conflating the Being of the Creator with that of the creature when referring to God as *forma omnium* ("the form of all things"). In fact, he merely intended to show that the absolute One becomes multiple in its self-communication and that participated being is

1. *Enchiridion Symbolorum Definitionum et Declarationum de rebus fidei et morum,* editio XXXVI, ed. Henricus Denzinger and Adolfus Schönmetzer (Freiburg im Breisgau: Herder, 1965), #3023.

2. These terms are difficult to translate but refer to nature as creative dimension (*natura naturans,* "nature naturing") and nature as a created or produced reality (*natura naturata,* "nature natured").

destined to return to this original unity. The doctrine that God is the form of all things was formally condemned in the writings of Amaury de Bène.[3]

Nicholas of Cusa was never formally charged with pantheism. But Johannes Wenck, in his attack on *De docta ignorantia*, repeated in fact some of the accusations that had been made against Meister Eckhart, first by the archbishop of Cologne and later by the Papal Court in Avignon. In his *Apologia doctae ignorantiae*, a response to Wenck's *De ignota litteratura*, Cusanus rejected Amaury's position, not because he considered the expression *forma omnium* necessarily erroneous (he himself had used *forma formarum* ["form of forms"]), but because Amaury failed to distinguish the creature's contracted being from God's absolute Being. In the same text Cusanus defended Eckhart against misinterpretations.

Indeed, with respect to the critical distinction, Cusanus's position is close to Eckhart's. I shall argue that in most essentials he followed Eckhart's metaphysics, though he articulated the distinctions more precisely, avoiding the use of the misleading Thomist terminology that makes the reading of the German mystic so difficult. Moreover, I hope to show that the Cusan thinker, by adding the crucial distinction between perspectival and absolute knowledge, dispelled much of the ambiguity that surrounded the Thuringian master's writings. Neither of them can be suspected of pantheism if read in the proper ontological context, though both of them held a position on creation that deviated from the traditional one. Eckhart clearly distinguishes God's Being from the creature's *esse ab alio* ("dependent being"), as he calls it, while Nicholas leaves no doubt that the divine *esse* ("being"), though all-inclusive, can be participated only in modes that imply *otherness*. Eckhart's influence on Cusa can hardly be exaggerated. One needs only look at the extensive notes he wrote in the margins of his Eckhart codex in Kues to realize how seriously Cusa studied Eckhart's work.

3. Dermot Moran, "Pantheism in Eriugena and Cusa," *American Catholic Philosophical Quarterly* 64, no. 1 (Winter 1990): 131–52.

Eckhart

Eckhart refers to the creature's being as *esse ab alio*. The term *esse*, for Eckhart as for Avicenna, refers to the *quidditas* ("whatness") of a being, *quod quid est* ("what something is"). Hence when Eckhart calls God *esse ipsum* ("being itself"), he means not Aquinas's *actus existendi* ("act of existing"), but rather the intelligible *essence* of God. That *esse* is all-comprehensive and without distinction. The creature participates in that same divine *esse*, but in a limited way. This limitation *distinguishes* it from other beings as well as from God. But since the creature's *esse* is God's own *esse*, the original description of the creature as *esse ab alio* needs to be qualified. Only the fact that the creature's *esse* is *received*, rather than inherent in its own nature, makes it *ab alio*. Vladimir Lossky, in his profound study of Eckhart's metaphysics, quotes a statement attributed to the Master at the trial conducted by the archbishop of Cologne: *"In omni creato aliud est esse ab alio, aliud essentia non ab alio"* ("In every created entity, [its] being is distinct from that of another; [its] essence is not.")[4] The Thomist terminology *(esse* opposed to *essentia)* confuses the issue but leaves no doubt about the divine quality of the *essentia* (to which he normally refers as *esse*). Significantly, to justify his position Eckhart refers to Avicenna and Albert of Cologne rather than to Thomas Aquinas.

What St. Thomas refers to as the act of existing is for Eckhart *id quo est*, that through which the divine *esse* (i.e., *essentia*) becomes *infused*. The fact that the creature *receives* the divine essence justifies Eckhart in calling it *ab alio*, that is, coming from *without*. At the same time, since the creature's being is God's own *esse*, it is most *intimate* to the creature. Indeed, that divine *esse* constitutes its very *form* (the *forma formarum* of Eriugena!). Ontologically, then, the creature's entire content is divine; only the limitation of its ability to receive that content is the creature's own. Yet looking at the matter *phenomenologically*, that is, as the created mind experiences its finitude, its *essence* appears as a finite receptacle of God's own Being. Here the fact that God's *esse* is being *communicated* to a finite recipient becomes primary. Whether considered from an ontological or from a phenomenological standpoint, the act of creation is not one of *external*, effi-

4. Vladimir Lossky, *Théologie négative et connaissance de Dieu chez Maître Eckhart* (Paris: Vrin, 1973), 152.

cient causality, but consists in the *formal* communication of God's very Being. The creature participates in God's *esse*. Still, since God's formal presence in the creature is entirely *dependent* on God's uncreated Being, one many claim that creation is also the effect of an efficient cause. The causal action, however, occurs *within* God, and the effect remains immanent in the divine Cause. As Bernard McGinn puts it: "[Eckhart's] explicit treatments of creation return again and again to the central message that the key to understanding creation is to grasp that it takes place *in Principio*—in the Divine Logos, or in God himself *(in seipso)*."[5] This also implies that creation occurs in God's *eternity*, a thesis that led to new charges at the papal trial in Avignon. Eckhart answered them by distinguishing the divine act from its creaturely reception. In the limited creature, eternity breaks open into time. Though both the creature's *essence* and *that through which* it comes to be are divine, it only *participates* in God's Being and thereby is limited and distinct from God's own Being.

Eckhart's mystical theology implies a dialectical opposition between the transcendental ideas of Being, Unity, and Truth as they are in God and in the creature. We will examine each of these and then turn to the closely related question of the image.

(1) *Esse*. In the Prologue to the *Book of Propositions,* Eckhart writes: *Esse Deus est* ("Being is God").[6] This statement obviously does not refer to the act of existence, but to *Being,* as it is properly predicated of God alone, namely, as *essential* Being that is beyond immanence and transcendence. Hence Eckhart's repeated assertions that God alone is Being and creatures are nothing. Indeed, creatures possess no being of their own. "All creatures are a pure nothing."[7] Yet if we use the term being phenomenologically, applying it to the finite entities we know, God is not *a* being. In the German sermons Eckhart emphatically states this without qualification:

5. Bernard McGinn, "Do Christian Platonists Really Believe in Creation?" in *God and Creation: An Ecumenical Symposium,* ed. David Burrell and Bernard McGinn (Notre Dame: University of Notre Dame Press, 1990), 199.

6. Meister Eckhart, *Die deutschen und lateinischen Werke herausgegeben im Auftrage der deutschen Forschungsgemeinschaft* (Stuttgart/Berlin: Kohlhammer, 1936–), 1:166 [ET: Master Eckhart, *Parisian Questions and Prologues,* trans. Armand Maurer (Toronto: Pontifical Institute of Medieval Studies, 1974), 93]. Hereafter the Latin works in the critical edition are cited as *LW.*

7. *Sermon 4, "Omne datum optimum . . . ,"* in *Meister Eckhart: Teacher and Preacher,* ed. Bernard McGinn, trans. Frank Tobin (New York: Paulist Press, 1986), 250.

"Whatever has being, time or place does not touch God. He is above it. God is in all creatures, insofar as they have being, and yet He is above them."[8]

(2) *Unum. Deus unus est* ("God is one") is the title of a Latin sermon. In it Eckhart declares God to be pure self-identity and as such distinct from creation. In the *Commentary on the Book of Wisdom,* the dialectic becomes more complex.[9] If God is one, He must be indistinct from all things. Yet by being indistinct God differs from creatures, which are distinct from each other. So God's very indistinctness distinguishes God from creation. In the German sermon *Nolite timere* ("Do not be afraid"), the dialectic between God as indistinct and distinct appears very clearly:

God *becomes* when all creatures say "God"—then God comes to be. When I subsisted in the ground, in the bottom, in the river and fount of the Godhead, no one asked me where I was going or what I was doing: there was no one to ask me. When I flowed forth, all creatures said "God."[10]

(3) *Intellectus* ("intelligence"). God's self-identity implies that self-understanding coincides with Being. In the creature the two are separate. Yet in the act of thinking those creatures that are capable of self-consciousness may attain identity both with themselves and with God. The intellect, then, is the faculty of union.

(4) *Imago* ("image"). A fourth opposition in the dialectic between Creator and creature is that between the *like* and the *unlike.* It differs from the transcendental one between identity and distinctness insofar as it refers only to resemblance and difference. In his *Commentary on Exodus,* Eckhart spells out the terms of the dialectic.[11] Since God is all-inclusive, no otherness exists with respect to God. Hence, in one sense, nothing is as similar to God as the creature, since they share one Being. But since the creature only participates in that divine Being and, as such, is *other* than God, nothing could be more dissimilar. This appears to exclude the traditional doctrine of the person as *image* of God. Yet in a Latin sermon on the words of

8. *Sermon 9,* "Quasi stella matutina . . ." in *Meister Eckhart: Teacher and Preacher,* 256.

9. *LW* 2:481–94; *LW* 3:477–506; trans. Bernard McGinn, in *Meister Eckhart: Teacher and Preacher,* 166–70, 182–87.

10. *Meister Eckhart: Sermons and Treatises,* ed. and trans. M. O. C. Walshe, 3 vols. (London: Watkins and Dulverton, 1979), 2:81.

11. *LW* 2:1–227; trans. Bernard McGinn, in *Meister Eckhart: Teacher and Preacher,* 41–146, especially 81–84.

Matthew 22:20, "Whose are this image and inscription?" Eckhart considerably qualifies his position.[12] Eckhart gives the question an entirely new meaning by referring to the description of God's Son in Colossians 1:15 as "the image of the invisible God." This Image emerges when the inner "boiling" of God's nature overflows into a distinctness of hypostases within the divine unity. The Son as perfect Image of the Father possesses the fullness of the Godhead as well as the dynamic power that drives his humanity back to that divine unity. The human mind, a finite product of the divine overflowing, is an image of that perfect Image in which it partakes. It is impelled by the same drive to its origin, the divine Image.[13] Here Eckhart develops an entire theology of the image which his *Commentary on Exodus* appeared to question. He distinguishes likeness from image, citing Augustine's word that likeness is found in every creature, but image only in intellectual beings.[14] This of course does not solve our problem since an image is a more intimate likeness than what is merely a likeness and what Bonaventure called a "trace." I shall return to this point in discussing Cusanus, who treats the presence of the image in negative theology more coherently than Eckhart. Yet before moving to Cusanus, we need to consider another sermon that sheds additional light on Eckhart's notion of image.

In his German sermon *Quasi vas auri solidum* ("Like a vase of solid gold"), Eckhart introduces a much needed distinction:

Every image has two characteristics. The first is that it takes its being immediately from that of which it is an image. It issues from it naturally coming forth from its nature like a branch from a tree. . . . You should know that the simple divine image which is pressed unto the soul in its innermost nature acts without a medium. . . . The second characteristic of an image can be learned by concentrating on the image's similarity [to its object]. Here notice especially two things. First, an image is not from itself, nor is it for itself, just like an image that is received in the eye is not from the eye and has no being in the eye.[15]

---

12. *Sermo XLIX* in *LW* 4:421–28; trans. Bernard McGinn, in *Meister Eckhart: Teacher and Preacher*, 234–38.

13. Cf. Donald F. Duclow, "'Whose Image Is This' in Eckhart's *Sermones*," *Mystics Quarterly* 15, no. 1 (1989): 29–40.

14. *Sermo XLIX* in *LW* 4:421–28; trans. Bernard McGinn as "Whose are this image and inscription?" in *Meister Eckhart: Teacher and Preacher*, 235.

15. *Sermon 16b, "Quasi vas auri solidum,"* trans. Frank Tobin, in *Meister Eckhart: Teacher and Preacher*, 276–77.

Similarity can exist only between the creature and God as *manifest,* not between the manifest and the unmanifest One. Yet the unmanifest dwells in
the manifest. The image of God in the creature ultimately consists in the
presence of God, as already Origen had declared in his *Homily on Numbers.*
The soul is an image of God because she houses that primal Image of
God, the divine Word.

Cusanus

Turning now to Cusanus, we notice that he follows Eckhart's metaphysics on all essential points. In the *Apologia* he resumes the dialectic of
the image. With Eckhart he holds that the image possesses no perfection
of its own: all comes from the original. He also repeats that God is no
particular being, yet that God is *omne quod est* ("all that is"). Yet, better
than Eckhart, he realizes how much depends on defining the *relation* between the terms and how little on the terms taken by themselves.

The crucial text in the question of pantheism is Cusanus's *De li non aliud.* Nicholas refers to God as *non aliud* because *non aliud* is the only term
that defines itself rather than being defined by another. Though not a
name (God is beyond names), it is a more adequate *symbol* than Being or
One in that it indicates the direction which the mind ought to follow in
thinking about God.[16] It is preferable to Being, because God is beyond all
beings. Cusanus considers it superior even to the Neoplatonic term *One,*
because "one" is still understood in opposition to *not one.* The argument,
as several others in this text, is specious: the only reason why *non aliud* excludes otherness is that it simply describes itself as non-other without giving any content to that term. Still, Cusanus's thesis remains important.
That God is not-other with respect to all that is implies neither that God
simply coincides with everything, nor that God is a particular being, but
that God differs from the creature only through the finite's non-being. As
Jasper Hopkins argues in the introduction to his excellent translation of
this demanding text, Cusanus's non-other refers to the *identity* of God and
the creature rather than to the absence of difference. A more accurate ex-

---

16. Jasper Hopkins, *Nicholas of Cusa on God as Not-other: A Translation and an Appraisal of
De li non aliud* (Minneapolis, Minn.: Banning Press, 1983), 122–23.

pression than "not-other" would be God is *not different* from."[17] If the
term "not-other" be taken in the absolute sense, God could not be not-
other than anything without annihilating all otherness, and this would indeed be pantheism.

Cusanus means that "in all things God is all things even though He is
none of these things."[18] If the not-other would cease to be, all other
things would also vanish, not only the actual but also the possible, that is,
their non-being would cease as well as their being.[19] Here appears the reason why Cusanus considers the term "not-other" a more adequate name
for the first principle than "Being": because not-other comprehends non-
being as well as being. Yet more importantly, the priority of the first principle is in the *essential* order. Only in that sense does its priority over being
as well as non-being make sense. Cusanus explicitly defines the *non aliud*
as the *essence of essences*[20] or the *quidditas* of all things.[21] This, of course,
implies that the dependence of finite beings upon God is primarily a formal one, a participation, rather than one of efficient causality. The opposition between Cusanus's metaphysics of *unity* and Aquinas's metaphysics
of Being is nowhere more obvious than in *De li non aliud*.

The question, then, arises, how there can still be otherness if God is
the not-other who embraces everything. Obviously not because God *causes* otherness. In *De docta ignorantia* Cusanus writes:

Since they [things] cannot be the maximum, it happens that they are diminished,
other, distinct, and the like, none of which [characteristics] have a cause. Therefore, a created thing has from God the fact that it is one, distinct. . . . However, it
does not have from God (nor from any positive cause but [only] contingently) the
fact that its oneness exists in plurality, its distinctness in confusion, and its union
in discord.[22]

In *De ludo globi* Cusanus is even more explicit: "God does not create otherness."[23] Thomas P. McTighe concluded therefrom that *alteritas* is not even
a principle, but an ontological state of being stemming from the fact that

---

17. Ibid., Introduction, p. 15. See also 162–63, n. 46.

18. Ibid., 50–51.   19. Ibid., 52–53.

20. Ibid., 68–69.   21. Ibid., 56.

22. *De docta ignorantia* II, in *Nicholas of Cusa on Learned Discourse,* trans. Jasper Hopkins
(Minneapolis, Minn.: Banning Press, 1985), 91.

23. *De ludo globi,* Book II; in Nikolaus von Kues, *Philosophisch-Theologische Schriften,* ed.
Leo Gabriel, trans. Dietlind and Wilhelm Dupré (Vienna, 1964–67), 3:308.

creatures are incapable of fully participating in God's Being. Though divine perfection communicates itself unstintingly and undiminishedly, the radiation from a unitary essence must necessarily break open into pluralism and *alteritas* ("otherness"). This occurs not because of the *essence,* which remains undivided, but because of a quality that is extrinsic to the essence. McTighe identified that negative quality with the principle of non-being in Plato's *Sophist.*[24] Otherness is inherent in createdness. Yet otherness does not define the creature's essence and self-identity. Paradoxically the same divine self-identity constitutes God's own as well as the creature's unique essence. The creature's essence, then, consists neither in its distinctness from others (a negative quality) nor in its existence (a contingent fact), but in its coincidence with God's essence. Multiplicity is not due to essence but is a mode of non-being. The contingency linked to createdness is the source of the creature's otherness.

This, of course, does not resolve the problem inherent in Cusanus's notion of creation. The traditional understanding refers to creation as a free act of God's will. Yet how can one consider an act "free" that consists in a necessary self-communication? Cusanus might, of course, answer that the *necessary* is not opposed to the *free,* as long as the act is not influenced by any agent outside God. Nor is it obvious how any act of a necessary Being could be other than necessary. But the concept of necessity excludes an act of choice wherein God decides to create or not to create. As for the *will* of God, when accused of holding the position that Wenck questioned in Cusanus's philosophy, Eckhart had answered that in God the will cannot be distinguished from the intellect, or for that matter from any other divine attribute. Nonetheless, Cusanus rather surprisingly asserts in *De venatione sapientiae* that "because the eternal Divine Mind is free to create or not to create either in this way or in that, it determined, as it willed to [*ut voluit*], and of itself, and from eternity, its own omnipotent act."[25] Hans Blumenberg considers these words inconsistent with Cusanus's position in *De docta ignorantia.*[26] Though Blumenberg may be

24. Thomas P. McTighe, *"Contingentia* and *Alteritas* in Cusa's Metaphysics," *American Catholic Philosophical Quarterly* 64, no. 1 (Winter 1990): 55–72, especially 59–67.

25. *De venatione sapientiae,* ch. 27; "On the Pursuit of Wisdom," in *Nicholas of Cusa: Metaphysical Speculations,* trans. Jasper Hopkins (Minneapolis, Minn.: Banning Press, 1998), 209.

26. Hans Blumenberg, *The Legitimacy of the Modern Age,* trans. Robert M. Wallace (Cambridge, Mass.: MIT Press, 1983), 520 and 656, n. 57.

right about a conflict in the *expression*, I think he misinterprets its significance. The conflict is due not to a "return" to nominalist philosophy, but rather to a stress on the intrinsic contingency of creation considered in itself.

In the end, I believe that the notion of *perspective* decisively distinguishes Cusanus's theology from pantheism and also from Eckhart's mysticism. He develops the notion epistemologically in *De coniecturis* and ontologically in *De visione Dei*. In *De coniecturis* he assumes that our knowing occurs always from a certain viewpoint, one that could be replaced by another one, and hence that it is intrinsically perspectival. The human mind never fully grasps reality: its knowing never overcomes the opposition with being. It remains a *coniectura*. Yet our conjecturing renders us aware of a higher truth: in becoming conscious of the perspectival quality of our knowledge, we also become, however negatively, aware of what lies beyond it. "Therefore, the unattainable oneness-of-truth is known by surmising otherness; and the surmising otherness is known in and through a most simple oneness-of-truth."[27] In the fact that perspectival knowledge refers to divine unity, the mind realizes its intrinsic relatedness to truth. In conjecturing and construing hypotheses the mind is led to reflect upon its own nature.

In *De visione Dei* Cusanus performs a more fundamental, ontological reflection on perspective. Here he shows that knowing itself is grounded in that *through which we know*, even though that is not a direct object of knowledge. He illustrates his thesis by means of a painting of Christ he sent to the monks of Tegernsee. The eyes of the icon face the viewer, who therefrom concludes that he perceives it correctly and that his vision is the only correct one. Yet others at the opposite side of the room report the same experience. The viewer is then forced to conclude that his vision is perspectival while the icon remains unchanged and includes all perspectives. From any angle the eyes of Christ look at the viewer without undergoing perspectival shifts.

In the symbolic experience of the viewer's changing view of the icon of Christ and the icon's steady glance, the mind understands that its seeing is no more than an imperfect image of Christ's seeing. Thus the icon

27. *De coniecturis*, Book I, Prologue; in *Nicholas of Cusa: Metaphysical Speculations*, trans. Jasper Hopkins (Minneapolis, Minn.: Banning Press, 2000), 2:149.

of Christ, the divine Image of God, awakens the mind to the fact that the mind itself is an imperfect (perspectival) image of that divine Image. By the same token it understands that the imperfect image owes its entire being to that which it represents. "In that you [God] see all creatures you are seen by all creatures. . . . The being of a creature is, at once, your seeing and your being seen."[28] Yet the mind is not a static image, but a living, dynamic one. Wilhelm Dupré puts it well: "We ourselves are the image which needs to be formed and developed. . . . Whether man is an image of God depends on how he turns into this image."[29] As the mind comes to understand itself as an image, it desires to grasp that which it represents and thus to move ever closer to an identity with its divine Original. The mind's vocation consists in *growing toward the Image,* according to Eckhart. Ruusbroec built his entire mystical theology on this idea.[30]

Under the metaphor of *seeing,* Cusanus here resumes the dialectic of *intelligere* and *esse* as it was first developed by Eckhart. In and through the activity of the *intellectus,* the mind approximates its divine model in which *intelligence* coincides with *esse.* The nature of this process lies in the words of 2 Corinthians 3:18, which Cusanus took as motto for his Latin sermon 251: *"Nos revelata facie gloriam Domini speculantes, in eamdem imaginem transformamur a claritate in claritatem tanquam Domini spiritu."* ("For us, as He has revealed his face, we all reflect as in a mirror the glory of the Lord; we are transfigured into His likeness, from splendor to splendor; such is the influence of the Lord who is Spirit.") Is the mind itself able to attain the perspectiveless vision of which the seeing of the icon is an image? Cusanus answers that the mind's highest capacity, the *intellectus,* surpasses the perspectival knowledge of the senses and even the knowledge of *ratio* ("discursive reasoning"), which transcends perspective. Yet *ratio's* knowledge beyond perspectives remains without positive content. It merely refers to the unknowable source of all knowing. Still, the mind thereby understands that its knowing originates in a source that lies be-

28. *De visione Dei,* ch. 10, 41; in *Nicholas of Cusa's Dialectical Mysticism: Text, Translation, and Interpretive Study of De visione Dei,* trans. Jasper Hopkins (Minneapolis, Minn.: Banning Press, 1985), 165.

29. Wilhelm Dupré, "The Living Image of God: Some Remarks on the Meaning of Perfection and World Formation," in the following essay.

30. Cf. Louis Dupré, *The Common Life: The Origins of Trinitarian Mysticism and Its Development by Jan Ruusbroec* (New York: Crossroad, 1984).

yond itself. That source remains "unseen" but contains all seeing and all that can be seen within itself.

The preceding establishes a total dependence of human knowledge on a divine source. The Source is perfect; the human knower imperfect. Though the creature's knowing asymptotically approaches the divine coincidence of knowing and being, it never attains this coincidence. The question now arises how this dynamic *growing toward* the Image may be reconciled with Cusanus's statements in *De li non aliud* of an unqualified ontological identity of God's Being with the creature's. I find no better explanation for this than the distinction that Eckhart adopted from Augustine and that was in some form or other repeated by a number of spiritual writers (most memorably by Bonaventure), namely, that *likeness* may be found in all creatures but *image* only in spiritual ones.[31] Ruusbroec, whose *Spiritual Nuptials* Cusanus probably knew, directly or indirectly, wrote: 'The first and highest unity is that which we have in God, for all creatures depend on this unity for their being, their life, and their preservation. . . . This unity is in us essentially, by nature, whether we are good or evil."[32] But he distinguishes this unity from the one that distinguishes the mind from all other creatures, particularly when the mind becomes divinely enlightened and understands itself as an image of God that "grows toward the Image." Cusanus was well aware of this distinction. In a Latin sermon entitled *Ubi venit plenitudo temporis* ("When came the fullness of time"), he writes: "Only the intellect is like a living image that is susceptible to the taste of life in itself, that is, of true life of which it is an image. . . . [It] discovers by discovering itself as image, the truth, the exemplar, and the form which gives it its being to the effect that it exists as image."[33]

This sheds light on the confusion that surrounds the notion of likeness. Likeness refers to the general *presence* of God in everything. But only in a spiritual being is that likeness an image of God. Though God's presence is always total, the mode of that presence varies according to the

31. Cf. *Sermo XLIX* in *LW* 4:421–28; trans. Bernard McGinn, in *Meister Eckhart: Teacher and Preacher*, 235.

32. John Ruusbroec, *The Spiritual Espousals and Other Works,* trans. James A. Wiseman, O.S.B. (New York: Paulist Press, 1985), 72.

33. *Sermo CLXIX*, "Ubi venit plenitudo temporis, misit Deus Filium suum," Codex Vaticanus Latinus 1245, fol. 63[rb].

degree of participation. Intellectual beings participate at a higher degree in God's life, and they may increase their capacity of participation as they become more aware of their being *images* of God. This increase results from the mind's intellectual endeavors but also, and above all, from the infusion of divine grace. Yet no degree of participation reaches *absolute* unity between the mind and God. Cusanus maintains an insurmountable distinction between God and the created mind, and this places his position beyond any suspicion of pantheism.

It must be conceded, though, that in describing the relation between Creator and creature, Cusanus occasionally uses expressions that may seem to make God *intrinsically* dependent on creation. Thus, in *De visione Dei* he writes: "Your seeing, Lord, is your essence" *(Visus tuus, domine, est essentia tua).*[34] This passage might be read as referring to the absence of distinctions in God: God's "seeing" (i.e., *intellectus*) is God's Being. But the context suggests that a stronger interpretation is needed, for a little later Cusanus writes: "Your seeing is Your creating and You do not see anything other than Yourself but are your own object, for You are (1) the perceiver, (2) that which is perceived, and (3) the act of perceiving. If so, then how is that you create things that are other than Yourself? For You seem to create Yourself, even as You see Yourself?"[35] And further: "Your creating is Your being."[36] God's Being here appears as God's creative seeing. Again, the problem consists not in the fact that the act of creating coincides with God's Being (since there are no distinctions in God), but in the fact that a necessary creation appears to entail a *need* for otherness in God's very essence. As I argued before, God remains free even while acting *necessarily,* as long as no *other* being forces God to act. Yet in creation, as Cusanus's question indicates, God appears to be compelled to act by the need for otherness in his own Being. This, of course, causes no problem in Neoplatonic philosophy, yet Christian theology, while repeating the Neoplatonic principle *Bonum est diffusivum sui* ("The good is its own self-diffusion"), nevertheless insists that God is free to create or not to create.

At the very least, the texts of *De visione Dei* imply that the presence of

---

34. *De visione Dei,* ch. 9, 35; Hopkins, 154–55.
35. Ibid., ch. 12, 50; Hopkins, p. 175.
36. Ibid.

finite minds makes a difference to God's very Being. The reflective glance by which humans return God's creative seeing of them opens up a dimension within God's Being that would not have existed without it. It enables God to see Himself in the seeing of the creature. In creating, then, God initiates a reciprocal relation to the creatures. This position has long been embraced by process theology. But it remains far from the accepted doctrine of St. Thomas that God has no *real* relation to the creatures.

Conclusion

Cusanus never was a pantheist, no more than Eckhart. But their views on the relation between God and creation differ from the common doctrine on causality. For them, that relation did not primarily consist in one of efficient causality, but in a more intimate divine presence that came closer to a formal cause. God's total presence to each creature constitutes its very being. The problem of a divine causality that descends "from above" (as in Aristotelian and Neoplatonic cosmologies), which made it so difficult for the Church to accept Galileo's theory, did not exist for Cusanus. All parts of the universe are equally present to God who empowers them through His own Being. The creature's true identity, then, consists in this immanent divine Being. *Otherness* exists not in God, but in the imperfect participation of the creature in divine fullness.

In the end in their "panentheism" Eckhart and Cusanus remain faithful to Aquinas's fundamental insight concerning the intimate presence of God as the Being of all beings. In the *Summa theologiae* St. Thomas raises the question whether God is in all things. He answers: "Being is innermost in each thing and most fundamentally present within all things, since it is formal in respect of everything, found in a thing. . . . Hence it must be that God is in all things, and innermostly."[37] To the question how God is thus present in all things, St. Thomas replies that God is present "as the cause of the being of all things." Yet he does not specify the nature of this divine causality. Is it formal, or efficient, or both? Cusanus avoids that ambiguity in his radical equation of God's immanent presence with a person's identity. Hence God is present through a formal, or at least a

---

37. *Summa theologiae*, I, 8, a. 1, c.

quasi-formal, causality. He also avoids the ambiguity that results from Eckhart's persistent use of a Thomist terminology for expressing an immanent presence conceived in a Neoplatonic metaphysics.

In *De li non aliud* and in *De visione Dei,* Cusanus justified the insight that had dominated Christian mysticism since Origen, namely, that the mind's being the image of God means that God is immanently present in it. Of this presence the finite mind can never have more than an imperfect awareness: it perceives various aspects of that presence but never the whole. Nonetheless, God's total vision (which coincides with his total presence) makes the creature's perspectival one possible. As the Psalmist wrote: *In lumine tuo videbimus lumen* ("In your light we see light").[38]

38. Psalm 35(36):10.

Wilhelm Dupré

5. THE IMAGE OF THE LIVING GOD
Some Remarks on the Meaning of Perfection
and World Formation

In considering the metaphor of man as a living image of God, I am taking up a theme central to the thought of Nicholas of Cusa (1401–1464). One of the reasons for focusing on Cusanus is the six-hundredth birthday that we commemorated in 2001. But more important than this external reason is the relevance of his ideas to the contemporary understanding of reality and what it means to be a human being. In the light of the questions that inspired him to think about the most elementary features of humanity, we discover that the problems of his age are still at hand and that the solutions he tried to formulate deserve the effort of continuous considerations. Like the people of the fifteenth century, we too tend to live and shape our lives by blithely ignoring the forces and insights that sustain us in our humanity. Like them, we should therefore have a vested interest in the elucidation of our situation, or as Cusanus said, in becoming learned about our ignorance. Cusanus treats prominently in his works self-knowledge, the experiences of human finitude, and the desires and striving for actual well-being and ultimate perfection. His treatment of these issues became paradigmatic because and inasmuch as he pushed them to their ultimate limits. As a pragmatist *avant la lettre,* he appreciated deeply the philosophical significance of common life, with its imageries and practical abilities, both as he saw in it the expressions of what he called the sound mind *(mens sana)* and as he symbolized it himself in the figure of the *Layman.*[1] Cusanus had a keen eye for the experiences of ordinary existence. But as he focused on these ex-

---

1. See H. Blumenberg, *Die Legitimität der Neuzeit* (Frankfurt: Suhrkamp, 1966), 506ff.; and M. Álvarez Gómez, "La mente como imagen viva en Nicolás de Cusa," in *Mente, Conciencia y Conocimiento,* ed. M. del Carmen Paredes Martín (Salamanca: Ediciones Universidad de Salamanca, 2001), 11ff.

periences in the light of the coincidence of opposites and contradictions, he felt free to question all and everything and to analyze the human condition by reconstructing it from its very beginnings.

I begin my paper with a brief reference to the notion of man as image of God. In the next step I discuss the meaning of the living image both as an idea of its own and as essential feature of being human. Against the background of these considerations, I will then focus on some consequences of understanding man as a living image of God.

Man as Image of God

The idea that human beings should be understood as images of God belongs to a long tradition of religious imagination and theological as well as anthropological reasoning.[2] In the biblical accounts of the beginning, we are told that

God said, Let us make man in our image, after our likeness; and let them have dominion . . . over all the earth. . . . So God created man in his *own* image, in the image of God created he him; male and female created he them.[3]

This statement must be seen in contrast to the belief of several surrounding cultures that took it for granted that the king was God's representative on earth and like other idols, image and God in his own right. But in contrast to Mesopotamian and Egyptian beliefs, the biblical text claims the same status and dignity for all human beings. By calling man an image of God, the Bible thus affirms the kingly nature of every person. At the same time it undermines the worship of idols: first, by bringing the cult of kings back to its true meaning; and second, if we relate to this cult as it has been part and parcel of the belief in many gods, by showing the illusory assumptions of pagan practices.[4]

---

2. See the article by D. Schlüter, W. Hogrebe, R. Tiedemann, and E. Stenius in *Historisches Wörterbuch der Philosophie,* ed. J. Ritter (Darmstadt: Wissenschaftliche Buchgesellschaft, 1971), s.v. "Bild" 1:913–21, as well as W. Pannenberg, *Anthropologie in theologischer Perspektive* (Göttingen: Vandenhoeck 1983), 40ff.

3. Genesis 1:26, 27. Cf. also Genesis 5:1, 2: "In the day that God created man, in the likeness of God made he him; Male and female created he them; and blessed them, and called their name Adam, in the day when they were created."

4. See Christoph Dohmen, *Das Bilderverbot, seine Entstehung und seine Entwicklung im Alten Testament* (Königsstein / Ts.: Peter Hanstein Verlag, 1985).

In the Christian period the association between image and dignity is not lost, but it is superseded by soteriological and philosophical interests. A basic theme is the obfuscation of the divine image in man as the result of the Fall and its restoration by Christ. From a philosophical point of view, one is interested in the relationship between image and creation, and, since all phenomena are in one way or another *eidola* (images), in the archetype or the exemplar of these images. Moreover, the Bible tells us also that "the Lord God formed man of the dust of the ground, and breathed into his nostrils the breath of life; and man became a living soul."[5] In this light, it is expected that all efforts were made to connect the two creation accounts and to interpret the first story in terms of an almighty artist who painted his images and let his sculptures *be* whatever they were, that is, not as images painted on canvas or created of separate materials, but as images and sculptures that existed in their own right, without the otherness that is needed when objects come into being by human art and workmanship.

The foremost reason for speaking of images becomes thus the experience of likeness. If we look at human beings and compare them with other animals, or with plants, we observe clear similarities in one group and considerable dissimilarities with regard to other groups, with many shades in between. And since how we draw the lines and what we would like to emphasize are up to us, similarities and dissimilarities can be grouped in various and very different ways. By using a mirror or other optical device, we discover the image in terms of virtual identity. We realize that the world of objects can be distinguished from itself in terms of a mirror-image because and to the extent that the image of its appearance (in reality) coincides with the appearance of this image (in the mirror). The world is there as we see it, though what we see looks like the image seen in a mirror. But we could also approach reality by comparison to an artist who paints a portrait or a landscape that looks more or less like the original, or is hardly recognizable in the picture. And, if we look at each other and become aware of eyes that look at us, either in other people or the icon of the all-seeing in Cusanus's *De visione Dei,* the gaze adds ontological depth and meaning to our image experiences.[6] Thus, a likeness makes us speak

5. Genesis 2:7.

6. See Clyde Lee Miller, "God's Presence: Some Cusan Proposals," in *Nicholas of Cusa on*

of images. In each case, however, the meaning of the likeness is very fluid, and the image can be defined through a broad spectrum of possible meanings. In fact, if we concentrate on the difference between image and original, we might as well say that every object that stands for something else is an image of its original inasmuch as it represents this original in the (imagined) confirmation of a specific difference. Though the meaning of this understanding is extreme, it is nevertheless of such a kind that likeness might easily be recovered by the extension of differences.

An additional impetus to the development of the theory of images was given by the doctrine of the Holy Trinity. With the doctrine of one God in three persons (Father, Son, and Spirit), the Son appears as the uncreated image of the Father in which or according to which everything is and has been created. The archetype of man as image of God is the Christ who as human being among human beings connects humanity with its divine origin. But because the divine Logos is reason and cause of everything, it is the whole of all creation that finds its place in God's uncreated image as well.[7]

The Trinitarian theory of the image thus provides a framework that makes it possible to refer to God as common focus and, if we keep track of the difference between image and exemplar, at the same time as the unquestionable vanishing point of all reality. With regard to St. Augustine, one could even speak of an ontology in which the difference between image and original is the constitutive principle of every being because and inasmuch as this difference forms the essence of reality.[8] Moreover, since the meaning of the Trinity is not complete without the Spirit, who, according to the Western Christian creed, proceeds from Fa-

---

Christ and the Church, ed. G. Christianson and T. M. Izbicki (Leiden: E. J. Brill, 1996), 241–49, at 242–43, as well as the essay by Bernard McGinn in this volume.

7. As to Cusanus see his "Vernacular Sermon on the *Pater Noster,"* *Sermones I* (1430–1441), ed. R. Haubst et al. (Hamburg: Meiner, 1991), trans. Frank Tobin (as in this volume), nr. 19: "And just as the three words signify the Holy Trinity and in the three words the Holy Trinity is meant, so also does each and every thing that exists have an image of God and the Holy Trinity in it through which image the thing is; for no thing is anything except insofar as and to the extent that it is an image of God."

8. See J. Mader, *Aurelius Augustinus. Philosophie und Christentum* (St. Pölten–Wien: Verlag Niederösterreichisches Pressehaus, 1991), 366–67, and his earlier work *Die logische Struktur des personalen Denkens. Aus der Methode der Gotteserkenntnis bei Aurelius Augustinus* (Vienna: Herder, 1965), 135ff.

ther and Son, the uncreated image of all reality is such that it allows for various movements within creation both as things are different and as we might think of man in terms of spiritual perfection. Deformity is in this regard not only a quality that confirms the divine origin of every being, but also a task that, when we think of ourselves, recalls the work of the divine Spirit who inspires us to strive for holiness and perfection. In contrast to the eternal movement (and non-movement) of the Spirit within the Holy Trinity, we can therefore point to the temporal movements of more or less permanence that concur with the created image in a variety of ways that determine it in modes of multiple developments of being and becoming. What turns things into images is the connection between them in variable relations to their origin. The meaning of God is mediated in the structure as well as by the dynamics of totality.

The Idea of a Living Image

I mention these features because the notion of man as image of God has been a self-evident assumption of the tradition in which Cusanus grew up. Moreover, it is important to be aware of the all-encompassing meaning of this notion and the understanding of images that arises in connection with it. Indeed, whereas the idea of the triune God pushes and draws Cusanus to the ultimate limits of thinking, his appreciation of images in terms of likeness, being, and abstract representation makes him focus on a wide range of image experiences—from geometrical figures and conceptual relations to metaphorical intimations and iconic representations.[9] Cusanus's philosophy is heavily indebted to signs and images in their own right (and not merely as problems of a nominalistic ontology). The image is the place in which truth appears.[10] It is through images and

9. See R. Haubst, *Das Bild des Einen und Dreieinen Gottes in der Welt des Nikolaus von Kues* (Trier: Paulinus, 1952); N. Henke, *Der Abbildbegriff in der Erkenntnislehre des Nikolaus von Kues* (Münster: Aschendorff, 1969); G. v. Bredow, "Der Geist als lebendiges Bild Gottes," MFCG 13 (1978): 58–67; P. Moffitt Watts, *Nicolaus Cusanus. A Fifteenth-Century Vision of Man* (Leiden: E. J. Brill, 1982), 87ff.; N. Herold, "Bild, Symbol und Analogie: die 'Modelle' des Nikolaus von Kues," in *Pragmatik,* Band I: Pragmatisches Denken von den Ursprüngen bis zum 18. Jht, ed. H. Stachowiak (Hamburg: Meiner, 1986), 299–318; R. Haubst, *Streifzüge in die cusanische Theologie* (Münster: Aschendorff, 1991), 263ff.; and M. Álvarez Gómez, "La mente como imagen viva en Nicolás de Cusa," 11–28.

10. Cf. Wilhelm Dupré, "Das Bild und die Wahrheit," MFCG 18 (1989): 125–58.

their structures that we are able to search for truth and find the names that bring thoughts, experiences, and knowledge into perspective.

The three books of *De docta ignorantia* (1440) are the first treatise in which Cusanus connected his inquiries into the basic structure of the human condition and its presuppositions with a comprehensive reflection on symbolic relations and what it means to understand the human being and the totality of all things in the light of Trinitarian questions and assumptions. They were followed by two books on *De coniecturis* (1443–1445), or what he called the *ars coniecturalis* ("the art of conjecture"). This project represented his attempt to cope with truth by concentrating on the artistic composition of human deeds and perceptions in a twofold sense: as free expressions of the self and as ways to recover the meaning of reality through various modes of self-understanding and world conception. Finally, the project was brought to a conclusion in his three dialogues of 1450, that is, in his *Idiota de sapientia, Idiota de mente,* and *Idiota de staticis experimentis* ("The Layman on Experiments with Weight"), in which the idea of the living image turned into the focus of his investigations.

With Raymundus Sabundus, an early contemporary of Cusanus who died in 1436, one could of course argue that man is a living image because and inasmuch as he is alive and carries features of the divine original. It is possible that Cusanus knew the passage of the *Theologia naturalis sive liber creaturarum* ("A Natural Theology or Book of Creatures," which was written about 1430) in which Sabundus described man as *imago Dei viva* ("a living image of God"), in order to emphasize human dignity and the obligation to love God and, as far as one's neighbor is concerned, God's image.[11] But even if Cusanus could easily agree with Sabundus's (and Gregory of Nyssa's) view, he had something else in mind. To be sure, what fascinated Cusanus was the Trinitarian structure of the processes that constitute us in our humanity and the idea that the human being is actually a second God. This second God, he maintains, creates his own world by copying the divine artisan through the imitation of nature

---

11. See M. van der Meer, *"Mens imago viva". De betekenis en de historische context van de term "mens imago viva" in de* Idiota de mente *van Nicolaus Cusanus* (M.A. thesis, Nijmegen, 2001), 34. Gerda von Bredow points to Gregory of Nyssa (*De hominis opificio* 4, PG 44, 136C) as the source of this idea. See G. von Bredow, "Der Geist als lebendiges Bild Gottes," MFCG 13 (1978): 58.

in the forms of civil existence and the works of his mind as well as his hands.[12] But the same thought also worried him because of the obvious imperfections and shortcomings of and in creation.[13] Even if we accept the idea that the world is the perfect image of God's infinite simplicity or that there is only "one infinite form of forms of which all forms are images,"[14] this idea makes sense only when we think of things in their timeless totality. If we take them in their temporal succession, they turn out to be fleeting instances of being and becoming, of varying permanence, and with the distinct qualification of more or less. What we perceive can be greater or smaller. What we are and do is marked by better and worse.

Cusanus seeks the solution to this problem in a thought-experiment. Since the notions we form are realities in their own right, we do not only have to take them in their specific forms and modes of objectivity, but we can also think of them as they assume various shapes and become instances that could display a life of their own. In accordance with the axiom "that each part of a power is in fact [an expression of] the whole pow-

12. Following Aristotle and St. Paul, Cusanus formulates his assessment of the human situation like this: "The political life is good that consists in the rule that we do to others what we would like to be done to us. . . . But the contemplative life which is without conflicting oppositions, full of bliss and eternal, is the true life of the thinking spirit. The life of the flesh opposes the life of the spirit [and] like lust opposes contemplation. If we live in accordance with the flesh, we die as far as the spirit is concerned. Reason comes close to animality. If we live in accordance with the spirit, then the life of the flesh will begin to die. However, if we live in accordance with the composition of the two lives, then we shall lead a human and political life where everything is done at its time, first in terms of animal life, then in terms of the divine life, and finally in terms of human life." *Sermo* CXCVII, "Debitores sumus," Cod. Vat. Lat. 1245, fol. 111[va].

13. See, for instance, Nicholas of Cusa, *De docta ignorantia* I 23 (I, 276;h I, nr. 71), in which he tackles the problem with a rhetorical question: "Quomodo enim posset esse ibi aliquid imperfectionis, ubi imperfectio est infinita perfectio et possibilitas infinitus actus, et ita de reliquis?" and ibid. II 2 (I, 322; h I, nr. 98), in which he states that corruptibility, divisibility, imperfection, and such are properties which do not derive from eternal being, after he has made his point (again by means of a rhetorical question): "Quomodo enim id, quod a se non est, aliter esse posset quam ab aeterno esse?" When quoting Cusanus, the references in parentheses refer, first of all, to the volume and page number, respectively, of: Nikolaus von Kues, *Philosophisch-theologische Schriften,* ed. Leo Gabriel and trans. Dietlind and Wilhelm Dupré (Vienna: Herder, 1989). After this I also cite the corresponding volume and paragraph in the edition of the Heidelberg Academy of Sciences (indicated by h). All translations in English are by the author.

14. *De docta ignorantia* II 9 (I, 380; h I, nr. 149).

er,"[15] he thinks of oneness as it is present in a number and plays with metaphors like "a living unity," "a living number," "a living measure," "a written law that turns out to be alive," "a living description," "a living voice," "a living sight," "a living spark," "a living mirror," and so forth, as instances in which the power of thought *(vita intellecutalis)* supposedly functions as the soul of these *entia rationis* ("entities of reason"). In the same vein he introduces also the idea of "a living image"[16] and connects it with the projection of the absolute art as subsisting creativity. Imagine, he tells us, that this art is that of an accomplished artisan who wanted to produce the best possible picture. What would he do? He could go on painting, and whatever he produced would be a perfect expression of his art. But he could also think of making a picture that would be alive and capable of imitating his craft. By its very nature the quality of such a picture would consist in the works that the picture produces on its own accord. Because this added quality includes the preceding ones, the living picture is obviously the more perfect image, even if the result is such that the picture's own products will never match the artisan's works. Or as Cusanus puts it:

No matter how perfect an image will be that cannot be more perfect and more in conformity with its exemplar, it is not as perfect as any imperfect image which has the power to conform itself ever more and without limitation to its inaccessible exemplar. In this it imitates infinity as best as it can. It is as if a painter made two portraits: the one, a dead image, would be very much like him, whereas the other, being alive, would be less like him, although of such a nature that it could make itself continuously more like him once it has been set in motion by its object. Nobody would hesitate to say that the second picture is the more perfect one because and inasmuch as it imitates the art of the painter in a higher degree.[17]

Assimilation and Creativity

The envisaged combination of perfection and imperfection in the internal dynamics of a living image is a strong indication of the possibility

---

15. Nicholas of Cusa, *De coniecturis* II 16 (II, 176; h III, nr. 158): "[Q]uaelibet pars virtualis de toto verificatur . . ."

16. Nicholas of Cusa, *Idiota de sapientia* I (III, 438; h V, nr. 18); *Idiota de mente* VII (III, 542; h V, nr. 106).

17. *Idiota de mente* XIII (III, 592; h V, nr. 109).

that perfection can be reconciled with imperfection if and to the extent that the contrasts between them connect with the emergent potential of freedom and creativity. Thus the thought-experiment proves its value by explaining the meaning of infinity in finite things. But because the idea of a living image is in itself a configuration of various meanings, we can also approach it as a symbol that stands for itself and see whether, and in what sense, it is compatible with the meaning of being human. The connection between this symbol and the meaning of being human is in itself a conjecture rather than the result of necessary relations. Whatever the worth and value of this connection, it depends on a test of self-reflection within the horizon of our experiences and on our ability to recognize the living features of the thought-experiment in our experiences.

In fact when Cusanus first introduces the metaphor of the living image, he connects it with the human assimilation to wisdom: "this assimilation which occurs naturally in our spirit and through which it finds rest only in wisdom itself, is like a living image of that wisdom."[18] By focusing on assimilation, Cusanus refers to the various processes that affect us in our being, but in which we relate also to the world around us and the semantic universe within us, both inasmuch as these processes are expressions of our desires and as they mark all forms of perception. But no less important is also the ability to live as cultural or civil beings, and to be creators of our own world. Assimilation itself is a two-way operation: in being assimilated to what we perceive, we assimilate ourselves and the objects of perception to our own notions and likings. "The power of being assimilated and the power to assimilate, and the connection between them, is in essence one and the same thing."[19] What we see is what we perceive and apperceive because it is mediated in the mind that recognizes itself in conjunction with the processes of assimilation.

An example by which Cusanus tries to explain these basic relations is the making of a spoon:

The layman [artisan] took a spoon in his hand and said: "A spoon has no model outside the idea of our mind. Though a sculptor or painter takes his exemplars from things which he tries to depict, I, by contrast, bring forth spoons and trays from wood and pots from clay. In this I do not imitate the shapes of any natural

18. *Idiota de sapientia* I (III, 438; h V, nr. 18).
19. *Idiota de mente* XI (III, 572; h V, nr. 133).

thing [but the principles of nature itself]. Forms like those of spoons, trays and pots are accomplished by human art alone. Therefore, my art is more perfect than the imitative art of created figures. And in this it is more similar to the infinite art."[20]

Whether we look at the general conditions of being human or consider the full range of human deeds and accomplishments, in either case we come upon the mind as the place where the various movements of our being are brought together and where the idea of a living image presents itself as core event that structures the human potential in its possibilities. As the mind conceives of this event, it is up to the human being to become one with its meaning. At first, the life of this image resembles a person who sleeps, as Cusanus says. But once it has been aroused by sense perceptions and admiration, its movements will become all-comprehensive. It is as if one brought to life the angle of a highly polished diamond in which the forms of all things were reflected. By looking at itself, it would find resemblances of all things, with the help of which it could make notions of everything.[21]

Human beings are an image of God because and to the extent that they keep the living image in themselves as principle of their humanity. The living image is pure and without obfuscation. We find it and become one with its meaning as we relate to ourselves in the originality of our origin and follow the hints of increasing deiformity.[22]

Completing the Image

With the localization of the living image in the center and original dimension of the human mind, Cusanus succeeds in finding a point from which it is possible to think of successive incorporations of the same principle and to outline a picture of reality as symbol of all and everything. The thought is by and large a synthesis between the Neoplatonic and

20. *Idiota de mente* II (III, 492; h V, nr. 62). See also G. von Bredow, *Im Gespräch mit Nikolaus von Kues* (Münster: Aschendorff, 1995), 255.

21. *Idiota de mente* V (III, 518; h V, nr. 85)

22. See G. von Bredow, *Im Gespräch,* 253. Inasmuch as the hints of increasing deiformity are focused in Christ, one could also say that Christ is (as J. Hopkins points out in his essay in this volume) the exemplar of the living image both in the sense that Christ connects God and creation and that the "Christ in us" connects humanity with its divine origin.

Christian traditions. To begin with the picture of reality, it should be noted that the human being is actively involved in the formation of this symbol and that its outline is no less an expression than it is an impression of being human. As Cusanus puts it: that it is the outcome of *assimilari,* of being assimilated, as well as of *assimilare,* that is, of active assimilation. Moreover, when I speak of "successive incorporations of the same principle," I am referring to Cusanus's idea that we can think of different images being alive, depending on the force that enlivens them, whether this force is pure intelligence with regard to the intellect, or the intellect with regard to reason, or reason with regard to sense perception, or sense perception with regard to the body. In each of these instances, we form images of particular kinds under variable conditions. They relate to experiences that make it necessary to acknowledge the divine in the picture of reality both as we come to think of reality and as we make it by connecting various elements in the form of this picture. In the configuration of things, an image is always also a configuration of differences. With each element we can combine different perspectives, and it is through different perspectives that we become aware of new combinations of elements.

What I would like to emphasize by these rather abstract qualifications is the threefold nature of the concept of the image. It seems to me that the implications of this theory of the image can be understood in terms of its (1) theoretical, (2) practical, and (3) affective significance.

As to its theoretical significance, I would like to point out that the image, in whatever form we might think of it, is not only an expandable configuration of elements subject to continuous modifications and revisions, but that it offers itself also to the investigations of limits and the reconstruction of reality in the light of these investigations. In exploring the world, we form images of the world and make use of self-constructed models and sequences of images in order to describe and analyze our findings. The investigation of limits refers to mathematical considerations of infinity. But Cusanus does not stop there. For him it is an issue that concerns all aspects of reality, the universe in its totality, as well as the conditions of being and understanding.[23] If the God-symbol stands for

23. When Cusanus notes in *Idiota de mente* IV (III, 506; h V, 74) that the mind is not the unfolding of the eternal enfolding but an *imago complicationis divinae* ("an image of the divine enfolding"), all he wants to say is that the human mind is not God, but that the mind's

and collects the investigations of limits, it is God whom he seeks and finds through the thought-experiment of the living image. Man in turn is the place where the living image of God appears in forms of concrete manifestations. On an abstract level we can think of God as the unimaginable antecedent of all images, but to do so we have to reach the limit of thinking and do justice to its meaning. At this juncture, the images of mind and perception become indications of the infinite truth that appears in them and transcends them in their finite configurations.[24]

---

creative power is mediated in its being God's image. The meaning of *complicatio* ("enfolding")–*explicatio* ("unfolding") applies to all creatures, including human beings. But whereas God creates in an essential sense, humans do so only by assimilation. Inasmuch as things lack the creative power of the mind they are no images of the divine enfolding as timeless and unconditional beginning of all unfolding. However, if we approach them as they fall under the power of the word, and thus, as they appear in the light of the mind, there can be no doubt that they, too, are "images of their proper and true exemplar which is ineffable" (*Idiota de mente* II [III, 498; h V, nr. 67]). Since the image is the place where truth appears, and because truth is the object of the mind, we cannot speak of images without referring to the mind that perceives the truth which is part of them. Whether we think of the mind or not, when we become aware of the world in multiple images, we have entered the realm of meaning and become dependent on the mind as it shapes and reshapes the conjectural features of reality—and thus, as it turns into the exemplar of its own deeds and images. Infinite mind and truth are beyond reach. But to the extent that they appear in the finite truth of finite minds, they turn into a symbol that permits us to approach reality in the light of this symbol. Therefore, if the mind is God's image because this image defines itself originally as mind, then it is obvious that everything else that presents itself to the mind becomes God's image in the assimilation processes of this mind. "For, inasmuch as things participate in the mind that comes after the mind's simplicity *(post simplicem mentem de mente participant)*, they participate also in the image of God. Hence, whereas the mind is by itself God's image, all that follows the mind is so only through the mind" (*Idiota de mente* III [III, 504; h V, nr. 73]).

24. See also *De venatione sapientiae* XVII (I, 76, 78; h XII, nr. 50): "Everything is in the mind in accordance with its mode of being because goodness, greatness, truth and so forth are all in everything, in God God, in the mind mind, in the sense sense. . . . Because cognition is assimilation, the mind finds everything within itself as in a living mirror gifted with intellectual life. When the mind looks at itself, it sees all that has been assimilated within itself. And this assimilation is the living image of the creator and of everything. Because the mind is a living and thinking image of God, who is no-other of any other thing, the mind discovers what its exemplar means if it turns toward itself and knows that it is such an image. Without doubt, it recognizes its God whose likeness it is. In its own conceptual goodness it realizes that God's goodness whose image it is, is greater than it is able to conceive or to understand. Likewise, if it observes that its greatness encompasses everything intellectually, it realizes that the exemplary greatness of its God, whose image it is, exceeds all limits because God is without end, and so forth. Above itself the mind sees also intelli-

The practical significance of the image concept consists in the combination of freedom and necessity in the formation of images. In connection with the first point, we could refer here to the idea of a *scientia experimentalis* ("a science of experiment/experience"), as Cusanus suggested in the last of the three dialogues of 1450, *Idiota de staticis experimentis*. Because of the implicit freedom of imagination, we can design all sorts of frameworks and see whether they will help us to find useful relations between various phenomena and to discover new possibilities of measurement with regard to these relations. But even more important is the realization that we ourselves are the image that needs to be formed and developed as we relate to our deeds and become one with the manner in which we unfold our own being. Whether man is an image of God depends on how he turns into this image by following his desires and elevating himself to infinity. Cultural achievements and the works of art are part of this process. But its first and decisive meaning is the work of art that we are as persons and communities, as civil and ethical beings, as beings who know of God and commit themselves to the meaning of this knowledge. It is a process that begins where the mind turns toward itself and makes use of itself because and inasmuch as it is a living image of God. But because it is an "autopoetic" process we could also say that the mind becomes aware of God as it discovers its true nature in the course of this process.

Finally, turning to the "affective significance of the image," I think, first of all, of the essentially human connection between *cognoscere,* to understand, and *diligere,* to feel attracted and to love. Even in its beginnings, it is the whole image that wants to come to completion and that provides in its desires the basis and the parameters of our achievements as well as of our failures. Like Aristotle before him, Cusanus is convinced that God and nature do nothing in vain and that understanding is not possible if the mind does not love what it is doing. In the second place, I think of the experiences of beauty both as beauty affects us spontaneously and as we

---

gences which are more lucid and capable of receiving the divine, whereas below itself it observes sense perception which is darker and less capable of the divine. What satisfaction the intellectual pursuit has to offer if it relates to itself and tries to deepen itself unceasingly, is shown by the discoveries of theologians, philosophers, and mathematicians which have been variedly preserved in their writings."

connect it with truth and happiness. Cusanus speaks of the ineffable joy that we experience when we touch the unity of infinite truth in the variety of true insights. He points, for example, to the pleasing variety of colors that shines forth in oneness and to voices that echo in unison and concordance. As he puts it:

> The case is similar with regard to every sense, all reason, and all intelligence. . . . [The one who touches the unity of infinite truth] sees intellectually in the otherness of visible things the unity of all beauty, hears the unity of all harmony, tastes the sweet unity of every delectable thing, apprehends the unity of all causes and reasons, and embraces everything with intellectual joy in the truth which alone he loves.[25]

Conclusion

Much of what Cusanus says sounds exaggerated in our ears and seems to make sense only if we contrast it with the cultural and religious background of his age. But in spite of these difficulties, I think that the metaphor of the living image is an idea that brings the meaning and experiences of humanity into perspective and inspires us to give the aesthetic dimensions of our being the credit they deserve. I mean this not in the Kierkegaardian sense that beauty should be subservient to ethics and religion. Beauty is rather a principle and criterion that concerns all human activities and that tells us what it means to be human and cultural.

25. *De coniecturis* II 6 (II, 116; h III, nr. 105). See also *Sermo* CCLI, "Nos revelata facie gloriam Domini speculantes in eandem imaginem transformamur a claritate in claritatem tamquam a Domini spiritu," Cod. Vat. Lat. 1245, fol. 188vb–189ra: "Remember that our mind is a figure and manifestation of God's beauty. In itself it folds together all perceivable beauty which is beneath it. And the same holds true of all other things. If you are careful, you will see that there is no perceivable beauty, nor discernment, nor order, if the mind has been removed. All this exists in the world of the senses because of the judgment of the mind. In this sense the mind is not of this world but is its perfection, which is higher than this world. If you look at the world, you look down and below you. If the mind turns to itself in full circle, it finds no beauty and adornment which it had not seen in its own being as in the figure and form of all forms and figures. Much remains to be said that I have partly discussed elsewhere. But don't neglect the idea that freedom dwells in the mind, as the mind holds the principle of its actions within itself and is the lord of its action as Damascenus says. The mind has this freedom because it has been created in accordance with the image of God. If you consider it closely you will discover that the first cause put its likeness as cause into freedom in such a way that it should be a living image or cause that has been caused."

Whether the result will concur with the idea of man as God's image is not a problem that can be solved once and for all but a question that needs to be asked ever anew, for this question invites us to reconsider the answers as well as the questions that have been asked and given. If we think of the answers Cusanus gave, the perspectives in which they have been presented not only become guides to his questions, but, more than anything else, challenge us to restart the investigation of limits in our own way. But whatever our own convictions and insights, inasmuch as beauty is self-sufficient and divine, I am inclined to say that the result speaks earlier than the theory that follows. With Cusanus we could quote the Bible: "Ye shall know them by their fruits"[26] and point out that through experimentation we shall come to know what is true or false.[27]

In a historical setting Cusanus belongs to the age of premodernity. Many of his thoughts give a foretaste of later developments. At the initial stage of postmodern developments, it becomes intriguing to think about alternatives to the history as we know it. Of course, what has happened cannot be redone. But still, if we think truly about alternatives, the thoughts themselves might not be lost if they help us to find significant perspectives for our own age. It seems to me that the idea of the living image needs to be discussed in just this context, for this idea in its original meaning provides strong and promising motives to evaluate the past as well as the present.

To conclude the discussion of the living image let me quote a passage from a sermon in which Cusanus summarizes the main points of this essay:

Consider the fact that the intellectual nature is the only one that is capable of true life. For nothing but the intellect can understand that it is alive. Only the intellect has the ability to be sight, not like a sense-organ which sees other things but not itself, but as living sight which sees itself and in itself all other things. Therefore only the intellect is like a living image that is susceptible to the taste of life in itself, that is, of true life, of which it is an image. The living image which has been enlivened by intellectual life discovers, by discovering itself as image, the truth, the exemplar, and the form which gives it its being to the effect that it exists as image. And this is the true life of the image which dwells in it as truth in the im-

---

26. Matthew 7:16.

27. *Sermo* CXCVII, "Qui facit voluntatem Patris mei, qui in caelis est, ipse intrabit in regnum caelorum," Cod. Vat. Lat. 1245, fol. 110va.

age. That is the reason why the intellect which understands itself as living image has the power to assimilate itself increasingly to its exemplar, and to ascend continuously to a greater union with its object, that is, truth, in order to find most pleasing rest. The image that understands itself as image cannot find rest outside the truth whose image it is. It enters into error, confusion, and death if it is cut off from the influence that gives intellectual life and being to the image. Nevertheless, like a real eye in darkness, it remains an image that has died as far as the sweetness of its life is concerned. Since God is good and wanted to show the richness of his glory, he created everything for the intellectual nature to which alone an act of displaying (*ostensio*) becomes possible because only the intellect has an eye which can see truth. There is nothing but truth which God can show in all his riches. Therefore, he ultimately sowed a kind of divine seed after he had made all other creatures, namely, the intellectual nature, as it is beautifully revealed in the book of Genesis. There we read that he set man above all other creatures. By breathing he put a living image into him. This way we should understand the difference between the intellect and the other creatures, because this breath was the breath of life. From this breath the soul has been made as it lives in conformity with the divine life which knows that it is alive. Through this event man has been made a living image of God. That this admirable life-force is a divine seed in the form of a living image, we experience in ourselves because and to the extent that we are creators by assimilation. Just as God the creator creates and forms truly through thought and thinking, we produce the resemblances of things through our intellect and show in the arts that we work with resemblances. And in the same way that God enfolds in his actuality everything which is or can be, our intellect enfolds the resemblances of all things in its power and explicates them by assimilation. This is what understanding means. To stimulate this seed and to make it bear the fruits of cognition, many incentives are given to the intellectual nature, to the effect that God shows the riches of his glory. God has given—and gives—men many gracious gifts. They are the gifts of the spirit, because God the Spirit gives them to our spirit. They are graces and illuminations which have no other purpose than to make sure that the grain does not remain mere potency in this earth, but that it grows and bears fruit.[28]

28. *Sermo* CLXIX, "Ubi venit plenitudo temporis, misit Deus Filium suum," Cod. Vat. Lat. 1245, fol. 63ra–63rb.

Karsten Harries

6. ON THE POWER AND POVERTY
OF PERSPECTIVE
Cusanus and Alberti

Were it possible, I would have begun this essay by showing an episode from Roberto Rosselini's *The Age of Cosimo de' Medici*, a film dating from 1972. Its third part focuses on Leon Battista Alberti. Included is a meeting between Alberti and Cusanus, supposed to have taken place in Florence at the time of the council that fleetingly reunited the Eastern and the Western Church. In the film it is the mathematician and doctor Paolo Toscanelli who appears to have brought Cusanus and Alberti together. The scene begins with a brief consideration of some of Toscanelli's achievements as geographer and astronomer. Suggesting his indebtedness to Toscanelli, Cusanus goes on to sketch some of the key ideas of *De docta ignorantia,* a book the attentively listening Alberti of the film tells us he has read.[1] In the film's next episode Alberti explains the perspective construction he had put down in *De pictura* ("On Painting").[2] Rosselini thus presents Toscanelli as the mediating figure between the Cardinal's cosmological vision and his teaching of the coincidence of opposites, on the one hand, and Alberti's perspective construction, on the other.

The film presents Cosimo de' Medici's Florence as the beginning of a new world, in which money and mathematics gain an altogether new significance. Rosselini thus places us on the threshold of our modern world. Like Cosimo de' Medici, the Alberti of the film appears to have already crossed that threshold.[3]

---

1. In fact, an actual discussion of *De docta ignorantia* (1440) is quite improbable given the presumable date of the fictional meeting.

2. The treatise was later translated by Alberti himself into Italian and thus frequently bears the title *Della pittura*.

3. The following discussion follows and, especially in its concluding section, advances

When I first saw the scene showing Toscanelli, Cusanus, and Alberti engaged in conversation, I was a bit surprised. Although I have long been convinced that there must have been meetings between Alberti and Cusanus, there is no documentary evidence for such a meeting. Alberti does not figure much in the secondary literature on Cusanus. There are more references to Cusanus in the literature on Alberti, most importantly in Giovanni Santinello's *Leon Battista Alberti,* published in Florence in 1962.[4]

That Cusanus was indeed interested in Alberti's theory of perspective is shown by the fact that he owned a copy of Alberti's later *Elementa picturae* ("Elements of Painting"). And Alberti, too, knew the work of Cusanus: one of his mathematical treatises, *De lunularum quadratura* ("On Squaring [the circle] by Means of Little Moons"), derives very directly from a treatise by Cusanus. Their shared interest in mathematics would thus appear to have been one thing that joined Cusanus and Alberti, their interest in the power of perspective another.

Did the two ever meet? Circumstantial evidence suggests that they must have known each other. Again and again they were in the same places at the same time, first in Padua, where Alberti had been sent when he was only ten or eleven to attend the school of the humanist Gasparino Barzizza, just at the time as Cusanus, three years older, arrived from Heidelberg to attend what was then the leading university in Europe. To be sure, there is no reason to assume that he would have met the young Alberti at that time. Still, it cannot be ruled out altogether: people matured early in those days. Later their paths were to cross again in Ferrara and Florence, at the Jubilee in Rome in 1450, and especially in the years 1459 to 1464, when both were residing in Rome.[5]

---

the discussion of Cusanus and Alberti that occupies a central place in my *Infinity and Perspective* (Cambridge, Mass.: MIT Press, 2001).

4. Giovanni Santinello, *Leon Battista Alberti. Una Visione Estetica del Mondo e della vita* (Florence: Sansoni, 1962). See especially the Appendix, "Nicoló Cusano e Leon Battista Alberti: Pensieri sul bello e sull'arte," 265–96. See also Giovanni Santinello, *Introduzione a Niccolò Cusano* (Roma-Bari: Laterza, 1971; 3rd ed. 1999).

5. Santinello, *Leon Battista Alberti,* 265–66. In *Leon Battista Alberti: Universal Man of the Renaissance* (Chicago: University of Chicago Press, 1969), Joan Gadol observes that "In the late 1450's Cusa's home in Rome was a gathering place for men of science like Peurbach, Regiomontanus, and Toscanelli; Alberti must have been a member of this group" (196–97, n. 68). See also Ernst Cassirer, *Individual and Cosmos in Renaissance Philosophy,* trans. Mario Domandi (New York and Evanston: Harper and Row, 1963), 50; and Leonardo Olschki, *Die*

That Cusanus must have met the somewhat younger Alberti is suggested by the fact that they befriended many of the same people.[6] Most important, they were both close to Paolo Toscanelli, who, a friend also of Brunelleschi, shared their interest in perspective. Toscanelli is now believed to have been the author of a treatise entitled *Della prospettiva* ("On perspective") (in the Ricciardi library) that once had been included among Alberti's works. "Cast as a summary, in 'vulgar' Italian, of the key concepts of medieval optics," it was written presumably earlier than *De pictura*.[7] Toscanelli also was among those responsible for the revival of interest in geography, more especially in producing more accurate maps, an interest shared by both Cusanus and Alberti. Rosselini's film alludes to the rumor that he was the author of the chart that first encouraged Columbus to seek the East by going west.

That Alberti and Cusanus both dedicated works to Toscanelli, Alberti the *Intercoenales* ("Dinner Pieces") of 1429, Cusanus his first two geometrical treatises, *De transmutationibus geometricis* ("On Geometrical Transformations") of 1450 and *De arithmeticis complementis* ("Complementary Arithmetical Considerations") of the same year, shows the high esteem in which both held the Florentine polymath. Cusanus had first met Toscanelli in Padua. They remained friends, and Toscanelli was the doctor at his bedside when Cusanus died in Todi in 1464. We have Toscanelli's critique of one of Cusanus's mathematical writings and also a little dialogue by Cusanus, *Dialogus de circuli quadratura* ("Dialogue on Squaring the Circle"), which is based on a discussion between the two that took place in Brixen in 1457.

⋙

But why am I even interested in joining Cusanus to Alberti, that is, in looking at the work of the Cardinal from the vantage point of Alberti? My reason is, I suspect, not so very different from that which led Rosselini to stage the meeting between the two in his film. I, too, understand Alber-

Literatur der Technik und der angewandten Wissenschaften vom Mittelalter bis zur Renaissance (Leipzig, Florence, Rome, Geneva: Olschki, 1919), 42, 81, and 108.

6. Among them Enea Silvio Piccolomini, later Pope Pius II, Giovanni Andrea de Bussi, Tommaso di Sarazana, who was to become Pope Nicholas V, Nicolò Albergati, bishop of Bologna, and Ambrogio Traversari. See Santinello, *Alberti*, 266.

7. Hugo Damisch, *The Origin of Perspective*, trans. John Goodman (Cambridge, Mass.: MIT Press, 1995), 71.

ti as one of the founders of our modern world, a world whose material wealth is shadowed by spiritual poverty. More specifically, I understand Alberti's *De pictura* as a work that helped inaugurate what Heidegger came to call "The Age of the World Picture." "Picture" is understood here as something produced by the subject, something that has its center in and receives its measure from the subject.[8] Heidegger, to be sure, was thinking not of Alberti, but of Descartes and of his promise of a method that would render us humans the masters and possessors of nature. But, as I hope will become clear in the course of this essay, in important ways Alberti's perspective construction is a precursor of that method. To confront Alberti with Cusanus is to invite our age, this "Age of the World Picture," to recognize the poverty that shadows its power, to become learned about its ignorance. We refuse that invitation at our peril. Cusanus is thus for me not just a person of historical interest, but a thinker who can help us to open windows in the house modernity has built, windows to transcendence. In this sense Cusanus figured already in my dissertation, the conclusion of which sought in Cusanus's *non aliud* an answer to the problem of nihilism.[9]

But if such remarks are not to remain unsupported, though perhaps suggestive, assertions, I need to say more, first of all about Alberti's perspective construction and its significance.

Addressed first of all to painters and those interested in understanding the practice of painting, Alberti's theory of perspective teaches us how to create convincing representations of what we see, of what appears as it appears, given a particular point of view. What such painting represents are not the objects themselves, but their inevitably perspective-bound appearances. These appearances have their measure in the perceiving eye.

It is important here to keep in mind the artificiality of Alberti's construction: To put geometry in the service of his construction, Alberti assumes monocular vision and a flat earth. The violence this does to the way we actually see is evident. Normally we see with two constantly shift-

8. Martin Heidegger, "Die Zeit des Weltbildes," *Holzwege,* Gesamtausgabe, vol. 5 (Frankfurt am Main: Klostermann, 1977), 75–113.

9. Karsten Harries, "In a Strange Land: An Exploration of Nihilism" (Ph.D. diss., Yale, 1961), 141–68.

ing eyes, and Alberti knew of course that our earth is a globe. Given his assumptions, it is easy to come up with a proof of the correctness of Alberti's construction. For the sake of achieving a certain mastery of appearances, the perspectival art of Alberti subjects what it presents to a human measure that has itself been subjected to the demand for ease of representation. Alberti's understanding of the art of perspective offers itself thus as a figure of Cartesian method. Perspectival painting prefigures the scientific representation of nature.

We are provided with at least a sketch of what was to come in the last of Cusanus's *Idiota* dialogues, *Idiota de staticis experimentis,* in which Cusanus, too, calls for a mathematical treatment of nature.[10] This may be understood as just another corollary of his Platonism. But this Platonism takes here a very practical turn, as Cusanus throws out numerous suggestions as to how the power of mathematical measures might be put to use. What matters are not the details, but the general direction: number gives us the key to how to represent and to learn more about the workings of nature. Like ruler and clock, the weight-scale helps us to redescribe nature in a way that makes it more commensurable with our mind's mode of operation. Implicit in such calls for a mathematization of the science of nature is a shift from the heterogeneity of the immediately experienced world to the homogeneity of a world subjected to the measure of number. With Cusanus this privileging of mathematics has its foundation not in the nature of things, but, as he points out in *De possest,* in relation to the nature of human understanding. We can imagine a being who knows what is by means of genetic definitions, somewhat in the way that the definition of a circle gives us a rule for its construction. But we do not construct the world we experience. In this respect a tree is very different from a circle. What we construct is never more than a similitude, an enigma, an image, or a picture. By their form such pictures should conform to the nature of the human spirit. They should thus be as comprehensible as possible. But they should not be confused with the things pictured: these we shall never adequately comprehend. For ease of representation and the power such representation gives us, our understanding here distances

10. English translation, *On Experiments Done with Weight-Scales,* in Jasper Hopkins, *Nicholas of Cusa on Wisdom and Knowledge* (Minneapolis, Minn.: Banning Press, 1996), 319–71 (h V, N. 161–195, pp. 221–241).

itself from a much richer experience. There is a sense in which both Alberti's perspective construction and the mathematical approach to nature advocated by Cusanus's *idiota* mean a derealization of the real.

Alberti's perspective construction brings to mind the painter criticized in Book X of the *Republic*. As Alberti was to do, Plato there likens him to a godlike magician, able to make not only all "the works of the other workmen, . . . but plants and animals, himself and all other things—the earth and heaven, and the things which are in heaven or under the earth," even the gods. Plato's Socrates goes on to suggest that such magic is indeed quite easy: all we need do is "turn a mirror round and round."[11] Imitating only the appearances of objects that are themselves but imitations of the forms, the artist is thus said to be thrice removed from reality. It is a charge invited especially by the perspectival art inaugurated by Alberti. How can we take seriously such an art's claim to serve the truth? It is easy to understand Jacques Maritain when he mourns the rise of Renaissance art based on the newly gained mastery of perspective.[12] Artful pictorial illusion invites us to mistake it for reality and to forget its merely artificial being. Artifice substitutes simulacra for reality, as the artist usurps the place of God, substituting for God's creation his own. Maritain would thus have us consider the single step that carries us in some museum from the rooms of the primitives to those holding the masters of the Renaissance as a crossing of the threshold that separates anthropocentric modernity from the theocentric Middle Ages.

That Alberti has already crossed this threshold is shown by his rejection of the use of gold in painting. To understand what is at issue here we should consider the significance of the gold background that was introduced into Western painting just before 1000. Perhaps the only artistic innovation of comparable importance was the stained glass window. Together they furnished medieval art with two critical metaphors—"critical" in the sense that they allow us to approach the essence of this art. The gold background has metaphorical power and hints at eternal blessedness as it helps to establish the timeless significance of representations drawn

11. *Republic* X 596. Trans. Benjamin Jowett.

12. Jacques Maritain, *Art and Scholasticism, and the Frontiers of Poetry*, trans. Joseph W. Evans (New York: Scribner, 1962), 52.

from the mundane. It invites us to look at what we see from a "spiritual perspective." I am using this expression, borrowed from Friedrich Ohly, deliberately.[13] Alberti's perspective invites us to look through the material painting as if it were transparent, that is, as a window through which we can see whatever the painter has chosen to represent. But this is very much a human perspective, which has its center in the observer: what we see is appearance for us. The spiritual perspective of medieval art would have us look through the painting in a very different sense—through the material to its spiritual significance. Alberti's art is incompatible with this spiritual perspective. A God-centered art gives way to a subject-centered art. The turn to perspective here means a loss of transcendence. And the same can be said of what Heidegger calls "The Age of the World Picture."

Key here is insight into the relativity of appearance, which has its center in and receives its measure from the perceiving subject. Such insight is as characteristic of Cusanus as it is of Alberti. The following passage from *De pictura* reads as if it could have been written by the Cardinal:

It would be well to add to the above statements the opinions of philosophers who affirm that if the sky, the stars, the sea, mountains and bodies should become— should God so will, reduced by half, nothing would be diminished in any part to us. All knowledge of large, small; long, short; high, low; broad, narrow; clear, dark; light and shadow and every similar attribute is obtained by comparison.[14]

Magnitude provides Alberti with his paradigm. We cannot know the absolute size of things; indeed, we do not even know what such absolute size might mean. Our understanding of the size of some object is relative through and through. Alberti goes on to give a number of examples, such as Aeneas, who stands head and shoulders above other men, but seems like a dwarf next to Polyphemus. He states:

Thus all things are known by comparison, for comparison contains within itself a power which immediately demonstrates in objects, which is more, less or equal.

---

13. Friedrich Ohly, *Schriften zur mittelalterlichen Bedeutungsforschung* (Darmstadt: Wissenschaftliche Buchgesellschaft, 1977), 15, 35–37.

14. Leon Battista Alberti, *On Painting*, trans. and intro. John R. Spencer (New Haven and London: Yale, 1956), 55. See Mark Jarzombek, *On Leon Battista Alberti* (Cambridge, Mass.: MIT Press, 1989).

From which it is said that a thing is large when it is greater than something small and largest when it is greater than something large.[15]

Cusanus was to observe seven years later in *De docta ignorantia* with quite similar words that our understanding relies on comparison:

However all those who make an investigation judge the uncertain proportionally, by means of a comparison with what is taken to be certain. Therefore, every inquiry is comparative and uses the means of comparative relation.[16]

All inquiry presupposes a great deal that is taken to be certain and allowed to go unchallenged. It presupposes something that may seem like a stable ground, the ground furnished by our language and the associated concepts. But this ground, if Cusanus is right, is ultimately no more stable than the earth on which we stand, an insight that provides Cusanus with a paradigm: it is in fact a shifting ground. To recognize this is to become learned about one's ignorance. The ancients are said to have lacked such learned ignorance.

It has already become evident to us that the earth is indeed moved, even though we do not perceive this to be the case. For we apprehend motion only through a certain comparison with something fixed. For example, if someone did not know that a body of water was flowing and did not see the shore while he was on a ship in the middle of the water, how would he recognize that the ship was being moved?[17]

Cusanus here invites the reader to engage in a simple thought experiment that must have held for him also a very personal significance. As he tells the reader in the letter to Cardinal Cesarini that he appended as a kind of epilogue to *De docta ignorantia,* the fundamental thought of that book came to Cusanus in the winter of 1437–38, "at sea en route back from Greece,"[18] where he had worked toward a reconciliation of the different perspectives that divided the Eastern and the Western Church. Recent memories of the haggling at the Council of Basel, of the way the different parties there focused on what divided them, rather than on their com-

---

15. Alberti, *On Painting,* 55.

16. Nicholas of Cusa, *On Learned Ignorance,* trans. Jasper Hopkins (Minneapolis, Minn.: Banning Press, 1981), I, 1, p. 50 (h I [1932], p. 5, lines 14–16).

17. Ibid., II, 12, pp. 116–117 (h I, p. 103, lines 13–17).

18. Ibid., dedicatory letter to Cardinal Cesarini, p. 158 (h I, p. 163, lines 7–8).

mon goal, the unity of the Church, must also have colored what he then experienced.

And because of the fact that it would always seem to each person (whether he were on the earth, the sun, or another star) that he was at the "immovable" center so to speak, and that all the other things were moved: assuredly, it would always be the case that if he were on the sun, he would fix a set of poles in relation to himself; if on the earth, another set; on the moon, another; on Mars, another; and so on.[19]

Like the painter's perspective, the poles by which we orient ourselves are fictions, created by us. As such, they reflect what happens to be our particular point of view.

In the beginning of the cited passage, Cusanus appeals to the principle of learned ignorance. The ancients are said to have lacked "learned ignorance." What they failed to understand was the full extent of the power of perspective. Such ignorance let them mistake perspectival appearance for reality. Their geocentric cosmology was born of this mistake. The earth, to be sure, appears to be the stable center of our life-world. This appearance makes it natural to believe that it must therefore also be at the cosmic center. But it would be equally natural for someone on the moon or on Mars or on any other star to proclaim whatever heavenly body they happened to be on to be the center of the cosmos. Rest and motion are relative concepts. What we take to be fixed depends on our point of view. Every attempt to seize an absolute center has to suffer shipwreck on the reef of infinity. Our life-world to be sure has its center, a center established by the accident of our body's location. In this sense the earth provides us humans with a natural center. But that center does not bind reflection. And the same can be said of the body that places us on this earth, assigns us terrestrials our point of view, and provides us with a natural measuring rod.

In this connection both Alberti and Cusanus appeal to Protagoras. Let me cite first Alberti: "Since man is the thing best known to man, perhaps Protagoras, by saying that man is the mode and measure of all things, meant that all the accidents of things are known through comparison to

19. Ibid., II, 12, pp. 116–117 (h I, p. 103, lines 17–21).

the accidents of man."[20] We meet with a similar reference in his *Libri della famiglia* ("On the Family"), dating from roughly the same time. In this rehabilitation of the sophist, which challenges both Plato and Aristotle, humanistic self-assertion in the face of the decentering threatened by meditations on infinity finds striking expression.

We find the same rehabilitation of Protagoras in Cusanus, who explicitly defends the sophist against the critique of Aristotle in *De beryllo,* which appeared in 1458. Did Cusanus here borrow from the younger Alberti?[21] I suspect that Cusanus had read *De pictura* when he began work on *De docta ignorantia.* Be this as it may, Cusanus's meditations on infinity have to lead to a denial of any absolute center or measure in the realm of creatures. This loss in turn generates the demand for a new center, a new measure. The decentering that is a consequence of thoughts of the infinity of God invites a humanist recentering. Cusanus invites us to understand the anthropocentrism of the Renaissance as a response to the decentering power of reflection on the infinity of God. The rehabilitation of Protagoras belongs in this context, although such a rehabilitation cannot have been based on much more than what was suggested by the much-quoted line that man is the measure of all things. Neither Plato's *Protagoras* nor his *Theaetetus* were then available. For Alberti's purposes, that one line was all he needed.

There are striking similarities between the ways Alberti and Cusanus appeal to Protagoras. Here Cusanus in *De beryllo:*

Thirdly, note the saying of Protagoras that man is the measure of things.[22] With the sense man measures perceptible things, with the intellect he measures intelli-

20. Alberti, *On Painting,* 55.

21. It is worth noting that both in places wrote Pythagoras, where they should have written Protagoras. Cusanus may have been misled by a copy of Bessarion's translation of Aristotle's *Metaphysics* that he owned, although he points out the confusion in a marginal note. But should we consider this a mere confusion? As we shall see, Cusanus's understanding of mathematics invites a blurring of the distinction between Pythagoras and Protagoras. See the following note.

22. Cusanus had written "Pytagorae." This was corrected in the critical edition by Ludwig Baur with the interesting comment: "Nicolaus scripsit Pytagorae. Hunc errorem inde repetendum esse puto, quod in codice Cusano 184 fol. 71 r in translatione Metaphysicae a Bessarione redacta legitur: 'Pytagoras omnium rerum hominem mensuram aiebat'; sed in codice additur; 'Credo dici debere Protagoras.'" Quoted in Santinello, *Leon Battista Alberti,* 287, n. 44.

gible things, and he attains unto supra-intelligible things transcendently. Man does this measuring in accordance with the aforementioned [cognitive modes]. For then he knows that the cognizing soul is the goal of things knowable, he knows on the basis of the perceptive power that perceptible things are supposed to be such as can be perceived. And likewise [he knows] regarding intelligible things that [they are supposed to be such] as can be understood, and [he knows] that transcendent things [are to be such] as can transcend. Hence, man finds in himself, as in a measuring scale, all created things.[23]

To the extent that we can know things at all, they must be capable of entering our consciousness, either as objects of sense, or as objects of thought, or as mysteries that transcend the power of reason. Just as the painter's representation of the world has its center in the perceiving eye, the world as we know it has its center in the knowing subject. And if this suggestion that the human being is the center of things known ascribes a quasi-divine creativity to man, this should not seem too surprising, given that according to the biblical tradition God created man in his own image. Cusanus understands this image character first of all in terms of man's ability to create a second world, the world of concepts, which allows us to measure what we experience. Rather like Alberti's perspective construction, this second world provides the linguistic or logical space in which what we perceive has to take its place if it is to be understood at all. Cusanus therefore continues:

Fourthly, note that Hermes Trismegistus states that man is a second god. For just as God is the creator of all real beings and of natural forms, so man is the creator of conceptual beings and of artificial forms that are only likenesses in his intellect, even as God's creatures are likenesses of the Divine intellect.[24]

Like Alberti, Cusanus insists here on the godlike character of man. As God's creative reason unfolds itself in creation, so the human intellect unfolds itself in whatever it knows. The known world resembles the world created by Alberti's painter.

Later in *De beryllo* Cusanus returns to Protagoras:

23. Nicholas of Cusa, *On [Intellectual] Eyeglasses,* trans. Jasper Hopkins, in Jasper Hopkins, *Nicholas of Cusa: Metaphysical Speculations* (Minneapolis, Minn.: Banning Press, 1997), 36–37 (h XI [1988], N. 6, p. 8).
24. Ibid., 37 (h XI, N. 7, p. 9).

There still remains one thing: viz., to see how it is that man is the measure of all things. Aristotle says that by means of this [expression] Protagoras stated nothing profound. Nevertheless, Protagoras seems to me to have expressed [herein] especially important [truths]. I consider Aristotle rightly to have stated, at the outset of his *Metaphysics,* that all men by nature desire to know. He makes this statement with regard to the sense of sight, which a man possesses not simply for the sake of working; rather, we love sight because sight manifests to us many differences. If, then, man has senses and reason not only in order to know, then perceptible objects have to nourish man for two purposes: viz., in order that he may live and in order that he may know. But knowing is more excellent and more noble, because it has the higher and more incorruptible goal. Earlier on, we presupposed that the Divine Intellect created all things in order to manifest itself; likewise the Apostle Paul, writing to the Romans, says that the invisible God is known in and through the visible things of the world.[25]

This, to be sure, hardly sounds like a critique of Aristotle. Quite the opposite: Cusanus sounds like a humanist Aristotelian when he here, and not only here, embraces the visible things of the world in all their variety as an epiphany of the Divine. Trinkaus is right to link this passage to Alberti's invocation of *la più grassa Minerva* ("a little richer, or fatter, wisdom") to suggest a new emphasis on visible form.[26] But what impresses Cusanus here is not just the beauty and wealth of the visible, but the way all we see is dependent on the fact that we possess eyes. Aristotle is said to have seen this very point: namely, that if perceptual cognition is removed, perceptible objects are removed. For he says in the *Metaphysics:* "If there were not things that are enlivened, there would not be either senses or perceptible objects."[27]

And the same holds for the objects of our knowledge. Is Protagoras then not right when he

stated that man is the measure of things? Because man knows—by reference to the nature of his perceptual [cognition]—that perceptual objects exist for the sake of that cognition, he measures perceptible objects in order to apprehend, perceptually, the glory of the Divine Intellect.[28]

25. Ibid., 68 (h XI, N. 65, pp. 75–76).

26. Charles Trinkaus, "Protagoras in the Renaissance: An Exploration," in *Philosophy and Humanism: Essays in Honor of Paul Oskar Kristeller,* ed. Edward P. Mahoney (New York: Columbia University Press, 1976), 203. On the phrase *la più grassa Minerva,* see John R. Spencer's introduction to his translation of Alberti's *On Painting,* 18–19.

27. Nicholas of Cusa, *On [Intellectual] Eyeglasses,* p. 70 (h XI, N. 69, p. 80).

28. Ibid.

The being of whatever presents itself is a being relative to the human perceiver and knower. Cusanus charges Aristotle with having failed to pay sufficient attention to such relativity and as a consequence to have failed to do justice to Protagoras.

Consider once more Aristotle's critique of Protagoras, where that very critique may have encouraged humanists who had come to associate the Stagirite with the scholasticism they rejected to give the maligned sophist a kinder reception.[29]

Knowledge, also, and perception, we call the measure of things, for the same reason, because we come to know something by them—while as a matter of fact they are measured rather than measure other things. But it is with us as if someone else measured us and we came to know how big we are by seeing that he applied the cubit-measure a certain number of times to us. But Protagoras says man is the measure of all things, meaning really the man who knows or the man who perceives, and these because they have respectively knowledge and perception, which we say are the measures of objects. They are saying nothing, then, while they appear to be saying something remarkable.[30]

Aristotle insists that more fundamentally our knowledge of things has its measure in these things. They are, as it were, the natural measures of knowledge. It is as if we were handed a yardstick and decided by that how tall we were.

For Cusanus, too, our knowledge begins with perception. But perception does not give us an unmediated access to God's creation. Even the yardstick example invites more questions than may at first appear. Does our understanding of the length of a "yard" not presuppose an understanding of its relationship to our body? That relationship becomes explicit when we say: "a yard is three feet." Perception already imposes a human measure on whatever presents itself to our senses. And this dependence on the subject is compounded by the way perception is entangled in understanding. To be sure, when I call this an oak-tree, the proposition's truth or falsity would seem to be decided by whether this tree is indeed an oak-tree. Cusanus, however, might ask whether, when I see this object as an oak-tree, such seeing is not itself dependent on the humanly

29. Cf. Charles Trinkaus, "Protogoras," 193.

30. Aristotle, *Metaphysics* X, 1, 1053a31–1053b4. Trans. W. D. Ross.

created concept "oak-tree," as it is dependent on the makeup of our eyes. From the very beginning we have subjected appearance to our human measures.

One could, to be sure, challenge Protagoras by invoking Cusanus's own doctrine of learned ignorance. There is, indeed, as Aristotle recognized, a sense in which knowledge and perception must be said to measure things. But do we not lose the distinction between appearance and reality when we make man the measure of all things? Was Cusanus's teaching of learned ignorance not meant to block precisely such an undue self-elevation of the human knower by reminding us that the final measure of all human knowing is God? Consider Plato's remark on Protagoras in the *Theaetetus,* a remark Cusanus is unlikely to have known, since Ficino finished his translation of that dialogue only some years later: "He says, you will remember, that 'man is the measure of all things— alike of the being of things that are and of the not-being of things that are not.' . . . He puts it in this sort of way, doesn't he, that any given thing 'is to me such as it appears to me, and is to you as it appears to you,' you and I being men?"[31] Plato already accuses Protagoras of confusing appearance and reality; or, of confusing perceiving and knowing.

But for Cusanus the seeming obviousness of this distinction is rendered questionable by a higher-order reflection: does the knower, too, not impose his human measures on what he claims to know? It is precisely because of this that Cusanus, like Alberti, calls man a second God, that is, a creator of conceptual forms in which he mirrors or unfolds himself and by means of which he reconstructs or recreates in his own image the manifold presented to his senses.

In his *Idiota de mente* Cusanus thus has his layman conjecture "that mind [*mens*] takes its name from measuring [*mensurare*]."[32] Elsewhere Cusanus appeals to Albertus Magnus, who, relying on a false etymology, had tied the word *mens* (mind) to *metior* (to measure).[33] He could also have ap-

31. Plato, *Theaetetus* 152a. Trans. F. M. Cornford.

32. Nicholas of Cusa, *The Layman on Mind,* trans. Jasper Hopkins, in Jasper Hopkins, *Nicholas of Cusa on Wisdom and Knowledge* (Minneapolis, Minn.: Banning Press, 1996), 171 (h V, N. 57, p. 90).

33. See Maurice de Gandillac, *Nikolaus von Kues, Studien zu seiner Philosophie und philosophischen Weltanschauung,* trans. Karl Fleischmann, vom Verfasser grundlegend über-arbeitetete Ausgabe (Düsseldorf: Schwan, 1953), 152. Gandillac refers to a sermon from 1455 (CLXVII, 509) where Cusanus appeals to Albertus Magnus, *De anima.*

pealed to Thomas Aquinas.[34] But important here is not the etymology, but the view that the proper activity of the *mens* is *mensurare*. But if so, where does such measuring find the proper measures? According to Cusanus we find the most fundamental measure within ourselves, where Cusanus is thinking first of all not of the body, but of the mind itself. Plato already had understood thought as a process seeking unity.[35] Sight, as we saw, furnishes us only ever different aspects of things. What then are these things in truth? Demanded is an understanding of the being of the thing in question that would allow us to gather these perceived aspects into a unity. Quite in the spirit of Plato, Cusanus, too, understands the human intellect as essentially in between that unity that draws it and the manifold of the world to which it is tied by the body and its senses and desires. This lived tension of the one and the many demands resolution. The human being demands unity and is yet prevented from seizing that unity by the manifold in which contradiction is always present. The manifold must therefore be brought under a unity. In its attempt to seize that unity, the intellect can succeed only to the degree to which it succeeds in applying this measure to the manifold.[36]

The nature of this process is made more explicit in the very beginning of the first of the *Idiota* dialogues, *Idiota de sapientia*.[37] Having proclaimed, citing Scripture, that wisdom cries out in the streets, the layman calls the orator's attention to the activities that take place in the marketplace: money being counted, oil being measured, and produce being weighed. In each case a unit measure is applied to what is to be measured. And can we not observe something of the sort wherever there is understanding? The activities observed on the marketplace invite the thought that just insofar as he is the being who measures, the human being transcends the beast. *Animal rationale* comes to be understood first of all as *animal mensurans.*

How then do we measure? The layman points out that we always measure by means of some unit, that is to say, by means of the one. The

---

34. See de Gandillac, *Nikolaus von Kues,* 152, who refers us to *De veritate,* X, art. 1, In sent. I, 35, 1: "Mens dicitur a metior, metiris."

35. Plato, *Republic* VII 524e–525a.

36. Cf. Ernst Cassirer, *Philosophie der symbolischen Formen* (Berlin: Cassirer, 1923), I, 9.

37. Nicholas of Cusa, *The Layman on Wisdom,* trans. Jasper Hopkins, in Jasper Hopkins, *Nicholas of Cusa on Wisdom and Knowledge,* 90–93 (h V, N. 5, pp. 8–10).

paradigm of all knowing is thus counting, a thought familiar to both Aristotle and Aquinas.[38] But both, as we have seen, insist that man is more fundamentally measured than measure. And something like that must be true if we are not to confuse reality and fiction—and is indeed presupposed by Cusanus when he suggests that we seek to see and understand in order to better appreciate the glory of the Divine Intellect. As a Christian thinker, he never loses sight of the importance of the distinction between God's creative knowledge and human re-creative knowledge. The human knower may indeed be likened to Alberti's painter, but we should not forget that this is a painter who paints creation in order to lead himself and others to a greater appreciation of the beauty of creation, which remains the ground of his re-creation.

All this implies that, as is indeed obvious, even if counting is constitutive of measuring, the latter nevertheless cannot be reduced to the former. Counting is not yet measuring. Thus if unity is indeed the primary measure, that primary measure must be incarnated in some concrete unit measure if there are to be activities such as weighing flour or measuring the length of a piece of cloth. And these concrete measures are not given to us by the human mind; they must be established by human beings in response to the world in which they live. The *braccio* that plays such an important part in Albert's perspective construction provides a good example. That measure, an arm's length, is read off the human body. In that sense it has its foundation in an already ordered nature. Not that a different unit of length might not have been chosen instead, which reminds us that such measures are indeed humanly created, but not *ex nihilo*. That just this measure is chosen has to do with the way the arm offers itself naturally when we measure cloth. Other activities might have suggested the foot or the digit of a finger as the appropriate measure.

And does something similar not hold for our words or concepts? They too are, to use one of Cusanus's favorite terms, conjectures. Incidentally, Maurice de Gandillac suggests that in the Latin *coniectura* Cusanus hears

---

38. See Aristotle, *Metaphysics* X, 1, 1053b4: "Evidently then, being one in the strictest sense, if we define it according to the meaning of the word, is a measure, and especially of quantity, and secondly of quality." Also Thomas Aquinas, *Summa Theologica* I, 11, 2, in *The Basic Writings of St. Thomas Aquinas*, 2 vols., ed. Anton C. Pegis (New York: Random House, 1945): "One implies the idea of a primary measure; and number is multitude measured by one."

the German *Mut-massung* it translates, which suggests a measuring with the mind. We can call such conjectures human creations, provided that we keep in mind that, like *braccio* and "foot," they are created not *ex nihilo,* but in response to certain experiences of an already ordered reality.

We have no way of understanding God's creation as He understands it. Things are not available to us in their truth. And yet that truth, the truth of things, measures our truth. But for that to be possible it must somehow present itself. But how is such presentation to be thought? Can it be comprehended? As soon as there is experience there is also the interpreting activity of the human mind. Constitutive of whatever we experience is thus our way of understanding it, our human perspective. This Cusanus takes to be the profound insight of Protagoras. But if there is a sense in which the human mind can be called a living unity that unfolds itself in measure and number, such an unfolding must respond to a world it has not created if it is not to substitute arbitrary invention for understanding. The unfolding of the living unity that we ourselves are must at the same time be a loving return to the unity that illuminates the countless particulars that make up our world.

But this means that whatever presents itself to our senses must present itself as already illuminated by *logos.*[39] If the mind is to gather some perceived manifold into a unity, that manifold must present itself as inviting such a gathering. In his perspective construction Alberti turns to the body to furnish him with measures to mediate between the eye's point of view and what is to be represented. Cusanus similarly recognizes the need for measures to mediate between the mind, thought as an unfolding unity, and what is to be represented. Here, too, successful representation of the world in which we find ourselves requires that we furnish ourselves with measures that will allow us to take the measure of what is to be represented. But such measures must be fitting. To be such, the mind that creates these measures must do so in response to what it would measure. In what, then, do these measures have their ground? A Platonist could point to the forms, but Cusanus is too persuaded by the wisdom of Protagoras to be able simply to accept that suggestion. In *De beryllo* Cusanus thus does not hesitate to criticize Plato's understanding of the forms:

39. Plato, *Timaeus* 69b–c. See Elizabeth Brient, "The Immanence of the Infinite: A Response to Blumenberg's Reading of Modernity" (Ph.D. diss., Yale, 1995), 113–16.

Know, too, that I have found, as it seems to me, a certain additional failing on the part of [those] seekers of truth. For Plato said (1) that a circle can be considered insofar as it is named or defined—insofar as it is mentally depicted or mentally conceived—and (2) that from these [considerations] the nature of the circle is not known, but (3) that the circle's quiddity (which is simple and incorruptible and free of all contraries) is seen by the intellect alone. Indeed, Plato made similar statements regarding all [such things].[40]

Cusanus challenges the Platonic claim that we have an intellectual vision of mathematicals and of the other forms as independent realities. "For if Plato had considered that [claim], assuredly he would have found that our mind, which constructs mathematical entities, has these mathematical entities, which are in its power, more truly present with itself than as they exist outside the mind."[41] Mathematics has its foundation in the unfolding of the human mind. "For example, man knows the mechanical art, and he has the forms of this art more truly in his mental concept than as they are formable outside his mind—just as a house, which is made by means of an art, has a truer form in the mind than in the pieces of wood. For the form that comes to characterize the wood is the mental form, idea, or exemplar."[42] But unlike Plato, Cusanus sees no reason to reify the idea of the house and to give it an independent reality. Plato's forms, just like mathematicals, are understood as human creations. For Cusanus already, as later for Descartes, there is a sense in which we understand things precisely only to the extent that we can make them.

That human beings, when looking for a form of representation that would do justice to the workings of their own mind, should have turned to mathematics is only to be expected. That holds especially for our attempts to understand the workings of nature. But we should remember that according to Cusanus the comparative transparency of such a mathematical representation of the world has its foundation in the chosen form of representation. This raises the question whether the other side of such transparency, as in the case of Alberti's perspective construction, is not the elision of the substance of reality, which must escape such comprehension.

40. Nicholas of Cusa, *On [Intellectual] Eyeglasses*, 62 (h XI, N. 55, p. 62).
41. Ibid., 62 (h XI, N. 55, p. 63).
42. Ibid., 62 (h XI, N. 56, p. 63).

Cusanus would have us understand that the concepts embodied in our language are human creations. But he would also have us see that they may not be understood as creations *ex nihilo*. To give us insight into the world, our measures must respond to that very world in which and to which we apply them. But if so, experience may not be reduced to a mere perception of *sensibilia*. The fitting establishment of such measures requires an altogether different kind of perception, a perception that bears a certain resemblance to a perception of forms, even though Cusanus found what he took to be Plato's reification of the forms inadequate. But what sort of perception could that be, a perception that invites or calls for concepts and words that in turn are then applied to the perceived? The following remarks offer no more than a pointer that calls for further discussion.

In his *Idiota de mente* Cusanus has his layman—that he is a craftsman is significant—offer the philosopher the example of a spoon to help the latter to a better understanding of the nature of mind.[43] Hollowing out the wood, the layman shapes it, until finally the form of spoon-ness shines forth fittingly, *convenienter resplendeat,* that same form that in varying degrees shines forth *(relucet)* in all spoons. When the art of the craftsman succeeds in shaping the wood in such a way that the form shines forth fittingly, we call his work beautiful.

And does something similar not hold also of what is not a product of human work? In the sermon *Tota pulchra es, amica mea* ("You are entirely beautiful, my beloved") of 1456[44] Cusanus, invoking the authority of Ci-

43. Nicholas of Cusa, *The Layman on Mind,* 179 (h V, N. 63, pp. 96–98).

44. Giovanni Santinello, "Nicolai De Cusa: Tota pulchra es, amica mea (Sermo de pulchritudine). Introduzione ed ediz. critica," *Atti e Memorie dell' Accademia Patavina* 71 (1959): 21–58. Page and lines references are to this edition. A French translation, "Sermon: Tu es toute belle, ma bien-aimée," appeared in Francis Bertin, *Nicolas de Cues, Sermons Eckhartiens et Dionysiens, Introduction, traduction, notes et commentaires* (Paris: Les Éditions du Cerf, 1998), pp. 317–85. The critical edition is now available as *Sermo* CCXLIII (h XIX/3, pp. 254–263) in the edition of the Heidelberg Academy of Sciences. Following Santinello, Bertin emphasizes how much of the sermon is made up of passages lifted from Ambrogio Traversari's translation of Dionysius's *De divinis nominibus* and from Albertus Magnus's commmentary on that text. Toscanelli had brought the former to Cusanus in 1443, on behalf of Pope Nicholas V. See Nikolaus von Cues, *Vom Nichtanderen, De Non Aliud,* trans., intro., and notes by Paul Wilpert, Schriften des Nikolaus von Cues in deutscher Übersetzung, Heft 12 (Hamburg: Felix Meiner, 1987), 14, n. 6. See also Giovanni Santinello, "Nicolò

cero as cited by Albertus Magnus, points out that we call the human body beautiful *ex resplendencia coloris super membra proportionata*.[45] *Proporcio* and *resplendencia* are taken to define the beautiful: "id quod materiale est in pulchritudine, puta proporcio, et formale puta resplendencia: primum quia unitas, secundum quia lux."[46] Proportion means unity; resplendence means a spiritual light. A beautiful body is likened to a light, an observation that we find already in Xenophon's *Symposium,* where the beauty of the young Autolycus is likened to a light at night that draws all eyes. To liken beauty to light is to suggest that beauty renders the beautiful more visible. Beauty lets us see.[47] But ever since Plato, understanding has been understood in the image of sight. If light lets us see, must there not also be a higher light that lets us understand? It is this simile that is presupposed by the example of the ruby Cusanus offers us in *De li non aliud* to help us to a better understanding of his thought of God as the not-other.

You see this carbuncle stone, which the peasants call a ruby. Do you see that at this third hour of the night—at a very dark time and in a very dark place—a candle is not needed because there is light in the stone? When this light wants to manifest itself, it does so by means of the stone. For in itself the light would be invisible to the sense [of sight]; for it would not be present to the sense and so would not at all be sensed, because the sense perceives only what is presented to it. Therefore the light which is in the stone conveys to the light which is in the eye what is visible regarding the stone.[48]

Cusano e Leon Battista Alberti: Pensieri sul bello e sull'arte," in Santinello, *Leon Battista Alberti.*

45. "because of the resplendences of color over its proportioned members." Giovanni Santinello, "Nicolai De Cusa: Tota pulchra es, amica mea," 51, 5–6.

46. "By material beauty I understand proportion, by formal beauty resplendence; the first because [it is] unity, and the second because [it is] light." Ibid., 56, 23–25.

47. Cf. Plato, *Phaedrus* 250d: "Now beauty, as we said, shone bright amidst these visions, and in this world below we apprehend it through the clearest of our senses, clear and resplendent. For sight is the keenest mode of perception vouchsafed us through the body; wisdom, indeed, we cannot see thereby—how passionate would had been our desire for her, if she had granted us so clear an image of herself to gaze upon—nor yet any other of those beloved objects, save only beauty; for beauty alone this has been ordained, to be most manifest to sense and most lovely of them all." Trans. R. Hackforth.

48. Nicholas of Cusa, *On God as Not-Other: A translation and an Appraisal of* De li non aliud, trans. Jasper Hopkins (Minneapolis, Minn.: Banning Press, 1987), p. 79 (h XIII [1944], pp. 23–24, lines 27–4).

The light in the stone answers to the light in the eye, which, without it, could not see. But the light in the ruby, no more than its glowing red, is said to be neither its essence nor its substance. That substance cannot be seen, does not present itself to our eyes.

The substance, which precedes accident, has nothing from the accidents. But the accidents have everything from the substance, since they are its accidents—i.e. the shadow, the image of the substantial light.[49]

The light by which we see thus figures the substantial light that gathers this thing so that it is not other than just this thing, as it gathers all things. And while this light is invisible, Cusanus yet insists that it shows itself in the visible, and more clearly in some than in others. Thus "the substantial light of the carbuncle shows itself more clearly—as in a closer likeness—in the glow of brighter splendor" (in clarioris fulgore splendentiae se clarius ostendit).[50] What is here called fulgor splendentiae ("the glow of brighter splendor") is the ground of Plato's construction of the forms. But this fulgor splendentiae is splendor formae ("the splendor of form"), is beauty. In the visible world experiences of the beautiful open windows to the transcendent ground of our knowing.

Following Albertus Magnus, Cusanus, too, defines the beautiful as splendor forme, sive substancialis sive accidentalis, super partes materie proportionatas et terminatas ("the splendor of the form, either substantial or accidental, upon the proportioned and bounded parts of matter").[51] That definition invites a distinction between two kinds of beauty, one where the splendor formae is substantial, the other where it is accidental. The beauty of the spoon is an example of the latter. As Cusanus says in De ludo globi of his globe:

Deus dator est substantiae, homo accidentis, seu similitudinis substantiae. Forma globi data ligno per hominem, addita est substantiae ligni. ("God is the giver of substance, man the giver of the accident, or the likeness of substance. The form of the globe that is given to the wood by man is brought to the substance of the wood.")[52]

49. Nicholas of Cusa, On God as Not-Other, p. 81 (h XIII, p. 24, lines 16–18).
50. Nicholas of Cusa, On God as Not-Other, p. 81 (h XIII, p. 24, lines 18–20).
51. Giovanni Santinello, "Nicolai De Cusa: Tota pulchra es, amica mea," 51, 3–4.
52. Nicholas of Cusa, De ludo globi (h IX, N. 25, p. 29); The Game of Spheres, trans. and intro. Pauline Moffit Watts (New York: Abaris, 1986), 66–67. Translation modified. See also Santinello, Leon Battista Alberti, 272, nn. 14, 15.

The beauty of the human body is an example of substantial beauty. As we read in *De ludo globi:* "the whole shines forth [*relucet*] in all its parts since each part is part of the whole; and so the whole human being shines forth in the hand that stands in the right proportion to the body; but the entire perfection of the human being shines forth more perfectly in the head."[53] Cusanus likens the human being to a kingdom gathered into one by its king. The body's beauty is the splendor of such a gathering. Just as "Trajan's power shines forth [*relucet*] in the preciousness" of his column, which his will defined and delimited, God's power shines forth in the well ordered universe[54] and in each of its parts—most perfectly, according to Cusanus, in the human being, the being that "enfolds intellectual and sensible nature and encloses all things within itself, so that the ancients were right in calling it a microcosm or a small world."[55] It is the only being that "can suitably be elevated to the Maximum by the power of the maximal, infinite God." Thus the sermon *Tota pulchra es, amica mea* concludes by calling Christ, the bridegroom of the Song of Songs, *pulchritudo absoluta.*[56] Such beauty calls the bride, the soul, with the most beautiful word, *amica,* beloved. But our soul experiences something of this call, the call of the divine *logos,* in all that is beautiful. The beauty of creation opens windows in the house our reason has built.[57] Only by our thus opening ourselves to what lies outside that house can our life and thought gain the measures that are a presupposition of all responsibility.

53. Nicholas of Cusa, *The Game of Spheres,* 74–75 (h IX, N. 42, p. 47). Translation modified.

54. Nicholas of Cusa, *On God as Not-Other,* 71 (h XIII, p. 20, lines 22–23).

55. Nicholas of Cusa, *On Learned Ignorance,* III, 3, p. 131 (h I, p. 127, lines 1–3).

56. Giovanni Santinello, "Nicolai De Cusa: Tota pulchra es, amica mea," 58, 11. Not altogether unrelated is Kant's claim that the human being alone can furnish an ideal of beauty. Cf. Immanuel Kant, *Kritik der Urteilskraft,* A 55–56.

57. Only after having completed this essay did I discover that with this train of thought I had been unpacking something I had written in my dissertation (Harries, "In a Strange Land," 153–54) more than forty years ago: "When I see an object in its ineffable particularity, I see it in the mode of the *non aliud.* . . . Rephrasing Kierkegaard's dictum we can say: purity of heart is to see one thing: the beautiful. Whenever I look at something and see it as some object among others, I see it not as it is in itself, not in the mode of the *non aliud,* and its beauty escapes me. It follows from this definition of beauty, that anything can become beautiful if I look at it in the right way. A tree, a cloud, and old roof can appear to me as nothing other than what it is. Without the notion of another, I can no longer think of possibility. But 'where I touch on reality without its transformation into possibility, I touch on transcendence'" [Karl Jaspers, *Philosophie,* 3 vols. (Berlin: Springer, 1932), 3:9]."

Walter Andreas Euler

7. AN ITALIAN PAINTING FROM THE LATE FIFTEENTH CENTURY AND THE *Cribratio alkorani* OF NICHOLAS OF CUSA

The original working title of this paper was "The Christology of the *Cribratio alkorani.*" While working on my presentation, however, I came upon a short article among my papers about a painting in Sassoferrato, Italy, from the late fifteenth century, whose proximity to the ideas of Cusanus's *Cribratio alkorani* is fascinating. Since it is likely that only a very few Cusanus scholars know about the painting at all, and since I consider it to be—along with the *Cribratio alkorani*—one important document in the Christian examination of Islam, I could not resist the temptation to put this painting at the beginning of my article. In making the comparison between the content of the image with Cusanus's *Cribratio alkorani,* I will provide a brief sketch of the Christological considerations in Cusanus's text.

An Analysis of the Painting

In 1992 Wolfgang Speyer, the classical philologist and historian of religion at the University of Salzburg, published a short article in the journal for Christian art *Das Münster* entitled "The Three Monotheistic World Religions in Dialogue: On an Unknown Image from the Quattrocento."[1] The article includes a reproduction of the image and a two-page description of the painting from the Franciscan cloister Santa Maria della Pace in Sassoferrato. Speyer dates the image to the late fifteenth century in central Italy.

---

1. Wolfgang Speyer, "Die drei monotheistischen Weltreligionen in Gespräch: Zu einem unbekannten Bild des Quattrocento," *Das Münster. Zeitschrift für christliche Kunst und Kunstwissenschaft* 45 (1992): 215–16; reprinted in Speyer, *Religionsgeschichtliche Studien* (Hildesheim-Zürich-New York: Olms, 1995), 184–88.

Painting of the Three Haloed Figures. Franciscan Convent of Santa Maria della Pace, Sassoferrato. Photo by Il Kim.

According to Speyer's analysis (which I follow with the exception of a few details), the elements in the painting are of significance. In the painting three middle-aged men are sitting in front of a green draping curtain on a chest-like bench. Each wears a beard, which is expressive of masculine dignity and a sign for the philosophic life. The three wise men are sitting on the same level, and each is adorned with a halo symbolizing their enlightenment through the Holy Spirit. Divine inspiration in each case found its expression in a book. According to the self-understanding of each of the three religions represented, these books are Holy Scripture, testaments that reveal God. While the book of the man on the left side remains closed, the book of the man sitting on the right is open just a crack, and the book of the man in the middle is completely open. In this way it is made clear that it is the middle book that imparts divine revelation perfectly.

The respective postures of the three figures are very important. The man on the right is resting his chin on his right arm and is looking off into the distance. According to Speyer, this attitude is meant to express an air of reflection and of expectation. The wise man in the middle is the principal actor in the picture, as is made clear by his finger and hand gestures, and he is explaining something to the man on the left, who is listening to him. Of central importance is a small detail in the representation of the wise man on the left. Next to his shoulder appears the head of an animal with a small dark horn. This is a demonic, apocalyptic being that is meant to symbolize a danger associated with the person and the pronouncement of the man seated at the left.

The three men represent the founders of the three religions: Judaism, Christianity, and Islam. Moses sits on the right, Jesus Christ in the middle, and Mohammed on the left.[2] The gesture of Mohammed's right hand, extending his index finger, reveals him to be a prophet of the singularity and unity of God, a prophet who, through the Qur'an, led the Arab people away from polytheism. Jesus Christ refers Mohammed to the divine Trinity through his hand and finger positions. In addition, the distinctive posture of his naked feet symbolizes the overcoming of death through the resurrection. Moses, for his part, gazes at Jesus full of expectation and desire. In this way, the artist expresses the familiar Christian theme of the fulfilling of the Old Testament hope for salvation through the coming of the Messiah, Jesus Christ.

The theme of the painting is already very unusual in itself: it represents, if Wolfgang Speyer's interpretation is correct, the three religious founders on the same level, and, to a certain extent, the three find themselves in a spiritual dialogue. The representation of the prophet Mohammed is especially noteworthy. The traditional medieval image of Mohammed is represented in the painting by his shadow, the demonic animal, which brands Mohammed as a great seducer and misleader of humanity, as does the fact that his book is closed.[3] The Qur'an, as depicted by the artist, does not contain any divine revelation at all, and from that fact it would seem to follow that Mohammed cannot be recognized as a prophet. Against such a conclusion, however, stands the halo, which indeed unmistakably marks Mohammed as an inspired and holy person.

---

2. As Mr. Speyer told me in a letter dated August 4, 2000, his interpretation of the painting as a presentation of the three founders of religions has not been questioned so far.

3. Cf., e.g., Dante, *La divina commedia, Inferno* XXVIII, 31–35.

Note also the friendly expression on his face, which is directed to Christ in keen expectation. As Speyer rightly emphasizes, we have before us "a great advance in the understanding" of Islam. He goes on to say: "To that extent this Christian humanist painting corrects, to a certain degree, a conception of Islam that is widespread even today; indeed, it was not until the Enlightenment of the eighteenth century that a more fitting assessment of the prophet was arrived at in the West."[4]

Nicholas of Cusa's Evaluation of the Qur'an

The question arises very naturally, "What or who prompted the unknown artist to paint such an image?" "One could," writes Speyer, "think of a humanist like Nicholas of Cusa as the commissioner of the work, a humanist who attempts, in his text *De pace fidei,* to bring the representatives of the religions of the peoples of the world closer to a belief in the simultaneous unity and trinity of God."[5] Nicholas is clearly a candidate as the source of inspiration for the artist. Indeed, the motifs that are used in the painting are also to be found—as will be shown in what follows—in Cusanus's writing, to a certain extent in *De pace fidei* and even more so in his *Cribratio alkorani.*[6]

4. W. Speyer, "Die drei monotheistischen Weltreligionen im Gespräch," 216.

5. Ibid., 215.

6. On *Cribratio alkorani,* see Nicholas of Cusa, *Cribratio alkorani,* h VIII, *Praefatio editoris,* ed. L. Hagemann (Hamburg: Felix Meiner, 1986), vii–xxi; P. Naumann, Foreword to *Sichtung des Alkorans. Cribratio Alkoran,* by Nicholas of Cusa, vol. 1 (Leipzig: Felix Meiner, 1943), 5–76; G. Hölscher, "Nikolaus von Cues und der Islam," *Zeitschrift für philosophische Forschung* 2 (1947): 259–74; F. H. Burgevin, *Cribratio Alchorani: Nicholas Cusanus's Criticism of the Koran in the Light of His Philosophy of Religion* (New York: Vantage Press, 1969); G. C. Anawati, "Nicolas de Cues et le problème de l'Islam," in *Nicolò Cusano agli inizi del mondo moderno. Atti del Congreso internazionale in occasione del V centenario della morte di Nicolò Cusano,* ed. Giovanni Santinello (Florence: G. C. Sansoni Editore, 1970), 141–73; S. Raeder, "Der Christus des Korans in der Sicht des Nikolaus von Kues," in *Christentum und Islam,* ed. Willi Höpfner, 14 vols. (Wiesbaden: Verlag der Evang, Mission in Wiesbaden, 1971–82), 6:71–93; J. E. Biechler, "Christian Humanism Confronts Islam: Sifting the Qur'an with Nicholas of Cusa," *Journal of Ecumenical Studies* 13 (1976): 1–14; L. Hagemann, *Der Kur'an in Verständnis und Kritik bei Nikolaus von Kues* (Frankfurt am Main: Knecht, 1976); L. Hagemann, *Nikolaus von Kues im Gespräch mit dem Islam* (Altenberge: Oros Verlag, 1983); J. Hopkins, "The Role of *pia interpretatio* in Nicholas of Cusa's Hermeneutical Approach to the Koran," in *Concordia discors. Studi su Niccolò Cusano e l'umanesimo europeo offerti a Giovanni Santinello,* ed. G. Piaia (Padova: Antenore, 1993), 251–73.

Nicholas composed the *Cribratio alkorani* in Rome in 1460–61.[7] It is dedicated to Pope Pius II and was meant to serve him as a collection of material for his letter to Sultan Mehmet II, the conqueror.[8] Nevertheless, one would completely misunderstand Cusanus's text if one were to view the text exclusively as a repetition of anti-Islamic apologetics or simply as a polemic of the Middle Ages.[9]

It is true that one can find many of the commonplaces of the older apologetics in Cusanus's text, and he cites them readily and in detail.[10] The periodically polemical tone of the *Cribratio* and Cusanus's palpable tendency in numerous passages to defame and mock both the Qur'an and the person of Mohammed remain at a first glance in clear contrast to the famous Cusan irenic of *De pace fidei*. For this reason many scholars of Cusanus chose to keep silent about the *Cribratio* or simply to ignore it, rather than to confront the text and wrestle with its contents.

Nevertheless, Rudolf Haubst is right to count the *Cribratio alkorani* among the Cardinal's great later works.[11] Indeed, from the perspective of religious studies, the *Cribratio alkorani* represents an important methodological advance over his earlier work on peace in belief. While Cusanus does indeed refer back to the ideas of *De pace fidei* (especially in the second book of his investigation of the Qur'an), at the same time he characterizes them as providing a *pia interpretatio,* a pious, that is to say, a Christian, interpretation of the Qur'an.[12] In other passages, however, he

7. Cf. Nicholas of Cusa, *Cribratio alkorani,* h VIII, p. xiv. All subsequent references to this text are taken from this edition.

8. Ibid., p. 3, N. 1, lines 4–5; 9–10: "Sume, sanctissime papa, libellum hunc per humilem servulum tuum fidei zelo collectum, ut . . . cito quaedam rudimenta scitu necessaria ad manum habeas."

9. This misunderstanding can be found in N. Daniel's standard work, *Islam and the West: The Making of an Image* (Edinburgh: University Press, 1960), 277–78: "Cusa's *Cribratio* is rambling and repetitive, like Ricoldo's *Disputatio*. Here was a fresh mind working over old themes with varying success." J. Hopkins objects: "For *Cribratio alkorani* is neither rambling nor strikingly repetitive; and it accomplishes significantly more than working over old themes." J. Hopkins, *Nicholas of Cusa's* De Pace Fidei *and* Cribratio alkorani: *Translation and Analysis,* 2nd ed. (Minneapolis, Minn.: Banning Press, 1994), 14.

10. Nicholas names his applied sources in Prol. I of *Cribratio alkorani* (pp. 5–7, nos. 2–4). Cf. in detail L. Hagemann, *Der Kur'an,* 15–68.

11. L. Hagemann, *Der Kur'an,* vii.

12. The term *pia interpretatio* appears altogether four times in *Cribratio alkorani*. All four passages can be found in the second book: c. 1, p. 72, N. 86, line 4; c. 12, p. 95, N. 119, line 1; c. 13, p. 99, N. 124, lines 3–4; and c. 19, p. 125, N. 154, line 8.

remarks that the real intention of the Qur'an itself stands opposed to this Christian way of reading it.[13] Again, from the perspective of religious studies, Nicholas's summary of the contents of the Qur'an in the second chapter of the first book is truly remarkable.[14] This section, together with scattered references in other passages, documents the fact that Nicholas has an accurate grasp of Islamic self-understanding. At the same time, Cusanus intends his consciously Christian "inspection" or "sifting" of the Qur'an to break through to what he takes to be the true core of the holy book of the Muslims. The essence of this book remains hidden to them because, unlike the Cardinal, they do not take the Gospel, that is, the person of Jesus Christ who is the divine-human mediator, as the hermeneutical measure of their reading of the Qur'an.[15] Cusanus felt he was justified in this Christian sifting of the Qur'an since, following numerous medieval Christian apologists, he held or was happy to adopt the useful fiction that Mohammed was raised by a Nestorian Christian, that he himself was a Nestorian, and that it was only after his death that some Jewish anti-Christian changes were made in his original text of the Qur'an.[16]

As already mentioned, Nicholas was perfectly well aware, however, that this Christian interpretation did violence to the holy book of the Muslims in many passages and that it largely ignored Islam's own self-understanding. In his letter to John of Segovia of December 29, 1454, Cusanus explicitly admits, as a hermeneutical principle, a selective reading of the Qur'an. He writes there that Christians in debate with Muslims should try to interpret the Qur'an in view of their faith. "For," Cusanus goes on to say, "we find passages in the Qur'an which are useful for us. And the passages which are antithetical [to these], we will interpret according to the ones [which are useful to us]."[17]

13. Cf., e.g., ibid., I, c. 1, p. 24, N. 23, lines 14–18; I, c. 14, p. 56, N. 64, lines 10–12.

14. Ibid., I, c. 2 (pp. 24–28, nos. 24–27): "Quid continet Alkoranus secundum eius laudatores."

15. Ibid., Prol. I, pp. 11–12, N. 10, lines 1–5: "Intentio autem nostra est praesupposito evangelio Christi librum Mahumeti cribrare et ostendere illa in ipso etiam libro haberi, per quae evangelium, si attestatione indigeret, valde confirmaretur, et quod, ubi dissentit, hoc ex ignorantia et consequenter ex perversitate intenti Mahumeti evenisse."

16. Ibid., Prol. II, p. 13, N. 11.

17. *Epistula ad Ioannem de Segobia* ("Letter to John of Segovia"), h VII, p. 99, lines 22–25: "videtur quod semper ad hoc conandum sit quod liber iste [i.e. the Qur'an], qui apud eos est in auctoritate, pro nobis allegetur. Nam reperimus in eo talia quae serviunt nobis; et alia quae contrariantur, glosabimus per illa."

Again and again we perceive the ambivalence of Cusanus's verdict concerning both the Qur'an and the Prophet Mohammed. No doubt this results, in the final analysis, from the fact that the holy book of the Muslims lies very close to, but at the same time very far away from, Christian thought. On the one hand, the Qur'an refers extensively back to biblical tradition: the Qur'an regards Jesus as a great prophet and names him the "Word or Spirit of God."[18] It professes his birth from the Virgin Mary and attests to his miracles. On the other hand, the same book denies the crucifixion of Jesus,[19] polemicizes vehemently against the belief that Christ is the Son of God, and takes the Christian doctrine of the Trinity to be a polytheistic teaching. Moreover, the Qur'an views Jesus as the last precursor of Mohammed, whom the Qur'an calls the "seal of the prophets,"[20] that is to say, the last and greatest of the prophets.[21]

Considered from a Christian perspective, Islam could appear either as a primitive stage on the way to true Christianity or as a subtle but diabolical attempt to deny Christianity's core ideas. Both views are to be found in the writings of Nicholas of Cusa.[22] The ambivalence of the Qur'an as seen from a Christian viewpoint suggests a strategy of "sifting" through the holy book of the Muslims, as James Biechler put it, like a prospector hunting for valuable gold "nuggets" and criticizing the remainder.[23]

The unevenness of Cusanus's verdict on the Qur'an and the prophet Mohammed makes reading his *Cribratio* tiresome. Nevertheless, the *Cribratio* documents a fundamental advance over older Christian interpretations of Islam, which regard Islam only negatively and Mohammed as a hateful figure of the first order. For Cusanus both the Qur'an and Mohammed possess two faces, just as in our Italian painting the demonic tempter is juxtaposed with the halo's saintly light. But in contrast to the painting's depiction, Cusanus certainly does not view the Qur'an as com-

18. See, for example, Sure 4:171; 3:45.   19. Sure 4:157.

20. Sure 33:40.

21. Cf., e.g., H. Räisänen, *Das koranische Jesusbild. Ein Beitrag zur Theologie des Korans* (Helsinki: Missiologian ja Ekumeniikan, 1971).

22. Cf. note 16 above and note 31 below.

23. J. E. Biechler, "A New Face toward Islam," in *Nicholas of Cusa in Search of God and Wisdom: Essays in Honor of Morimichi Watanabe by the American Cusanus Society,* ed. G. Christianson and Th. M. Izbicki (Leiden: Brill, 1991), 199: "Nicholas 'sifts' (*cribrare*) the Qur'an to find those nuggets which reflect divine truth."

pletely closed to the truth of Jesus Christ. This can be made clear with a quick look at the statements Cusanus makes concerning both Mohammed and the Qur'an.

First of all, if considered in purely quantitative terms, Cusanus's polemical statements, which aim at defending Christianity against the claims of Islam, clearly stand in the foreground.[24] According to Cusanus, there are many reasons to doubt the legitimacy of the claim that Mohammed is a prophet. His coming was not foreseen in Scripture by the prophets and saints of the Old and New Testaments,[25] and neither did he have the power to perform miracles, a characteristic of prophets.[26] Indeed, Mohammed's status as a prophet is even more clearly brought into question, according to Cusanus, by Mohammed's own biography: his failure to achieve human greatness, his lack of moral integrity, and finally the manifest deficiencies of the Qur'an itself. Nicholas portrays Mohammed—very much in line with the prior Western tradition—as a man given over to sensual desires[27] and as a man who, in order to satisfy lust, even allowed divorce.[28] These essential characteristics of Mohammed have their counterpart, according to this reading, in the glorification of fleshly pleasures in the Qur'an's representation of paradise. By claiming the status of prophet, so the reading goes, Mohammed was seeking to serve not God, but rather his own personal glory,[29] for the sake of which he was even willing to resort to the use of force. Indeed his supposed reign as a prophet is understood, here, as grounded in acts of violence.[30] In all these ways Mo-

---

24. Cf. L. Hagemann, *Der Kur'an,* 85–115, 175–78; F. H. Burgevin, *Cribratio Alchorani,* 28–31.

25. Cf., e.g., Nicholas of Cusa, *Cribratio alkorani,* III, c. 3, p. 136, N. 168, lines 6–7: "nec in ambobus nec in altero librorum allegatorum [i.e., in the Old and New Testament] mentio fiat aut nominetur Mahometus."

26. Ibid., I, c. 2, p. 25, N. 24, lines 9–10, and I, c. 7, p. 40, N. 44, line 13. See also L. Hagemann, *Der Kur'an,* 89–95.

27. Cf., e.g., Nicholas of Cusa, *Cribratio alkorani,* I, c. 7, p. 40, N. 44, lines 11–12: "Mahometus vir muliebris, lubricus, totus huius mundi et sensibilium amator."

28. Ibid., II, c. 19, pp. 126–127, N. 156. On the Islamic background, see L. Hagemann, *Der Kur'an,* 96.

29. Cusanus speaks about Mohammed's *perversitas intentionis* (*Cribratio alkorani,* Prol. I, p. 12, N. 10, lines 4–5) since "Mahumeto vero non dei gloriam et hominum salutem sed gloriam propriam quaerente" (ibid., lines 6–7).

30. Ibid., III, c. 3, p. 137, N. 170, lines 1–2: "Est igitur ultima resolutio probationis omnium, quae in Alkorano leguntur, gladius." Cf., in addition, ibid., III, c. 3, p. 136, N. 168.

hammed is portrayed as the perfect antithesis of Christ. Cusanus's view of Mohammed would seem to lead to the conclusion that Mohammed was a tool of the devil. He is the *princeps huius mundi* ("a prince of this world"), who must also be regarded as the author of the Qur'an.[31]

Nicholas of Cusa evaluates the Qur'an in a similar manner. Cusanus rejects the idea of a divine origin for the holy book of the Muslims because of the ways in which it contradicts the previous revelation of the Old and New Testaments[32] and because of the complicated genesis of the Qur'an itself.[33] The stylistic perfection of the Qur'an's form, its *elegantia dictaminis,* which Muslims regard as an argument for the inimitability of the Qur'an, is, according to Cusanus, inconsequential in the face of the contradictory, uncertain, and the outright repulsive content of some parts of the text.[34] Nicholas sees the true character of Islam—in connection with the depiction of Mohammed's personal character—as revealed in the Qur'an's ethical and eschatological representations. Here, he holds, Islam reveals itself as the religion of the flesh, of lower sensibility, and of enmity with the spirit. According to Cusanus, it conceives of the blessedness of heavenly paradise as an eternal land of milk and honey or a garden of earthly delights and provides theological legitimization for polygamy, for the use of violence, and for war. In doing so, Cusanus concludes, it seduces and misleads its followers.[35]

31. Ibid., I, c. 1, pp. 23–24, N. 23. In a sermon Nicholas interprets Mohammed as the Antichrist's forerunner (*Sermo* CCX, h XIX/1, pp. 38–39, N. 20, lines 1–12): "Primam bestiam de aqua seu mari ascendentem posse Mahimmet intelligi, cuius nomen ex maiim, hoc est aqua, ortum est, et secundam bestiam esse antichristum, qui in specie agni et in verbo draconis veniet cum signis, ut ibidem. Dicit autem Iohannes in fine capituli 13 numerum nominis eius esse 666. Loquitur forte de prima bestia principali, scilicet Mahimmet, cuius imaginem facit secunda bestia adorare, qui in tot annis Arabum post Christum populum seduxit." The apocalyptic view of Mohammed was very widespread in the Middle Ages. Cf. E. Benz, *Ideen zu einer Theologie der Religionsgeschichte* (Wiesbaden: Verlag der Akademie der Wissenschaften und der Literatur in Mainz, in Kommission bei F. Steiner Verlag, 1961), 20–21, and G. Rizzardi, "Maometto—anticristo nei commentari all'Apocalisse," *Renovatio. Rivista di teologia e cultura* 22 (1987): 59–87.

32. Cf. Nicholas of Cusa, *Cribratio alkorani,* I, c. 4, pp. 29–33, nos. 29–34: "Quod Alkoranus fide careat, ubi sacris scripturis contradicit."

33. Cf. ibid., I, c. 1, pp. 21–24, nos. 20–23: "De Alkorano et quod deus verus non sit auctor eius."

34. Ibid., I, c. 7, pp. 38–40, nos. 43–44.

35. Ibid., II, c. 18: "De paradiso," pp. 121–24, nos. 149–53, and II, c. 19, pp. 124–25, N.

Nicholas presents this picture of Islam in stark contrast to Christianity, which he depicts as a religion of the spirit that professes Christ to be the exemplar for all believers and teaches that the beatific vision of God is the most genuine expression of heavenly blessedness. Cusanus seeks to ground this interpretation of Christianity with the claim that Christianity is the legitimate heir of Abraham, the father of faith. It is the Christians who are the legitimate descendants of Abraham, Nicholas explains, for they stem from Isaac, the son of Sara, a free woman, and from Jesus Christ. And it is they who preserve Abraham's faith and, in Christ, have fulfilled the promise given to Abraham. On the other hand, Cusanus holds that the Muslims stem from Ishmael, the son of the slave woman Hagar, and so are bound to Abraham only according to the flesh.[36]

It seemed clear to Cusanus that the more knowledgeable and sensible Muslims were also aware of the obvious deficiencies both of Mohammed's character and of the Qur'an, and therefore merely pretended to believe in the teachings of Islam out of fear of persecution and death.[37] The *Cribratio* is thus directed first of all to these "wise men among the Arabs"[38] and the "teachers of the Qur'an"[39] who have the capacity for discernment. It is to these readers that the *Cribratio* hopes to reveal the difference between the Qur'an and the Gospel, whose truth, Cusanus believes, they themselves are seeking.

In accordance with Nicholas of Cusa's dual way of looking at Islam, a second aspect of his reading pushes the polemic to the side and constitutes the beginnings of a positive assessment of the Muslim religion. Here we encounter precisely the consideration alluded to earlier, namely, his conviction that, despite all the deficiencies and inadequacies of the Qur'an, the truth of the Gospel as well as the teachings of Christian faith can nevertheless be disclosed from it. Indeed, the Qur'an in this view presents a sort of "hidden Gospel."[40]

---

154. On Cusanus's image of the Islamic paradise, see in addition: *Sermo* X, h XVI, p. 219, N. 32, lines 27–28; *Sermo* CCL, h XIX/3, pp. 228–29, N. 2, lines 12–18; and *Sermo* CCLXXIV (271) in *Vier Predigten im Geiste Eckharts*, ed. and trans. J. Koch (Heidelberg: C. Winter, 1937), 136, lines 5–8.

36. Cf. Nicholas of Cusa, *Cribratio alkorani*, III, c. 11–16, pp. 155–74, nos. 195–219.

37. Ibid., I, c. 3, p. 29, N. 28, lines 15–18.

38. Ibid., II, c. 19, p. 128, N. 158, line 5.

39. Ibid., II, c. 15, p. 105, N. 131, line 1: "magistri legis Arabum."

40. Ibid., II, c. 19, p. 128, N. 158, lines 4–8: "Tamen omnipotens deus inter omnia illa

Hence Cusanus attempts—*pia interpretatione* ("through a pious interpretation")—to derive the Trinitarian conception of God and the hypostatic union of the person of Christ from the Qur'an itself. These were
truths, Cusanus holds, that Mohammed for pedagogical and pastoral reasons was not able to reveal perfectly to his idolatrous, uneducated, and ignorant compatriots.[41] Cusanus also attempts to demonstrate the positive,
spiritual meaning of sensualistic statements in the Qur'an, for example,
the statements about paradise, by giving them a metaphorical interpretation.[42] Nicholas even emphasized the historically correct fact that Mohammed was able to convert the Arabs to monotheism, a feat which the
Christians, who were active in Arabia before him, were themselves unable
to accomplish. This is yet another respect in which Cusanus's ideas are
also reflected in our Italian painting, which clearly refers to the belief in
one God taught by the Qur'an.[43]

Clearly the two groups of assertions about Islam, both the polemical
and the conditionally positive, stand in tension to one another, and this
tension has repeatedly proven embarrassing for readers of the *Cribratio
alkorani*. In my view, they are to be explained on the one hand by the Cardinal's connection to the medieval anti-Islamic tradition and on the other
hand by the actual guiding intention of his reading of the Qur'an. This intention is summed up in the concept of the *pia interpretatio* and takes
shape in and through his philosophy and his understanding of the Trinity
and Christ. It is here that he steps out of the shadows of the tradition to
gain a new perspective. How this is realized will be shown in what follows, using the example of the Cardinal's Christological theology of religion.

---

spurca et vana et sapientibus etiam Arabum abominabilia talia etiam inseri voluit, in quibus
evangelicus splendor sic lateret occultatus, quod sapientibus diligenti studio quaesitus se ipsum manifestaret." See S. Raeder, *Der Christus des Korans*, 85.

41. Cf., e.g., Nicholas of Cusa, *Cribratio alkorani*, I, c. 17, p. 63, N. 74; II, c. 12, pp. 95–96,
N. 119.

42. Cf., e.g., ibid., II, c. 18, pp. 123–124, nos. 152–153. Nicholas makes a similar argument in *De pace fidei*, c. 15, h VII, p. 48, line 6–p. 50, line 2, and in *Epistula ad Ioannem de
Segobia*, h VII, p. 99, lines 16–22.

43. Cf. Nicholas of Cusa, *Cribratio alkorani*, II, c. 12, p. 96, N. 120.

The *Cribratio Alkorani*'s Theology of Religion and Revelation

In the end, Cusanus's appraisal of the Gospel and of the Qur'an, of Jesus Christ and of Mohammed, is not made by superficial and aggressive polemics, but rather by his understanding of religion and of revelation. This is already made clear at the beginning of the *Cribratio*. In Prologue I, Nicholas describes in detail his many efforts since the time of the Council of Basel to collect authentic information about Islam and about the Qur'an.[44] He then immediately turns to a religious and philosophical consideration of the Good and humanity's way or path to that Good.[45] This short text contains, in an impressively concise manner, the essential elements of Nicholas's religious speculation as it developed from his early sermons.[46]

"We experience," Cusanus writes, "a certain striving present in us, which is named spirit because of its indwelling movement, and because the ground of this movement is the Good."[47] Where does this perceivable striving for the Good come from? It comes, according to Nicholas, from the Good itself, which is both the origin and the goal of the movement of spirit, and it is that alone in which this movement finds rest. This Good, argues Cusanus, cannot be a worldly good, since the spirit is never able to come to rest in this world.[48] In short, the Good that spirit seeks must be God.[49]

But how, then, does a human being attain God, the transcendent Good,

44. Ibid., pp. 5–7, nos. 2–4.

45. Ibid., pp. 7–12, nos. 5–9.

46. Cf. in detail W. A. Euler, *Unitas et Pax. Religionsvergleich bei Raimundus Lullus und Nikolaus von Kues,* 2nd ed. (Würzburg-Altenberge: Echter/Telos, 1995), 224–46, and Euler, "Proclamation of Christ in Selected Sermons from Cusanus's Brixen Period," in *Nicholas of Cusa and His Age: Essays Dedicated to the Memory of F. Edward Cranz, Thomas P. McTighe and Charles Trinkaus,* ed. C. Bellitto and Th. Izbicki (Leiden: Brill, 2002), 89–103.

47. Nicholas of Cusa, *Cribratio alkorani,* Prol. I, p. 7, N. 5, lines 1–2: "Experimur in nobis appetitum quendam esse, qui ob motum, qui in eo est, spiritus dicitur, quodque ratio motus ipsius est bonum."

48. Ibid., Prol. I, pp. 8–9, N. 6, lines 6–8: "scimus bonum illud non esse de regione huius sensibilis mundi quodque spiritus noster in hoc mundo ad quietem non perveniet."

49. Ibid., Prol. I, p. 9, N. 7, lines 8–10: "quod quidem bonum nominamus deum, ut, dum de ipso conferimus, nos mutuo intelligamus."

which his spirit seeks without ceasing? He needs a way, a path. He needs guidance, and this guidance or path would have to be just as good, in turn, as the sought-after Good itself.[50] But there are many ways to God. By this Nicholas means the many religions of humanity. So a legitimate doubt arises as to which of them in fact leads truly and perfectly to the goal.[51]

At this point in the text, Cusanus turns to the most famous descriptions of the path leading to community with God. He names the three great founders of religion, which our Italian artist also attempted to represent in his painting about the same time: Moses, Jesus, and Mohammed. Eusebio Colomer sees in this comparison of the three great founders a "silent play on the parable of the three rings, which was commonly known at the time."[52] Cusanus writes:

Moses had described a path (to God), but this path was neither taken up by everyone nor was it understood by everyone. Jesus illuminated and perfected this path; nevertheless, many even now remain unbelievers. Mohammed tried to make the same path easier, so that it might be accepted by all, even by idolaters. These are the most famous descriptions of the said path (to God), although many others were presented by the wise and the prophets.[53]

Considered in a purely descriptive sense (One could also say, "considered from the point of view of religious studies"), the three founders of religion are situated at the same level—just as they are in our painting. They all claim, each in his own manner, to know the way to the absolute and to be able to communicate it to others.

---

50. Ibid., Prol. I, p. 9, N. 7, lines 3–5: "Via autem, per quam in hoc mundo transire debemus, ut habilitemur ad apprehensionem desiderati boni, non debet esse nisi bona, et quae seducit mala erit."

51. Ibid., Prol. I, p. 9, N. 7, lines 6–8: "Sed cum multae possint viae esse, quae bonae videantur, manet haesitatio, quae sit illa via vera et perfecta, quae certitudinaliter nos ducit ad cognitionem boni."

52. Eusebio Colomer, S.J., *Nikolaus von Kues (+1464) und Ramon Llull (+1316). Ihre Begegnung mit den nichtchristlichen Religionen* (Trier: Paulinus Verlag, 1995), 18. Cf. W. Speyer, "Die drei monotheistischen Weltreligionen im Gespräch," 216.

53. Nicholas of Cusa, *Cribratio alkorani*, Prol. I, pp. 9–10, N. 7, lines 10–15: "Moyses quidem descripsit unam, sed non est ab omnibus recepta nec intellecta. Christus illam illuminavit et perficit multis tamen adhuc incredulis remanentibus. Mahumetus eandem viam, ut ab omnibus etiam idolatris reciperetur, faciliorem describere nisus est. Et haec sunt magis famosae descriptiones dictae viae, licet aliae multae sapientium et prophetarum factae sint."

Cusanus does not remain at this level but rather dares to choose among the three founders of religion. Neither Moses nor Mohammed regarded by himself, he argues, was able adequately to describe the way to God. As mere human beings—mere prophets (!)—they could never have seen this path alone. This was only possible, he holds, for the Son of God become man, Jesus Christ, who accordingly leads all who follow his way to salvation.[54] In summarizing his considerations, Cusanus writes:

> But Jesus, the son of the virgin Mary, the Christ whose coming was foretold by Moses and the prophets, has come and because he is ignorant of nothing has most perfectly revealed the often named way (to God), as even Mohammed attested. It is thus certain that whoever follows Christ and his way will succeed in seizing hold of the sought after Good.[55]

Christ, according to Cusanus, is more than a sign of divine truth; he is the coincidence of sign and that which is signified by the sign and is therefore the embodiment of true religion. His book, the Gospel—as we can ascertain in our painting—is perfectly open, that is to say, it contains pure divine revelation. This grounding of Christology in revelatory theology possesses structural significance for the argumentation of the *Cribratio alkorani*. Cusanus repeatedly emphasizes that only that divine messenger, or rather divine intermediary, can be believed who is himself more than a mere man.[56]

True religion, that is, the actual path to God, has at its center the Christological dogma of the hypostatic union of God and man in one person, which in turn presupposes a Trinitarian conception of God. In this dogma, religion fulfills itself. It is thus to be found in every concrete

---

54. Cf. ibid., Prol. I, p. 10, N. 8.

55. Ibid., Prol. I, p. 11, N. 9, lines 1–5: "Iesus autem virginis Mariae filius Christus ille per Moysem et prophetas praenuntiatus venturus venit et viam saepe dictam, cum nihil ignoraret, perfectissime propalavit attestante etiam Mahumeto. Certum est igitur, quod, qui Christum et viam eius sequitur, ad comprehensionem desiderati boni perveniet."

56. Cf., e.g., ibid., I, c. 16, p. 60, N. 69, lines 5–9: "Nam cum nullus nuntius, qui est purus homo, sit talis, quod necesse sit sibi credi, cum omni rationali creaturae quantumcumque veraci deus veraciorem creare possit, manet haesitatio, an illis quis talem fidem dare, quod ipsos sequi debeat"; II, c. 16, pp. 109–110, N. 136; and III, c. 11, p. 157, N. 196, lines 4–7: "Sola una est perfectissima via seu lex ad unicum perfectissimum finem perducens, quae alia esse non potest quam illa, per quam Christus, qui omnium perfectissimus, ivit et docuit eundum."

religion, though in very different degrees of clarity; and so it is also to be found in Islam. For this reason, Nicholas of Cusa searches tirelessly throughout the Qur'an for links with his understanding of religion. He believes that he has found these in the supposed maximal statements that the Qur'an makes concerning the person of Christ: that he is the "Word and the Spirit of God," the "highest ambassador of God,"[57] and the "face of all people."[58] The description of Jesus as the Word and Spirit of God is in fact to be found in the Qur'an,[59] but there it is not interpreted as an acknowledgment that Christ is the Son of God, as is the case in the Christian tradition. The two other predicates stem from errors in the Latin translation of the Qur'an that Cusanus used.

On the other hand, Nicholas knew perfectly well that the Christian and Islamic understandings of religion are not compatible with one another in the end. Islamic religion emphasizes the infinite distance between creator and creation, between God and humanity, and therefore clearly rules out the possibility of a divine-human mediation.[60] The Christian conception of religion is therefore rigorously personalistic and is fundamentally based on the idea that man was made in the image of God and that this image character is perfected in the person of Jesus Christ, since in Christ image and exemplar meet, as Nicholas of Cusa explains, for example, in the last chapter of *De visione Dei*.[61]

57. Cf. ibid., I, c. 16, pp. 59–61, nos. 68–71: "Quod Christus quia verbum et legatus summus dei est dei filius" and I, c. 18, pp. 64–65, nos. 75–76: "Quomodo Alkoranus intelligi debet Christum esse spiritum et animam dei." On Jesus as *verbum Dei,* cf. in addition Prol. II, p. 16, N. 15, lines 7–8 and I, c. 12, p. 50, N. 58, line 5. On *omnium prophetarum maximus,* cf. I, c. 8, p. 41, N. 45. On *summus nuntius,* cf. I, c. 15, pp. 58–59, N. 67.

58. Cf. ibid., I, c. 19, pp. 65–68, nos. 77–80: "Quomodo Alkoranus intelligi debet Christum esse virum bonum et optimum et 'faciem omnium gentium.'"

59. Cf., e.g., Sure 4:171; 3:45: "Word of God."

60. Cf., e.g., Nicholas of Cusa, *De docta ignorantia* III, c. 8, h I, p. 143, line 30–p. 144, line 5: "Vides, ni fallor, nullam perfectam religionem homines ad ultimum desideratissimum pacis finem ducentem esse, quae Christum non amplectitur mediatorem et salvatorem, Deum et hominem, viam, vitam et veritatem. Age quam absona est Sarracenorum credulitas, qui Christum maximum atque perfectissimum hominem de virgine natum et ad caelos vivum translatum affirmant, Deum negant. Obcaecati sunt profecto, quia asserunt impossibile."

61. Cf. Nicholas of Cusa, *De visione Dei,* c. 25, h VI, pp. 87–88, N. 116.

Conclusion

In conclusion, we have seen that Cusanus in his *Cribratio alkorani* undertakes a project that is just as daring as it is problematic: the attempt at an intensive theological dialogue with Islam. The bare fact that he studied the Qur'an at all—indeed several times over the course of his life[62]—and seriously attempted to understand it sets him apart from most other medieval Christian theologians and distinguishes him from his own contemporaries. Indeed, there have been very few important Christian authors even up to the present day who have seriously studied the religion of the Arabic prophet, a religion that is just as close to Christianity as it is far from it. And there are probably even fewer Christian artists who have ventured to depict the relationship between the three religious founders: Moses, Jesus Christ, and Mohammed. Perhaps it was the daring of Nicholas of Cusa that inspired our unknown painter and so contributed to the genesis of a very unusual work of art. In any event, both the painting by the unknown master and the work of Cusanus bear witness to the fact that here at the beginning of the third millennium, contemporary efforts at interreligious and intercultural understanding can fruitfully look back to and remember older models.

62. Cf. J. E. Biechler, "Three Manuscripts on Islam from the Library of Nicholas of Cusa," *Manuscripta* 27 (1983): 91–100.

Il Kim

8. A BRIEF REPORT ON THE PAINTING
OF THREE HALOED FIGURES

Preaching in his episcopal see of Brixen on the feast of All Saints in 1456, Cardinal Nicholas of Cusa confirmed the pivotal importance of painting to his understanding of reality:

Consider then a painter who, when he wants to depict something, e.g., a narrative of some sort, intuits the very concept of painting the thing and fashions a picture in the likeness of the idea that he intuits within himself. But until the intellect undertakes to depict the art of painting, it could depict nothing that can be painted according to any particular fashion, not the heavens, the earth, an animal, nor any other visible thing. Rather, [the intellect "paints"] an intellectual nature that is merely capable of art and can impress the principles of the pictorial art in itself so that there arises an image of the form of the pictorial art *(forma artis pictoriae)* as well as the form of the form of all things *(species specierum omnium)* that can be sensibly depicted.[1]

The act of painting provides a concrete image of a highly creative intellectual process that cannot, however, be depicted in images. Painting an image is a concrete expression of the foundational creativity within the pictorially barren but still fruitful chamber of the intellect. This sheer wonder in the face all creativity penetrates the core of Cusan thinking and, above all, thinking of the absolute. The analogy of the painter even

---

1. *Sermo* CCLI, Codex Vaticanus latinus 1245, fol. 188va–188vb: "Et considera consequenter quod pictor dum vult aliquid depingere puta historia aliquam, intuetur in conceptum rei pingendae et facit picturam ad similtudinem ideae, quam in se intuetur. Sed dum intellectus artem pingendi depingere institueret, tunc nihil quod pingi potest particulariter depingeret, quia non caelum, non terram, non animal, nec alliud visibile, sed intellectualem naturam, quae solum artis est capax, et artis pictoriae principia in ipsa imprimeret, ut fieret imago formae artis pictoriae et species specierum omnium quae sensibiliter possent depingi," as cited in M.-A. Aris, "'Praegnans affirmatio' Gotteserkenntnis als Ästhetik des Nichtsichtbaren bei Nikolaus von Kues," *Theologische Quartalschrift* 181 (2002): 107, n. 43.

leads to a Cusan notion of reality that M.-A. Aris calls "the knowledge of God as an aesthetics of the invisible."[2]

No philosopher who took so seriously the intellectual content of images and of painting deserves to be studied from within the history of art except also in terms of the rigor of art criticism. In other words, it would not do justice to the intellectual caste of Nicholas's own theory of painting to conclude precipitously and without further comment the discussion of his place in the history of art. The point of this essay is far more modest than the elaboration of a Cusan basis for a principle of art criticism. Rather, we turn to a critical examination of the painting mentioned in the previous essay that has in recent scholarship been closely associated with the figure of Nicholas of Cusa.

The painting of three haloed figures [Fig. 1] had been unknown to most art historians until the German philologist Wolfgang Speyer published an article entitled "Die drei monotheistischen Weltreligionen in Gespräch: Zu einem unbekannten Bild des Quattrocento" in 1992, asserting that the painting was created in the fifteenth century and that it exemplified Cusanus's sympathetic attitude toward the Qur'an.[3] As far as I know, no other article on the painting has been published. This article is a report based on my observation of the original painting that I conducted in January 2003 in Sassoferrato.

The painting measures 131cm by 85cm. Drawn on canvas in oil by an unknown artist in middle Italy, it is today kept in the Franciscan convent of Santa Maria della Pace, a religious house founded in 1502 on the outskirts of Sassoferrato near Urbino. According to Father P. Stefano Trojani of the convent, no one living can clearly understand the meaning of the painting, and there is nothing about the painting's provenance on record. It is not known, therefore, for what purpose the painting was created and how long it has hung on these walls.

---

2. M.-A. Aris, "'Praegnans affirmatio' Gotteserkentnis als Ästhetik des Nichtsichtbaren bei Nikolaus von Kues," *Theologische Quartalschrift* 181 (2002): 97–111. On the general topic of Cusanus's aesthetics, see the Introduction (and especially the sources cited in notes 7 and 32), as well as the contributions of K. Harries and W. Dupré, to this volume.

3. Wolfgang Speyer, "Die drei monotheistischen Weltreligionen in Gespräch: Zu einem unbekannten Bild des Quattrocento," *Das Münster. Zeitschrift für christliche Kunst und Kunstwissenschaft* 45 (1992): 215–16; reprinted in Speyer, *Religionsgeschichtliche Studien* (Hildesheim-Zürich-New York: Olms, 1995), 184–88.

The painting is in poor shape, particularly on the right-hand side, and the bottom of the painting has lost significant amounts of pigment, revealing the base foundation. The sides of the painting are bordered by a perimeter roughly two inches wide, with little pigmentation. The top and the bottom perimeters show an off-white foundation, but the left and right perimeters have a gradation of color, starting from pale yellow-green at the bottom to off-white in the middle and to a light blue on the top. On the yellow-green part of the left perimeter, there is a drawing of wolf-like animal in gray. In the middle of the right perimeter, there is a rough sketch of a tall tree, again in gray. It is possible that the canvas had some kind of preliminary drawing of a landscape and that it was cut and reused for the painting. The painting is loosely attached on the perimeters by nails to a wooden rectangular support.

Even a casual inspection of the back of the canvas reveals that the areas surrounding the three figures were repainted at a later date. These areas include the deep green drapery behind the figures, the horizontal plane on which a bench is situated, the deep green drape that covers the right thigh of the right figure, and the proportionally too small feet of the left and right figures. On the back, these areas contain a completely different type of paint, which is more absorbed within the thread of the canvas. The three haloes are also later additions. Again, from the back of the canvas, one can tell that originally there was one more figure partially depicted on the right of the right figure; indeed, even from the front, the lower right side of the figure and his drape can be traced. This suggests that the painting was originally connected horizontally to another canvas, showing at least a few more figures. At some point, then, the painting might have been separated from a larger canvas, heavily repainted by some other artist, and its meaning altered.

The present painting depicts three figures that are given almost equal prominence, for each one is seated on the same horizontal plane. The reproduction accompanying Speyer's article crops the left end of the painting; however, the original shows a corner of a bench made of either stone or wood. The artist used the same *modello* for the middle and right figures, simply rotating the *modello*. Although only the middle figure is portrayed with feet bare, more than likely the left and right figures were also originally depicted without shoes. Having been added later, the shoes in the present painting appear to be too small. The original artist was, unfortunately, not good at anatomy. The hands are disproportionately large relative to the faces. The middle figure's left leg looks flat, and the relationship between his crossed feet and legs is not well defined. Worse still, the left figure's left hand is not connected to his forearm.

Although Speyer dates this painting to the year 1500 at the latest and claims that it was contemporaneously inspired by Cusanus's writing, the painting should be dated toward the second half of the sixteenth century or even later, based on the following observations.

First, painting on canvas in oil, while not unknown, was still rare in the late fifteenth century, when painting in tempera on wood was a more common practice. Second, stylistically this painting strongly reveals the Manneristic techniques of the sixteenth century. For example, the middle figure's posture is very elegant and stylistic. The lower body with crossed feet is frontal, while his torso is twisted to show the profile of his face. And third, all three figures, particularly the middle one, have extremely elongated fingers. Moreover, color combinations of clothes with bright red, yellow, orange, and blue, as well as highly stylized drapes, also share a part of Manneristic vocabulary. Finally, all three figures are clearly engaged in some sort of intellectual activity. The dramatic eye contact, such as that between the left and middle figures in this painting, is often found in sixteenth-century and later paintings.

The painting is thought by Speyer to portray from left to right: Mohammed, Christ, and Moses. This conclusion is based on his observation that only the central figure (displaying the sign of the Trinity with his fingers) is shown with feet bare (a symbol of the Resurrection), and that only his book is fully opened. The partially opened book held by the right figure, Speyer asserts, indicates the relative importance of the Old Testament for Christians. The left figure, whose gesture with his right index finger indicates monotheism, is accompanied by a demon, says Speyer, and his book is completely closed, indicating its uselessness to Christians. Yet the same left figure is conversing with the central figure, Christ, and therefore, Speyer asserts, is Mohammed holding the Qur'an. Speyer further argues that because of the equal treatment of the three monotheistic religions and the conversation between Christ and Mohammed, the painting reflects Cusanus's sympathetic, though complex, attitude toward Judaism and Islam, which was a theological perspective uncommon in the fifteenth century.

Close observation of the painting suggests, however, that it has a different theme. I agree with Speyer that the central figure is Christ. He is wearing a typical combination of blue and red robes. By placing his right index finger upward and at the same time making a triangle, he is explaining Oneness and the Trinity. The fully opened book shows some text with rubrics, symbolizing his teachings; with the exception of a few words, the letters are indiscernible. The left figure pointing toward the opened book, Speyer's Mohammed, is actually accompanied by a reclining ox, whose left horn we can clearly see. The ox, a symbol of the traditional author of the Third Gospel, is gazing at Christ's hands, which leads me to conclude that the left figure is actually St. Luke. The book held by the evangelist is still closed because his Gospel is to be written well after the death and resurrection of Christ.

The right figure, who is meditating with his eyes cast upward, seems to be speculating on the future. Wearing a conical cap, he rests his right elbow on his almost closed book. The cap resembles the Jewish head covering with a pointed center that was worn by Jews during the high and late Middle Ages. This figure is indeed Moses, as Speyer asserts. In Christian iconography, Moses has been often depicted with a halo, and sometimes with a cap, as a pre-Christian saint.[4] His book, a symbol of the Old Covenant between God and the Jews, is almost closed, because now through Christ the New Covenant between God and all mankind has manifested itself. Among the writings within the New Testament, the Gospel of St. Luke particularly stresses the good deeds of gentiles praised by Christ; examples are the story of Jesus healing a Roman officer's servant and the parable of the Good Samaritan.[5]

From an art historian's point of view, this work is not that of a great master, yet the image itself is very unusual because of the depiction of Moses, Christ, and St. Luke together. It is, however, possible to connect

4. For examples of Jews depicted in the Middle Ages, see Heinz Schreckenberg, *The Jews in Christian Art: An Illustrated History*, trans. John Bowden (New York: Continuum, 1996), 77 (fig. 4), 79 (fig. 7), 112 (fig. 2), 113 (figs. 3–5) [German original: *Die Juden in der Kunst Europas: Ein Bildatlas* (Göttingen: Vandenhoeck and Ruprecht, 1996)].

5. See Luke 7:1–10 and 10:25–37, respectively.

this painting with the theme of Franciscan poverty. Historically, the Gospel of St. Luke has a special importance for Franciscans; it emphasizes the necessity of not only spiritual humility, but also material poverty: an important tenet of Franciscan faith and practice. For example, when one reads the teachings of Jesus recorded both in Matthew 5:1–17 and Luke 6:17–38, it is clear that Matthew stresses a Jesus who cares for people in spiritual hunger, presenting his words as: "How blest are those who know their need of God" and "How blest are those who hunger and thirst to see right prevail." Luke, by contrast, emphasizes a Jesus who looks after people who lack *material* comforts: "How blest are you who are in need" and "How blest are you who now go hungry."

There are some connections between Luke's emphasis on poverty and certain stories associated with Moses.[6] When Moses returned from Mount Sinai after receiving the Ten Commandments, he found that the Israelites had rebelled against the monotheistic and aniconic worship of God and were making sacrifices to, and prostrating themselves before, an image of a golden calf cast by Moses' brother Aaron after the form of the Egyptian god Apis. Moses destroyed the idol and replaced it with the Ark of the Covenant.

During the Renaissance, worship of the golden calf by Israelites was decoded as a symbol of corrupt life and materialistic luxury. For example, the painting of *The Worship of the Egyptian Bull God, Apis* by a follower of Filippino Lippi (1457–1504),[7] which depicts ecstatic worshippers who dance and sing to music, is interpreted as a satirical caricature of the court of Pope Alexander VI Borgia. Infamous among his contemporaries for his self-indulgences and for making his court painter, Pinturicchio, cover his apartment in the Vatican with the images of Apis, Pope Alexander claimed that the bull was his ancestor. In this painting of three haloed figures, it is therefore reasonable to think that Moses was regarded by Franciscans who saw this painting as a man who strictly denounced the materialistic approach to life.

In Luke 18:18–30, the Gospel writer tells the story of an affluent Jewish leader who asked Jesus what he must do to receive eternal life. The man claimed that ever since he was young he had continually obeyed all

6. See, for example, Exodus 32.
7. National Gallery, London, 4905.

Ten Commandments given to Moses. In response Jesus recommended that the man needed to do one more thing, saying: "Sell all you have and give the money to the poor, and you will have riches in heaven; then come and follow me." The story is followed by a famous admonition by Jesus: "How hard it is for rich people to enter the Kingdom of God! It is much harder for a rich person to enter the Kingdom of God than for a camel to go through the eye of a needle." Bearing all of this in mind, I have concluded that this painting of these three haloed figures functioned as a means of convincing Franciscan friars of the importance of the mendicant order's fundamental mission: absolute renunciation of material wealth.

I would argue that it is now clear that the painting is not related to Cusanus's writings about Islam. This very unusual image, depicting Moses, Christ, and St. Luke, has great significance, however, as a pedagogical tool used to inspire friars who lived their lives following Christ, in poverty.

Thomas Prügl

9. THE CONCEPT OF INFALLIBILITY IN NICHOLAS OF CUSA

In his *Dialogus concludens Amedistarum errorem* ("Dialogue Resolving the Error of the Amedists"), a polemical work that Nicholas of Cusa writes to justify his ecclesiological and political turnaround, the Disciple reminds the Master that he has still to explain the argument of infallibility. The Master, trying to evade the issue, answers: "This seems so unimportant to me that I have decided to ignore it."[1]

Although—or indeed because—Cusanus tries to lay a false scent, it is worth studying his ecclesiology, paying particular attention to the concept of infallibility. I shall suggest that for Cusanus infallibility is one of the most essential characteristics of the Church, comparable to consent, representation, and reception. This is obvious just from the frequency Cusanus uses the words *infallibilis* ("infallible") and *infallibilitas* ("infallibility") and related terms such as *indeviabilitas* ("inerrancy"), *errare non posse* ("incapacity for error"), and *privilegium veritatis* ("prerogative of truth").[2]

Late medieval ecclesiology in general evinces a high degree of interest

---

1. "Adeo parvi momenti apud me est, quod eam preterire statui." *Dialogus concludens Amedistarum errorem ex gestis et doctrina concilii Basiliensis* [hereafter, *Dialogus*], ed. Erich Meuthen, MFCG 8 (1970): 11–114, here: N. 25, p. 104. Special thanks to Andrew Irving (Notre Dame), who read and helped to improve this paper.

2. In Cusanus's early work *De usu communionis,* I have found nine occurences of *infallibilitas/infallibilis.* In his major work *De concordantia catholica* the term occurs more than twenty times. In *De auctoritate praesidendi* ("On the authority of presiding"), I counted three instances, and in the *Dialogus* the term is discussed in a lengthy paragraph, in which I counted thirteen appearances of the terms. Our topic is discussed in passing in the monographs of Morimichi Watanabe, *The Political Ideas of Nicolas of Cusa with Special Reference to His "De Concordantia Catholica"* (Geneva: Droz, 1963), 78, 93f., 105; in some more detail in Paul E. Sigmund, *Nicholas of Cusa and Medieval Political Thought* (Cambridge, Mass.: Harvard University Press, 1963), 168–76 (infallible council) and 272–74 (infallible pope); Gerd Heinz-Mohr, *Unitas christiana. Studien zur Gesellschaftsidee des Nikolaus von Kues,* ed. J. Lenz (Trier: Paulinus, 1958), 66–72 (papal *magisterium* and *Ecclesia Romana*).

in the notion of infallibility. Especially in the writings of the conciliarists, the word "infallibility" occurs with increasing regularity.[3] We are misguided if we try to understand this term in the precise way that modern ecclesiology does, that is, as a quality of church magisterium as pronounced by the last two Vatican Councils.[4] In the Middle Ages the concept of infallibility has a much wider range of meaning. Its starting point is the conviction that the Church will never undergo a complete destruction. Medieval thinkers consider the Church to possess what we moderns would call "indefectibility" and are inclined to assertions of the inerrancy of certain persons or institutions within the Church due to a special guidance of the Holy Spirit.[5] A closer study of what Cusanus understands by this no-

3. "Ihren Höhepunkt erreicht die Unfehlbarkeitsdiskussion auf dem Konzil von Basel." Hermann Joseph Sieben, "Ein Hauptstück: Die Theorie vom unfehlbaren Konzil (1378–1449)," in Sieben, *Traktate und Theorien zum Konzil: Vom Beginn des Großen Schismas bis zum Vorabend der Reformation (1378–1521)* (Frankfurt/Main: Knecht, 1983), 149–207, in particular pp. 165–77, here at 65. Erich Meuthen once observed: "Je deutlicher die Existenz des Konzils von der Anerkennung durch die Mächte abhing, desto rigider und undifferenzierter verhielten sich die Basler bei der Postulierung ihres Unfehlbarkeitsdogmatismus, der die damaligen Formulierungen päpstlicher Inerranz weit hinter sich ließ." Erich Meuthen, "Konsens bei Nikolaus von Kues und im Kirchenverständnis des 15. Jahrhunderts," in *Politik und Konfession. Festschrift für Konrad Repgen,* ed. Dieter Albrecht (Berlin: Duncker and Humblot, 1983), 11–29, here at 25. About the idea of infallibility in the Middle Ages in general, see also Angel Antón, *El misterio de la Iglesia. Evolución historica de las ideas eclesiologicas,* vol. 1: *En busca de una eclesiología y de la reforma de la Iglesia* (Madrid-Toledo: Biblioteca de Autores Cristianos, 1986), 406–33; Paul de Vooght, "Esquisse d'une enquête sur le mot 'infaillibilité' durant la période scolastique," in *L'infaillibilité de l'église. Journées oecuméniques de Chevtogne, 25–29 sept. 1961* (Chevtogne: Éditions de Chevtogne, 1962), 99–146, particularly 122–27; Amadeo Molnár, "Infaillibilité et indéfectibilité de l'Eglise," *Communio Viatorum* 14 (1971): 155–64; Hermann Schüssler, *Der Primat der hl. Schrift als theologisches und kanonistisches Problem im Spätmittelalter* (Wiesbaden: Steiner, 1977), 159–224.

4. Jean-François Chiron, *L'infaillibilité et son objet. L'autorité du magistère infaillible de l'église s'étend-elle aux vérités non révélées?* (Paris: Cerf, 1999); Francis A. Sullivan, *Magisterium: Teaching Authority in the Catholic Church* (Mahwah: Paulist Press, 1983); Avery Dulles, "Infallibility: The Terminology," in *Teaching Authority and Infallibility in the Church: Lutherans and Catholics in Dialogue VI,* ed. P. C. Empie, T. A. Murphy, and J. A. Burgess (Minneapolis, Minn.: Augsburg, 1980), 69–80; Yves Congar, "Infaillibilité et indéfectibilité," *Revue des Sciences Philosophiques et Théologiques* 54 (1970): 601–18 (reprinted in Congar, *Ministère et communion ecclésiale* [Paris: Cerf, 1971], 141–65.)

5. Most studies in this area are primarily concerned with the development of the dogma of papal infallibility. The broader meaning of the notion of infallibility is frequently ignored. See, e.g., Brian Tierney, *Origins of Papal Infallibility 1150–1350: A Study on the Concepts of Infallibility, Sovereignty and Tradition in the Middle Ages* (Leiden: Brill, 1972), and Yves Congar, "Saint Thomas Aquinas and the Infallibility of the Papal Magisterium (*Summa Theol.,*

tion of infallibility may shed some light not only on his ecclesiology, but also on the development of the notion of infallibility since the Middle Ages.

As a rule, infallibility is usually a concern when the authority of the church is challenged: this is also the case with Nicholas of Cusa. Depending on the targets of his concerns, we may distinguish three occasions in which he stresses infallibility: (1) when he writes against the Hussites, (2) when he reflects on councils criticizing papalist claims, and (3) when he eventually considers the limits of conciliarism. Using this distinction, the chronology of his developing ecclesiology is also easily discernible.[6]

"Anti-Hussite" Infallibility
Infallibility and Liturgical Rite

Shortly after being incorporated at the Council of Basel as a member of the deputation of faith, Cusanus is assigned to a team led by John of Ragusa that has to deal with the Hussites' request that all participants of the Mass receive the cup. This task is the source and context for Cusanus's opusculum *De usu communionis contra Bohemos* ("Concerning the Practice of Communion against the Bohemians").[7] With regard to the Hussites,

---

II-II, q. 1, a. 10)," *Thomist* 38 (1974): 81–105 (reprinted in Congar, *Thomas d'Aquin: sa vision de théologie et de l'Église*, no. 8 [London: Ashgate, 1984,]).

6. This division reflects the outlines of Sieben's research ("Ein Hauptstück"). Sieben studied the medieval discussions about conciliar infallibility according to places and periods: Paris (1378–), Oxford/Prague (1378–), Pisa/Konstanz (1409–), Basel/Rome (1432–), Basel/Prague (1432–), Rome/Ayton (1449–).

7. p II, fol. 5ʳ–13ᵛ. In Cusanus's library in the Hospital at Kues, there still lies the copy of Ragusa's speech on the Eucharist, complete with Cusanus's lengthy notes in the margins (Codex Cusanus 166, fol. 1–21ᵛ). Cusanus wrote a short paper based on these notes against John of Rokycana, the Hussite representative and defender of the Hussite praxis. The short paper by Cusanus was only a preparatory work for the larger and more detailed *Contra Bohemorum errores: De usu communionis*, which, according to Erich Meuthen, was written in the second half of 1433 when the Hussites had already returned from Basel to Bohemia. Cusanus, therefore, probably sent this work from Basel to Prague—a reason why in later times it was considered a letter. The shorter preparatory work is known only in one manuscript: Prague, Library of the University, IV H 17 (781), fol. 57ᵛ–60ʳ. Cf. *Acta Cusana: Quellen zur Lebensgeschichte des Nikolaus von Kues*, vol. I.1, ed. Erich Meuthen, Hermann Hallauer (Hamburg: Meiner, 1976), no. 170. For the longer treatise, see *Acta Cusana*, no. 171; Hermann Hallauer, "Das Glaubensgespräch mit den Hussiten," MFCG 9 (1971): 53–75, particularly 73. Hallauer found two manuscripts of *De usu communionis*: Trier, Stadtbibliothek

Cusanus wants to stress some points that he considers not well enough developed by Ragusa's official speech.[8] For this purpose he does not invest much time dealing with the eucharistic questions or problems of pastoral theology, as one might expect from the title. Instead he insists on the reliability of the liturgical rite and on infallibility. The combination of liturgical rite and infallibility seems surprising, but the explanation of liturgical rites as a reliable practice of the Church points to the center of Cusanus's concept of infallibility. Whatever the Church decides to be part of its rite, it never succumbs to error. The Church is unable to commit heresy by changing its rite. The rite is an expression and an effect of the authority of the Church.[9] But who and what institutions can claim to represent this au-

---

704/906, fol. 85ʳ–97ᵛ, and Munich, Bayerische Staatsbibliothek, Clm 3071, fol. 15ᵛᵇ–23ʳᵃ. The Paris edition of Cusanus's works (p) presents the treatise as two distinct letters, thus dividing it in two parts (*epistola* II and III). In the Munich manuscript Clm 3071, the beginning of *epistola* III is marked only by a short indent. The first sentence of *epistola* III in p ("Quamquam satis constat ex priore epistola . . .") must be read according to Clm 3071, fol. 19ᵛᵇ: "Quamquam satis aperte constat ex predictis . . ." Clm 3071 is a small manuscript with only twenty-three sheets, originating from the Benedictine monastery of Andechs. This manuscript erroneously attributes the opusculum to John of Capistran, who together with Cusanus also preached against the Hussites in 1452–1454. Cf. Hallauer, "Das Glaubensgespräch." The only other text in the manuscript beside Cusanus's is the *Disputatio de sacramento eucharistie* of Lanfranc of Canterbury (fol. 1–15ᵛᵃ).

8. On John of Ragusa's ecclesiology, see J. Santiago Madrigal Terrazas, *La Eclesiología de Juan de Ragusa O.P. (1390/95–1443): Estudio e interpretación de su Tractatus de Ecclesia* (Madrid: Universidad Pontificia Comillas, 1995). The *Oratio de communione* is discussed at 168–86 and the question of infallibility at 179–81 and 348–52. See also Johannes Laudage, "Certum est quod papa potest errare. Johannes von Ragusa und das Problem der Unfehlbarkeit," in *Studien zum 15. Jahrhundert. Festschrift für Erich Meuthen*, ed. Johannes Helmrath, Heribert Müller, and Helmut Wolff, 2 vols. (München: Oldenbourg, 1994), 145–68.

9. Nicholas of Cusa, *De usu communionis*, p fol. 7ʳ, Clm 3071, fol. 17ᵛᵃ. "Certe hoc te non moueat, quod diuersis temporibus alius et alius ritus sacrificiorum et eciam sacramentorum stante ueritate inuenitur scripturasque esse ad tempus adaptatas et uarie intellectas, ita ut uno tempore secundum currentem uniuersalem ritum exponerentur mutato ritu iterum sententia mutaretur . . . Christus enim . . . mysteria [Clm 3071: ministeria] pro temporum uarietate dispensat et que singulis temporibus congruunt uel occulta inspiratione uel euidentiori illustratione suggerit." Cusanus held this conviction throughout his life: cf. *Dialogus*, n. 27, ed. Meuthen, 105: "Aliquando enim tota ecclesia habuit unam formam baptizandi, secundum quam omnes salvabantur; post hoc alia est introducta, et tunc, si quis secundum priorem baptizatus fuisset, non salvabatur. In hiis ergo mutationibus saluti nichil deperiit." For the larger context of changes of sacramental and liturgical rites in the middle ages, see Georg Avvakumov, *Una fides, diverso ritu. Die rituelle Eigenart der Ostkirche als Problem der lateinischen Theologie 1053–1300* (Berlin: Akademie, 2002).

thority? Cusanus has to turn to those authorities that the Hussites are ready to accept: sacred Scripture, the practice of the Lord and the apostles, and the practice of the primitive Church.[10] He warns his opponents not to play the practice of the primitive Church off against the practice of the Church in later times, because the authority of the Church to fix its liturgical rules is the same at every stage in its history. Furthermore, he warns them not to oppose the authority of the Lord to that of the Church, because both are related to each other. There would not exist any command of the Lord, if the Church did not accept it as such. Therefore the Lord's commands become valid only by their reception by the Church.[11] He considers the authority of sacred Scripture analogously, saying that its impact would be insignificant if the Church did not receive it. If the Church did not acknowledge it as the word of God, Holy Scripture would remain a "dead letter." This idea was very common in late medieval ecclesiology and is based on the famous Augustinian adage: "I would not believe the gospel unless the Church moved me." Therefore Cusanus considers the practice, the rite, and especially the reception of and by the Church as a "sound refuge" for the faithful. And by this expression, *solidum refugium,* he understands nothing other than the infallible rule of the Church.[12]

10. The famous "Judge of Eger," who pointed out the rules for the theological debates between Hussites and Catholics at Basel, is printed in Johannes Dominicus Mansi, *Sacrorum Conciliorum Nova et Amplissima Collectio* (Paris 1901–1921; reprinted Graz: Akademische Druck- und Verlagsanstalt, 1960–1962), T. 30, 145f.

11. Nicholas of Cusa, *De usu communionis,* p fol. 7ᵛ: "Dico nulla esse Christi precepta quam per ecclesiam pro talibus accepta ut prehabitum est. Si igitur constat ecclesiam illa precepta ut talia laudare, illis ut Christi preceptis obediendum nemo ambigit. . . . Et non est hec mutatio tanquam a minori auctoritate quam Christi precipientis dependens, quoniam ecclesia, que est corpus Christi et eius spiritu uegetatur, non aliud agit quam Christus uult . . . et propterea hec ligandi et soluendi potestas non minor est in ecclesia quam in Christo."

12. *De usu communionis,* p fol. 7ʳ–7ᵛ: "Ubi erit solidum refugium peregrinantium? Certe in alio nullo quam in militantis ecclesie usu atque approbatione siue hoc sit circa scripturam et eius auctoritatem atque intellectum siue extra scripturam in consuetudine accepta per ecclesiam. In his enim firmitas est ut in solida petra ac ueritatis columna. . . . Et ita uia cuiusque in ecclesia existentis est, ut per ecclesiam ad scripturam eius intellectum aut usum non scriptum se conuertat, non ut per scripturarum auctoritatem ad ecclesiam pergat." See also ibid., fol. 7ʳ: "Fatuum est ergo argumentum uelle uniuersalem ecclesie ritum ex scripturis predecessorum arguere. Legitur enim apostolos non tradidisse fidem per scripturas sed per uocalem impressionem breuissimi symboli. . . . Unde scripture de bene esse regiminis ecclesie etiam incepte et continuate nequaquam de essentia existere possunt quia per

Now, the Hussites would not contest that the Church has authority and that the Church is able to use it in a legitimate manner. But is that authority in itself always and everywhere infallible? Is not the Church obliged to verify its deeds and words by the words and commands of the Lord? Is not Holy Scripture in a much more eminent way the infallible rule for the Church than vice versa? There, however, is the decisive difference of Cusanus's ecclesiology; the Church for him is the foremost authority of revelation. In opposition to the Hussites, he presumes infallibility within the Catholic Church, because it embodies the true Church. What are the criteria for the true Church? Cusanus would answer: the Chair of St. Peter (*cathedra Petri*) and the priesthood, or more precisely, the priesthood in its greater part (*maior pars sacerdotum*). Let us consider each more closely.

"Cathedra Petri" and "Sacerdotium"

In the treatise against the Bohemians, the word "infallibility" is employed first when Cusanus introduces the idea of *cathedra Petri*. He writes:

And as an infallible rule of our salvation Christ gave to the Church this power and authority, so that we can not stray from the way of our salvation if we remain within the unity of the Church, which follows the Chair of St. Peter and by means of which we are connected to Christ the head even through bad successors [of St. Peter].[13]

---

imperium alicuius tyranni Antichristi omnes cremari et de mundo tolli possent." Cusanus will repeat this idea, which stresses the "sense" of Scripture over its "letter," in his epistles to the Hussites (*Epistola VII ad clerum et litteratos Bohemiae*, p II, fol. 20ʳ): "Ex praemissis constat, quod tota catholica ecclesia non potest ad litteram scripturarum obligari licet semper ad spiritum. Quando enim littera non seruit aedificationi et spiritui, recepit id quod magis seruit spiritui." The reference to Augustine is "Ego vero evangelio non crederem, nisi me catholicae ecclesiae commoveret auctoritas." *Contra epistolam quam vocant "fundamenti,"* nr. 5, in St. Augustine, *De utilitate credendi et alia,* ed. J. Zycha, Corpus Scriptorum Ecclesiasticorum Latinorum 25 (Vienna: CSEL, 1891–92); also published in Carl Mirbt and Kurt Alland, *Quellen zur Geschichte des Papsttums und des Römischen Katholizismus,* 6th ed. (Tübingen: Mohr/Siebeck, 1967), 170 (no. 369). The primacy of the Church over Scripture nevertheless continued to be controversial in the late Middle Ages. For example, Henry of Ghent considered Scripture more important than the Church: "Simpliciter et absolute magis credendum est sacrae scripturae quam ecclesiae." Gerhard von Bologna, following Thomas Aquinas, connects both authorities with the *auctoritas Dei:* "Credens non recte credit ecclesiae nec scripturae nisi propter auctoritatem Dei." These texts are quoted in de Vooght, "Esquisse," 106f. In the anti-Hussite context, however, the focus is on the primacy of the Church.

13. Clm 3071, fol. 17ᵛᵃ; p fol. 6ᵛ–7ʳ (here Clm 3071 preserved the better text.): "Et pro

What is the meaning of this dense and complex statement? The infallible rule to which Cusanus alludes is not the Church itself but the authority of the Church. The Church, which possesses in its authority and power an infallible rule, follows and depends on the Chair of St. Peter. The *cathedra Petri*, however, consists of the long line of the successors of St. Peter, the good as well as the evil. Through this unbroken succession is established a direct, even physical, contact with Christ, the head of the Church. Infallibility is within the Church, but the Church is based on the Chair of St. Peter. In his treatise against the Hussites Cusanus identifies *cathedra Petri* to a large extent with the papacy. But the papacy need not necessarily be identified with the Roman bishop, because Rome could easily be destroyed by the infidels. This is why Cusanus will not equate the Chair of St. Peter with the See of Rome. Rather *cathedra Petri* aims at the principle of a perpetual, hierarchically structured episcopacy with a supreme bishop. The Chair of St. Peter would always remain with this supreme bishop wherever his residence, Rome or elsewhere. The generally recognized primacy of the Roman Church in this perspective means nothing other than the fundamentally hierarchic and monarchic structure of the Church. The indefectibility of the Church is guaranteed in the existence of a supreme bishop who always gathers around himself the majority of the faithful.[14]

This interpretation of *cathedra Petri*, which closely connects the papacy with the episcopacy, receives further support in *De concordantia catholica*. In his major ecclesiological work Cusanus focuses upon the role of the

---

infallibili regule salutis nostre Christus hanc tradidit ecclesie potestatem et auctoritatem, ut, cum in unitate cum ipsa persistimus, que cathedre Petri adheret et per quam per successores etiam malorum Christo capiti alligatur, errare a via salutis non possimus."

14. P fol. 8[r-v]; Clm 3071, fol. 18[vb]–19[ra]: "Nolo tamen ut ex loco auctoritatem arguamus, cum possibili sit aliquando ibi non futurum pontificem aut urbem opprimi ab infidelibus aut desolari, sed ex prioritate episcopi super ceteros in quo prior principatus et altior super quosque existit. . . . Et tamen si casu Roma deficeret, ibi ueritas ecclesie remanebit ubi erit principatus et Petri sedes modo predicto. . . . Et licet sepe multi schismatica diuisione ab illa romana ecclesia recesserint, numquam tamen fuit quin maior fidelium numerus in unitate illius romane ecclesie ex fidelibus et primo episcopo compacte perseueraret. Quare in ea nostre saluti necessaria remansit hactenus et remanebit ueritatis columna." Against a common opinion that in times of crisis the faith of the Church could be reduced and found only in an old woman (*vetula*), i.e., the so-called "rest-argument" of Ockham, Cusanus considered the principle of majority to be a definite fact of ecclesiology. The true Church would always be found in the majority.

whole episcopacy that represents the *cathedra Petri*. *Cathedra Petri* is the *principatus regitivus* ("chief post or hegemony of governance"), which is not limited to the supreme bishop and highest ruler but is that in which the whole episcopacy is involved. From this perspective *cathedra Petri* means the principle of presidency in the Church generally, which is realized in each single bishop and even more in the whole episcopacy. By this change of emphasis, the episcopacy too becomes the principle of infallibility and indefectibility.[15]

Cusanus addresses the rivalry between papacy and episcopacy as subjects of infallibility in a short *quaestio* in his treatise against the Hussites. He formulates the problem this way: "Where and why is infallible truth within the Church?" There are two possible reasons: either the Church derives its infallibility from the Roman See, which has this truth as a divinely conferred privilege and which confers this infallibility on the Church, or infallibility is found within the episcopacy, which does not receive it directly from God, but from the Church, since the episcopacy "embraces" *(amplectitur)* the Church. In the first case it would be an infal-

---

15. Nicholas of Cusa, *De concordantia catholica,* I, 14, h XIV (1964), p. 76: "Est itaque verum unam esse cathedram Petri, quoniam cathedra principatum regitivum significat in ecclesia. Et sicut in ipsa cathedra Petri tres primi patriarchae leguntur sedisse, scilicet Romanus, Alexandrinus et Antiochenus, ita et cum illis omnes subiecti episcopi." Ibid., p. 77: "sic est omnium episcoporum unius episcopatus una cathedra, in qua primo sedet Romanus." The notion of *praesidentialitas* is discussed in *De concordantia catholica* I, 9, p. 65: "Quare sacerdotium ita ad praesidentiam relatum habet suae praesidentiae animam, scilicet cathedram, et spiritum, scilicet angelum, ad instar prioris. Unde ex hoc trahitur, quod veritas praesidentiae et cathedrae ex hoc est infallibilis." Cf. also idem, *De auctoritate praesidendi in concilio generali,* ed. Gerhard Kallen, Cusanus-Texte II.1, Sitzungberichte der Heidelberger Akademie der Wissenschaften, Philosophisch-historische Klasse, Jahrgang 1935/36, 3 (Heidelberg: Winter, 1935), p. 18 (2nd *consideratio*). The conception of the indefectibility of the episcopacy is shared by John Gerson. Indeed, he probably was the source of Cusanus's opinion. Cf. Jean Gerson, *De auctoritate concilii,* ch. 3, in *Œuvres complètes,* vol. 6, ed. Palémon Glorieux (Paris: Desclée, 1965), 6:115: "Collegium omnium episcoporum christianorum non posse errare in fide et schismate maculari est certa fide credendum." See also Sieben, "Ein Hauptstück," 158f. The notion of *cathedra* in patristic thought, another important source for Cusanus, is explored in Pierre Batiffol, *Cathedra Petri. Études d'histoire ancienne de l'Église* (Paris: Cerf, 1938), and Werner Marschall, *Karthago und Rom: Die Stellung der nordafrikanischen Kirche zum Apostolischen Stuhl in Rom, Päpste und Papsttum* 1 (Stuttgart: Hiersemann, 1971). For the origin of the modern formula *ex cathedra,* see Yves Congar, *Die Lehre von der Kirche. Von Augustinus bis zum Abendländischen Schisma* (Freiburg/Breisgau: Herder, 1971), 65.

libility "from above," in the second case "from below." Having introduced his query, Cusanus refuses to give a solution, saying: "We need not investigate this question here." A rivalry between papacy and episcopacy is of no help in the effort to convince the Hussites and lead them back into the Catholic Church.[16] Instead he favors a complementary solution that appeals to obedience and trust and that tries to bracket both alternatives. Hence infallibility is granted and guaranteed by the mutual dependency of bishops (including the Pope) and Church. Bishop and community are as form and matter, from which arises the infallible Church. In the end Cusanus's concept of infallibility is based on his underlying theory of consent. Or, to put it more strongly: consent is the ground of infallibility within the Church.[17]

In *De usu communionis* Cusanus will neither criticize the Pope nor defend the episcopacy or the council against papal claims. He tries rather to reject the Hussite attack against priestly and hierarchic authority. Hence, he reflects not only on *cathedra Petri* but also on priesthood *(sacerdotium)*. In the second part of *De usu communionis,* the concept of *sacerdotium* is the focus of Cusanus's attention. Now it is the *sacerdotium* that is the subject of infallibility, because it continues the legacy of Christ and because it contains in its body the episcopacy and the *cathedra.* At first glance this idea seems to be only a variation of our previous considerations, but the ideas of *cathedra* and episcopacy are only historical concretions of the more fundamental concept of *sacerdotium.* In his mystical—or rather ty-

16. Nicholas of Cusa, *De usu communionis,* p fol. 9ʳ; Clm 3071, fol. 19ʳᵃ: "Nec est opus hoc loco inuestigare an ideo ueritas infallibilis sit in ea ecclesia quia ad sedem illam unitur, tamquam a sede riuus ille ueritatis priuilegialiter emanet, uel quia episcopatus ille ecclesiam amplectitur, ideo ille episcopatus ab ecclesia infallibilitatem sortiatur, aut neutrum horum; quoniam puto quod hoc non sit ad nostrum propositum necessarium, licet credam ex mutua adherentia exsurgere infalliblitatem."

17. Ibid.: "Unde etsi in ecclesia quedam appareat materialitas in quantum subiectiue consideratur ad regimen principum et in primate formalitas ut ex ipsis tamquam materia et forma constituatur infallibilis illa ecclesia catholica quasi ex utroque consurgens; tamen in parte ecclesie quaedam prioritas uidetur, ut Ieronimus ait 95 di. Olim et 93 di. Legimus. Sicut et in aliis naturalibus ubi forma educitur de potentia materie ita de potentia ecclesie educitur ille primatus qui eoipso quod eductus est respectiue se habet ad ecclesiam propter quam est, et diuino gaudet presidentiali priuilegio ex successione. Et iam ista sufficiant quam breuissime dicta ut sciamus ex mutuo complexu ecclesie et primatus ueritatem ecclesie persistere infallibiliter."

pological—view of the Church, which is based on the Pseudo-Dionysian idea of prototype and image *(exemplar)*, the priesthood is among the three constitutional parts of the Church militant. It is the core institution of the Church on earth that connects the faithful with the divine sphere represented by the sacraments. It is like the soul in the body.[18] Analogously to his earlier-expressed ideas about the papacy, Cusanus discovers within the priesthood a succession that goes back to the first priest, Christ. Both the theological way of mediation, the administration of sacraments, and the historical way, succession, establish the indefectibility of the priesthood: "Nor is there ever a failing in this kind of a legitimate succession of the priesthood since the whole Church necessarily would be errant."[19] The everlasting priesthood is the reason for the Church's indefectibility, and

18. Cusanus first mentions these typologies in the second part of his treatise *De usu communionis (epistola* III), p fol. 11[v]; Clm 3071, fol. 21[rb]. A more detailed version is found in *De concordantia catholica* I, 6. In his *Tractatus de auctoritate praesidendi,* he repeats only the threefold scheme of the Church militant, but with special emphasis on the *sacerdotium.* In this work Cusanus focuses on the priesthood to such an extent that he deems the ordination of priests among the most important sacraments: "Sacramentum ordinis in ipsa ecclesia est de prioribus sacramentis, quoniam per ipsum sacerdotium constituitur, et per sacerdotium alia sacramenta conficiuntur et ministrantur" *(De auctoritate praesidendi,* ed. Kallen, p. 18). This is a remarkable phrase in a work on the Eucharist! Especially in *De auctoritate praesidendi* the priesthood is presented as the nucleus of the true Church. The priesthood itself is the Church that never will perish. It is a *corpus mysticum* on its own, which has the power of the keys. Because of Christ's legacy truth is forever granted to the priesthood; indeed the Church has truth only through the priesthood. The laity participates in this truth by loyal consent: "Quoniam omnis populus fidelis est in potentia sacerdotali, cui obedire tenetur et credere" (ibid.). Influenced by Cusanus, Henry Kalteisen called the priesthood the *ecclesia sacerdotalis,* which is a legitimate representation of the Church. Cf. Kalteisen, *Lectiones* (Bonn, Universitätsbibliothek, ms. S 327), fol. 57[r]: "Ecclesia potest tripliciter considerari: Uno modo ut universalis, secundo ut sacerdotalis, tercio ut conciliaris"; Thomas Prügl, *Die Ekklesiologie Heinrich Kalteisens OP in der Auseinandersetzung mit dem Basler Konziliarismus* (Paderborn: Schöningh, 1995), 142, 231, 284. Cusanus too calls the priesthood an *ecclesia sacerdotalis* (in *De concordantia catholica* II, 18 [N. 156, 13], p. 191, but he conceives of it as a mystical body (see *De auctoritate praesidendi,* ed. Kallen, p. 16 [2. consideratio]). Cusanus's vision of the priesthood is discussed in Klaus Reinhardt, "Die Repräsentanz Christi und der Christgläubigen im kirchlichen Amt," MFCG 21 (1994): 183–202.

19. Nicholas of Cusa, *De usu communionis,* p, fol. 11[v]: "Nec umquam deficit talis successio legitima sacerdotii cum necessario tota deficeret ecclesia." See also ibid., fol. 13[r]: "Commune sacerdotium capiens sui regiminis motum a sancto Spiritu, quoniam sanctissimum est, ex Christi legatione—non obstante quod quidam peccatores sint in ministratione—errare non potest."

consequently the priesthood gains infallibility in the sense of inerrancy, since if the priesthood were to err, the Church would perish too.[20]

Potestas Ecclesiastica

Thus far we have approached Cusanus's concept of infallibility following his arguments against the anti-hierarchical ecclesiology of the Hussites. He is mostly replying to their underlying assertion that the ancient Roman Church had abandoned the precepts of the Lord. Now, let us take a closer look at Cusanus's more specific notion of infallibility. His considerations concerning the rites of the Church reveal that he aims neither at a certain charism of Church leaders nor at the magisterium of the Church. Invoking infallibility, he refers to a high degree of reliability and certainty of the salvific ministry of the Church. With regard to the concrete issue of the day, Cusanus wants to emphasize that the decision of the Church to withhold the cup from the faithful does no harm to them. In terms of grace and salvation, it is not detrimental to receive the consecrated bread without the cup. Although the sacramental sign seems deficient, the faithful are not deceived by this limited rite of communion; they are not "cheated" out of the sacramental effects, but they can trust the Church's infallibility. This assertion of infallibility is a response to uncertainty about personal salvation and to the suspicion of ritual error.

To underscore the importance of unreserved confidence in the Church's decisions, Cusanus never tires of repeating the rule: *Nemo ad impossibile obligatur.*[21] The obligation simply lies in the mandate of the Lord

20. Nicholas of Cusa, *Tractatus de auctoritate praesidendi,* ed. Kallen, pp. 16–18 (*consideratio* 2): "Ipsum sacerdotium habens hanc Christi regitivam legationem, constituit unum corpus mysticum, et hoc corpus habet unum episcopatum et unam cathedram. . . . Sic sacerdotium errare non potest, cui illa legatio commissa est, quoniam per errorem sacerdotii erraret tota ecclesia." In *De concordantia catholica* I, 8–10, and II, 18, Cusanus also discusses the *sacerdotium,* although not in the concentrated form as in *De auctoritate praesidendi.* Even while emphasizing the notion of priesthood, Cusanus also highlighted other important aspects such as the principle of majority, which is more likely achieved in a large group of priests than in single bishops or even the Pope. Furthermore, we should further bear in mind that Cusanus's own self-confidence and assurance resulted from his priesthood and his membership in an infallible college. On this subject, see Thomas Prügl, "Successores apostolorum. Zur Theologie des Bischofsamtes im Basler Konziliarismus," in *Für euch Bischof—mit euch Christ. Festschrift für Friedrich Kardinal Wetter zum siebzigsten Geburtstag,* ed. Manfred Weitlauff and Peter Neuner (St. Ottilien: EOS, 1998), 195–217.

21. "Nobody is bound to do the impossible." Cf. *De usu communionis,* p fol. 13ʳ; Clm

to follow the doctrines of those who are in charge of the *cathedra*.[22] Because of this dominical mandate, the faithful can be assured to have an infallible rule in the dispositions of the Church. This understanding of infallibility becomes obvious also by examining the language Cusanus employs: he speaks of *firmitas* ("steadfastness"), *solidum refugium,* and *securitas* ("safety"). Indeed it seems that Cusanus is not interested in single dogmas or doctrines of faith but in a generally respected obligation, reliability, and validity of Church orders. Infallibility is the reason for faithful obedience and therefore a quality of Church power, that is, of *potestas ecclesiastica* rather than of *magisterium* ("teaching authority").[23]

3071, fol. 22[va]: "Quare non cadit deceptio quo ad fidelem populum etiam per malum sacerdotem. . . . Alioquin si in hoc hesitatio esse posset duo inconuenientissima [p: maxima inconuenientia] sequerentur, scilicet aut totam ecclesiam errare posse aut fidelem ad impossibilia obligari." See also *Dialogus*, N. 19, ed. Meuthen, p. 97: "Nemo enim ad impossibile obligatur, et in omnibus obligatur unusquisque catholicae ecclesiae se conformare. Nemo igitur decipitur quoad anime salutem, qui ecclesie sequitur." In the apparatus Meuthen noticed parallels in Cusanus's letter to Thomas Ebendorfer (text in *Acta Cusana*, N. 481, p. 347): "Unde si commissa est ecclesia uni summo pastori Petro et eius successori . . . tunc non debuerunt fideles obligari ad impossibile. . . . Necessarium est dicere, quod summus prelatus et pastor non possit seducere fideles in doctrina; nam si posset seducere, nulla esset firmitas fidei neque certitudo, an in fide esset ecclesia." Also in Cusanus's long speech from 1442 *(Summa dictorum):* "Ymmo si errarent, adhuc est ibi salus; non enim potest fidelis ad impossibile obligari" (*Acta Cusana*, N. 520, p. 405). This argument Cusanus continued to deem decisive when he returned to the dispute with the Hussites in 1452–1454. He reproached the Hussites that their priests did not have legitimate power and therefore deceived the faithful. Cf. *Epistola V ad Bohemos* (dating from June 27, 1452), p II, fol. 15[r]: "Et cum nullam habeant potestatem ligandi et soluendi populum decipiunt." *Epistola VII ad clerum et litteratos Bohemiae,* ibid., fol. 20[r]: "sed fides ecclesiae non decipitur quo ad animarum salutem in rituum diuersitate." For the historical situation and the circumstances of Cusanus's letters to the Hussites, see Hallauer, "Glaubensgespräch," 57ff.; Johannes Hofer, *Johannes Kapistran. Ein Leben im Kampf um die Reform der Kirche,* 2 vols. (Heidelberg: Kerle, 1964), 2:57–146; and F. M. Bartoš, "Cusanus and the Hussite Bishop M. Lupá," *Communio Viatorum* 5 (1962): 35–46.

22. Cf. Matthew 23:2–3.

23. This is also the opinion of Guido Terreni, an earlier advocate of papal infallibility. Terreni, however, does not support personal papal infallibility, but he says that the Pope cannot err in determinations of faith if he uses the advice of the cardinals. This inerrancy is important for the maintenance of the "infallibility" of faith and the reliability of church authority. Cf. Guido Terreni, *Quaestio de magisterio infallibili Romani Pontificis,* ed. Bartolomaeus M. Xiberta (Münster: Aschendorff, 1926), 16f.: "ad salvandum certitudinem et infallibilitatem fidei christianae ac stabilitatem auctoritatis ecclesiae . . . papa, ad cuius auctoritatem pertinet determinare sentencialiter et declarare que ad fidem pertinent non

Such an interpretation is lent further support when we look at Cusanus's exegesis of the most important biblical text concerning infallibility, Matthew 23:2–3: "The scribes and the Pharisees occupy the chair [*cathedra*] of Moses. You must therefore do and observe what they tell you; but do not be guided by what they do, since they do not practice what they preach." The context of *cathedra* seems to refer to the magisterium of the Church. But even as Cusanus speaks in this context of *veritas cathedrae* ("the truth of the chair"), he is referring to a degree of obedience rather than to an intellectual quality.[24] The truth of such obedient abiding in the infallible authority will be stronger and more reliable than any conviction of (subjective) rightness based upon (personal) intellectual knowledge. If, for example, on the basis of false witnesses an ecclesiastical judge excommunicates an innocent person, this innocently excommuni-

---

possit cum consilio dominorum cardinalium errare." It is not the Pope that is infallible, but only faith and Holy Scripture. On the authority of the Church, the faithful firmly believe that Holy Scripture contains "infallibly the truth" (ibid., 17, 27f.). About Terreni see Thomas Turley, "The Ecclesiology of Guido Terreni" (Ph.D. diss., Cornell, 1978); Turley, "Infallibilists in the Curia of Pope John XXII," *Journal of Medieval History* 1 (1975): 71–101; Thomas Izbicki, "Infallibility and Erring Pope: Guido Terreni and Johannes de Turrecremata," in *Law, Church and Society: Essays in Honor of Stephan Kuttner,* ed. Kenneth Pennington and Robert Sommerville (Philadelphia: University of Pennsylvania Press, 1977), 97–111; and Tierney, *Origins of Papal Infallibility,* 238–72. Compared to these late medieval doctrines of infallibility, the thirteenth-century theologians had a quite different use of the term. For Thomas Aquinas, faith, the personal act of believing as well as the objective and formulated faith of the Church, relies upon the "divine truth" (*Summa theologiae* II-II, 1, 1). Only God's knowledge and the "rule of faith" derived from it are infallible: "Quod cadit sub praescientia divina, habet quandam necessitatem infallibilitatis." *Summa theologiae* II-II, 1, 3, ad 2; and particularly I, 14, 13. Cf. Ulrich Horst, *Papst—Konzil—Unfehlbarkeit. Die Ekklesiologie der Summenkommentare von Cajetan bis Billuart* (Mainz: Grünewald, 1978), 8. Bonaventure too describes only God's pre-knowledge as infallible (*Breviloquium,* I, 8, nr. 3–4): "Deus cognoscit contingentia infallibiliter." Also cf. ibid., I, 8, nr. 6 and Prologus §5 as well as Bonaventura, *Sermo theologicus* IV "Unus est magister vester," nr. 6. Cusanus is still familiar with this use of the word. Cf. *De concordantia catholica* I, 5, (N. 28, 2), p. 49, where he mentions the infallible ordination of God.

24. Nicholas of Cusa, *De usu comunionis,* p fol. 8ʳ; Clm 3071, fol. 18ᵛᵇ: "Veritas enim cathedre per Christum alligata est, quando dixit 'Supra cathedram Moysi sederunt scribe et pharisei; que dicunt facite,' non personis, quia ait 'que faciunt facere nolite.'" *Tractatus de auctoritate praesidendi,* ed. Kallen, 16: "Unde assignavit sacerdotio cathedram unam Moysi legislatoris, in qua unitate cathedre de veritate certificavit ecclesiam. . . . Ex istis patet, quod potestas ligandi et solvendi a Christo sacerdotio tradita est ipsis secundum premissa ex Christi missione et legatione quoad judicium credita."

cated person would not lose the grace of the sacraments from which he or she has been excluded. Obedience and obedient renunciation of the sacraments, rather than any rebellion against the authority of the Church, will promote somebody's salvation. This example shows that infallibility is not a gift or charism of the ecclesiastical judge, who can be deceived, but an assurance for the faithful, who will infallibly attain salvation, despite the error of the church minister.[25]

Truth must be based upon authority, and authority evinces reliability. True authority, which ultimately is an authority coming from God or Christ, must therefore be infallible authority, that is, an authority the faithful need not worry to trust, whatever the circumstances.

Anti-papalist Infallibility

While in the opusculum against the Hussites we encounter just traces of anti-papalist infallibility and only at the initial stages, this is the very topic of *De concordantia catholica*. Part of the reason is that *De usu communionis* had refrained from developing a conciliar theory; indeed, the authority of universal councils is barely mentioned.[26] *De concordantia catholi-*

---

25. Ibid., p fol. 9ʳ; Clm 3071, fol. 19ᵛᵃ: "Quare ecclesia pro tempore iudicans ita expedire uti agit irreprehensibiliter sequenda est, quia fidem habet et mandata seruat etiam si in hoc iudicio aliquid exequens [Clm 3071: expedientis] deciperetur, sicuti cum iudex falso testimonio circumuentus excommunicat insontem, cum nihil agat in quo cor suum eum reprehendat . . . et eapropter se a corpore domini separans, non perdit gratiam aut uitam quam ex sacramento consequeretur, sed ecclesie etiam decepte obediendo in omissione salutem consequitur."

26. The only council Cusanus mentions in the treatise against the Hussites is Lateran IV. This council, however, plays a pivotal role in Cusanus's argument. Toward the end of the treatise, Cusanus resumes a long chain of arguments conclusively showing that the actual rite of communion in the (Roman) Church is infallible because it was also confirmed by this great and famous synod, over which Pope Innocent III presided: "Solet etiam a uobis curiose superflue tamen queri quis Romanus pontifex aut quale concilium ritui unius speciei auctoritatem primo prestitit. Et licet infallibilis nostre salutis regula in istis per Augustinum post Basilium, 12 de ecclesiasticis, conscripta, merito sufficeret, tamen ut curiositati etiam superflue satisfiat, dico quod magna et plenaria totius orbis et uniuerse ecclesie synodus anno Christi 1215 in ecclesia Lateranensi Rome Innocentio illo tertio literatissimo diuine et humane legis peritissimo presidente hunc ritum non communicandi infantes et sub una specie fideles per c. Omnis utriusque sexus approbauit." *De usu communionis*, p fol. 13ᵛ; Clm 3071, fol. 22ᵛᵇ.

ca's objective, on the other hand, amounts to an attempt to encapsulate a theory of the infallible council of the universal Church. However, before Cusanus focuses upon the infallible council he has to deal with the notion of *Ecclesia Romana* ("Roman church"), which is known to be traditionally linked with claims of papal indefectibility.

Ecclesia Romana

As confirmed by numerous canonistic texts from the earliest centuries, the Roman Church is believed to be the indefectible testimony of the Church's tradition and its faith: it has avoided any stain of heresy and therefore enjoys the privilege of inerrancy.[27] How does Cusanus interpret this tradition? Following a widely accepted canonistic interpretation first articulated by Huguccio, Cusanus maintains a broad meaning of *Ecclesia Romana*. For him the Roman Church is not a clearly defined entity but realizes itself in different degrees. Thus Cusanus distinguishes five such degrees:[28]

27. Cf. *Decretum Gratiani,* di 21, c. 3 (Quamvis), di. 22, c. 1 (Omnes); C. 24 q. 1, cc. 9–18, in *Corpus Juris Canonici,* ed. Aemilius Friedberg, 2 vols. (Leipzig: Tauchnitz, 1879; reprint ed., Graz: Akademische Druck- und Verlagsanstalt, 1959), 70, 73, 969–72; Brian Tierney, *Foundations of the Conciliar Theory: The Contribution of the Medieval Canonists from Gratian to the Great Schism* (Cambridge University Press, 1955; enlarged ed., Leiden: Brill, 1998), 36–46; Walter Ullmann, "Cardinal Humbert and the Ecclesia Romana," *Studi Gregoriani* 4 (1952): 111–27 (reprinted in Ullmann, *The Papacy and Political Ideas in the Middle Ages,* no. 1 [London: Ashgate, 1976]); John T. Gilchrist, "Humbert of Silva Candida and the Political Concept of Ecclesia in the Eleventh Century Reform Movement," *Journal of Religious History* 2 (1962): 13–28; Yves Congar, "Ecclesia Romana," *Cristinanesimo nella storia* 5 (1984): 225–44; Horst Fuhrmann, "Ecclesia Romana—Ecclesia universalis," in *Rom im hohen Mittelalter: Studien zu den Romvorstellungen und zur Rompolitik vom 10. bis zum 12. Jahrhundert. Reinhard Elze zur Vollendung seines siebzigsten Lebensjahres,* ed. Bernhard Schimmelpfennig and Ludwig Schmugge (Sigmaringen: Thorbecke, 1992), 41–45; and Klaus Schatz, "The Gregorian Reform and the Beginning of a Universal Ecclesiology," *Jurist* 57 (1997): 123–36, particularly pp. 134–36. For the term *Ecclesia Romana* in John of Ragusa, see Madrigal Terrazas, *La eclesiología de Juan de Ragusa,* 311–17; in Johannes de Torquemada, see Karl Binder, *Wesen und Eigenschaften der Kirche bei Kardinal Juan de Torquemada O.P.* (Innsbruck: Tyrolia, 1955), 88–93; and in Henry Kalteisen, see Prügl, *Die Ekklesiologie Heinrich Kalteisens,* 195–202.

28. *De concordantia catholica* I, 17 (N. 68), p. 89f. John of Ragusa distinguished within the notion of *Ecclesia Romana* a material and a formal aspect. Considered under the material aspect *Romana Ecclesia* comprises the Pope as head of the cardinals, the diocese of Rome, the Western Patriarchate, and the laws the Pope promulgates according to his respective functions. The formal aspect includes within its purview all the faithful, the universal council,

1. *Ecclesia Romana* as the Apostolic See, which is identical with the Pope;

2. *Ecclesia Romana* that embraces the Pope as the Bishop of Rome and his diocese;

3. *Ecclesia Romana* meaning the Pope as an archbishop and metropolitan united to his Church province;

4. *Ecclesia Romana* as equivalent to the Pope as the patriarch of the Western Church and his western patriarchate;

5. and, last, *Ecclesia Romana* as all the faithful unified under their head, the Roman Church.

Two of the definitions in this list are of particular interest. In the first meaning, which is concerned only with the person of the Pope, Cusanus avoids using the term *Ecclesia Romana,* because, for him, the term "Church" demands both a shepherd and a flock who are unified in consent. The Roman Chair on its own does not fulfill this prerequisite. In the fifth meaning, where *Ecclesia Romana* is seen in all the faithful, Cusanus avoids defining the Pope as head of the Church. Instead the head, which in this meaning corresponds to the body of the universal Church, is not the Pope, but, surprisingly, the Roman Church.

The privilege of inerrancy is granted only to that reality of *Ecclesia Romana* specified in the fifth and last interpretation, where *Ecclesia Romana* is identified as the universal Church. For all the other degrees of realization of *Ecclesia Romana* this privilege is valid only in a lesser, limited way. The more *Ecclesia Romana* approaches the universal Church, the greater the intensity that Cusanus ascribes to its infallibility. Thus we are confronted with the rather odd phenomenon that we may call "comparative" or "graduated" infallibility.[29] This idea considers infallibility as a dynamic reality, linked to the reliability, authority, and representative realization of various forms of Church. However, is this not a contradiction of the con-

---

and its laws and decrees. John of Ragusa, *Tractatus de Ecclesia,* ed. Franjo Šanjek (Zagreb: Hrvatska Dominikanska Provincija, 1983), 17–19 (= lib. I, c. 2). Cf. Madrigal Terrazas, *La eclesiología,* 316f.; Sieben, "Ein Hauptstück," 168; and Werner Krämer, *Konsens und Rezeption. Verfassungsprinzipien der Kirche im Basler Konziliarismus* (Münster: Aschendorff, 1980), 379.

29. *De concordantia catholica* I, 17 (N. 68, 1), p. 89: "Sed istae veritates graduationes habent." The term "comparative infallibility" is Sigmund's (*Nicholas of Cusa,* 172) and Watanabe's (*The Political Ideas,* 93). At the beginning of Book II of *De concordantia catholica* (II, 4 [N. 79, 2], p. 106), Cusanus uses the word *infallibilis* again in the comparative. Here he

cept of infallibility in itself? Surely, either something is infallible or it is not. As "infallibility" and "fallibility" are contradictory terms, there can be neither a middle course nor a mediation: *tertium non datur.*

On the other hand, this model of "differentiated" or "comparative" infallibility, to which I know of no correlate, makes clear that Cusanus does not consider the concept of infallibility as a term of logic or epistemology. For him, infallibility indicates a degree of realization of the Church, in which there can be more or less perfection. Hence, this concept of infallibility fits in very well with the one we came across in the treatise against the Hussites, in which Cusanus insisted upon the reliability and, even more, upon the certainty of Church doctrine. Furthermore, such "graduated" infallibility provides a criterion of superiority, while at the same time, maintaining the certainty of salvation in any local or particular church.

The different realizations of *Ecclesia Romana* have their equivalents in corresponding councils. Before we turn to the universal council, which has the highest authority in the Church, let us consider the council of the Roman Patriarchate.[30] This council, which also represents the Roman Church, is the proper council of the Pope. Only by means of this council is the Pope able to decide on controversies of faith. Thus, according to Cusanus, every assertion of papal infallibility must be related to the council of the Roman Patriarchate. Its decisions have a very high degree of certainty: Cusanus says they are *tutissima* ("most secure"). They are valid, reliable, and thus infallible, or infallibly trustworthy, statements of the Church. The reason for the faithfulness of the Roman Church consists in its observation of the old canons and traditions. Neither a special divine gift nor the Pope, who can fall into heresy, vests the Church's decisions with infallibility, but a conservative and attentive attitude toward the old traditions does so.[31]

A higher degree of infallibility than the patriarchal council of the Pope

stresses the importance of consent for the quality of conciliar decisions: "quanto maior concordantia, de tanto infallibilius iudicium."

30. *De concordantia catholica* II, 7 (N. 92–95), pp. 121–26. Cusanus's idea of the patriarchal council influenced John of Ragusa. Cf. Hermann Josef Sieben, "Non solum papa definiebat nec solus ipse decretis et statutibus vigorem praestabat. Johannes von Ragusas Idee eines römischen Patriarchalkonzils," in *Studien zum 15. Jahrhundert*, 123–44; Santiago Madrigal, *La eclesiología*, 206–12.

lies only in the council of the universal Church. In Cusanus's words, its decisions are *infallibilius* ("more infallible") and *tutius* ("more secure"): this simply means that it has higher authority and is superior to the patriarchal council.[32] Although Cusanus's distinction between patriarchate and universal Church could be employed to sketch out the perspectives of Church communion even in terms of modern ecumenism, he shares the medieval conviction that the universal Church has been reduced to the borders of the Roman patriarchate. He regrets this development not only in view of the universal Church but also in view of the universal council because, as a result of this decline, the difference between patriarchate and universal council has de facto disappeared. In his eyes, this is a primary cause of the struggles between the Council of Basel and Pope Eugene IV, since "many"—Cusanus knows about the widespread support for the Pope—will recognize Basel not as a universal council but only as a council of the Western Patriarchate.[33]

Concilium Universale

Although the Pope is not the head of the universal council, he plays a prominent role in it. He, for example, summons and presides over it. However, as soon as the council of the universal Church legitimately is initiated, it has authority over the Pope. It can depose and punish him not only for heresy but also for other crimes.[34] This authority of the universal

---

31. *De concordantia catholica* II, 20 (N. 178, 23–27), p. 216f.: "ipsa Romana ecclesia canonicas et synodicas sanctorum patrum sanctiones inviolabiliter atque irrefragabiliter retinet. . . . Ecce ex hoc habes causam firmitatis apostolici Romani iudicii ex inviolabilium canonum irrefragabili observantia esse."

32. Ibid., (N. 95, 8–11), p. 126: "Iudicium fidei, quod per papam et hoc concilium fit, esse tutissimum inter omnia particularium congregationum iudicia, licet infallibilius sit et tutius iudicium universalis concilii totius ecclesie." Since the first days of conciliarism, the infallibility of the universal council was used as an argument for its superiority. See the examples of Konrad of Gelnhausen and Heinrich of Langenstein quoted by Sieben, "Ein Hauptstück," 152: "Die Superioritätsfrage ist ein Motiv, das die Entfaltung der Lehre von der Unfehlbarkeit der Konzilien mächtig vorantreibt."

33. *De concordantia catholica* I, 7 (N. 95, 14–16), p. 126: "Hodie autem, prohdolor, catholicae universalis ecclesiae et patriarchalis Romanae sedis unum est concilium, cum tota ecclesia redacta sit ad unum illum tantum patriarchatum." Cusanus repeats his quest at the end of *De concordantia* (II, 20, [N. 190, 4–8], p. 232): "Hodie autem, quia universalis ecclesie, heu, ad solum patriarchatum Romanum redacta est, et quod quondam generale patriarchale tantum et subiectum Romano pontifici fuit, hodie est universale universam fideli-

council depends to a large extent on its infallibility. With greater perspicacity than other conciliarists, Cusanus works out the interdependence of authority and infallibility. In his eyes, infallibility does not entail a special *habitus* ("disposition") of faith nor a divine assistance in certain situations. Rather it is part of the power of the keys. To be precise, it is the divine guarantee for the execution and reliability of the power of the keys. Both senses of authority—power of the keys and infallibility—are granted to the whole Church and not to a single person alone. The concept of the infallible power of the keys is Cusanus's response to the idea of papal plenitude of power. As an infallible power, it is given to the Church as a whole.[35]

But under what conditions is this authority of the Church to be activated? Cusanus specifies two conditions: consent and representation. Whenever the priesthood gathered in a universal council legislates with unanimity and consent, a law gains binding force. Indeed, "the higher the concordance the more infallible the judgement."[36] This means, however, that the consent of the Pope is also required, especially in controversies of faith. This special competence of the papal office is the reason why Cusanus concedes to the Pope the title he has found in the acts of the Fourth Ecumenical Council: *princeps in episcopatu fidei.*[37]

---

um ecclesiam repraesentans, hinc cum hoc novum sit, dubitatio orta est."

34. Ibid., II, 2; II, 18 (N. 161, 1–5), p. 197: "Quare concluditur universale concilium rite adunatum, licet graduationes inter se habere possit quo ad iudicia, est tamen semper maioris auctoritatis et minoris fallibilitatis quam papae tantum. Ex quo sequitur corollarie universale concilium etiam in alio quam haeresis casu deponere posse."

35. Ibid., II, 18 (N. 156, 4–10), p. 190f.: "Potestas ligandi et solvendi et infallibilitas et indeviabilitas propter Christi assistentiam usque in consummationem saeculi est in ipsa catholica vera ecclesia. Cum autem Romanus pontifex sit membrum illius ecclesiae, quae corpus Christi mysticum est, et infallibilitas non cuilibet membro, sed toti ecclesiae promissa est, tunc, non dubium, potestas indeviabilis ligandi et solvendi totius ecclesiae est supra potestatem Romani pontificis."

36. Cf. ibid., II, 4 (N. 78, 1–2), p. 105: "Verum quia dixi, quod, si ex concordantia procedit diffinitio, tunc ex sancto Spirito processisse creditur" and ibid. (N. 79, 1–2), p. 106: "Ecce concordantiam maxime in his quae fidei sunt, requiri, et quanto maior concordantia, de tanto infallibilius iudicium."

37. "A prince in the episcopacy of faith." Cf. *De concordantia catholica* II, 15 (N. 136, 4–7), p. 170: "Fateor de constitutionibus fidem tangentibus verum esse, quod, sedis apostolicae auctoritatis nisi interveniat, ratae non sunt, immo et ipsius pontificis Romani consensus intervenire debet, cum sit princeps in episcopatu fidei." Controversies about faith are the proper reason to convoke councils. Beside this primary task (ibid., II, 9) there are also other

Consensus must be achieved not only among the single persons gathered in a council but also between the respective "head" of a Church and its council. That means that a diocese is represented in the consent of bishop and diocesan council, and the universal Church is represented in the consent within the universal Church. Analogous to what we have seen in the concept of *Ecclesia Romana,* the representation of the Church in councils can reach varying degrees of intensity or perfection. The more participants a council gathers, the more complete its representation and the more closely it approximates the truth. Truth in this context means a full realization of the Church. Supposing that all the faithful are gathered in a council, this assembly would be a perfect representation of the Church, for Church and council would be completely identical. This idea of "representation by identity" as opposed to "representation by delegation" provides another argument to concede higher infallibility to the universal council than to the Pope. While the universal council by its members and widespread universal participation provides a representative accumulation of the Church, the Pope on his own is a far cry from representing the Church in this way. As a single person he emerges as only a faint—Cusanus calls it *confusissima* ("a very confused")—representation of the Church.[38]

---

matters *(extra materiam fidei)* of minor importance with which the council has to deal (ibid., II, 8). This centrality of theological concerns and faith in councils corresponds to the Pope's title as *princeps in episcopatu fidei,* which originally occurs in a letter of the emperors Valentinian and Marcian to Pope Leo I (*Acta Conciliorum Oecumenicorum* II/3, 17). Cusanus mentions it first in *De maioritate auctoritatis* ("Concerning the majority of authority"), no. 7 (text in *Acta Cusana,* no. 174). It was taken up again in *De concordantia catholica* I, 15 (N. 61, 17–19), p. 80. Other occurrences include: *Acta Cusana,* no. 481 (letter to Thomas Ebendorfer), p. 346 (cf. particularly footnote 46); *Acta Cusana* no. 599 (answer for the German king, 1444), p. 481f. (cf. particularly footnote 103). Henry Kalteisen also uses this title as a welcome affirmation of his monarchical concept of the papal office. Cf. Henry Kalteisen, *De ecclesia,* edited in Thomas Prügl, *Die Ekklesiologie Heinich Kalteisens,* 281, and his *Consilium,* in ibid., 336.

38. *De concordantia catholica,* II, 18 (N. 158, 1–5. 12–15. 16f), p. 194: "Sicut Petrus unice et confusissime figurat ecclesiam, qui deviabilis est, quod tunc inter petram et Petrum sunt plures graduationes repraesentationum et significationum, quousque in petra deveniatur a confusissima repraesentatione et figura usque in veritatem per media certa et veriora. . . . Quanto illa synodus minus confuse plus tendendo in veritatem repraesentat, tanto eius iudicium plus a fallibilitate versus infallibilitatem tendit et semper maius est iudicio unici Romani pontificis confusissime figurantis. . . . Quare papae iudicium minus stabile et magis fallibile praesumi quam ipsius et aliorum." The same idea is expressed more concisely in *De*

Inspiration

Our reading of Cusanus's idea of infallibility so far underscores that he understands it as an integral part of the power of the keys. Through the consent of the priesthood, the power that rests potentially in the Church is actualized. It is therefore up to the priests to determine the degree of reliability and even infallibility that they want to give to a decision. Compared to that idea of infallibility being inherent to the body of priests, it seems that the concept of infallibility is found wanting when it is understood as a result of divine assistance and inspiration in certain doctrinal actions. Cusanus, however, is well aware of that idea, too. He adopts the current views of Basel conciliarism, which in part relies on rather naive ideas of inspiration.[39] Cusanus himself is convinced that Christ is present in the midst of the gathered Fathers if the rules for the celebration of universal councils are faithfully observed and if conciliar decisions are reached by consent and concordance. This kind of decision making would be inspired by the Holy Spirit and may be considered infallible.[40]

---

auctoritate praesidendi, h XV, p. 28: "Licet papa representet totam ecclesiam, sicut concilium sacerdotium representat, tamen verior est ipsa representatio concilii quam pape, quia pape est remotissima, concilii proxima. Unde representatio concilii, cum plus appropinquet ad veritatem ecclesie et certiori modo representat eandem, tunc etiam prefertur confuse representationi papali in auctoritate et judicio." For the theories of representation in Cusanus, see Hasso Hofmann, *Repräsentation. Studien zur Wort- und Begriffsgeschichte von der Antike bis ins 19. Jahrhundert* (Berlin: Duncker and Humblot, 1974), 286–321. Hofmann observed quite correctly that Cusanus's idea of graduated representation *(graduationes repraesentationum),* which derives from Neoplatonic and Pseudo-Dionysian metaphysics, evades juridic and legal definition. Ibid., 310. See also Rudolf Haubst, "Wort und Leitidee der 'repraesentatio' bei Nikolaus von Kues," in *Der Begriff der repraesentatio im Mittelalter,* ed. Albert Zimmermann (Berlin, New York: de Gruyter, 1971), 139–62; Maurizio Merlo, *Vinculum Concordiae. Il problema di rappresentanza nel pensiero di Nicolò Cusano* (Milan: Angeli, 1997), particularly ch. 2: "Graduatio repraesentationum" and ch. 3: "Rappresentazione e consenso nella chiesa"; Claudia Lücking-Michel, *Konkordanz und Konsens. Zur Gesellschaftslehre in der Schrift "De concordantia catholica" des Nicolaus von Cues* (Würzburg: Echter, 1994), particularly 157–86.

39. In a homily for the feast of St. Thomas Aquinas delivered on March 7, 1435, Johannes de Torquemada sneered at the hysteria of inspiration at the Council of Basel: "Nemo nobis blandiens et in tantam securitatem concedere volens de hoc sacro concilio iuxta Ieremiam <7:4> dicat 'Templum Domini, Templum Domini est', Spiritus sanctus errare non potest! Fateor hoc, sed nos non sumus Spiritus sanctus." Thomas Prügl, "Die Predigten am Fest des hl. Thomas von Aquin auf dem Basler Konzil. Mit einer Edition des *Sermo de sancto Thoma* des Johannes de Turrecremata OP," *Archivum Fratrum Praedicatorum*

It would seem that the idea of conciliar inspiration in Nicholas Cusanus owes more to the conciliar enthusiasm among the Basel Fathers than to his own vision of the Church. We may have an example of this in chapter twenty of the second book of *De concordantia catholica,* in which Cusanus comments on some recent events in Constance and Basel. The council's success in the years 1433–1434, when Cusanus composes *De concordantia catholica,* is considered as a proof of the inspiration and the guidance of the Holy Spirit. Although during the first years Basel did not make any doctrinal decisions, Cusanus is convinced that from the beginning of the Council, every action has been inspired by the Holy Spirit.[41] In the same way that he develops the idea of infallibility in order to reject papalist claims, he refers to divine inspiration:

If the Holy Spirit said that it wished to inspire the Council at this time, how can Pope Eugene say that this is true only if he wishes it to be and not otherwise? As if the inspiration of the Holy Spirit were in the power of the Roman pontiff so that it would grant its inspiration only when the pope wished.[42]

At this point at least, Cusanus abandoned his scholarly sobriety in order to join in Basel's public polemics.

---

64 (1994): 145–99, here at 197.

40. Nicholas of Cusa, *De concordantia catholica,* II, 3 (N. 77, 1–6), p. 103: "Ecce nunc essentialia ad universale concilium, ubi universalia tractari debent, quod non secrete, sed publice omnibus liberrima detur audientia, et si tunc concordanti sententia aliquid fuerit diffinitum, per sanctum Spiritum censetur inspiratum et per Christum in medio congregatorum eius nomine praesidentem infallibiliter iudicatum." See also ibid., II, 9 (N. 101, 1–6), p. 136; II, 20 (N.182–184), p. 222–224; and II, 34 (N. 248: 8–11), p. 291: "Universale vero concilium dictans talem conclusionem consensu et legatione omnium fidelium necessario ex Christi assistentia et sancto Spiritu inspirante vere et infallibiliter dictat eandem." Also ibid., II, 20 (N. 172, lin. 3–5), p. 209f.: "Rectiores enim et indeviabiliores regulas nemo invenire poterit quam Spiritus sanctus, universalium conciliorum inspirator." See further *De auctoritate praesidendi,* ed. Kallen, p. 24: "scimus Spiritum sanctum dictare sententiam." Already in *De usu communionis* (p fol. 13ʳ) Cusanus wrote: "Commune sacerdotium capiens sui regiminis motum a sancto Spiritu, quoniam sanctissimum est, ex Christi legatione non obstante quod quidam peccatores sint in ministratione errare non potest."

41. *De concordantia catholica* II, 20 (N. 183, l. 4–5), p. 223: "Omnia acta a principio per inspirationem Spiritus sancti firmiter credamus."

42. Ibid., II, 20 (N. 184, lin. 12–17), p. 224: "Si Spiritus sanctus dixit se Basileae hoc tempore in universali concilio velle inspirare, dum ederentur decreta praetactorum conciliorum, quomodo potest papa Eugenius dicere hoc verum esse, si ipse velit, et non alias? Ac si inspiratio foret ipsius sancti Spiritus in potestate Romani pontificis, quod tunc, quando ipse velit, inspiret." The English translation is taken from Nicholas of Cusa, *The Catholic Concor-*

Anti-conciliarist Infallibility

In the *Dialogus,* the work in which Cusanus tries to justify his break with the Council of Basel, the *Discipulus* asks for the reason for the superiority that the Council claims over the Pope: "What reason of superiority do they give?" The Master replies: "Infallibility—because they say that the Church cannot err but the pope can."[43] By this answer Cusanus admits how fundamentally the idea of conciliarism relies upon infallibility. He has realized, and he acknowledges, that "infallibility" is the core term and the battle cry of the conciliarists. This may have been also the reason why he has abandoned the word and has changed his language about infallibility after his turnaround in Church politics and ecclesiology. He subsequently ignores the term but not its contents.

Let us consider to what extent Cusanus has changed his mind and specify the new coordinates of his concept of infallibility. Infallibility depends on the representation of the Church. Here is the *Grundprinzip* of Cusanus's ecclesiology, one that he has never changed. However, he abandons the idea of "representation by identification," returning instead to his original understanding of representation, which relies on consent.[44] According to the new premises of Cusanus's ecclesiology, the consent of the Pope becomes decisive for a valid representation of the Church in a universal council. Without the Pope's consent, its decisions would not be infallible. Even if this seems only a slight correction of his earlier convic-

---

dance, ed. and transl. Paul E. Sigmund (Cambridge: Cambridge University Press, 1991), 140. At the end of *De concordantia catholica* II, 20, Cusanus, however, sounds more gently disposed towards the Pope, admonishing the council: "Quare hoc sacrum concilium absque passione cum summa mansuetudine se habere debet in ordine ad Romanum pontificem: non se ex privilegio universalis concilii in tantum erigat, de quo potius [prohdolor] dolendum esset, quod obliviscatur subiectionem patriarchalem, in qua semper fuit, secundum quam in papam fidelem nihil posset." Ibid., (N. 190, lin. 8–13), p. 232.

43. *Dialogus* N. 18, ed. Meuthen, p. 95: "Discipulus: Quam rationem assignant superioritatis? Magister: Infallibilitatis, quoniam aiunt ecclesiam deviare non posse, sed bene papam, concilium autem representare ecclesiam. Et quia necesse est, quod sit eadem potestas in representante et in representato, ideo infallibilitas est in concilio." For Cusanus's opinions after 1437, see also Arnulf Vagedes, *Das Konzil über dem Papst? Die Stellungnahme des Nikolaus von Kues und des Panormitanus zum Streit zwischen dem Konzil von Basel und Eugen IV.* (Paderborn: Schöningh, 1981), 116–28.

44. Continuing the Master's answer, the *Discipulus* in the *Dialogus* (ibid., N. 18) ob-

tions, in fact it amounts to the rejection of conciliar superiority. As a council that lacks the Pope's consent is no longer infallible, it cannot claim superiority over the Pope.

Neither the Pope nor the members of a universal council are infallible as long as they are considered single, private persons.[45] The possibility of a heretic Pope has never been denied by Cusanus, but now he is more aware of the fact that councils too have erred in faith. According to his new opinion, it is even more likely that a council should fall into error than a Pope. In this affirmation, which he attempts to confirm using examples from history, Cusanus abandons a key argument of his former concept of infallibility, namely, the principle of majority.[46] On the other hand, this revision means that the Pope is the appropriate entity to make new decisions on the faith and to explain it, a prerogative that Cusanus minimizes in De concordantia catholica.[47]

In his anti-conciliar writings, Cusanus makes the object of infallibility more precise. Only those doctrines and decisions are infallible that neces-

serves: "non recte intelligunt repraesentationem." The main intention of the Dialogus is just to demonstrate that the conciliarists at Basel have lost the true representation of the Church. As long as there is no true representation any more, neither is there a true council.

45. Dialogus, N. 25, lin. 5–8, ed. Meuthen, p. 104.

46. Ibid., N. 28, p. 105: "Discipulus: Satis ex hiis intelligo argumentum infallibilitatis nichil facere. Nam etsi magnus numerus episcoporum presumatur minus errasse, tamen compertum est in Arimino contrarium. Nichil igitur infallibilitas dicit numerositas, ut propter infallibilitatem prima sedes subici debeat." The same idea is found in the letter to a Carthusian monastery: "Ubi Romano pontifici aliqua pars adheret, eciam si multo maior pars ab ipso recederet, illa pars pontifici unita ecclesiam facit et sic per consequens concilium." The whole passage within this text is important: "Septima questio: Quid, si in concilio pauci pape adherent et multi contra?" Cf. Acta Cusana, no. 468, p. 310f. The argument concerning erring councils also occurs in Cusanus's speech at the diet in Nürnberg 1438. Cf. Acta Cusana, no. 375, pp. 244–47. Compare these texts with Cusanus's earlier statements about erring councils, e.g., in De concordantia catholica II, 15 (N. 136, lin. 8–15), p. 170f., and ibid., II, 5, in which he discusses Ephesus and Rimini at length.

47. In De concordantia catholica the Pope alone is the least significant court to declare matters of faith because he represents the Church only in a faint manner. His letters to universal councils are not considered as authoritative doctrine but as material to be examined: "Similiter invenitur epistolas et scripturas Romanorum pontificum ad concilium missas universale concilium examinasse" (De concordantia catholica II, 20 [N. 176, lin. 1–2], p. 216). In contrast to this earlier conviction, Cusanus emphasizes the Pope's importance for the magisterium in the letter to Thomas Ebendorfer: "Dico quod hucusque doctores tam theologi quam iuriste tenuerunt in declaratione novi articuli sententiam Romani pontificis, qui dicitur princeps in episcopatu fidei, necessariam. . . . Idem dicitur quo ad diffinicionem fidei; et

sarily are required for salvation *(ea quae ad necessitatem salutis pertinent)*. Not everything a Pope or a council defines comes under that classification. Cusanus also refrains from discussing the whole range of *potestas ecclesiastica* in terms of infallibility.[48]

The concepts of *Ecclesia Romana* and *cathedra* that Cusanus has previously considered as realizations or representations of the universal Church receive again their primarily papal interpretation. Cusanus uses them as synonyms (or at least near synonyms) of *Sedes Apostolica*. Increasingly, the "Apostolic See" itself, which consists of the Pope and the college of the cardinals, is understood to enjoy infallibility.[49] The a priori claim of being infallible *(argumentum infallibilitatis)* is no longer valid for councils. Indeed, the conciliarists' proudest trump card works in favor of the Pope rather *(potius)* than the council.[50] Nonetheless Cusanus remains skeptical with regard to papal infallibility. The rejection of conciliar infallibility does not necessarily lead to papal infallibility. Cusanus purports only a tendency, a possibility, and an assumption that the Pope might be infallible. In other words, his assertions are cautious. Compared to the council, the Pope's determinations are deemed *more likely* to be infallible. Nonetheless, infallibility not only has shifted from a conciliar to a papal prerogative but serves to criticize shortcomings of conciliar theory.

To what extent has Cusanus really changed his ecclesiology? He has not abandoned his leitmotifs of consent and representation, but he rearranges and accentuates them to another end. The result is negative. There is no infallibility without the Roman Pontiff. Beside this general adjustment of his theory, he takes up new arguments from the papalist party, accepting, for example, the conclusions drawn from the enumeration of heretical councils: councils have erred more frequently than Popes.[51] In his ecclesiological writings after 1437, Cusanus is generally less optimistic

reperitur, quod in omni dubio fidei apostolica sedes prior diffinivit et postea hanc diffinitionem ad concilium misit cum potestate se exponendi, si fides illa immutaretur." *Acta Cusana,* no. 468, lin. 107–112, p. 346.

48. *Dialogus* N. 26, p. 104.; ibid., N. 28, lin. 20f, p. 106.

49. Ibid., N. 29, lin. 2, p. 106; ibid., lin. 19f., p. 107; *Acta Cusana,* no. 408, p. 272; *Acta Cusana,* no. 468, lin. 122–124, p. 312: "Constat Romanum pontificem cum multis adherentibus sibi, maxime cardinalibus secum apostolicam sedem facientibus, cui a Christo veritas propinquius alligata est."

50. *Dialogus* N. 29, p. 106: "Ista clarissime ostendunt argumentum infallibilitatis potius concludere pro Romano pontifice et Romana ecclesia quam pro aliis membris ecclesie aut

about infallibility. As long as there is no need and as long as there is no danger for the faithful, neither Pope nor council should proceed to dogmatic decisions. If only the Pope alone is opposed to deciding a pending question of faith, the Church rather should abstain from pushing for that definition. On the other hand, Cusanus sees no danger in a dogmatic decision that the Pope alone, without or even against the Church's consent, intends to proclaim because in this case the Church will not accept his doctrine. Cusanus remains skeptical about papal infallibility until the end of his life.

Summary

It is no surprise to see that after the break with the Council of Basel Cusanus has changed and modified his ideas about infallibility. It is, however, more astonishing to realize that his concept of infallibility has a broad range of meanings. Let us sum up four of them.

1. The most important meaning of infallibility in Cusanus stems from a soteriological context. He considers the certainty of salvation through the lens of the authority of the Church. This idea of infallibility depends on a sacramental model, especially upon the notion of *ex opere operato* ("the objective character of the sacrament"). Just as grace is conferred by the sacraments, an equally reliable and infallible salvation is guaranteed if the faithful observe the orders of the Church.[52]

2. Cusanus considers infallibility, by extension, as a quality of the pow-

concilii ac quod ipsa Petri sedes etiam propter demeritum presidentis numquam conculcari deberet."

51. The "Latrocinium" of Ephesus is mentioned in Dialogus N. 10, p. 83.

52. This idea is also perfectly expressed in Pierre de Versaille's *Cedula "Ad probandam"*: In this view the Church is predominantly established and structured by the sacraments, "que sunt signa uisibilia, cum quibus habet pactum infallibile, quoad eorum positionem in esse certam infundit gratiam"; edited in Thomas Prügl, "Antiquis iuribus et dictis sanctorum conformare. Zur antikonziliaristischen Interpretation von Haec sancta auf dem Basler Konzil," *Annuarium Historiae Conciliorum* 31 (1999): 72–143, here at p. 128, lin. 18–20. Sieben ("Ein Hauptstück," 175) saw Henry Kalteisen's deliberations about the infallible council as an application of sacramental theology. Cusanus quotes Kalteisen's speech against the Hussites from 1433 in his *Dialogus* N. 24, p. 102f.; also N. 31, p. 108f. See particularly Meuthen's references in the apparatus. In *Dialogus* N. 26, p. 104, Cusanus, citing Kalteisen, pointed out that even unholy church leaders cannot diminish or damage the

er of the keys. This power is infallible because it is authorized and warranted by God and therefore has the highest degree of reliability. As in the first case, we can discern in this concept of infallibility an analogy between sacramentality and Church authority.

3. Within this general notion of infallibility as part of church authority, the Roman Church (*Ecclesia Romana* in all its realizations) and the universal council share the privilege of inerrancy. That privilege, however, presupposes broad consent within the Church, especially the consent among the members of a council and the consent between council and Pope. The ambiguity of the concept of infallibility, which fluctuates between reliability and inerrancy, enables Cusanus to develop the idea of "graduated" or "comparative infallibility," one that depends on respective degrees of representation and realization of the Church.

4. In terms of the biblical foundation of the concept of infallibility, Cusanus relies on several scriptural texts. The most important are Matthew 16 and 18, in which Jesus confers the power of the keys to Peter and the apostles. However, Cusanus combines the biblical data with other models of argument, such as the theory of inspiration. This theory is based on the exegesis of Matthew 18:20: "Where two or three are gathered in my name, I am in the midst of them." While this biblical text is one of the most important authorities to underscore conciliar infallibility, after 1437 Cusanus pays more attention to another word of the Lord, namely, Luke 22:32, in which the Lord prays for the faith of St. Peter. This scriptural text, which has contributed heavily to the development of the dogma of papal infallibility, gains important influence especially in the Dominican tradition following Thomas Aquinas. In *De concordantia catholica* Nicholas mentions its pro-papal exegesis only as an opinion of Albert the Great; in his later writings, however, he is more eager to acknowledge its importance.[53]

Church's infallible power because it is a *gratia gratis data* given also to them. For Kalteisen's ideas of the infallibility of the universal council, expressed especially in his *Oratio de praedicatione verbi Dei*, see Prügl, *Die Ekklesiologie Heinrich Kalteisens,* 76–80, and Sieben, "Ein Hauptstück," 173–75.

53. In his answer to Thomas Ebendorfer, Nicholas finds in the prayer of the Lord for St. Peter the guarantee that, personal error notwithstanding, no Pope could ever dogmatize a heresy: *Acta Cusana* no. 481, lin. 113f., p. 346. See also *Acta Cusana*, no. 408, lin. 58, p. 271. His earlier opinion is expressed in *De concordantia catholica* I, 14: "Nam licet Christus rogaverit, ut non deficeret fides Petri, qui pro sua reverentia exauditus est, et licet hoc

The experience in Basel leaves Cusanus skeptical about infallibility. The definition of papal infallibility at the First Vatican Council does not meet the principles of Cusanus's concept of infallibility because it neglects the importance of consent and reception of the Church within the process of dogmatization. Perhaps in 1870 Nicholas would have reminded the Vatican Fathers of the words of his colleague Henry Kalteisen, a Dominican, who, being himself influenced by Cusanus, replied to the Basel fathers: *"Quod papa cum ecclesia statuit, hec est infallibile."*[54]

---

exponatur de fide ecclesiae, tamen etiam per aliquos, puta Albertum Magnum super eodem passu, de fide Petri et eius successoribus intelligitur, quia in eis finaliter non deficiet. Per alios autem, ut Gorra exponit, intelligitur de fide Romanae ecclesiae." In *De auctoritate praesidendi*, ed. Kallen, p. 14, Cusanus declares that Christ has prayed not only for the apostles, but for all the faithful. For Albertus Magnus's opinion on the papal primacy, see Ulrich Horst, "Albertus Magnus und Thomas von Aquin zu Matthäus 16, 18 f. Ein Beitrag zur Lehre vom päpstlichen Primat," in *Albertus Magnus: Zum Gedenken nach 800 Jahren: Neue Zugänge, Aspekte und Perspektiven,* ed. Walter Senner (Berlin: Akademie, 2001), 553–71. The ecclesiological impact of Luke 22:32 is explored in Brian Tierney, "A Scriptural Text in the Decretals and in St. Thomas: Canonistic Exegesis of Luke 22:32," *Studia Gratiana* 20 (1976): 361–78.

54. "That is infallible, what the Pope decides together with the Church." Henry Kalteisen, *Consilium de auctoritate pape et concilii generalis,* ed. in Prügl, *Die Ekklesiologie,* 368.

Cary J. Nederman

IO. EMPIRE MEETS NATION

Imperial Authority and National Government in
Renaissance Political Thought[1]

The study of Renaissance political thought by both historians
and political philosophers in recent decades has concentrated
disproportionately upon civic republicanism—to the point, indeed, that
one might well be surprised to discover that thinkers of the *quattrocento*
knew of, let alone embraced, any other political doctrine.[2] Yet in truth—
and *pace* a long line of scholars including, most recently, the contributors
to the volume *Republicanism: A Shared European Heritage*[3]—civic republicanism was, practically speaking, a historical dead end. The way forward
in shaping the political landscape of modernity lay instead with the territorial nation-state, organized usually around monarchic power and legal-

1. Versions of this paper were presented to the Australia and New Zealand Medieval
and Early Modern Studies Association 2003 conference in Melbourne, Victoria, and to the
Renaissance Society of America 2003 conference in Toronto. I appreciate and have endeav-
oured to integrate into the text the many suggestions and critical comments that the paper
attracted in these two venues. My special thanks to John Headley for stimulating the composition of the paper by organizing a session on empire for the Renassiance Society of
America and inviting me to participate.

2. James Muldoon, *Empire and Order: The Concept of Empire, 800–1800* (New York: St.
Martin's, 1999), 108–10.

3. Republicanism has been a dominant theme among historians of European political
thought of the last generation. It was central to two of the most influential of these, John
Pocock and Quentin Skinner, whose *The Machivellian Moment* and *Foundations of Modern Political Thought*, respectively, placed civic republicanism and attendant concepts at the center
of Western political thinking. This tendency crystallizes in the lately published *Republicanism: A Shared European Heritage,* ed. Martin van Gelderen and Quentin Skinner, 2 vols.
(Cambridge: Cambridge University Press, 2002). It should be noted, however, that some
countervailing tendencies are also evident in recent scholarship, for example, Maurizio Vi-
roli, *From Politics to Reason of State: The Acquisition and Transformation of the Language of Politics 1250–1600* (Cambridge: Cambridge University Press, 1992) and *Renaissance Civic Humanism,* ed. James M. Hankins (Cambridge: Cambridge University Press, 2000).

bureaucratic authority—qualities far removed from republican values. Thus, the civic republican tradition had relatively little to contribute to the theorization of the nation-state during the fifteenth and later centuries, its urban-centered citizen-patriot embodying an ethos quite distinct from the population of subjects inhabiting the geographically extensive nation-state.[4] When authors used the language of civic republicanism in the context of territorial nations, such as in the case of James Harrington's *Oceania* (1656), the result was a fundamental transformation in the populist and publicly vital characteristics that energized the civic republicans of the Renaissance.[5]

In asserting the historical limitations associated with civic republicanism, however, I do not wish to imply that thinkers with deep connections to Renaissance humanism made no contribution to the exploration and explanation of the parameters of national political life.[6] For alongside the republicanism of some humanists, we find others who directly confronted the nation as a viable and vigorous unit of community. Ironically, perhaps, a number of the humanists associated with this position fell into a camp that we might term "imperial humanism," inasmuch as they sub-

4. Hence, there has been something of a backlash against the interpretation of the so-called Atlantic Republican system by Gordon Wood and John Pocock and its diffusion in North America. For one outstanding example, see Paul Rahe, *Republics Ancient and Modern: Classical Republicanism and the American Revolution* (Chapel Hill: University of North Carolina Press, 1992).

5. James Harrington, *The Commonwealth of Oceana; and a System of Politics*, J. G. A. Pocock, ed. (Cambridge: Cambridge University Press, 1992). See Jonathan Scott, "The Rapture of Motion: James Harrington's Republicanism," in *Political Discourse in Early Modern Britain*, ed. Nicholas Phillipson and Quentin Skinner (Cambridge: Cambridge University Press, 1993), and Gary Remer, "James Harrington's New Deliberative Rhetoric: Reflection of an Anticlassical Republican," *History of Political Thought* 14 (1995): 532–57.

6. Historians of a certain stripe are likely to join John Headley in recoiling at my use of "nation-state" as a kind of equivalent for "territorial state" or the like on the grounds that "it is misleading to talk of the nation state and nationalism prior to 1789" (private correspondence). It is not possible for me to defend in the present context my equation of "territorial state" with "national state" during the late medieval period. Instead, I commend the skeptical reader to several works of scholarship that set out to refute a wholly modern origin for the nation state, including Adrian Hastings, *The Construction of Nationhood: Ethnicity, Religion, and Nationalism* (Cambridge: Cambridge University Press, 1997); Antony Black, *Political Thought in Europe 1250–1450* (Cambridge: Cambridge University Press, 1992), 108–11; and Bernard Guenée, *States and Rulers in Later Medieval Europe*, trans. Juliet Vale (Oxford: Blackwell, 1985), 49–65.

scribed to a belief in the natural and spiritual unity of the human race (or at any rate its Christian segment). While such universalism might seem prima facie unfertile ground for fruitful reflection on the nation, some imperial humanists—faced with the undeniable reality of autonomous national states—were induced to examine how such nations might legitimately exist without undermining the unity of the universal community under a single empire and emperor. In the present paper, I shall consider two such imperial humanist accounts of national identity and autonomy, those proposed by Nicholas of Cusa in *De concordantia catholica* (1433–1434) and Aeneas Sylvius Piccolomini in *De ortu et auctoritate imperii Romani* ("On the Origin and Authority of the Roman Empire," 1446).

In one sense, Nicholas and Aeneas represent distinct imperial humanist strategies for analyzing and explaining national political order: the former adopts an explanation of national government founded on public consent, the latter on imperial authorization. Yet at a more fundamental level, Cusanus and Piccolomini share a common core principle: the nation as a form of *political* organization is based on will and rooted in convention, rather than deriving from any natural or spiritual source. Unlike the *Respublica Christiana* or the universal human race, both of which lend a justification to imperial regimes that requires no further human action, nations are artificial and impermanent creations that depend for their existence entirely upon the determination of human beings. This also distinguishes the imperial humanist conception of national community from the ideas of previous medieval authors who had adopted some version of the Aristotelian explanation of *natio* on the basis of natural linguistic, environmental, and/or ethnological diversity within the human species.[7] In articulating such voluntary/conventional origins of national government, then, Nicholas and Aeneas identify an important precondition necessary for the more general trend in later centuries away from accounts of political order derived directly from either Christian or naturalistic precepts in favor of human authority itself as the sole legitimate fount for the exercise of political power.

---

7. See Black, *Political Thought in Europe*, 111–13.

Nicholas of Cusa

To implicate Nicholas of Cusa in the formulation of the doctrine of the national state might seem a bit far-fetched. After all, scholars have generally associated Nicholas with a commitment to a version of universalism that would leave little room for independent political units. Paul Sigmund has remarked that "the yearning for a universal empire and universal church, and the hopes for the universal agreement among men which characterized *De Concordantia Catholica,* remained with Nicholas until his death."[8] Likewise, Morimichi Watanabe discerns Nicholas's "failure to recognize the emergence of the nation-state, which had been gradually gaining ground in Europe."[9] Jeannine Quillet finds in Nicholas "a basis and sanction for the progressive development of a 'universal commonwealth' as the utopian conclusion of an ecumenism whose theoretical foundations he propounded with a boldness that goes well beyond Dante's anticipatory ideas."[10] And Bernard Guenée implicates Nicholas in a renewal of "the old idea of universal Empire" from which "confusion was created which was ultimately responsible for the persistence of the German dream of universal hegemony."[11] Yet Nicholas, as we shall see, proves to be far more restrained and nuanced in his attitude toward imperial universalism and far more congenial toward nationalism than these comments suggest, precisely as a result of the founding principles that he enunciates to explain political rule.

On the face of it, there seems to be little that distinguishes Nicholas's political doctrines from preceding advocates of universal empire such as Dante.[12] In *De concordantia catholica,* Cusanus emphasizes the rational foundations of the earthly social and political community. Insisting that rational faculties distinguish human beings from animals, he asserts that

8. Paul Sigmund, *Nicholas of Cusa and Medieval Political Thought* (Cambridge, Mass.: Harvard University Press, 1963), 292.

9. Morimichi Watanabe, *The Political Ideas of Nicholas of Cusa with Special Reference to De Concordantia Catholica* (Geneva: Droz, 1963).

10. Jeannine Quillet, "Community I: Community, Counsel, and Representation," in *The Cambridge History of Medieval Political Thought c. 350–c. 1450,* ed. J. H. Burns (Cambridge: Cambridge University Press, 1988), 544–45.

11. Guenée, *States and Rulers in Later Medieval Europe,* 17.

12. Cf. Dante Alghieri, *Monarchy,* trans. and ed. Prue Shaw (Cambridge: Cambridge University Press, 1996).

"the exercise of their reason" led men to form associations, adopt laws, and appoint rulers.[13] Human reason, Nicholas maintains, provides access to the precepts of natural law that guide all valid political institutions and powers. But reason is not equally distributed among human beings. Cusanus remarks that some people are "better endowed with reason," so that these "wiser and more outstanding men are chosen as rulers by the others to draw up just laws by the clear reason, wisdom and prudence given to them by nature and to rule the others by these laws."[14] Consequently, Nicholas posits a strict distinction between the wise few and the foolish multitude, which dictates that the latter can play no direct role in their own rule. He says, "Almighty God has assigned a certain natural servitude to the ignorant and stupid so that they readily trust the wise to help them preserve themselves."[15] Reason dictates the dominance of the few over the many, and thus the rule of a small governing elite over the subjected masses.

If reason justifies government in general, then specifically imperial government derives from its superior, spiritual calling. Cusanus constructs a hierarchy of regimes stretching from the king of the Tartars—who "is the least worthy because he governs through laws least in agreement with those divinely instituted"—through Islamic governance to Christian monarchs. On top of the pyramid, "according to the standard of holiness of rule, I maintain that the authority of the empire is the greatest."[16] He reasons that the chief purposes of all rulers, and especially of Christian kings, are the maintenance of religion and the promotion of eternal ends; all other goals of government are "subservient." Thus, "our Christian empire outranks the others, just as our most holy and pure Christian religion is highest in holiness and truth. And just as every kingdom and prince should care for his kingdom, so the emperor should care for the whole Christian people."[17] Other Christian princes are therefore beneath the Roman emperor and must submit to him in matters concerning the protection of Christ's Church.[18] Given Nicholas's polemical intention to lend

---

13. I follow Paul Sigmund's excellent translation of *De concordantia catholica*: Nicholas of Cusa, *The Catholic Concordance*, trans. and ed. Paul Sigmund (Cambridge: Cambridge University Press, 1991), sec. 269.

14. Ibid., sec. 127.   15. Ibid., sec. 271.
16. Ibid., sec. 348.   17. Ibid., sec. 349.
18. Ibid., secs. 349–52.

support to the efforts of the Emperor Sigismund to intervene in the Council of Basel, he could hardly have adopted any other position.[19] It is the emperor, in his view, to whom the duty pertains to enforce conciliar decrees. Hence, imperial authority must extend to all Christian believers: "Because he is guardian of the universal faith and the protector of universal statutes [canons] which could not be effectively executed without a ruler over all, and since the universal statutes respecting the Christian faithful bind all faithful Christians to maintain and apply them, all are subject to the emperor's rule insofar as he is established to maintain those directives."[20] Such a universal jurisdiction stems from the fact that "the whole Christian people" transferred power to him to act as enforcer of canon law and "guardian of the faith."[21] In these matters, little room would appear to be afforded for national governments to exist as anything other than local agents of the emperor.

Yet Cusanus is careful to stipulate that the honor due to the Empire, and hence its universalistic character, pertain only to its status and functions in the spiritual realm. Previously in *De concordantia catholica,* he had acknowledged that political rule also naturally and necessarily involves nonreligious functions that properly pertain to Christian and non-Christian regimes alike.[22] Natural reason and the survival of the incompetent multitude demand the existence of political order and communal law. In performing these duties, it seems, the emperor's authority does not derive from God and the Christian people. How, then, does any particular regime emerge to provide these services? He claims that all people—even the most ignorant—are held to assent to the terms of their governance, both originally and on a continuing basis. According to Nicholas, the "enslavement" of the ignorant to the wise does not undercut the voluntary character of political arrangements. It may be true that "those better endowed with reason are the natural lords and masters of the others but not by any coercive law or judgment imposed on someone against his will." This is because human beings possess a natural equality in their power and freedom.

Since all are by nature free, every governance . . . by which subjects are compelled to abstain from evil deeds and their freedom directed towards the good through

19. See ibid., secs. 380–424.
20. Ibid., sec. 355.
21. Ibid., secs. 353, 352,
22. Ibid., secs. 268–69.

fear of punishment can only come from the agreement and consent of the subjects. For if men are equal in power and equally free, the true properly ordered authority of one common ruler who is their equal in power cannot be naturally established except by the election and consent of the others, and law is also established by consent.[23]

This famous passage has elicited much comment from scholars who find themselves drawn to its apparently modern overtones. Brian Tierney has referred to Cusanus's "almost Rousseau-ish faith in the righteousness of the community,"[24] while Antony Black declares that "the idea of a shared human nature and reason *is* used to give an apparently democratic view" that bears "striking similiarity to John Locke."[25] Likewise, for James Blythe, "Nicholas is one of the first to combine what is in all respects a mixed constitution with the social contract and the doctrine of the separation of powers."[26] Such observations certainly overstate the volitional basis of political community, which Nicholas does not deem to be participatory in character.[27] The consent of the masses has the wholly formal character of silent submission and deference. Insofar as the wise enjoy privileged access to the reason by which all are governed, there is no cause for public deliberation on the part of the multitude. The wise remain instead the natural trustees of the common good: "The rule of the wise and the subjection of the ignorant are harmonized through common laws that have the wise as their special authors, protectors, and executors, and the concurrent agreement of all the others in voluntary subjection."[28] Law and rulership rest upon the rational foundation of natural law that the wise few are particularly qualified to discover and uphold.

What the principle of consent does contribute, however, is a powerful justification for national variations in political rule. Because political order and law depend upon human volition, at least in their temporal applications, valid systems of government must always be traced to public con-

---

23. Ibid., sec. 127.

24. Brian Tierney, *Religion, Law, and the Growth of Constitutional Thought 1150–1650* (Cambridge: Cambridge University Press, 1982), 67.

25. Black, *Political Thought in Europe*, 182.

26. James M. Blythe, *Ideal Government and the Mixed Constitution in the Middle Ages* (Princeton: Princeton University Press, 1992), 257.

27. See Cary J. Nederman, "Rhetoric, Reason, and Republic: Republicanisms—Ancient, Medieval, and Modern," in *Renaissance Civic Humanism*, 261–62.

28. Nicholas of Cusa, *The Catholic Concordance*, sec. 275.

sent apart from spiritual authorization. This also implies that political arrangements are historically mutable and capable of reorganization over time. Consent, then, becomes the touchstone of national diversity in political rule. The emperor's "power to command," Cusanus asserts, "does not extend beyond the territorial limits of the empire under him," citing a decree of the Carolingian Emperor Louis, who, although he "describes himself as emperor, . . . issues commands only to the inhabitants of the kingdom of France and the Lombards who were his *de facto* subjects."[29] Even the claim made on behalf of the Roman emperor "to be lord of the world as ruler of the empire that the Romans once conquered by their valor" must be tempered by the fact that Rome never extended its conquests to the larger part of Asia and Africa that, if not heavily populated (to Nicholas's knowledge), are of great geographic expanse.[30] The only reasonable conclusion is that the phrase "lord of all the world" must be interpreted narrowly and figuratively in its application to the emperor: "If rulership is only rightly possessed through the elective agreement of the subjects as argued above, then he is only lord over those who are actually subject to him and we should conclude that the emperor is lord of that part of the world over which he exercises effective authority."[31] Cusanus never questions the legitimacy of the political rights enjoyed by the many kingdoms of the world beyond the boundaries of the Western Empire, nor does he insist upon a global reach (even potentially) for the temporal authority of the emperor. This is implied, for example, in his explanation of the emperor's right to arrange the seating of other temporal princes in attendance at a general council: "The ranking of the secular participants depends on the emperor, since everyone, including those not otherwise subject to him, is under him in the council because of his role as protector of the council. Therefore he has jurisdiction over all of them."[32] But that jurisdiction stems purely from the sacral dimension of the imperial majesty. The emperor's duty as protector of the catholic faith has no corollary in a secular responsibility for all the peoples of the earth, because the latter requires public consent that has not been given, whereas the permission of the body of Christian believers authorizes the former.

Consequently, Cusanus clearly believes that the scope of the imperial

---

29. Ibid., sec. 343.
31. Ibid., sec. 347.
30. Ibid., secs. 343–46.
32. Ibid., sec. 406.

jurisdiction in Europe possesses a purely political (that is, historical and conventional) character. In a series of chapters tracing the decay of the Empire since the time of Emperor Otto I, *De concordantia catholica* demonstrates how the extent of the emperor's authority has both grown and shrunk according to the provinces that have placed themselves under its guardianship. Initially, the domains under Otto I's command included "the kingdom of Italy and the Lombards, the kingdom of Burgundy" as well as "the kingdom of the Germans of which his father, Henry, is supposed to have been the first king."[33] Gradually, other peoples—Cusanus names the Hungarians, Bohemians, Danes, Norwegians, Poles, and Prussians—placed themselves under the Empire on account of its unparalleled ability to make effective its laws and uphold communal peace and order.[34] Their rulers, in Cusanus's account, became imperial functionaries: "It was also decreed at that time that princes, dukes, and counts should be appointed to public office at the command of the emperor and should be removable at his will with an obligation to give an account of their ministry to the public treasury."[35] He describes virtually a "golden age" of imperial majesty and honor in which "everything tended to the public good."[36] In more recent times, by contrast, the Empire is in a state of decline and decay. Not only have those nations that once submitted to the emperor and his laws withdrawn their consent because peace is not maintained, but even the imperial princes within Germany have asserted their autonomy and claimed rights formerly reserved for the emperor.[37] Nicholas laments,

A mortal disease has invaded the German empire and unless an antidote is found at once, death will surely follow. You seek the empire in Germany and you will not find it. As a result others will take our place and we will be divided and subjected to another nation.[38]

Hence, he calls for immediate reform of the Empire to promote its recovery. Yet such a restored empire would be by no means a universal (or even trans-European) one: it encompasses only Italy, Lombardy, Burgundy, and the whole of Germany—that is, the original extent of Otto I's jurisdiction[39]—of which Nicholas had earlier said "our empire is composed" and

33. Ibid., sec. 483.
35. Ibid., sec. 491.
37. Ibid., sec. 496–504.
39. Ibid., sec. 508.

34. Ibid., secs. 485–87.
36. Ibid., sec. 495.
38. Ibid., sec. 507.

which "have maintained fidelity and loyalty to it."[40] Such reform is a far cry from the universalism that is sometimes ascribed to Cusanus. And indeed, the closing chapters of *De concordantia catholica* read like nothing so much as a blueprint for the building of a federated nation, with proposals for national and regional assemblies (complete with a sophisticated balloting system), a customs union, fiscal administration and tax-gathering, and a paid national army.

Thus, the exalted aspirations of revivifying the territories of the original Roman Empire and of restoring the emperor to the status of the "lord of all the world" are nowhere on display in *De concordantia catholica*. Nicholas recognizes that the foundation of popular consent to earthly government means that even if such a far-flung empire did once legitimately exist, its validity has been eroded by later patterns of communal choice. While he may value universality as a quality necessary for the sake of the Church, he recognizes that the shifting and wholly conventional nature of political volition means that such a global system of temporal government cannot be justified as the permanently "best" or "ideal." Cusanus's emphasis on the "historicity" of secular political life, and hence of the inescapable diversity of systems of rule, may indeed be viewed as a recurring theme in his social thought. As I have discussed elsewhere, Cusanus's appeal to the historical character of nationality in *De pace fidei,* written twenty years after *De concordantia catholica,* constitutes one of the central pillars upholding his conception of religious toleration.[41] In the later work, Nicholas in fact praises the peaceful expression of national pride through different forms of religious rites (non-Christian as well as Christian) typical of each nation without denying the truth of a single set of universal religious principles. Thus, Cusanus throughout his career had confronted and explained the nation-state in terms far more realistic and coherent than those for which he is generally credited. As in all forms of government, national jurisdictions arise from acts of public will: they have a valid claim on obedience inasmuch as those subjects who submit to them have given their prior assent.

40. Ibid., sec. 484.

41. Cary J. Nederman, *Worlds of Difference: European Discourses of Toleration, c. 1100–c. 1550* (University Park: Pennsylvania State University Press, 2000), 89–95.

Aeneas Sylvius Piccolomini

Although he was an almost exact contemporary and, at times, a close political ally of Cusanus, Aeneas Sylvius Piccolomini adopted a strategy quite different from Nicholas's to the negotiation of the relationship between universal empire and the organization of political life along national lines. Specifically, Piccolomini's approach to imperial authority, expressed most succinctly in his *De ortu et auctoritate imperii Romani,* appears more traditional in its arguments and deployment of sources than Cusanus's. Indeed, given Piccolomini's outstanding humanist credentials—he eventually ascended to the papacy as the famed "humanist pope" and enjoyed a reputation for his writing similar to his almost exact contemporaries Matteo Palmieri, Lorenzo Valla, and Francesco Patrizi—many commentators have been surprised by the apparently conventional character of his ideas in *De ortu.* Thus, Ewart Lewis concludes that the treatise is little more than a useful compendium of standard arguments favoring the Roman Empire,[42] while J. H. Burns claims that it "adds little to the traditional stock of imperialist ideas."[43] Antony Black finds the work's universalistic imperial claims so implausible that "it could hardly have been meant seriously" and is "marked by flattery and conceit."[44] In contrast, James Muldoon and I have both argued that *De ortu* is indeed a serious work of humanist political theory inasmuch as it extends widely espoused Ciceronian principles in a self-consciously anti-republican direction.[45] Thus Aeneas Sylvius was perhaps the quintessential expositor of what I earlier in this paper called "imperial humanism."

At first glance, Aeneas's Ciceronianism appears to work directly against a national system of sovereign states. *De ortu* regards nationalism as a source of the disintegration of the principles of mutual association and common benefit upon which society itself is built. Nationalism is in-

42. Ewart Lewis, *Medieval Political Ideas* (London: Routledge and Kegan Paul, 1954), 465.

43. J. H. Burns, *Lordship, Kingship and Empire: The Idea of Monarchy 1400–1525* (Oxford: Clarendon Press, 1992), 115.

44. Black, *Political Thought in Europe,* 107, 108.

45. Cary J. Nederman, "Humanism and Empire: Aeneas Silvius Piccolomini, Cicero, and the Imperial Ideal," *Historical Journal* 36 (1993): 499–515, and Muldoon, *Empire and Order,* 110–12.

compatible with the rational foundations of social and political life that stem from human nature, a claim that arises directly out of Aeneas's adherence to Ciceronian premises. Thus, in Aeneas's view, national sovereignty and particularism cannot be reconciled with human nature itself. By contrast, only a world empire performs the functions necessary for the maintenance of social bonds among human beings and is therefore uniquely consistent with the natural endowment of mankind. Piccolomini unequivocally asserts that Roman dominion "takes its origin from the rational faculty of human nature itself, which is the best guide of how to live and which all must obey."[46] From this precept of rationality, Aeneas thinks that he detects an inherent weakness in political arrangements associated with localized distribution of power. Since there are a plurality of such territorial units, each of which defines (and often tries to expand) its geographical boundaries or sphere of jurisdiction, they inevitably came into conflict. And since there was no means of arbitration among such co-equal powers, the resolution of disputes between them occurred by means of armed engagements. Thus, the political model of an independent network of states is incompatible with the very purpose for which civil justice was instituted, namely, the maintenance of harmonious relations among human beings. As Aeneas remarks, "With wars clattering and raging, city was not able to meet with city, nor province with province, and that sweet and most pleasant commerce of human society was prohibited."[47] The decentralized distribution of royal power ultimately produces an effect exactly contrary to that intended. Diverse and particularized regimes run afoul of the universality of nature, and the ordained end of political power will thereby never be achieved. In empire alone does political power finally attain a form consistent with the universalistic tendencies of sociability implicit within human nature.

Later in *De ortu*, Aeneas returns to a Ciceronian critique of the claims of national regimes and their defenders to be independent of imperial control. He observes that one of two grounds are ordinarily advanced for such an exemption from subjection to the Empire : either liberty has been

---

46. *De ortu* has been translated by Thomas Izbicki and me in *Three Tracts on Empire: Engelbert of Admont, Aeneas Silvius Piccolomini and Juan de Torquemada* (Bristol: Thoemmes Press, 2000). I will use this English version (here at 95).

47. Ibid., 97.

conceded by the superior authority of an emperor or it has been earned by meritorious virtue.[48] In both instances, the case for autonomy rests on a readiness to shatter the bonds of human sociability, the maintenance of which is the primary purpose of the exercise of political power. Even admitting that an emperor might have ceded some of his prerogatives to inferior governments, still all such grants are cancelled because of their incompatibility with the natural law dictates of universal justice:

> Since, as we have previously stated, it is agreed that Empire was established in accordance with the law of nature and that monarchy is necessary to the preservation of peace and the administration of justice, it is certain that such privileges, which confer power upon a multitude of authorities, are invalid. For discord is born of this, frequent robberies occur, [and] various forms of murder are committed without number, since, once the peace has been upset, then wars spring up on all sides with no individual greater than all others, who could impose a limit on disputes with the rule of law.[49]

Society itself crumbles when divided by concessions of liberty, reverting to those Hobbesian conditions that obtained prior to the creation of a single world empire. But since political power is pointless or arbitrary unless it contributes to the promotion of communal intercourse, such reversion cannot be justified by even the most thoroughly documented and complete grant of freedom given by an emperor to a nation or its rulers.

Similar considerations exclude merit as a legitimate rationale for the assertion of national sovereignty. Aeneas allows that during the dark days of the Empire, certain men may have recovered imperial territories from barbarian domination and thereby claimed hegemony over a given province as the reward for their courage and skill. He does not deny that such a liberator and his heirs should be permitted to serve in the role of imperial vicar in these reclaimed lands. But the authority enjoyed by recoverers of imperial territories is at best that of a protectorate; *de facto* possession and rule does not confer *de jure* lordship *(dominium)*. Indeed, if such *dominium* were claimed, these men would be thieves and usurpers rather than defenders of the Empire. No merit of persons or families can displace the fact that political power must be exercised according to a universal plan if it is be employed in a manner congruent with the legitimate

48. Ibid., 102.
49. Ibid., 103.

standards of reason and justice.[50] The application of authority independent of the emperor by even the most virtuous individual "shatters the dignity of monarchic power, produces schism within the empire, and takes away all the harmony of human society."[51] The emperor is thus obliged to assert his imperial rights over any lesser ruler who believes that he has earned autonomous power over a realm because of his own good deeds or those of his ancestors. If the division of the Empire into national units is not to be destructive of social order, the governors of nations must acknowledge their lack of sovereignty and their primary duty to defer and submit to their imperial master.

Up to this point, Piccolomini seems to have presented a compelling and philosophically rigorous defense of the universalistic view that "all peoples, all nations, all kings and princes should submit with willing souls to your sovereignty."[52] Yet he never calls for the elimination or suppression of national governments or kingdoms. Indeed, he remarks at one point, "We do not deny, nevertheless, that the power of kings and other princes is great."[53] Rather, he wishes to propose a different and far more plausible and subtle relationship between empire and nation, one still derived from his basic premises. Since autonomous and self-subsistent states, if left to their own devices, will inevitably fall into conflict, which is incompatible with natural social concord, the primary purpose of empire is to assure that the justice upon which human order rests is everywhere upheld. In other words, Aeneas objects not to the existence of nations per se, but to forms of nationalism (such as claims of permanent exemptions and privileges) that are antithetical to pacific human association. The only way to put a stop to such conflictual nationalism is to insist that specific governments have power because it has been explicitly conferred by a political superior—the emperor. Hence, "It belongs to the Roman Emperor to grant privileges to cities, princes and kings on account of both merit and pressing circumstances; but, it is agreed, these are such that they in no way undermine the strength of the imperial power, nor extinguish it."[54] All assertions of national jurisdiction derive from and may be referred to an overarching universal authority that created the nation and

50. Ibid., 103–4.
51. Ibid., 104.
52. Ibid., 101.
53. Ibid., 104.
54. Ibid., 104.

exists in order to protect it. Just as the nation comes into existence for Cusanus at a historical moment by a determinant act of (popular) volition, so for Piccolomini any and every nation on earth has been formed by a political act, a legal grant from the emperor. For the former, the source of authorization is "from below"; for the latter it is "from above." But in both instances, the nation emerges from human will and no other source.

Nor does the human (imperial) origin of national governments imply that their existence is capricious or arbitrary. Their creation is referred by Piccolomini to the common good of humanity. He clearly believes that privileges of ruling a nation are conferred by the emperor with a view to ensuring that public peace and social harmony are upheld. Therefore, so long as this goal is realized, the emperor ought not and will not remove jurisdiction and power from any regime that he has authorized. "Privileges are not to be removed—nor are they to be modified—without reasonable cause," Aeneas Sylvius maintains. "Whatever privileges have been granted justly and remain just are to be observed without detriment to the republic."[55] Admittedly, it remains up to the emperor to determine in the final analysis whether justice is being served, since he is the court of last resort and ultimate judge in all such matters. But Piccolomini seems unconcerned that the emperor will abuse his power. Evidently, he believes that the fear of God's wrath and eternal punishment, not to mention a sincere desire to imitate Christ's lordship, constitute all of the restraint that the emperor requires.[56] Whatever the case, Aeneas seems confident that nations consistent with the maintenance of peace and justly ruled may reasonably expect the confirmation and defense of their privileges by the imperial majesty. Indeed, having the emperor ensure and warrant a justly exercised national jurisdiction only strengthens the claims that legitimate rulers enjoy against usurpers and hostile subjects, as well as foreign enemies.

Piccolomini's greater concern is the potential perfidy of princes who imagine that they have no one to answer to on earth. In making his case for imperial supremacy, he wants to emphasize that the purpose of such power is to render the governors of nations subject to certain moral and legal limits that otherwise would be absent.[57] In other words, the Empire

---

55. Ibid., 105.
56. See ibid., 107, 111–12.
57. Ibid., 102–3.

represents for Piccolomini the introduction of the rule of law into the international arena, not the sweeping away of national units of rule altogether. "If we were living under one head," he observes, "if we recognized only one supreme prince in temporal affairs, the best sort of peace would flourish everywhere on earth; and all of us would enjoy sweet concord."[58] This role of international policeman seems to be played in two sorts of cases. First, it is the emperor's duty to pacify by legal as well as military means those conflicts between nations that would otherwise rage unabated in the absence of some single and final arbiter of just causes. Piccolomini's emperor is more like the United Nations than Julius Caesar, not a conqueror or expansionist but a supreme court and executor of peaceful solutions to disputes. Arguably, the absolutist overtones that sometimes emerge from the pages of De ortu reflect its author's desperate need to promote respect and honor for the Empire on the part of the diverse nations that require an imperial superior as a constraint on their own militaristic and expansionist pretensions.[59] Second, Aeneas licenses the emperor to interfere in the internal politics of nations when the oppression of subjects by their governors occurs. Since national rulers "are under the Empire," he asserts, "their correction, when they become tyrants, pertains to the Roman Emperor. We assert that the cases of kings are to be referred to Caesar, and that all are to be constrained to obey the Emperor for the common good."[60] The emperor as the universal ruler is the universal source of justice, and all who are repressed or unjustly treated by their superiors may refer their cause to him.[61] Claims of national sovereignty afford no valid defense for abuse of one's people. In turn, because imperial majesty is legitimately imposed only on account of the dictates of human nature and for the sake of social harmony, the emperor may not refrain from protecting the weak against the strong and the injured against the iniquitous.

In sum, Piccolomini's imperialism is of a chastened sort in comparison with, say, Dante's in the prior century. Aeneas sees the Empire not as antithetical to, but rather as complementary with and even entailed by, more localized units of political power. While for him universal empire is the one truly natural form of government, this does not mean that national

58. Ibid., 103.
60. Ibid., 104.

59. Ibid., 109–11.
61. Ibid., 112.

regimes are utterly without legitimacy. Rather, precisely because they are "unnatural," that is to say, conventional or artificial, they require the political affirmation and regulation of the one system of governance that is truly consistent with human nature. Yet *De ortu* quite clearly harbors no romantic aspirations such as Dante possessed of a return to direct world government on the model of the classical Roman Empire. Piccolomini realizes quite fully that those days are forever lost and that the political landscape has shifted to a network of national kingdoms. Within such a world, the Empire still has a vital role to play—a fact, however, that can be overlooked only at peril to human peace and global political order. There is a very profound and surely relevant point to be gleaned from Aeneas's fear that national states left unchecked and to their own devices will likely wreak havoc on one another and on their own populations. Recent history continues to prove his prognosis correct.

Conclusion

The examples of Nicholas of Cusa and Aeneas Sylvius Piccolomini demonstrate how genuine intellectual commitment to the idea of a universal empire did not preclude acceptance and justification of the national state system that had clearly enveloped Europe by the fifteenth century and was eventually to embrace the globe. This lesson is one that remained salient in later years—and should be so today. As James Muldoon has pointed out, despite the tendency to think of the "modern world as the age of the state, in fact, the most extensive period of imperial development was from the sixteenth to the nineteenth centuries."[62] Nations and empires grew together in practice, and so the theory of empire never really ceased to be relevant.[63] Indeed, one might argue that from a number of perspectives this insight remains as true at the dawn of the twenty-first century. In a recent *New York Times Magazine* article, Michael Ignatieff asks, "What word but 'empire' describes the awesome thing that America is becoming? It is the only nation that polices the world through five military commands; . . . guarantees the survival of countries from Israel to

62. Muldoon, *Empire and Order,* 114.

63. See also Anthony Pagden, *Lords of All the World: Ideologies of Empire in Spain, Britain and France c. 1500–c. 1800* (New Haven: Yale University Press, 1995).

South Korea; drives the wheels of global trade and commerce; and fills the hearts and minds of the entire planet with its dreams and desires."[64] These imperial functions—now made truly universal—contain quite obvious echoes of the imperialism defended by Cusanus and Piccolomini. It was not an expansionist or a territorial dominion so much as a benign force for the moral and/or social improvement of humanity. So perhaps it is not so odd that we retain an interest in the imperialist theories of national government even as we submit republicanism to the ash heap of irrelevancy. For it seems that Nicholas and Aeneas have proven in many ways more prescient about the issues that drive the real world of politics than civic republicans old and new. It is the tension—sometimes creative, sometimes destructive—between empire and nation that persists in animating the leading edge of political life globally.[65] So we may have much yet to learn from the imperial humanists who have been long neglected.

64. Michael Ignatieff, "The Burden," *New York Times Magazine,* January 5, 2003, 22. Similar views have been expressed also by the syndicated columnist Clarence Page, "If This Country Isn't an Empire, Then What Is It?" *Houston Chronicle,* March 23, 2003, among others.

65. For some further provocative reflections on the continuing relevance of empire, see John M. Headley, "The Universalizing Principle and Process: On the West's Intrinsic Commitment to a Global Context," *Journal of World History* 13 (2002): 291–321.

Paul E. Sigmund

II. MEDIEVAL AND MODERN
CONSTITUTIONALISM
Nicholas of Cusa and John Locke

The study of political theory involves the analysis of the origin and historical development of central concepts of government. One such concept is that of constitutionalism, which has a long history in Western political thought. This paper will examine the development of the idea of constitutionalism and evaluate a current debate about the relation of the medieval and modern forms of that concept. We will use the writings of Nicholas of Cusa (1401–1464), George Lawson (1598–1678), and John Locke (1632–1704), to identify elements of continuity and of change in constitutionalist thinking.

The term "constitutionalism" has been defined in a variety of ways. The chapter with that title in the *Cambridge History of Political Thought, 1450–1700* describes it as a nineteenth-century neologism, which draws on a much older term, "constitution," to denote the advocacy of "a system of checks upon the exercise of political power" that provides "institutionally determined limits" on government.[1] Carl Friedrich's text on *Constitutional Government and Politics* speaks in similar terms of "effective regularized restraints" on governmental action,[2] although Friedrich understood those restraints as going beyond the merely institutional, in a more dynamic and processual direction. Friedrich did not devote much attention to the medieval origins of constitutionalist thought, but his Harvard colleague Charles McIlwain, in his lectures on *Constitutionalism, Ancient and*

1. Howell A. Lloyd, "Constitutionalism," in *The Cambridge History of Political Thought, 1450–1700*, J. H. Burns and Mark Goldie, eds. (Cambridge: Cambridge University Press, 1991), 254–55.

2. Quoted in Paul E. Sigmund, "Carl Friedrich's Contribution to the Theory of Constitutionalism," in *Constitutionalism*, ed. John Chapman and J. Roland Pennock (New York: New York University Press, 1979), 32.

Modern, argued that in the Middle Ages, while the king had an area of discretion in administration *(gubernatio)*, there were clearly recognized limits to his authority in the area of law and rights *(jurisdictio)*. He distinguished between medieval and modern constitutionalism by the absence in the medieval case of institutional sanctions against errant rulers, other than the threat or use of revolutionary force.[3]

More recent scholarship has argued for continuities between the two periods, especially in the area of constitutionalism, understood as institutional controls on the ruler, and of the related themes of popular sovereignty and individual rights. Challenging the assumption that the central concepts of liberal constitutional democracy emerged only in the modern period, scholars have argued that the foundations of individualism, rights, institutional restraints on power, and popular participation can be traced to the twelfth-century canonists, thirteenth-century parliamentarians, and fourteenth- and fifteenth-century conciliarists. While the massive six-volume *A History of Medieval Political Theory in the West* by the Carlyle brothers as well as Ewart Lewis's *Medieval Political Ideas* had earlier provided documentary evidence that in the Middle Ages the community was seen as the source of law and legitimate authority, more recent writing has linked the late Middle Ages to the institutionalization of community control in ways that previously had been thought of as distinctively modern.[4] The late medieval period was identified as the source of modern ideas of individual rights, consent, representation, and a popular role in legislation.

The link between fifteenth-century conciliarism and seventeenth-century constitutionalism was made as early as 1907, in John Neville Figgis's book, *From Gerson to Grotius.*[5] Beginning in the 1950s, it was reasserted and developed by Brian Tierney, who extended the chronology of influence back to the twelfth century, arguing that conciliarist constitutionalism developed its principal arguments out of the much older canon law

---

3. Charles Howard McIlwain, *Constitutionalism: Ancient and Modern,* rev. ed. (Ithaca, N.Y.: Cornell University Press, 1947), 84ff.

4. R. W. Carlyle and A. J. Carlyle, *A History of Medieval Political Theory in the West* (Edinburgh and London: W. Blackwood and Sons, 1928–36); Ewart Lewis, *Medieval Political Ideas* (New York: Knopf, 1954).

5. John Neville Figgis, *Studies of Political Thought from Gerson to Grotius 1414–1625* (Cambridge: Cambridge University Press, 1907; 2nd rev. ed., 1916).

tradition beginning in the twelfth century.[6] Other studies of the conciliar writers analyzed the canonist influence on specific conciliar writers and traced the path of influence of conciliarist constitutionalism through the University of Paris from the Protestant exiles from Queen Mary's persecution and the French Huguenots to the English civil war and Locke's *Second Treatise of Civil Government* in the 1680s. Citing Harold Laski's claim that there is "a direct road" from the claim of conciliar superiority made by the Council of Constance (1414–1417) to the assertion of parliamentary supremacy in the Glorious Revolution in England in 1688, Francis Oakley argued from texts and history for continuity between medieval and modern constitutionalism.[7] In the most influential assertion of the same thesis, Quentin Skinner devoted the first of two volumes to late medieval constitutionalist ideas that, he argued, provided *The Foundations of Modern Political Thought.*[8]

In the area of rights, in the 1940s and 1950s Jacques Maritain linked contemporary rights theories to an updated version of Aquinas's writings on natural law.[9] More recently scholars have traced the origins of the idea of individual "subjective" rights to canon law texts,[10] the writings of the fourteenth-century theologian William of Occam[11] or the fifteenth-century conciliarist Jean Gerson.[12] Their scholarship effectively refuted the arguments of Leo Strauss and his followers that had found the origins of modern natural rights theory in the writings of Thomas Hobbes and John Locke.[13]

In the 1990s, however, the linkage between medieval and modern the-

6. Brian Tierney, *The Foundations of the Conciliar Theory* (Cambridge: Cambridge University Press, 1955).

7. F. W. Oakley, "Figgis, Constance, and the Divines of Paris," *American Historical Review* 75, no. 2 (Dec. 1969): 368–86.

8. Quentin Skinner, *The Foundations of Modern Political Thought,* vol. 1 (Cambridge: Cambridge University Press, 1978).

9. Jacques Maritain, *The Rights of Man and the Natural Law* (New York: Scribners, 1943); Maritain, *Man and the State* (Chicago: University of Chicago Press, 1951).

10. Brian Tierney, *The Idea of Natural Rights: Studies on Natural Rights, Natural Law and Church Law, 1150–1625* (Atlanta: Scholars Press, 1997).

11. Michel Villey, *Formation de la pensée juridique modern* (Paris: Editions Montchretien, 1975).

12. Richard Tuck, *Natural Rights Theories: Their Origin and Development* (Cambridge: Cambridge University Press, 1979).

13. Leo Strauss, *Natural Right and History* (Chicago: University of Chicago Press, 1953).

ories of constitutionalism was questioned by Cary Nederman,[14] who argued against the "Neo-Figgisite" continuity thesis that had now become what he called "a new orthodoxy" enshrined in such works as the *Cambridge History of Political Thought, 1450–1700*.[15] Maintaining that conciliarist thought did not differ from other medieval theories in stressing the rule of law and the community origin of authority and thus should not be singled out for special attention, he then outlined four characteristics of modern constitutionalism that mark a "decisive break" between medieval and modern versions of that idea. He enumerated them as an impersonal view of government, public control over rulers, specific and imprescriptible rights for citizens, and individualized free consent.[16] Taking the writings of Jean Gerson at the Council of Constance as representative of conciliarist thought, he argued that none of the characteristics named above appeared in Gerson's thought and that the only limit on the ruler's power was the threat of deposition by the Church acting through the council in a corporate capacity to deal with an extraordinary situation. For Gerson, Nederman asserted, the faithful were subjects rather than citizens, and the papacy was viewed as divinely instituted. Furthermore, he maintained that the action of the council as the corporate representative of the whole Church in extreme cases such as that presented by multiple claimants to the papacy is conceptually distinct from the modern assertion of a regularized system of legal institutions to limit the ruler, as well as the modern recognition of a right of individuals to consent and representation.

In response, Francis Oakley argued that if Nederman's "sweeping" case is correct, "some of us have put in a good deal of misdirected effort over the years."[17] Oakley claimed that Nederman misrepresented both fifteenth- and seventeenth-century constitutionalism. According to Oakley,

---

14. Cary Nederman, "Conciliarism and Constitutionalism: Jean Gerson and Medieval Political Thought," *History of European Ideas* 12 (1990): 189–209, and Nederman, "Constitutionalism—Medieval and Modern: Against Neo-Figgisite Orthodoxy (Again)," *History of Political Thought* 17 (Summer 1996): 179–94.

15. *The Cambridge History of Political Thought, 1450–1700*, ed. J. H. Burns and Mark Goldie (Cambridge: Cambridge University Press, 1991).

16. Nederman, "Conciliarism and Constitutionalism," 191, 193.

17. Francis Oakley, "Nederman, Gerson, Conciliar Theory and Constitutionalism: Sed contra," *History of Political Thought* 16 (1995): 2.

the fifteenth-century theories contained elements of individualism as well as corporatism and supported regularized institutional restraints on the Pope. Moreover, the writers of the seventeenth century, at least before John Locke, were largely corporatist in their conception of the relation of the community to the king. Oakley also noted that Gerson himself attributed a generalized superiority of the council to the Pope, enabling it to remove even a guiltless Pope for the well-being of the Church. He concluded his criticism by endorsing the view expressed in Antony B. Black's *Political Thought in Europe, 1250–1750* that the whole period from the eleventh to the eighteenth century should be considered as "essentially a single epoch."[18]

Nederman had summed up his claims at the end of the article on Gerson by contrasting the "corporatist and spiritual tenor of medieval constitutionalism with the individualistic and secular tone of its modern successor," thus changing the terms of the debate. He also admitted that "perhaps other advocates of the supremacy of the Council will prove to be more 'modern' in their outlook."[19] The obvious alternative candidate as a conciliar constitutionalist is Nicholas of Cusa, and John Locke is generally recognized to be the most important representative of early modern constitutionalism. An examination and comparison of their constitutional theories, as well as those of George Lawson, who directly influenced Locke, should be helpful in evaluating the Nederman-Oakley debate.

In his reply to Oakley, Nederman quoted Cusanus at length to demonstrate the organic and corporatist character of conciliar thought, which, in its vision of the Church as a mystical body of functionally interacting and hierarchically organized parts, is far removed from modern secular individualism.[20] As this example indicates, one can find elements in Cusanus's political thought that are far removed from modern conceptions of politics and constitutionalism. This should not surprise us since his announced purpose in his seminal work *De concordantia catholica* is to describe a *concordantia* that is *catholica* in the tradition and practice of the

18. Antony B. Black, *Political Thought in Europe 1250–1450* (Cambridge: Cambridge University Press, 1992), 19, 191.

19. Nederman, "Conciliarism and Constitutionalism," 201.

20. Nederman, "Constitutionalism—Medieval and Modern," 190ff.

universal Church—both Eastern and Western—and that reflects certain underlying principles of social organization in both church and state. His political theory encompasses *both* hierarchy and equality, authority and freedom, papal primacy and conciliar supremacy, group consensus and individual consent, and implicit (virtual) and explicit representation. He recognizes the need for centralized authority and for decentralized administration, for the rule of law and the possibility of dispensation, for the recognition of the claims of intellectual superiority as well as decision making by the numerical majority and equal natural rights based on original freedom. When the second part of each of these pairings is emphasized, he appears to be a forerunner of liberal constitutional democracy. When the first is emphasized, he seems very far removed from modernity. It is thus possible to use his writings to argue for either continuity or change between medieval and modern constitutionalism. The more modern aspects of his constitutionalist theory become more apparent as the argument of the *De concordantia catholica* develops and the major influences on his thinking move from the hierarchical views of Dionysius the Areopagite in Book I, to the corporatism of Gratian's *Decretum* and the records of the Greek councils in the first version of Book II, to the greater individualism and equalitarianism of the revised version of Book II, and to the unacknowledged influence of Marsilius of Padua in Book III. It is thus not surprising that Nederman's quotations in support of the organic, hierarchical, and corporatist characteristics of Cusanus's thought are taken from the earlier parts of the work.

Walter Ullmann, in his writing on medieval political theory, argues that Nicholas's *De concordantia catholica* combines both populist "ascending" and hierarchical "descending" approaches to the legitimation of government.[21] My own work on Nicholas of Cusa, originally written as a doctoral dissertation before Ullmann's book was published, described the *De concordantia catholica* as a combination of hierarchical elements drawn from Christian Neoplatonism with theories of consent drawn from canon law.[22]

If we single out only the hierarchical elements, Cusanus's theory seems

21. Walter Ullmann, *A History of Political Thought: The Middle Ages* (Baltimore: Penguin Books, 1965).

22. Paul E. Sigmund, *Nicholas of Cusa and Medieval Political Thought* (Cambridge, Mass.: Harvard University Press, 1963).

very medieval. Book I is influenced by Pseudo-Dionysius, the fifth-century Neoplatonist writer who in the Middle Ages was believed to have been a disciple of St. Paul. Dionysius invented the term "hierarchy" and described the *Ecclesiastical Hierarchy* as a reflection of the general order of the universe as well as the order among the angels.[23] However, Nicholas describes in Book I of the *De concordantia catholica* not one, but two hierarchies in the Church. The sacramental hierarchy is composed of three sets of three choirs: (1) bishops, priests, and deacons; (2) subdeacons, acolytes, and exorcists; and (3) readers, porters, and the tonsured.[24] The governmental hierarchy in the Church, however, is different. It still has nine ranks, but they are now: (1) Pope, patriarchs, and archbishops; (2) bishops, archdeacons, and deacons; and (3) priests, deacons, and subdeacons.[25]

There are corresponding hierarchies in the empire as well, and again they are described in two different ways. The emperor in his spiritual role as protector of the Church is over all Christians in a parallel position with the Pope, while in the temporal sphere he is first among the kings just as the Pope is first among the patriarchs. Dukes are parallel to archbishops and counts to bishops, and we are instructed to "proceed with the rest."[26] In the imperial council, the emperor is "head and first of all," followed by: (1) the kings, imperial electors, and patricians; (2) dukes, governors, and prefects; and (3) marquises, landgraves, and others.[27] There is a fixed pattern in both Church and empire that is described in organic and corporatist terms. The papacy was established by Christ "to maintain unity" and "to avoid schism." Although all bishops are equal in sacramental power, the Pope is "prince of the bishops" and "has rulership of all men in the church."[28] The emperor in his religious role is "the minister of God" and "vicar of Jesus Christ on earth."[29] The complicated pattern of parallel hierarchies in each case with a single head is distinctively medieval.

When Nicholas develops the conciliarist elements in his theory to argue for consent to law and government, he uses arguments that also ap-

---

23. Nicolai de Cusa, *De concordantia catholica,* ed. Gerhard Kallen, I, 6–8 (h XIV/1, N. 32ff.). (For an English translation, see *The Catholic Concordance,* trans. Paul E. Sigmund [Cambridge: Cambridge University Press, 1991, pb. 1995].)

24. Ibid., I, 7, N. 41.   25. Ibid., I, 8, N. 42.
26. Ibid., III, 1, N. 293.   27. Ibid., III, 35, N. 470–471.
28. Ibid., I, 5, N. 35; II, 34, N. 259, 261, and 264.
29. Ibid., III, 5, N. 341.

pear medieval at the outset. The council is superior to the Pope because it is a meeting of all the bishops, and the bishop "represents and symbolizes the church as a public person." The "particular churches are the mystical bodies of those who preside over them as representatives of Christ."[30] The council contains more "public persons," and "the more specific the headship, the more certain the representation,"[31] which makes the council more representative of the Church as a whole than the Pope alone. The electors of the empire represent and give the consent of the Roman people to the emperor without themselves being elected. The cardinals, who in Nicholas's scheme represent the provinces of the Church, are named by the Pope, although Nicholas proposes that the archbishops should choose them with the advice of the bishops.[32] Consent is tacit, and representation is virtual or absorptive in a way that is far removed from modern theory or practice.

At the beginning of Book III, Nicholas says that law must have "the consent of all,"[33] yet even here he asserts that the "ignorant and stupid" will accept the direction of the more intelligent "by a certain natural instinct" in consenting to laws "that have the wise as their special authors, protectors and executors and the concurrent agreement of all the others in voluntary subjection."[34] As in the case of his discussion of representation, his theory of consent amounts to the tacit acceptance of the rule of one's betters, rather than any individual act of the will.

Yet these medieval and authoritarian elements in his theory are counterbalanced by striking anticipations of more modern theories. The best known is his claim that consent is required for legitimate law and government because "all are by nature free" and because "men are by nature equal in power and equally free"[35]—an apparent rejection of hierarchy and what appears to be an anticipation of later contract theory. While not specifically endorsing numerical majority rule, Nicholas refers repeatedly to the rule of "the major part" when discussing the infallibility of the priesthood[36] and says that "ordinarily" and "normally" the major part should rule in the Church council.[37] In matters of doctrinal definition,

30. Ibid., I, 6, N. 17.
31. Ibid., II, 18, N. 163.
32. Ibid., III, 4, N. 325; II, 18, N. 164.
33. Ibid., III, pref., N. 270.
34. Ibid., III, pref., N. 271, 275.
35. Ibid., II, 14, N. 127.
36. Ibid., I, 8, N. 43; II, 4, N. 79; III, pref., N. 270.
37. Ibid., II, 4, N. 79; II, 15, N. 137.

moreover, the Pope must be consulted but should submit to the major part.[38] At the beginning of Book III, following his reading of Marsilius of Padua's *Defensor pacis,* he repeatedly endorses the rule of the "major part" in temporal affairs as well.[39] Most strikingly, he bases his theory of consent on "the common equal birth of all men and their equal natural rights."[40]

Did Nicholas of Cusa believe in majority rule in the modern sense? The canon lawyers spoke more often of "the greater and sounder *(sanior)* part," and Marsilius qualified the rule of "the weightier part" by adding "as to quality and quantity."[41] The term *maior pars* was frequently used in early modern political writings without denoting anything approaching universal suffrage, even in the establishment of the basic constitution. More often consent by the greater part was assumed when the leaders and corporate groups in a given society indicated their assent.[42] After his break with the Council of Basel, Nicholas himself criticized its procedures because the vote of an ordinary priest was counted the same as that of a cardinal.[43] Yet the incipient populism of his thought is expressed in such statements as "All power both spiritual and temporal rests potentially in the people"[44] and "Legislation ought to be adopted by those who are bound by it or by their representatives because . . . what touches all should be approved by all."[45]

His institutional proposals for the Church and the empire give expression to more modern constitutional forms. In the Church he proposes that elections be held at every level. Parish priests are to be elected or "at least some convenient provision should be made" for consent to their appointment. The diocesan clergy should elect the bishops with the consent of the laity. The bishops should elect the archbishops or metropolitans, and they in turn are to choose the cardinals, who "should elect the pope, if possible with the consent of the metropolitans."[46] The cardinals are also

---

38. Ibid., II, 15, N. 137.

39. Ibid., II, 34, N. 261; III. pref., N. 270, 276, 278, 283.

40. Ibid., III, 4, N. 331.

41. Marsilius of Padua, *The Defender of Peace,* trans. A. Gewirth (New York: Columbia University Press, 1956), I, xii, 3.

42. Sigmund, *Nicholas of Cusa,* 146.   43. Ibid., 264.

44. *De concordantia catholica,* II, 19, N. 168.   45. Ibid., III, Pref. N. 270.

46. Ibid., II, 18, N. 164.

to act as a "continuing council which legitimately represents the whole church," and they are to be consulted on matters that affect the whole Church.[47]

In addition to the universal and daily councils, Nicholas also discusses the council of the patriarchate of Rome, an institution that he finds useful in answering the texts cited by the canon lawyers in favor of papal superiority to the council, which, he argues, referred to the patriarchal council of Rome rather than the universal council. The patriarchal council is under the Pope, while the universal council is over him. "The power of the [universal] council is immediately from Christ, and it is in every respect over both the pope and the Apostolic See."[48] The council can remove him for heresy and "when he governs incompetently."[49] The councils in Nicholas's view are thus part of the regular governing institutions of Church (as the Council of Constance had conceived them in its decree *Frequens* [1415]), although the Pope also has inherent powers of administration that the council cannot take away from him.[50] Church laws should be made by the councils and by synods at lower levels, although papal decrees can acquire legislative force from custom and acceptance of the Church. The canons of the councils constitute the basic law of the Church, and papal decrees must not violate them.[51] Nicholas even gives the councils the power to review papal legislation to assure that it is in accordance with the canons of the universal councils and with natural law, arguing that otherwise the Pope could be both legislator and judge.[52]

Long after he moved from conciliarism to papalism, at the end of his life as a cardinal, Cusanus still advocated institutional checks on the Pope. The college of cardinals, however, replaced the universal council by representing the "consent of the whole church spread throughout the world" in electing the Pope and acting as "representatives of the nations" in constituting the "daily full council of the church."[53] Indeed, according to Pope Pius II's *Commentaries,* Nicholas insisted that the Pope could create cardinals only "with the consent of a majority of the college [of cardinals] and according to the decrees of the Council of Constance."[54]

47. Ibid., II, 18, N. 167.
49. Ibid., II, 18. N. 148.
51. Ibid., II, 20, N. 177.
53. Sigmund, *Nicholas of Cusa,* 298.

48. Ibid., II, 16, N. 148.
50. Ibid., II, 16, N. 162.
52. Ibid., II, 14, N. 129–130.
54. Ibid., 300.

In the case of the empire, in addition to the electors who meet to choose the emperor, the *Reichstag* should meet regularly, representing the nobility, the Church, and major corporate groups. Like the Pope, the emperor should have a daily council to give advice and consent to legislation.[55] Nicholas does not go further in proposing elective bodies in the empire because in contrast to the Church, the problem in the empire is the lack of centralized authority. To remedy that problem, he proposes the establishment of a standing army, a centralized tax system, and an imperial judiciary based on district courts.[56] In the election of the emperor, he proposes a system of preferential voting by the electors who are to rank the candidates numerically in the order of preference, a system that that he considers necessary when there are multiple candidacies.[57]

This brief summary indicates that Cusanus's thought contains striking anticipations of modern constitutional institutions. There is a sophisticated analysis of the powers of the papacy that moves far beyond the judgment of individual character mentioned by Nederman to a careful delineation of the respective jurisdictions of Pope and council. There is consent, often, but not always, corporate, and there is at least one example, that is, the election of the emperor, where numerical voting procedures are used. The Pope and other Church rulers are elected by bodies that in some sense are representative of the ruled, and they are responsible to them for the conduct of their administration and their observance of basic law. The emperor, while chosen by electors who are not responsible to the Roman people whom they are supposed to represent, nevertheless is to act through administrative and legislative councils and to create a judicial system to apply the law. If modern constitutionalism is defined in terms of institutional restraints on power, the *Concordantia* outlines a modern constitutionalist system for both the Church and the empire. In terms of Nederman's criteria of modernity, there is a concept of rulership as an office, public control over the ruler, natural rights—especially to participate in government and legislation in some manner—and, in a limited number of cases, individual consent.

Nicholas of Cusa's differences from modern constitutionalism have

---

55. *De concordantia catholica*, III, 12, N. 378.
56. Ibid., III, 33, N. 510ff.; III, 39, N. 552ff.
57. Ibid., III, 37, N. 535ff.

been described earlier. His proposal assumes a unity in church and state and the existence and acceptance of hierarchies in both areas, phenomena that are not possible or desirable in the modern world. Cusanus believes in a possibility of agreement and harmony *(concordantia)*, with the help of the Holy Spirit, that seems utopian in a later age. The parallelism between church and state that he envisions fails to distinguish between the nature of the goals and methods of secular rule and those of the life of the spirit.

And while one can find anticipations of modern notions of individual rights—especially the right to participate in some way in legislation and in the selection and evaluation of rulers—the contractualism, voluntarism, and pluralism of modern liberal thought are absent.

Yet one can overstate the differences between late medieval and early modern constitutionalism. For an example of seventeenth-century constitutionalism that shares many of Cusanus's assumptions, we can look at George Lawson, *Politica Sacra et Civilis,* a work of political and ecclesiological theory published in 1660 and read by John Locke in 1679, that is, shortly before he composed the *Two Treatises of Civil Government.*

Lawson mentions Cusanus by name, along with Jean Gerson and Pierre d'Ailly, the leading conciliarist writers from the Council of Constance. Like them Lawson builds his political and ecclesiological theory on the basis of a "free and voluntary" consent of the whole people to the constitutional structures of the church and state.[58] He cites Augustine and Cicero rather than legal sources but uses consent, as the lawyers did, as the source of the power of the community to enforce limits on its spiritual and temporal rulers.[59] He repeats the canonist/conciliar distinction between the corporate community as a whole *(omnes ut universi)* that establishes the ruler and basic law and as individuals *(omnes ut singuli)* who are subject to them. He also cites the examples of the Councils of Constance and Basel. Lawson is more willing than his medieval predecessors to tolerate diversity of forms of government, but his basic arguments for the derivation of authority from consent and the accountability of rulers are shared with the conciliarists whom he cites. It is true that, as in the case of

---

58. George Lawson, *Politica sacra et civilis,* ed. Conal Condren (Cambridge: Cambridge University Press, 1992), II, 5, 24.

59. Ibid., II, 5, 24; XII, 1–2, 163–67.

Richard Hooker, whose *Laws of Ecclesiastical Polity* is often quoted by Locke, the consent is given by the community rather than the individual, but it can also be withdrawn in cases of "tyranny in exercise, or acting to the dissolution of the fundamental constitution."[60] Lawson has thus not moved far beyond his conciliarist predecessors. The community can limit the rulers, and the parliament can enforce those limits as the representative of the community. There is therefore a distinct similarity between the fifteenth-century conciliarism of Nicholas of Cusa and the seventeenth-century constitutionalism of George Lawson.

There is less continuity in the case of John Locke, who wrote the *Two Treatises of Civil Government* in the early 1680s and published them in 1689. Locke replaces the earlier theory of community consent to the ruler and the constitution with an explicit social contract. This contract is exercised in the state of nature by free individuals who consent to government and a system of laws for the protection of their lives and property. In addition, the parallels between spiritual and temporal structures of authority evident in both Cusanus and Lawson are replaced by a sharp disjunction drawn in Locke's *Letter on Toleration* (1685) between the Church as a voluntary society concerned with individual salvation and the state as a coercive institution that promotes the material well-being of its citizens. Individual consent concerning the rule of law and the basic constitutional structure is given by a numerical majority—without hierarchical elements. The constitution should include a partial separation between the legislature and the executive as well as a property qualification for voting. If the ruler abuses his power, he can be held accountable by the legislature. If this is not effective, the people have a right to "appeal to heaven," that is, to carry out an armed revolution. If an individual's rights are violated, he can appeal to the majority to defend him.

Locke thus describes a much more individualistic theory of consent—although he must resort to tacit consent to demonstrate that it is given by everyone. He also has a more secular and more limited conception of the role of the state, which is denied any involvement in religion, except for this-worldly purposes. It is here, therefore, that the real break between medieval and modern constitutionalism takes place. Here too Neder-

60. Ibid., XV, 5, 226.

man's argument about a fundamental change has some validity—especially in his second formulation of the differences between the religious and corporatist character of medieval thought and the individualism and secularism of modern liberal thought.

We conclude that there is indeed considerable continuity between fifteenth-century conciliarism and seventeenth-century constitutionalism, but that a distinctively modern conception of constitutionalism appears only at the end of the seventeenth century, with the more secular liberal individualism of the political writings of John Locke.[61]

---

61. Paul E. Sigmund, *The Selected Political Writings of John Locke,* (New York: W. W. Norton, 2005).

Elizabeth Brient

12. HOW CAN THE INFINITE BE THE MEASURE OF THE FINITE?

Three Mathematical Metaphors from *De docta ignorantia*

Early on in *De docta ignorantia,* Nicholas of Cusa clearly states a fundamental principle of his speculative metaphysics: "[I]t is evident that there is no proportion between the infinite and the finite."[1] When two things stand in a proportional or comparative relationship, Cusanus holds, they agree in some respect, by virtue of which agreement they can be compared. At the same time, the two things maintain a degree of difference with one another, for otherwise they would fall into identity and would no longer be two distinct things. Indeed, Cusanus holds, number is a necessary condition of all comparative or proportional relation, that is, of whatever exists in the realm of the "more" and the "less," of the "this" and the "that," of the "similar" but "different." Further, only finite things can stand in a comparative or proportional relation because only finite things are determinate in this sense. The infinite, qua infinite, Cusanus asserts, "escapes all proportion."[2]

Nevertheless, Cusanus maintains that the Divine Infinite, the Absolute Maximum, "is the one, most simple, and most adequate measure of the whole universe and of everything existing in the universe."[3] What are we to make of this apparent paradox? On the one hand, there is no comparative relation *(nulla proportio)* between the infinite and the finite, and yet on the other hand, the infinite is the "one, most simple, and adequate measure" of finite things. In what sense is the infinite the *measure* for the finite?

---

1. Nicholas of Cusa, *De docta ignorantia* I, 3, N. 9 (h I, 8): "infiniti ad finitum proportionem non esse." I have used H. Lawrence Bond's translation of *De docta ignorantia* (hereafter cited as Bond) in *Nicholas of Cusa: Selected Spiritual Writings* (New York: Paulist Press, 1997), here at 90.

2. Ibid., I, 1, N. 3 (h I, p. 6); Bond, p. 88.

3. Ibid., I, 23, N. 72 (h I, p. 47); Bond, p. 120.

In order to address this question, I will examine three of the mathematical metaphors that Cusanus utilizes in order to explain how this proposition is possible. Each of the three highlights an important aspect of the way in which the infinite may be said to "measure" the finite.

The first metaphor is number itself. Cusanus uses the example of counting to indicate the way in which the superlative is always the implicit measure of the comparative. That is to say, our ability to recognize the comparative *as* comparative already implies an awareness of the superlative.[4] The second metaphor involves the consideration of the nature of the continuum and the division of a finite line in particular. Cusanus uses this example in order to indicate that the infinite is the measure of the finite insofar as the infinite is the *essence* of the finite. The third metaphor is that of an *n*-sided polygon inscribed inside a circle. As the number of sides on the polygon increases, it approaches coincidence with the circumference of the circle. Cusanus uses this metaphor to illustrate the way in which the infinite is the measure of the finite in the sense of being the *goal* and *perfection* of the finite. Here we also see Cusanus developing a conception of Christ as a limit-concept in order to think the relationship between two orders of infinity: the absolute infinity of God and the privative infinity of the universe. The metaphor is used to figure vividly the way in which the absolutely infinite acts as the measure for the privative infinity of unending approach to a limit.[5]

The Number Series

The first example is that of the number series or simple counting. Cusanus holds that the number series is finite.[6] By this he means that it is not possible to arrive at infinity by a successive increase of finite quantities.[7] I am not any "closer" to an end in the ascent at 10,000 than I was at 100. In-

---

4. In this context, see the related discussions in the papers by Karsten Harries and Louis Dupré included in this volume on the principle of perspective: to recognize a perspective as a perspective is already in some sense to think beyond that perspective.

5. In this paper I will touch on only these three mathematical metaphors. See also my book *The Immanence of the Infinite: Hans Blumenberg and the Threshold to Modernity* (Washington, D.C.: The Catholic University of America Press, 2002), part 3, sec. 2: "Cusanus' Use of Mathematical Metaphors," 188–204.

6. *De docta ignorantia* I, 5, N. 13 (h I, p. 12).

7. Ibid., I, 6, N. 15 (h I, 13); II, 1, N. 96 (h I, p. 63).

deed, this is an inherent characteristic of any number, that is, that it always stands in a comparative relationship to a greater positable number. Unending increase in the realm of the comparative, that is, in the realm of finite quantities that are comparatively greater or smaller, will never actually arrive at the infinite. Any number is by nature finite and hence potentially surpassable by a still greater number. That is just what we mean when we say that the number series is "unending," the progression is "potentially infinite," or the increase "goes on *ad infinitum.*" We do not mean that the number series comes to an end in some "infinite" or "maximal" number. Rather, no matter how large a given number may be, it remains "infinitely" distant from the end of the series, which is to say the series can have no end. In this sense the infinite stands as the measure for the potentially unending character of comparative increase.

It is the thought of the infinite, as the maximum that can never be reached by comparative increase, that grounds my understanding of the essential surpassability of any given finite quantity, that is, of the essentially comparative nature of number itself. Again, it is because I can think of the maximum as that which is not arrived at by comparative increase that I can understand what it means for something to be *merely* comparatively great and that I am able to recognize the comparatively great as *always* potentially surpassable by something still greater. In order to make this recognition, I am drawing on an implicit awareness of the absolutely great, of the superlative. Here the superlative is presupposed in the qualifiers "merely" and "always." It acts as the measure of the intelligibility of the comparative *as* comparative. While the infinite, qua infinite, transcends our understanding since it transcends all comparative relation, it is, nevertheless, understood "incomprehensibly" and implicitly in the very act of grasping the comparative *as* comparative. This is a persistent theme in Cusanus's thought, a theme that spans his corpus and that is perhaps given its most explicit and general formulation in *De apice theoriae* (1464). Here, Cusanus describes this intuition or awareness of the divine infinite as a kind of mental vision that surpasses the mind's power to comprehend but is nevertheless presupposed in that very power:

Hence, the simple vision of the mind is not a comprehensive vision, but it elevates itself from a comprehensive vision to seeing the incomprehensible. When, for example, it sees comprehensively one thing to be greater than another, then it elevates itself in order to see that than which nothing can be greater. And this is infinite, greater than all that is measurable or comprehensible.[8]

It is just this key insight, namely, that the superlative is the implicit measure of the intelligibility of the comparative, that Cusanus sees so clearly illustrated in the example of the number series in *De docta ignorantia*.

Indeed, there is in this example a second and equally important sense in which the superlative may be seen to act as the measure of the intelligibility of the comparative. This has to do with the way in which the superlative—now considered as minimum—is the ground or principle of all numbers. This becomes clear, Cusanus holds, when we attend to another important aspect of the number series. While it is the case that in ascending the number series, I can always posit a larger number, it is not the case that the descent back down the series is similarly open-ended. In fact, when descending the series of natural numbers, I do in fact arrive at a minimum beyond which there cannot be anything less, and this is unity *(unitas).*[9] Counting down, we arrive eventually at *one,* and oneness must be understood as the beginning of number, the being of number, and the unit measure by virtue of which all numbers are ordered in relationship to each other.

Cusanus is drawing here on the traditional Greek notion that *one* is not itself a number, but is the principle or ground of all number.[10] He follows the Neoplatonic view that oneness or unity is the inexhaustible source of all number and understands unity and number as standing in a *complicatio-explicatio* relationship.[11] Unity is the enfolding of all number, and number

8. Nicholas of Cusa, *De apice theoriae* 11 (h XII, pp. 124–125); trans. Bond in *Nicholas of Cusa,* 297. I am grateful to Lawrence Bond for directing me to this passage. For a discussion of the mind's vision in relation to its ultimate object *posse* and to number see also the Epilogue to *Compendium* 45–47 (h XI/3, pp. 33–36), especially sec. 46.

9. *De docta ignorantia* I, 5, N. 13 (h I, p. 12).

10. Ibid., I, 5, N. 14 (h I, p. 12); II, 3, N. 108 (h I, p. 70). See also Nicholas of Cusa, *De principio* 32, and Aristotle, *Metaphysics* X 1, 1052b 20–25: "For measure is that by which quantity is known; and quantity *qua* quantity is known either by a 'one' or by a number, and all number is known by a 'one'. Therefore all quantity *qua* quantity is known by the one, and that by which quantities are primarily known is the one itself; and so the one is the starting-point of number *qua* number."

11. The unfolding of number from infinite unity is a metaphor Cusanus uses repeatedly in *De docta ignorantia* for the way in which the plurality of distinct, finite, created things is unfolded from God.

is the unfolding of unity.[12] As the inexhaustible source of number, infinite unity or oneness is precisely that superlative that always outstrips the comparative greatness of any positable number. This is made clear in the following passage from *De coniecturis:*

> Behold with a depth of mind the infinite power of oneness [*unitatis infinitam potentiam*], for oneness is infinitely greater than is any positable number. For there is no number, howsoever large, in which the power of oneness is inactive. Since, then, through the power of oneness there can always be had a number greater than any [given] positable number, it is evident from the inexhaustible power of *the one alone* that oneness is omnipotent.[13]

No matter how high I count, I can always add one and still arrive at a greater number.

The power of oneness, however, is active in all number, great and small, in another fundamental sense as well. Number always indicates a plurality, and any given number must be understood to be composed of a plurality of units. The number three, for example, is composed of three units. It is not enough, however, simply to posit the three units separately (one, one, one), but they must be thought *together* as a *unity*. Hence number is a unified plurality, or a union of units.[14] Cusanus explains what he has in mind in the following passage from *Idiota de mente:*

> If you say [merely] that the number three is a composite of three units, then you are speaking as if someone were to say that the walls and the roof, separately, make a house. For if the walls exist separately and so too does the roof, then a house is not composed of them. Likewise, three separate units do not constitute the number three. Therefore, if you consider the units according as they constitute the number three, you consider them as united. And what, then, are three united units other than the number three?[15]

12. *De docta ignorantia* II, 3, N. 105 and N. 108 (h I, p. 69 and p. 70).

13. Nicholas of Cusa, *De coniecturis* I, 5, N. 18 (h III, pp. 23–24); trans.Jasper Hopkins in *Nicholas of Cusa: Metaphysical Speculation, Volume Two* (Minneapolis, Minn.: Banning Press, 2001), 156–57.

14. Euclid had defined number as "a multitude composed of units" (*Elements* VII Def. 2). Aristotle goes on to raise the question of what makes any given number or "multitude" itself a unity, i.e. one single number? See, e.g., *Metaphysics* VIII 3, 1044a 2–5, and VIII 6, 1054a 7–12. See Myles Burnyeat's helpful discussion in his commentary in *The Theaetetus of Plato* (Indianapolis and Cambridge: Hackett Publishing, 1990), 205–9. See also Boethius's definition of number: "Numerus est unitatum collectio, vel quantitatis acervus ex unitatibus profusus" (*De Institutione Arithmetica* I, 3, ed. G. Friedlein [Leipzig: B. G. Teubner, 1867; reprint ed., Frankfurt: Minerva GmbH, 1966]).

15. Nicholas of Cusa, *Idiota de mente* 6, N. 90 (h V, p. 68), trans. Jasper Hopkins in

Thus, oneness, or unity, is the generative *principle* of number both as the *unit* measure that grounds magnitude and makes quantitative comparison possible (the three units of the number three as compared to the four units of the number four), and also as that which *unites* the units into *one distinctive* plurality, that is, into a single, distinctive number (the number three or the number four). Without *oneness* "there would be no distinction between things; nor would order or plurality or greater and lesser be found in numbers; indeed, number itself would not exist."[16]

Hence, if the superlative as maximum is presupposed in the recognition of the essential surpassability of the comparative—in the inexhaustibility of the ascent—it is the superlative as minimum that is the presupposition of the order and comparative relationships that hold between distinctive numbers. And indeed, maximum and minimum coincide here, as the "infinite unity"[17] that is the beginning and end of all numbers:

Unity, however, cannot be number, for number, which admits a greater, can in no way be either simply minimum or simply maximum; but because unity is minimum, it is the beginning of all number, and because it is maximum, it is the end of all number.[18]

Reflection on the nature of number, and the number series, thus provides a first answer to the question of how the infinite can be the measure of the finite. It is the measure in the sense that the superlative is the measure of the merely comparative. The comparative is derivative of and presupposes the superlative. And our ability to recognize the comparative as comparative already implies an awareness of the superlative. That is to say, the finite is derivative of and presupposes the infinite. And our ability to recognize the finite as finite already implies an awareness of the infinite.[19]

Nicholas of Cusa on Wisdom and Knowledge (Minneapolis, Minn.: Banning Press, 1996), p. 215. See also Nicholas of Cusa, *De Coniecturis* I, 2, N. 8, and *De ludo globi* II, N. 109.

16. *De docta Ignorantia* I, 5, N. 13 (h I, p. 12); Bond, p. 93.

17. See ibid., I, 4, N. 11, and I, 5, N. 14.

18. Ibid., I, 5, N. 14 (h I, p. 12); Bond, p. 93.

19. Descartes utilizes this insight in his proof for the existence of God in his Third Meditation.

The Division of the Continuum

The second mathematical example to consider is that of the division of a finite line. Take a line and divide it in half. Take one of those halves and divide it in half as well. Again, take one of those halves and divide it in half, and so on. This example is clearly closely related to our previous example of counting, in that no matter how often I divide a line, I can *always* make another division and be no nearer an end in the process than when I first began. Like the ascent up the number scale, the descent in the division of the continuum to progressively shorter and shorter lines is potentially unending. The infinite can never be reached by such incremental addition (in the case of counting) or division (in the case of the continuum). Cusanus explicitly notes this parallel in the following passage:

> Since it is impossible to ascend to the simply maximum or to descend to the simply minimum, so that, as is evident with number and with the division of the continuum, there is no transition to the infinite, it is clear that for any given finite thing, a greater and a lesser, whether in quantity, power, or perfection, and so forth, necessarily can be given.[20]

There is not a progression of more and less to infinity. The more and less cannot apply to the infinite, which is beyond—indeed prior to and the ground of—all comparative relation. Again, we are able to understand that a greater or a lesser can *necessarily* be given because we have an implicit awareness of the superlative (the infinite as maximum and as minimum) that stands as the measure for the potentially unending character of comparative increase or decrease.

Cusanus believes, however, that if we attend carefully to the example of the division of the continuum, we will recognize another important sense in which the infinite acts at the measure of the finite. It is the measure, Cusanus holds, insofar as the infinite is the *essence* of the finite. What does he have in mind? Cusanus begins by asking us to consider an infinite line composed of an infinite number of segments, each one foot long, and another infinite line composed of an infinite number of segments two feet long.[21] The two infinite lines would have to be equal, Cusanus

---

20. *De docta ignorantia* II, 1, N. 96 (h I, pp. 63–64); Bond, p. 130.
21. Ibid., I, 16, N. 46 (h I, p. 32).

observes, despite the fact that two feet is twice the length of one foot, for one infinite line cannot be "longer" or "greater" than another infinite line. Otherwise it would be merely comparatively great and so finite rather than infinite.

Now at first it might seem that the lesson to be learned is that the two infinite lines must be equal because each is composed of an *infinite number* of finite segments. Thus we might be tempted to try to think about the example in the following way. We recognize that a line two feet long is twice the length of a one-foot line. But we also recognize that a line composed of two one-foot segments is the same length (namely two feet) as a line composed of one two-foot segment. Similarly, a line composed of four one-foot segments is the same length (namely four feet) as a line composed of two two-foot segments. Imagine continuing this parallel construction indefinitely. No matter how long the line (a line two hundred feet long, four thousand feet long, etc.) we would always have two lines of equal length, but one would be composed of "more" segments (namely twice the number of segments) than the other. But if both lines were composed of an "infinite number" of segments, this "more" would disappear. Both lines would be "infinitely long" precisely because they would both be composed of an infinite number of finite parts, each extending indefinitely.

This is not, however, what Cusanus has in mind. We recall that there can be no quantitative ascent or increase to infinity. Hence, the infinite line cannot be thought of as composed of an infinite number of *finite* parts. This becomes clear in the discussion following Cusanus's observation that an infinite line consisting of an infinite number of lengths of one foot would have to be equal to an infinite line consisting of an infinite number of lengths of two feet. Here, he goes on to explain:

Therefore, just as in an infinite line one foot is not smaller than two feet, so an infinite line is not longer than the length of one foot more than it is longer than the length of two feet. Indeed, since each part of the infinite is infinite, then one foot of an infinite line is interchangeable with the entire line, just as two feet would be.[22]

---

22. Ibid., I, 16, N. 46 (h I, p. 32); Bond, p. 108.

If the infinity of an "infinite line" were thought of as the result of its being composed of an infinite number of finite parts, then those finite parts could still be compared one to the other and assessed as greater or smaller. In such a supposedly "infinite line" one foot *would* be smaller than two feet. We might attempt to visualize such a line as composed of finite segments, but extending indefinitely in both directions, thus:

But this is misleading insofar as what we symbolically represent here is merely indefinite increase.

So how are we to understand the infinity of the infinite line if not as indefinite extension of finite increments? If a line is truly thought of as infinite, or maximal, it must be thought of as absolute extension. It has no fixed length that can be compared to the length of a given finite line. Indeed, insofar as it is truly infinite, the maximum and minimum coincide.[23] An infinite line coincides with a minimal line. That is why he asserts, in the passage cited above, that "an infinite line is not longer than the length of one foot more than it is longer than the length of two feet." Further, an infinite line, unlike a finite line, is "indivisible." That is to say, an infinite line cannot be divided into parts, "for the infinite, in which maximum and minimum coincide, has no parts."[24] It clearly follows that an infinite line cannot be composed of finite parts.

Cusanus often makes this same point—that the infinite is not a whole composed of distinct parts—by insisting that each "part" of the infinite must itself be infinite, so that each part coincides with the whole. That is why *in* an infinite line one foot is not smaller than two feet.[25] Each part of the infinite is infinite, so that "one foot of an infinite line is interchange-

---

23. Ibid., I, 17, N. 47 (h I, p. 33).

24. Ibid.; Bond, p. 108.

25. Cusanus makes a similar point about how we would have to conceive of a maximal or infinite number (*De docta ignorantia* II, 1, N. 96 [h I, p. 64]; Bond, p. 130): "Because each part of the infinite is infinite, the assertion that where we reach the infinite we find more and less implies a contradiction. For just as more and less cannot apply to the infinite, so they cannot apply to anything that bears some proportional relation to the infinite, because this thing also would have to be infinite. If by ascending one could actually arrive at an infinite number, two in such a number would not be less than a hundred, just as an infinite line consisting of an infinite number of lines of two feet would not be less than an infinite line consisting of an infinite number of lines of four feet."

able with the entire line, just as two feet would be [interchangeable with the entire line]." It is just this "interchangeability," which is recognized when we say—in the language of modern mathematics—that there is a one-to-one correspondence between each and every point on the one-foot line with each and every point on the infinite line (and similarly for any finite line segment). Each finite line is infinitely rich in this sense. And it is this infinite richness that grounds the potentially unending divisibility of all finite lines.

Cusanus explains as follows: although any given finite line is divisible, it cannot be so far divided that it is no longer a line. That is, in the division of the line we never come to some simple, atomic part that is not itself further divisible. Each division simply marks off a smaller line segment, which is itself still a line and is itself further divisible. A finite line is therefore not composed of atomic, nonlinear parts.

In its linear essence a finite line is, therefore, indivisible; a line of one foot is no less a line than is a line of one cubit. It follows, therefore, that an infinite line is the essence of a finite line.[26]

To *be* a line is to have this same linear integrity through and through, no matter how great or small its magnitude. Indeed, it is the linear integrity of the continuum, its inexhaustible richness, that grounds the potentially unending divisibility of all finite lines.

The indivisible, infinite line is present as a whole in all finite lines as their linear essence. Just as, in the infinite line, a one-foot line is not shorter than a two-foot line, so also the reciprocal holds:

in a line of two feet the infinite line is neither longer nor shorter than the two-foot line, nor in a line of three feet is it longer or shorter than a three-foot line and so on. Because the infinite line is indivisible and one, it is entire in each finite line.[27]

It is present, as their very essence, not insofar as one line differs in magnitude from another line but insofar as each line, no matter its magnitude, is still a line.[28] They each participate in its maximal indivisibility, its absolute linear integrity. In this sense, then, the infinite line is the precise measure

26. Ibid., I, 17, N. 47 (h I, p. 33); Bond, pp. 108–9.
27. Ibid., I, 17, N. 50 (h I, p. 34); Bond, pp. 109–10.
28. Ibid.

of each finite line. Cusanus finds this to be a helpful metaphor for describing the way in which the divine Maximum is the essence and hence the "most adequate and most precise measure" of all created things.[29] The divine maximum is the essence of each created thing and is wholly present in each finite thing, not insofar as one creature is distinct one from the other, but as the essential being of each thing. Every finite creature participates (albeit in a limited way) in the divine infinite.[30] It is for this reason that Cusanus describes each creature as a "finite infinity" or a "created god."[31] Each finite thing is a unique "contraction" of divine infinity.

The Inscribed Polygon

The third mathematical metaphor to consider is that of a many-sided polygon inscribed in a circle. This metaphor appears at the very beginning of Book I of *De docta ignorantia* and then again at a crucial juncture of Book III, and thus it serves as a sort of frame for the trajectory of the entire text. As we shall see, it incorporates both the previous examples and expands on them to illuminate a third sense in which the infinite acts as the measure of the finite: as its goal and perfection.

The inscribed polygon makes its first appearance in Book I, chapter 3, in order to help illustrate how it is that the precise truth of things is unattainable for a finite (human) intellect. Cusanus begins by reminding the reader that there is no proportion between the infinite and the finite and that whenever we encounter a greater and a lesser we do not reach the simply maximum. Now all finite things stand in comparative relations one to the other. One thing may be more or less similar to another thing than it is to some third thing. But no two finite things are "so similar and equal that they could not be still more similar *ad infinitum*."[32] This is because, as

29. Ibid., I, 16, N. 45 (h I, p. 32); Bond, p. 108. See also ibid., I, 17, N. 47 (h I, p. 33), and N. 50–51 (h I, pp. 34–35).

30. On the dynamics of this participation through the mediation of the universe, see *De docta ignorantia* II. For a discussion of this dynamic, see Brient, *The Immanence of the Infinite*, part 3, sec. 2: "The Intensive Infinitization of the Cosmos," 219–23. See also Regine Kather on the relation between the infinite and the finite and its cosmological implications in the next essay.

31. *De Docta Ignorantia* II, 2, N. 104 (h I, p. 68); Bond, p. 134.

32. Ibid., I, 3, N. 9 (h I, p. 9); Bond, 90.

we have seen, the divine infinite lies at the heart of the being of each created thing as its essence. Each finite thing is a unique contraction of divine infinity. Hence, among finite things only degrees of equality can be found, and "however equal the measure and the thing measured may be, they will always remain different."[33]

This holds for finite human intellectual measures as well.[34] Such measures inevitably fall short of attaining the precise truth of things that is their quiddity.[35] The infinitely rich "thisness" of a created thing is precisely what it is and nothing else. In this sense the truth of things is neither more nor less but "indivisible"; it is thus maximum equality, whereas the finite human intellect always stands in a relationship of "more or less" to the truth that it seeks. A finite intellect, Cusanus underscores, "never comprehends truth so precisely but that it could always be comprehended with infinitely more precision."[36] Cusanus then compares the relationship between the finite human intellect and truth to that of a many-sided polygon inscribed in a circle:

The intellect is related to truth as a polygon to a circle. The inscribed polygon grows more like a circle the more angles it has. Yet even though the multiplication of its angles were infinite, nothing will make the polygon equal the circle unless the polygon is resolved into identity with the circle.[37]

No matter how many sides and angles the polygon has, a polygon with a greater number of sides and angles can always be posited. Hence truth, as maximal equality and the very quiddity of the things themselves, stands as the measure of the adequacy of the finite intellect's (never-ending) approach to it.

This example incorporates the key insights of the two previous mathematical examples. Like the ascent up the number series and the descent in the division of the continuum, the multiplication of angles and sides of the inscribed polygon is a potentially unending process. Here, too, in the guise of maximal equality, the infinite stands as the measure for the potentially unending character of comparative increase. It is the indivisible

33. Ibid.
34. See *De coniecturis* I, Prologus, N. 2 (h III, p. 4).
35. *De docta ignorantia* I, 3, N. 10 (h I, p. 9).
36. Ibid., I, 3, N. 10 (h I, p. 9); Bond, p. 91.
37. Ibid.

singularity of the truth that is not other than itself, the simple "what it is" of things, which provides the measure for the merely relative adequacy of conceptual approximation. While the series of inscribed polygons provide better and better approximations of the circumference of the circle, it can never finally close the gap between polygon and circle. Indeed, no matter how many sides and angles it had, the polygon, as polygon, would remain "infinitely" distant from the indivisible simplicity of the circle that measures it. Just as in the example of counting and the division of the continuum, I am no nearer an end at 10,000 (sides) than I was at 10.

Nevertheless, in the example of the polygon, a crucial new element appears. The circle, here, is not simply a measure that allows us to recognize the comparative as comparative, that is, as relative to the maximal equality of the circle. It is, more importantly, thought here as the goal of a convergent series of polygons. As the polygon's sides and angles increase towards infinity, the polygon approaches coincidence with the circle. The polygon that "is resolved into identity with the circle" is a limit-concept that functions as the goal and perfection for the entire series. This limit-concept is alluded to only in passing at this point in the text, and the reader must wait until Book III for further elaboration. The immediate lesson that Cusanus draws from the inscribed polygon metaphor in Book I is that while the precise truth is indeed the goal of all intellectual striving, it is a goal that nevertheless remains ever out of reach for the finite intellect. "Truth is like the most absolute necessity, which can be neither more nor less than it is, while our intellect is like possibility."[38] Further, the recognition that all human measures are only relatively better or worse approximations of the truth and inevitably all fall short constitutes that recognition of our ignorance, which is of course at the same time a positing of the precise truth as an ever unattainable goal. Hence Cusanus concludes this discussion by remarking that "[t]he more profoundly learned we are in this ignorance the more closely we draw near to truth itself."[39]

Cusanus returns to the example of the inscribed polygon in Book III, and here focuses explicitly on the limit-concept only hinted at in Book I. Once again the many-sided polygon is a figure for human intellectual nature. Now the circle stands for divine intellectual nature, which is the ab-

38. Ibid., I, 3, N. 10 (h I, p. 9); Bond, p. 91.
39. Ibid.

solute truth and the absolute quiddity of all of creation. Christ, as both divine and human, is conceptualized as the limit of the series of n-sided polygons, the limit in which the "maximum polygon" is resolved into identity with the circle.[40]

Cusanus begins, just as he did in Book I, by contrasting the potentiality of the human intellect with the divine intellect, which alone is actually all things. "For the intellect in all human beings is potentially all things; it grows by degrees from potentiality to actuality, so that the greater it exists in act, the less it exists in potentiality."[41] He then goes on to posit the absolute limit of this movement of the human intellect from potentiality to actuality as a maximum intellect that exists in perfect actuality. This maximum intellect is conceived of as the limit at which conjecture coincides with the truth of things, thought with reality. But this coincidence of concept and reality is traditionally understood to be nothing other than divine creative knowledge itself. "[B]ecause the maximum intellect is the limit of the potentiality of every intellectual nature and exists completely in act, maximum intellect cannot exist at all unless it were intellect in such a way that it were also God, who is all in all."[42] Hence, Cusanus makes use of the theological conception of the hypostatic union of human nature with the second person of the Trinity (the creative Word of God) in Jesus Christ in order to conceptualize this limit. Christ, the God-man, is then conceived of as just that "maximum polygon" alluded to in Book I, the limit of the endless series of n-sided polygons that is finally resolved into identity with the circle:

It is as if a polygon inscribed in a circle were the human nature and the circle were the divine nature. If the polygon were to become a maximum polygon, than which there can be no greater polygon, it would in nowise exist per se with finite angles but only in a circular figure. In this way it would not have its own figure of existing, not even intellectually separable from the circular and eternal figure itself.[43]

---

40. Christ is thought here as the union of the absolute quiddity of all things and the contracted quiddity or universal contraction of all things, which is itself contracted in a unique manner in each finite being. As such Christ functions as the principle of ontological determinacy for creation. See *De docta ignorantia* III, 3, N. 199–202 (h I, pp. 127–29). For a detailed discussion see Brient, *The Immanence of the Infinite*, part 3, sec. 2: "Christ as Limit Concept and Measure," pp. 228–42.

41. *De docta ignorantia* III, 4, N. 206 (h I, p. 132); Bond, p. 180.

42. Ibid.   43. Ibid.

Here in Book III, then, the emphasis is no longer placed on the unattainability of precise truth for the finite human intellect, which can never arrive at the maximum by degrees. Rather the focus is placed squarely, now, on the "maximum intellect" in its function as the limit and perfection of human intellectual nature. As just noted, the maximum intellect is *"the limit of the potentiality* of every intellectual nature." In other words, it acts as a regulative ideal for the human intellect insofar as it is that state of actuality toward which every intellectual nature strives. Christ is thought of here as the limit and perfection of the unending potentiality of human intellectual existence.

Conclusion

In order to articulate the way in which the infinite may be understood to be the measure of the finite, Cusanus made use of three particularly helpful mathematical metaphors or examples: the number series, the division of the continuum, and the inscribed polygon. Each example illuminated important respects in which the infinite functions as the measure of the finite. The first example, that of the number series, illustrated the way in which the infinite, as superlative, functions as the measure for the intelligibility of the comparative. The superlative is presupposed in the recognition of the essential surpassability and relativity of the comparative. It also serves to ground the relative order and comparative relations that hold between distinct, finite things. The second example, that of the division and nature of the continuum, illuminated the way in which the infinite acts as the measure of the finite precisely because it is the essence of each finite thing. It is the presence of the infinite in the finite, which grounds the infinite richness of each utterly unique finite thing. Finally the third metaphor, that of the inscribed polygon, illustrates the way in which the infinite measures the finite as the goal and perfection of the finite. This last mathematical example is of particular interest insofar as Cusanus uses it in developing a limit-concept in order to conceive of the relationship between two orders of "infinity": the *absolute* infinite functions as the measure for the *privative* infinity of unending approach to it.

Cusanus uses each of these mathematical metaphors to illustrate general metaphysical principles that pertain to the relationship between the infinite and the finite, namely, between God and creation. He uses the example of the number series to figure the unfolding of creation in all its multiplicity from divine unity. His reflections on the nature of the continuum, in turn, serve to articulate his conception of the immanence of the infinite in the finite and illustrate important aspects of his metaphysics of contraction. Finally, the maximum polygon, which is resolved into identity with the circle, figures the link between the infinite and the finite—the locus of enfolding and unfolding—as a limit-concept, one in fact that posits the coincidence of the privative infinity of the universe with the absolute infinity of God.

Regine Kather

13. "THE EARTH IS A NOBLE STAR"

The Arguments for the Relativity of Motion in the
Cosmology of Nicolaus Cusanus and Their Transformation
in Einstein's Theory of Relativity

The Thesis: A Change in Cosmology

∞ In Book II of his treatise *De docta ignorantia,* Cusanus initiated a decisive transformation in the idea of the universe. For the first time in occidental cosmology, the universe loses every center. Neither the earth nor the sun, as even Nicholas Copernicus continued to maintain, is the center of the cosmos.

Concerning the decentering and the relativity of motion of the celestial bodies, Cusanus can be called a predecessor of Albert Einstein's theory of relativity. Nevertheless, the form of argumentation that leads Cusanus to his thesis differs completely from the method that Einstein practiced. And, as a consequence, the relation of the material and the spiritual dimension of reality is, as we will see, completely different.

The Method: A Speculative Form of Argumentation

To compare the cosmological concepts of Cusanus and Einstein, we must first recall their mode of argumentation. Cusanus does not yet separate the method of physical research and the method of theological argumentation. As in Plato's *Timaeus,* cosmology still deals with theological and physical questions as well. The subject matter of physics and theology is therefore also the same.

For Cusanus, it first has to be explained *that* the world is. Consequently, the starting point for the explanation of the structure of the universe is, as for all medieval thinkers before him, absolute being. "[W]hat is caused derives altogether from its cause and not at all from itself."[1] With-

1. Nicholas of Cusa, *De docta ignorantia* II, *incipit* in *Philosophisch-Theologische Schriften,*

out an absolute being as the ontological cause of the universe, *all* scientific research would be impossible.

Though God is the foundation of the universe through his being and by his creative power, he does not influence the motion of the stars in a physical manner by mechanical forces or, in a more modern sense, by electricity, gravitation, or magnetism. He creates the being of the finite things; he is their first reason and their final aim. To describe the universe, it is therefore not yet sufficient to explain the physical laws that govern the motion of the celestial bodies. Even the order of the stars reflects a spiritual meaning, for it is a visible sign of the relation of finite objects to infinite being. The meaning of causality therefore is not restricted to *causa efficiens* ("efficient cause") as in modern science but also implies *causa exemplaris* ("exemplary cause"), *causa formalis* ("formal cause"), and *causa finalis* ("final cause"). Cosmology not only has to explain *how* material structures of the universe have developed and *how* the celestial bodies are moving. It has to explain the specific form of the universe and, above all, its meaning.

Though Cusanus does not yet know the difference between the truth of being *(Seinswahrheit)* and the truth of scientific statements *(wissenschaftliche Wahrheit)* as it is discussed in the twentieth century, he does distinguish, as did Plato in the *Seventh Letter,* the truth of being from mathematical and physical statements. Only absolute being is immaterial and transcends time and space. It has no limitation, which means that it is not determined by a relation to anything else. It is therefore impossible to define absolute being precisely with rational concepts, which always are, as Plato has already mentioned in the *Timaeus,* occupied with determined objects. The only form of knowledge that may be adequate is a form of knowledge that transcends all mental concepts. But though it is impossible to explain what absolute being is in itself and how finite beings are grounded in it, man can know *that* it is the ontological foundation of the universe and therefore the foundation of every form of knowledge. "Therefore, it is fitting that we be learned-in-ignorance beyond our understanding, so that (though not grasping the truth precisely as it is) we may

---

ed. Leo Gabriel, trans. Wilhelm and Dietlind Dupré, 3 vols. (Vienna: Herder, 1982), 1:313. The English translation is taken from Nicholas of Cusa, *On Learned Ignorance,* trans. Jasper Hopkins (Minneapolis, Minn.: Banning Press, 1985), 87. Hereafter this translation will be referred to as Hopkins, *On Learned Ignorance.*

at least be led to seeing that there is a precise truth which we cannot now comprehend."[2]

In contrast to the form of knowledge that is adequate for absolute being, mathematical statements represent ideal, timeless, and (therefore) unchangeable rules. The idea of a circle, for example, is always the same. Only the images of this idea, for example, concrete circles painted on a wall, on paper, or on the ground, are never exactly identical. The ideal form never can be realized completely by a concrete representation. Though the rule for every circle is the same, every circle differs at least a little bit from all others. By the process of realization, the one ideal circle is multiplied into a lot of concrete circles.

In particular, the constitution of the universe cannot be explained by mathematics only. Cosmology deals with real bodies and real forces. Though we can recognize that they are grounded in absolute being and represent certain mathematical rules, statements about the physical world never can be reduced to mathematical statements. Physical statements refer to concrete events happening under very special conditions. As a consequence, two events will never be completely identical with one another. Statements about the physical order of the world can therefore never be as exact as purely mathematical statements. The lack of exactness is not the fault of the instruments of observation, the concepts of a certain theory, or the special method of research, but of the structure of the world. Only absolute being is not influenced by anything else. It is identical with itself and represents an absolute unity without any multiplicity. The universe, which has the reason for its existence in God and not in itself and which is bound to matter, time, and external causation, can never stay in pure identity with itself. All finite things have a certain lack of being be-

2. *De docta ignorantia* II, incipit in *Philosophisch-Theologische Schriften*, 1:312: "Supra igitur nostram apprehensionem in quadam ignorantia nos doctos esse convenit, ut—praecisionem veritatis uti est non capientes—ad hoc saltim ducamur, ut ipsam esse videamus, quam nunc comprehendere non valemus" (Hopkins, *On Learned Ignorance*, 87). See also *De docta ignorantia* II, 2: "For how could that which is not from itself exist in any other way than from Eternal Being? But since the Maximum is far distant from any envy, it cannot impart diminished being as such. Therefore, a created thing, which is a derivative being, does not have everything which it is (e.g., [not] its corruptibility, divisibility, imperfection, difference, plurality, and the like) from the eternal indivisible, most perfect, indistinct, and one Maximum—nor from any positive cause" (Hopkins, *On Learned Ignorance*, 90).

cause they do not exist only by their own reason. They are influenced and even generated and annihilated by other finite beings and underlie a permanent change.[3] Therefore it is impossible that two bodies have exactly the same shape, the same position in space, and the same relations to all other beings, and are moving in the same manner. All finite things differ from one another. For the universe a multitude of being is constitutive. "[R]ather, in all things difference according to place, time, complexity, and other [considerations] is necessary."[4]

Nevertheless, empirical knowledge is possible only because the objects it deals with are not only in a restless change. They also have a certain unity that they have received from absolute being. Therefore even empirical knowledge is related—in contrast to the modern concept of science—to infinite being as its foundation. Empirical knowledge is not a merely theoretical construction, nor can it be proven by the analysis of empirical data only. But though our knowledge about the universe has a foundation in absolute being, conceptual and mathematical knowledge can be only an approximation to the real essence of being. Empirical knowledge can attain only a relative aim; it will never be complete. Thus, it has to continue in an infinite process.

According to Cusanus, it is a necessary condition of knowledge that we are able to compare something with something else. Objects that are compared must belong to the same class. Only then can they enter into a certain relation to one another. If something can be compared with something else, the difference between the objects is not an absolute one; it can be bridged by many little steps. The continuity between finite things is a necessary condition for measurement by comparison.

The distance that separates infinite being from finite things cannot be measured because the infinite and the finite are separated by an unbridgeable gulf. This gulf cannot be closed by any empirical method nor by logical argumentation. The finite and the infinite belong to two different orders of being. Absolute being is beyond the smallest and the largest finite being as well. Therefore the existence of absolute being can be neither proven nor disproven by empirical science. It is, as Plato has said in the

---

3. Cf. ibid., II, 1, in *Philosophisch-Theologische Schriften*, 1:315.

4. Ibid., II, 1, in *Philosophisch-Theologische Schriften*, 1:317 (Hopkins, *On Learned Ignorance*, 88).

"analogy of the sun," beyond all finite being or, as Cusanus puts it, *supra opposita,* "beyond opposites."[5]

This idea implies that the distance between absolute being and every finite thing is the same. There is no privileged place in the universe or a privileged year in the current of time that is closer to God than another one. It depends not on a spatial or temporal distance nor whether God is near or distant to a finite being, but only on its inner structure. Though measurement is possible only between finite objects, it is nevertheless impossible to find an absolute measure. Nothing that is finite can gain the status of an absolute measure. Therefore neither the biggest nor the smallest thing can be found. As a consequence, the absolute identity of two finite objects is impossible, as is an absolute contradiction between them.[6]

Though the mediating position of mathematical truth still resembles the Platonic hierarchy of knowledge, there is already a certain hint here of the transformation of the function of mathematics into the function of modern science.[7] On the one hand, mathematics still is conceived as a step on the ladder to the timeless ideas of things, that is, to absolute being. On the other hand, it already represents the order of things, that is, the laws that relate them and that determine their position and their motion. In modern science, the laws of nature, which for Galileo Galilei and Johannes Kepler are written in mathematical letters, are no longer identical with the order of values. For the explanation of the motion of a body, no reference to its essence and its telos is made; it is caused only by external forces.[8] So mathematics changes from the representation of ideal forms, which are true, good and beautiful, into the analysis of functional

5. Plato, *Republic* 507c–509b; *De docta ignorantia* II, 1, in *Philosophisch-Theologische Schriften,* 1:315.

6. Cf. *De docta ignorantia* II, 1, in *Philosophisch-Theologische Schriften,* 1:319: "Der Aufstieg zum Größten und der Abstieg zum Kleinsten ist, damit kein Übergang ins Unendliche zustande kommt, schlechthin nicht möglich. . . . Daraus folgt, daß es für jedes gegebene Endliche sowohl in der Quantität als auch in der Mächtigkeit als auch in der Vollkommenheit und allem übrigen notwendig ein Größeres oder Kleineres gibt."

7. On the meaning of mathematics in Cusanus, see the essay by Elizabeth Brient in this volume.

8. Cf. A. Koyré, *Von der geschlossenen Welt zum unendlichen Universum* (Frankfurt am Main: Suhrkamp, 1980), 7f. (ET: *From the Closed World to the Infinite Universe* [Baltimore: Johns Hopkins University Press, 1957]).

relations.[9] Modern mathematics disconnects the idea of the good as an orientation for ethical decisions and as an aim in life from the idea of mathematical truth. The infinitesimal calculus that Gottfried Leibniz and Isaac Newton developed can analyze mathematically the transition between minimal distances, which Cusanus has already postulated.

The Relation of the Infinite to Finite Being

Cusanus explains the structure of the universe by the special relation of the infinite to finite being, not by the empirical observation of stars and their analysis by physical laws. The concept of an absolute being implies that it is impossible to determine it by a graduation of more or less, smaller or bigger, shorter or longer.

For just as more or less cannot befit the infinite, so [they cannot befit] something having any kind of comparative relation to the infinite, since, necessarily, this latter would also be infinite. . . . And so, [by comparison] there is not positable anything which would limit the Divine Power.[10]

Absolute being cannot be measured by anything else, and therefore it cannot be the object of scientific research. The infinite being has no limits at all, because, as already Plotinus has written and as Spinoza will write still some centuries later, "Omnis determinatio est negatio," that is, every determination implies already a negotiation of power. Being, which is determined, is no longer completely caused by itself. It is no longer *causa sui* and therefore not the foundation of the universe. To be limited by something else means that there is something that is in a certain respect more or less, stronger or weaker. Only something that has no limits at all may be infinite. But even if it were possible to go on without coming to an end, it would be impossible to reach the infinity of God. Cusanus elaborates an important difference in the concept of infinity. It is possible to

9. Cf. E. Cassirer, *Individuum und Kosmos in der Philosophie der Renaissance*, 2nd ed. (Darmstadt: Wissenschaftliche Buchgesellschaft, 1963), 7–48 (ET: *The Individual and Cosmos in Renaissance Philosophy* [New York: Harper and Row, 1963]).

10. Cf. *De docta ignorantia* II, 1, in *Philosophisch-Theologische Schriften*, 1:320: "magis et minus, sicut nec infinito convenire possunt, ita nec qualemcumque proportionem ad infinitum habenti. . . . Nihil est itaque dabile, quod divinam terminet potentiam" (Hopkins, *On Learned Ignorance*, 89–90).

speak of a quantitative and a qualitative form of infinity. The universe is infinite in a spatial and temporal respect, but it is not infinite in an absolute sense because the reason for its being lies outside of itself. Only God is pure actuality. Though without a spatial border, the universe is finite. All finite beings are characterized by becoming and fading away, life and death, and more or less actuality. There is always a certain resistance of matter against the realization of a pure idea. Not all that is possible can be realized.[11] The infinity of God cannot be reached by an infinite progress in space, time, or even power. Therefore there is no relation at all between the infinite and the finite being. God is, as Cusanus puts it, the *non aliud*. He is a being that transcends even the contrast of identity and alterity, which is, as Plato mentions in the *Sophist,* characteristic for the constitution of the world. This contrast already implies the relation between different things.

Though the gulf between finite and infinite things is unbridgeable, finite things participate in the infinite. Finite beings have received their being from God. Without him, they would not be; they would be nothingness. God could be without the finite world, but the world cannot exist without God.[12] Therefore finite beings are between God and nothingness. Though they are created by an eternal being, they are in time, are generated, and fade away. They have received their unity from God. Their lack of unity is therefore a measure for the distance from him.[13] So their real and unique measure is not the comparison with the qualities of other finite things. The only real measure is God himself.

Though all finite beings participate in God,[14] each one participates in him in its own manner.[15] Therefore every finite being is complete. It bears the measure for its being in itself so that it does not long to be another being.[16] By their special form finite beings are differentiated from one anoth-

11. Cf. ibid., II, 1, in *Philosophisch-Theologische Schriften,* 1:321.

12. Cf. ibid., II, 3, in *Philosophisch-Theologische Schriften,* 1:335–37, and II, 4, in *Philosophisch-Theologische Schriften,* 1:339.

13. Cf. ibid., II, 3, in *Philosophisch-Theologische Schriften,* 1:331, 333.

14. Cf. ibid., II, 3, in *Philosophisch-Theologische Schriften,* 1:337.

15. Cf. ibid., II, 2, in *Philosophisch-Theologische Schriften,* 1:329: "Die unendliche Gestalt ist nur auf endliche Weise aufgenommen, so daß jedes Geschöpf eine endliche Unendlichkeit oder ein geschaffener Gott ist und dies auf die bestmögliche Weise."

16. Cf. ibid., II, 2, in *Philosophisch-Theologische Schriften,* 1:329, 331: "Jedes Geschöpf als solches ist vollkommen." And: "Jedes geschaffene Sein ruht in seiner Vollkommenheit, die

er, but just this differentiation makes possible the relation between them and thereby the complex unity of the universe.[17] Complexity is possible only because of the multitude of being. The annihilation of multitude would therefore be the annihilation of the universe.

In his treatise *De visione Dei* Cusanus explained the relation of finite and infinite to some monks of the monastery of Lake Tegernsee. The title of this treatise has a double sense. It can be understood as the view of God himself, and it can be understood as man's view of God:

First of all, then, marvel at how it is possible that [the face] beholds each and every one of you at once. For the imagination of the brother who is standing in the east does not at all apprehend the icon's gaze that is being directed toward a different region, viz., toward the west or the south. Next, let the brother who was in the east situate himself in the west, and he will experience the [icon's] gaze as fixed on him in the west, just as it previously was in the east. But since he knows that the icon is stationary and unchanged, he will marvel at the changing of the unchangeable gaze. Moreover, if while fixing his sight upon the icon he walks from west to east, he will find that the icon's gaze proceeds continually with him; and if he returns from east to west, the gaze will likewise not desert him. He will marvel at how the icon's gaze is moved immovably. And his imagination will be unable to apprehend that the gaze is also moved in accompaniment with someone else who is coming toward him from the opposite direction. Now, [suppose that] wanting to experience this [phenomenon], he has a fellow-monk, while beholding the icon, cross from east to west at the same time that he himself proceeds from west to east. And [suppose] he asks the approaching brother whether the icon's gaze moves continually with him. Thereupon he will be told that the gaze is also moved in this opposite manner; and he will believe his fellow-monk. And unless he believed, he would not apprehend that this [simultaneous opposition of motion] was possible.[18]

To explain the relation between infinite and finite being, Cusanus chooses the concept of motion and rest, which is very important for his cosmology, too. He differentiates three ways in which the picture, an *icona Dei,* moves in relation to the monks who regard it:

es vom göttlichen Sein in Fülle erhalten hat und trachtet nicht danach, ein anderes Geschöpf zu sein, als ob es dadurch vollkommener wäre."

17. Cf. ibid., II, 2, in *Philosophisch-Theologische Schriften,* 1:325: "Von Gott ist dem Geschöpf zuteil geworden, daß es geeint, unterschieden und mit dem Gesamt verknüpft ist; je mehr es geeint ist, um so ähnlicher ist es Gott."

18. Nicholas of Cusa, *De visione Dei, praefatio* in *Philosophisch-Theologische Schriften,* 3:97. The English translation is taken from Jasper Hopkins, *Nicholas of Cusa's Dialectical Mysticism* (Minneapolis, Minn.: Banning Press, 1988), 115–17.

1. It is at rest for a person who is also at rest.

2. It is moving with a person who is also moving.

3. It is even moving in different directions for two different observers moving themselves in opposite directions, for example, to the east and to the west. That the view of the picture moves with both observers cannot be seen. It can be known only if they speak with one another about their experiences.

The *icona Dei* is a perfect illustration of the relativity of motion. First, every monk sees himself as the center of the world. He organizes motion and rest from his special point of view. If he feels at rest, the view of the picture is looking at him and also seems to be at rest relative to its environment. If he is walking from east to west, the view of the picture accompanies him. Relative to the observer, the view stays at rest, though it is moving, like the observer, relative to the environment. And if two monks are walking in different directions, each one has the impression that the view of the picture accompanies only him. One can notice that no one has a privileged position but that each moves relatively to the other not by sense perception, but only by the comparison of the experiences of different observers.

But though every one of them sees the *icona Dei* from his special point of view, all monks have a common point of reference, namely, the infinite being God himself. Only because God transcends the contrast of motion and rest can he appear as the unique point of reference for all the monks who move relatively to one another. At least by the infinity of God the multitude of finite perspectives is related. So the multitude of perspectives does not lead into a pure relativism, as in the philosophy of postmodernism. Nor has the multitude been split into the complementarity of perspectives, as in modern physics.[19] In the multitude of perspectives, a certain unity can be recognized, which for Cusanus is the condition that multitude can be.

Only God transcends the contradiction of rest and motion, identity and alterity, here and there. The view of God is therefore not bound to a spatial and temporal perspective. He does not see first this monk and then

---

19. Cf. W. Heisenberg, *Ordnung der Wirklichkeit* (München / Zürich: Piper-Verlag, 1989), and H. Primas, "Ein Ganzes, das nicht aus Teilen besteht," in *Neue Horizonte 92/93. Ein Forum der Naturwissenschaften,* ed. E. P. Fischer (München: Piper-Verlag, 1993), 81–111.

the next; he does not give more attention to this one and less to another one. He sees all of them at once. Therefore God is called the *Alles-Sehende,* the one who is "omnivoyant."[20] God transcends time, space, and matter. For this reason alone is he omnipresent. The act of seeing is not a reflex of an external stimulus. It is an act of consciousness that is constitutive for the world, its being, and its perceptibility. The eternity of the divine knowledge is defined in relation to a certain form of consciousness, one that differs from the human form of consciousness. The consciousness of God has the structure of complete self-reflexivity.

The view by which the monks regard the *icona Dei* is also an activity of consciousness. Only by this activity, which cannot be derived from the perceived objects, can the world be recognized.[21] But in contrast to the timeless knowledge of God, the knowledge of man is finite. It is limited by a spatial perspective, and it changes in time. Every man is living under certain historical, social, and geographical conditions that restrict his knowledge. Under the finite perspective of man, it is impossible to see all things at once. Man can see the different perspectives only one after the other, in succession. And while he changes from one perspective to the next, he has to leave his former perspective. All human knowledge therefore is in time. It is an infinite process, and that means it is finite and incomplete in its very structure.

This insight applies not only to the position of man in the universe and his relation to finite objects. It even applies to human knowledge of God. Though God is the same for every monk, he is recognized only by a certain perspective. For man there is no absolute standpoint, from which he could see at once the whole universe and its foundation in God. Therefore it is impossible that two individuals are looking at God and at the universe from exactly the same point of view. They differ from one another by their position in the world and their relation to one another and therefore by their knowledge too. Every person is an individual who cannot be replaced by another one. Again the finiteness of the world is the condition of differentiation. The difference between human beings can-

---

20. *De visione Dei,* 5, in *Philosophisch-Theologische Schriften,* 3:111.

21. Cf. Arthur Zajonc, *Die gemeinsame Geschichte von Licht und Bewußtsein* (Reinbek bei Hamburg: Rowohlt, 1994) [English original: *Catching the Light: The Entwined History of Light and Mind* (New York: Bantam Books, 1993)].

not be neglected; individuality belongs to the essence of every human be-ing.[22]

Cosmological Implications: The Relativity of Motion of Celestial Bodies

Cusanus derives by a strictly speculative form of argumentation a new idea of the cosmos from these methodological principles and the special relation between the infinite and the finite. In its implications Cusanus's idea is much more far-reaching than the physical models of Copernicus and Galileo. Einstein with his theory of relativity will be the first to devel-op a physical model of the universe that also denies every center of the universe.

If it is true, so goes the argument of Cusanus, that in the world no ab-solute measure can be found, it is the logical and inevitable consequence that no physical object can be completely at rest or move with an absolute velocity so that it could be the measure for the motion of other bodies. "[I]t is not the case that any motion is unqualifiedly maximum motion, for this latter coincides with rest."[23] So *every* celestial body must be mov-ing, the sun and the earth as well. Thus: "From these [foregoing consider-ations] it is evident that the earth is moved."[24] Already several decades be-fore Copernicus, Cusanus was convinced that the earth really is moving. For him, the motion of the earth is not, as Andreas Osiander, the writer of the foreword of Copernicus's *De revolutionibus orbium coelestium* ("On the revolutions of the celestial orbs"), had supposed, only a helpful hy-pothesis that could simplify the calculation of the positions of planets and stars.[25]

But how are the celestial bodies moving? He states:

---

22. It is above all Gottfried Leibniz who stresses in the *Monadologie* the idea that every being is singular.

23. *De docta ignorantia* II, 10, in *Philosophisch-Theologische Schriften,* 1:389 (Hopkins, *On Learned Ignorance,* 113).

24. Ibid., II, 11, in *Philosophisch-Theologische Schriften,* 1:395 (Hopkins, *On Learned Igno-rance,* 116).

25. Cf. J. Hamel, *Nicolaus Copernicus. Leben, Werk und Wirkung* (Heidelberg: Spektrum Akademischer Verlag, 1994).

It has already become evident to us that the earth is indeed moved, even though we do not perceive this to be the case. For we apprehend motion only through a certain comparison with something fixed. For example, if someone did not know that a body of water was flowing and did not see the shore while he was on a ship in the middle of the water, how would he recognize that the ship was being moved? And because of the fact that it would always seem to each person (whether he were on the earth, the sun, or another star) that he was at the "immovable" center, so to speak, and that all other things were moved: assuredly, it would always be the case that if he were on the sun, he would fix a set of poles in relation to himself; if on the earth, another set; on the moon, another; on Mars, another; and so on. Hence, the world-machine will have its center everywhere and its circumference nowhere, so to speak; for God, who is everywhere and nowhere, is its circumference and center.[26]

The argument is similar to what Cusanus developed in the description of the *icona Dei*. A point of reference is necessary to decide whether a body is in motion or at rest, whether it is moving slowly or quickly. Therefore, from its own position, a star seems to be at rest and all other stars seem to be moving around it. So it seems to be the center of the universe. The inhabitants of the planet Earth, for example, have the impression that the earth is at rest and that all other celestial bodies are moving around it. But the inhabitants of another planet would have the impression that their planet was at rest and that the sun, the moon, the earth, and all the other stars would move in a circle around their planet. On the basis of theological argumentation, Cusanus demonstrates for the first time in occidental history the relativity of motion of all celestial bodies.

The insight that we cannot find an absolute measure in the universe has a lot of consequences for our understanding of the whole structure of the universe. An absolute, ideal shape is as impossible as absolute precision. It is only an ideal for our knowledge and for the forms of things as well. So the universe cannot be a perfect ball as Aristotle thought, and the paths of the planets cannot be exact circles. As with everything in the world, the paths of the planets are only "more or less" circles. All things in the world are only the shadow of the ideal forms, an approximation.[27]

26. *De docta ignorantia* II, 12, in *Philosophisch-Theologische Schriften*, 1:397 (Hopkins, *On Learned Ignorance*, 116–17).

27. Cf. ibid., II, 12, in *Philosophisch-Theologische Schriften*, 1:397–99: "Die Erde ist also nicht sphärisch, . . . auch wenn sie zur Kugelgestalt hinstrebt. . . . Die Gestalt der Erde ist also edel und sphärisch, ihre Bewegung ist kreisförmig, sie könnte aber vollkommener sein."

This idea will be used by Kepler. In search for a mathematical formulation for the paths of the planets, he argued that they cannot be exact circles. They are less perfect than a circle and therefore only ellipses.

If it is impossible to find in the finite world an absolute being, then the universe has neither an absolute center nor a definite border. It cannot be a finite ball with the earth at rest in the center; and the circle of fixed stars cannot be a final border, as the medieval theologians had supposed.[28] Besides, it is impossible that not the earth but another star is the center of the universe, as Copernicus will suppose. Though Copernicus accepted the motion of the earth around the sun, he was, like the medieval thinkers, convinced that the universe was surrounded by the belt of fixed stars. In contrast to Copernicus, the universe for Cusanus has no center and is without any definite border. It is infinite in its spatial extension. Without a definite border, there is no "space" beyond the world.[29]

Already some decades before the theory about the motion of the earth of Copernicus and Galileo, the conclusions of Cusanus destroyed the union between the physical order of the universe and the order of salva-

28. In the cosmology of Hildegard von Bingen, for example, the world is surrounded by God, and the earth is at rest in the center of the universe. Cf. R. Kather, "Vollendetes Kunstwerk Gottes: Das kosmische Weltbild Hildegards von Bingen," in *Hildegard von Bingen: Prophetin durch die Zeiten zum 900. Geburtsjahr,* ed. Edeltraut Forster und die Abtei St. Hildegard, Eibingen (Freiburg: Herder, 1997), 198–210.

29. Cf. *De docta ignorantia* II, 11, in *Philosophisch-Theologische Schriften,* 1:391: "Nachdem wir die verschiedenen Bewegungen des Weltkreises betrachtet haben, ist es unmöglich anzunehmen, daß der Weltbau diese sichtbare Erde oder die Luft oder das Feuer oder irgendetwas anderes als festes und unbewegliches Zentrum besitzt. Denn man gelangt in der Bewegung nicht zum schlechthin Kleinsten, wie es der feste Mittelpunkt ist, weil das Kleinste mit dem Größten koinzidieren muß. Der Mittelpunkt der Welt koinzidiert also mit ihrem Umfang. Folglich hat die Welt keinen Umfang. Denn wenn sie einen Mittelpunkt hätte, hätte sie auch einen Umfang und darum in sich ihren Anfang und ihr Ende; sie wäre auf etwas anderes hinbestimmt und außerhalb von ihr wäre Ort und Anderssein. Das alles entspricht nicht der Wahrheit. Da es demnach unmöglich ist, die Welt zwischen körperlichem Mittelpunkt und ihrem Umfang einzuschließen, wird sie, deren Mittelpunkt und Umkreis Gott sind, nicht verstehend begriffen; zwar ist sie nicht unendlich, dennoch kann sie nicht endlich begriffen werden, da sie der Grenzen entbehrt, zwischen die sie eingeschlossen werden könnte. Da die Erde also nicht Mittelpunkt sein kann, kann sie auch nicht ohne jede Bewegung sein. Denn sie muß sich so bewegen, daß sie sich auch unendlich weniger bewegen könnte. Wie die Erde nicht der Mittelpunkt der Welt ist, so ist auch nicht die Fixsternsphäre ihr Umkreis, obwohl, wenn man Erde und Himmel vergleicht, die Erde dem Mittelpunkt und der Himmel dem Umkreis näher zu sein scheint."

tion. In medieval thinking the order of the world was identical with the order of salvation. In Dante Alighieri's *Divina Commedia,* for example, the path that leads to paradise first descends to hell, which is located in the center of the earth. After having passed the deepest circle of the hell, the way finally leads upward to paradise. After Dante has reached the surface of the earth again, he has to climb a high mountain. Then he has to cross the different circles of the planets until at last he reaches the belt of the fixed stars. After he has passed through that realm, he finally arrives in paradise. Since Aristotle the cosmos was divided into the sphere under the moon, which was not so complete, and a sphere above the moon, which was much closer to God. Only in the celestial spheres could mathematics really be applied, for the order of nature was disturbed by a lot of irregularities in the region under the moon. While the earth was formed by the dark and heavy elements, the stars were constituted by light and transparent ones. The hierarchy of the spheres expressed a hierarchy of being, which means a hierarchy of values too. The earth, though the center of the universe, lay at the greatest distance from God. Hell was hidden in the middle of it all. This place was reserved for those people had been damned, that is, who had turned away from God, not in a spatial but in a moral sense.

But if, as Cusanus argued, there is no absolute "down" or "above" and no "right" or "left," then every substantial difference between the celestial spheres has to be overcome. As a consequence, the same four elements have to be found in all stars, only in a different mixture. The universe is no longer divided into different spheres. The region under the moon is governed by the same laws as the region above the moon. The universe now is homogenous. By expressing the conviction that the same laws apply everywhere in the universe, Cusanus anticipates an idea that would be first formulated into a physical law by Newton. The law of gravitation determines the fall of an apple on the earth, the path of the moon around the earth, and the path of the earth and moon around the sun.

In a homogenous universe without any center, the earth is only one star among a lot of other stars. But for Cusanus the loss of the earth's privileged position implies no degradation. On the contrary, if no celestial body is nearer to God than another one, every one has the same value. The earth now is no longer the lowest place of the universe. It has now the position of a star, and this elevation entails a growth of dignity. "And because in the world there is no maximum or minimum with regard to perfections, motions, and shapes (as is evident from what was just said), it is not true that the earth is the lowliest and the lowest."[30] Moreover: "Therefore, the earth is a noble star which has a light and a heat and an influence that are distinct and different from [that of] all other stars, just as each star differs from each other star with respect to its light, its nature, and its influence."[31]

Nevertheless the loss of the spatial center implies for Cusanus not the loss of every center but a clearer elaboration of the concept of God. Cusanus stresses the difference between the material and the spiritual center of the universe, a distinction that the medieval thinkers had ignored. God is immaterial and eternal. So he cannot be located in space, neither in a certain planet, nor, as one might add today, in the brain. He is not at this place and not at another place. He is, as the picture of the *icona Dei* had demonstrated, everywhere simultaneously. Cusanus cites, as Giordano Bruno and Gottfried Leibniz would do some centuries later, a sentence that originates in the Neoplatonic philosophy: "Hence, the world-machine will have its center everywhere and its circumference nowhere, so to speak; for God, who is everywhere and nowhere, is its circumference and center."[32] Because God is not bound to matter, time and space, every star and every being is equidistant from him.

But the divine Logos is not only transcendent, he is also immanent in the universe. Therefore he is present in every star and in every being.[33]

---

30. Ibid., II, 12, in *Philosophisch-Theologische Schriften,* 1:399 (Hopkins, *On Learned Ignorance,* 117).

31. Ibid., II, 12, in *Philosophisch-Theologische Schriften,* 1:401 (Hopkins, *On Learned Ignorance,* 118).

32. Ibid., II, 12, in *Philosophisch-Theologische Schriften,* 1:397 (Hopkins, *On Learned Ignorance,* 117). Cf. D. Mahnke, *Unendliche Sphäre und Allmittelpunkt* (Halle: Max Niemeyer Verlag, 1937).

33. Cf. *De docta ignorantia* II, 4, in *Philosophisch-Theologische Schriften,* 1:341: "Wie Gott als der Unermeßliche weder in der Sonne noch im Mond ist, wenn er auch auf absolute Weise in ihnen das ist, was sie sind, so ist auch das Gesamt zwar nicht in der Sonne noch im Mond, aber es ist in ihnen das, was sie sind, in Verschränkung. Die absolute Washeit der Sonne ist der absoluten Washeit des Mondes gegenüber nichts anderes, nämlich Gott selbst, die absolute Seiendheit und Washeit von allem, die verschränkte Washeit der Sonne dagegen der verschränkten des Mondes gegenüber durchaus eine andere; denn die verschränkte Washeit eines Dinges ist nichts anderes als dieses selbst, ebenso wie die absolute

God himself is the immaterial center of the universe. In a nonspatial sense the universe is limited, but only by God; therefore, God is also the circumference of the universe.

[I]t is no less false that the center of the world is within the earth than that it is outside the earth; nor does the earth or any other sphere even have a center. . . . He who is the center of the world, viz., the Blessed God, is also the center of the earth, of all spheres, and of all things in the world. Likewise, He is the infinite circumference of all things.[34]

God may be found everywhere in the universe, at every place, and at every time.

Let us summarize. The relativity of motion was already known since Aristotle, but Cusanus was the first to apply this observation to the structure of the whole universe. Only a little shift in the argumentation expelled the earth from the center of the universe and led to a transformation of the whole relation of man to the universe and to God. The discovery of the relativity of motion of all celestial bodies is based not yet on empirical observations, but on a purely theological argument. It leads to the loss of every hierarchy of celestial spheres. In a universe without spatial borders, all stars are moving relatively to one another and influencing one another. But why is it that even in theology today we associate the idea of the motion and the decentering of the earth not with Cusanus but with Copernicus and Galileo? In the fifteenth century a new method for scientific research prevailed. Scientific statements had to be proven by systematic experiment and formulated in mathematical language. The new method led to the separation of physical und theological cosmology, a separation reflected in a famous statement ascribed to Galileo: "The paths of nature are not the way to God." The change of method, which separated the cosmology of Cusanus from that of modern science, is in my opinion the main reason why the decentering of the earth has not been associated with Cusanus. Since the birth of modern science, theological argumentation for the infinity of the universe has no longer been

---

Washeit dieses nicht ist. Daraus ergibt sich, daß die Selbigkeit des Gesamt in der Verschiedenheit besteht, wie die Einheit in der Vielheit. Das Gesamt ist nämlich verschränkte Washeit, die anders in der Sonne, anders im Mond verschränkt ist."

34. Ibid., II, 11, in *Philosophisch-Theologische Schriften*, 1:393 (Hopkins, *On Learned Ignorance*, 115).

seen as well founded. The epoch of Cusanus is separated from that of modernity by the way in which a statement has to be proven as true.

Nevertheless, the arguments of Cusanus are in a certain respect very important even today. They disprove the thesis that the loss of the center of the universe implied the ethical and spiritual disorientation of modern man, that is, what Friedrich Nietzsche called "his fall into nothingness" and Sigmund Freud a "narcistic illness." For Cusanus, and for Bruno as well, the expulsion of the earth from the center of the universe has, as we have seen, increased its dignity.[35] The infinity of the universe is a visible sign for the infinity of the creative power of God. If God, as is written in the Bible, is pure spirit, then, so the argument of Cusanus, the spatial center of the world cannot be identical with its spiritual center. Man is not, as Pascal has written, lost in the width of a universe governed only by mechanical laws. He can, as Cusanus and Bruno have argued, feel "at home" even in an infinite universe if its center is the divine logos himself. Man can find God everywhere in the universe and above all in his own spirit.

The Discovery of the Systematic Experiment as a New Method: Cusanus and Modern Science

It was again Cusanus, in his treatise *Idiota de staticis experimentis,* who for the first time developed the "program of an experimental science" that with Galileo became the method of modern science.[36] Not for scientific research, but for humanitarian reasons, medical therapy, agriculture, and juridical problems, Cusanus postulated that all objects that can be measured should be measured.[37] It is impossible to attain really exact data as long as one is dependent on the subjective estimation of the sensual qualities of things, for example, the heat or weight of a body or the intensity of solar rays. Different observers can get the same results only if the observations are made independently of their own feelings. To attain this

35. See, for example, Bruno's *Zwiegespräche vom unendlichen All und den Welten* (Darmstadt: Wissenschaftliche Buchgesellschaft, 1983), 36 (ET in Dorothea Waley Singer, *Giordano Bruno, His Life and Thought* [New York: Schuman, 1950]).

36. Nicholas of Cusa, *Idiota de staticis experimentis,* in *Philosophisch-Theologische Schriften,* 3:631. The English translation is taken from Jasper Hopkins, *Nicholas of Cusa on Wisdom and Knowledge* (Minneapolis, Minn.: Banning Press, 1996), 606–30.

37. Nicholas of Cuda, *Idiota de sanctis experimentis,* 3:627.

aim, a special method has to be applied. The qualities have to be measured under the same conditions in long series of systematically constructed experiments.

Experimental knowledge requires extensive written records. For the more written records there are, the more infallibly we can arrive, on the basis of experiments, at the art elicited from the experiments.[38]

The instruments of observation are not only a prolongation of sense perceptions. They not only widen the horizon of observation, but they transform the concept of experience in a characteristic manner. The qualities of things are transformed by the experimental method in a special manner; they are quantified.

There are far-reaching consequences to the program for the development of an experimental science that Cusanus does not yet mention. Special instruments are necessary to be able to attain exact data by measurement. For Cusanus the ideal technology was the scale. To improve the exactness of the data, the instruments also have to be improved. Progress in experimental science is therefore connected with a progress in technical development. And, at least to a certain degree, the progress in experimental science should support progress in the conditions of social life. While Aristotle in *Nichomachean Ethics,* Book VI, separated technical intelligence from the social and the scientific intelligence, Cusanus combines them for the first time in his program for an experimental science. Social progress now depends not only on the realization of ethical values but on a certain level of technical progress as well. Some centuries later Francis Bacon will postulate explicitly that scientific research should lead to new technical inventions, which in turn should improve the conditions of social life.[39] Since then the dynamics of modern society is based on the hope that scientific research and technical inventions might also support social progress.[40]

Objectivity in the scientific sense of the word can be reached only if a

---

38. Ibid., 3:631 (Hopkins, *Nicholas of Cusa on Wisdom and Knowledge,* 615).

39. Cf. F. Bacon, *Neues Organon der Wissenschaften,* ed. A. T. Brück (Darmstadt: Wissenschaftliche Buchgesellschaft, 1990), 60 (English ed.: *The New Organon,* ed. Lisa Jardine and Michael Silverthorne [Cambridge: Cambridge University Press, 2000]).

40. Cf. H. Jonas, *Technik, Medizin und Ethik. Die Praxis des Prinzips Verantwortung* (Frankfurt am Main: Surhkamp, 1987).

theory is based on those data that are completely independent of a reference to a human being, which means to all qualified sense perceptions, emotions, aims, and even values. Modern science tries to explain the world without any reference to the observing individual. It describes the world, living beings included, under the perspective of the third person. This statement is valid not only for classical mechanics but even for quantum theory, which has changed the relation of observer and observed fundamentally. But though the process of observation can no longer be ignored, the subjectivity of man is still completely irrelevant. The method of physics, which has been the ideal for all empirical sciences and, up to W. V. O. Quine, for the definition of truth as well, does not ask about the essence or the substance of a being. It only asks about the laws by which something can be explained. It does not ask *what* a being is and *why* it is, but only *how* something happens. As a consequence, the concept of causality is restricted to *causa efficiens*. The data gained by measurement are the basis for a theory that should be formalized by mathematics. Mathematical formulas represent the laws that determine the development of certain events. The transformation of the concept of experience and the new relation between experience and concept was therefore the condition for the development of modern science. It determined what since then is regarded as, on the one hand, an objective statement and, on the other, what has a certain meaning "only" for the feeling and thinking individual. Some centuries after Cusanus Descartes separated explicitly those qualities that depend upon the observing subject from those attributes that seem to belong to the object itself.

By contrast to the speculative method of Cusanus's cosmology, the new scientific method is based on the separation of the knowledge of facts from the knowledge of values. Values cannot be derived from facts that are scientifically explained, for values refer to man as a being who can realize the meaning of events and decide, at least to a certain degree, independently. An example is the famous formula of Einstein, which expresses the transformation of energy into mass: $E = mc^2$. The explanation of the physical process implies no information about the aims for which it should or should not be used. History has shown that this purely theoretical insight was also the basis for the construction of the atomic bomb.

But not only qualified perceptions, aims, values, and meaning, all of which depend on the perspective of the first person, cannot be tested by the empirical method. The divine spirit is equally incapable of being proven empirically, as Cusanus already had observed. The theory of modern science explains events that are happening in time and space.

Normally physical research is led by the conviction that there is a real world, which, at least in a certain respect, can be analyzed by the empirical method. To this degree even scientific theories have an ontological basis. But, as Kant has argued, the conditions of knowledge and of experience determine what is seen as "real." As a consequence of its method, modern cosmology does not deal with the question of whether the universe has a spiritual cause, how it can be interpreted, and where man can find an ethical orientation and an aim in life. The separation of science and ethics, as well as of science and religion, determines the fundamental difference between the cosmologies of Cusanus and Einstein.

The Relativity of Time, Space, and Mass in the Theory of Relativity

Let us briefly glance at the theory of relativity. Since the destruction of the medieval *ordo* and the cosmology of Cusanus and Bruno, the theory of relativity was the first attempt to explain the structure and the genesis of the whole universe by some simple principles. Like the cosmology of Cusanus, it is based on the equality of all systems of reference. No system has a privileged position. All systems are moving relatively to one another.

But modern cosmology depends on the empirical method. In other words, its statements have to be proven by measurement. But how can motion be measured if there is no background that is in absolute rest? And how can the velocity of different systems that are moving relatively to one another be compared? In contrast to Cusanus, modern physicists accept one velocity that seems to be the absolute maximum at least for all material objects, namely, the speed of light. It is the same in all inertial systems that are in a non-accelerated motion relatively to one another.

What will then happen if we use a signal of light to measure time in two different systems? Theory and experiment show that time passes more or less slowly in systems moving relatively to one another. This insight forced Einstein to give up the concept of an absolute time that is the same for all systems of reference. In contrast to Cusanus, not only the relativity of space but also the relativity of time have been discovered. Statements about temporal distances are always statements that refer to a certain system. But this form of relativity is independent from the subjectivity of the observer. For all individuals who refer to the same system, temporal distances between two events are the same.

Also spatial distances are different in systems that are moving relatively to one another. Length, too, is not invariant against the transformation from one system to another. And even the mass of a system changes depending upon its relative velocity. The model of the universe based on the theory of relativity implies the relativity of space, time, and even mass.

Though the concepts of time, space, and mass of classical mechanics differ from those of the theory of relativity, classical mechanics is not wrong. The concepts of classical mechanics apply to another frame of reference than those of the theory of relativity.[41] To this degree, the theory of relativity (and quantum theory as well) has demonstrated that there are limits to the validity of concepts *(Gültigkeitsgrenzen)*. Not only the method of physics but also the concepts of physical theories determine what we recognize as "reality." If the frame of a concept changes, the concept of experience and of reality changes too.

The Separation and Completion (or Coordination) of Methods in Einstein's Thinking

Because of the method of modern physics, the theory of relativity can be the basis only for the explanation of the material structure of the universe. It analyzes the physical laws that determine the development of the atomic particles, galaxies, stars, and planets. This model of the universe therefore does not imply the spiritual dimension that Cusanus described. It cannot give an answer to the question of whether or not the universe has meaning, and it cannot give an ethical orientation to man.[42]

41. Cf. P. Mittelstaedt, *Philosophische Probleme der modernen Physik,* 7th rev. ed. (Mannheim: Bl.-Wiss.-Verlag, 1989), 16–45.

42. On the history of the relation of philosophical and physical cosmology, see R. Kather, *Ordnungen der Wirklichkeit. Die Kritik der philosophischen Kosmologie am mechanistischen Paradigma* (Würzburg: Ergon-Verlag, 1998).

Nevertheless, the theory of relativity gives an impulse to correct the "Copernican turn in the theory of cognition" that Kant initiated. For Kant the human subject is the final starting point for the discovery of the world. The explanation of nature has to begin with the reflection on the categories and concepts man uses. The conditions for the possibility of knowledge explain how we see nature. Man, according to this aspect of Kant's heritage, can recognize nature only by certain methods and concepts; therefore, his knowledge is finite. The categories of the human mind, the method of research, and even the frame of concepts that one employs determine our interpretation of reality. If, as has been recognized by the theory of relativity and also by quantum theory, the fundamental concepts of time, space, substance, and causality change, our concept of physical reality changes too.

Nevertheless Kant's insight led to a purely anthropocentric perspective on nature. The physical cosmology developed by the theory of relativity elaborates the opposite point of view: the universe is prior to man in a temporal and ontological sense. Without the universe and the laws of nature that govern its development, man would not be alive and therefore also would be unable to think. In a certain respect the universe is a condition for the possibility of cognition. To understand the "position of man in the cosmos," we need the insight of the conditions of cognition that Kant revealed, as well as the opposite point of view, which shows that man is by his body also a part of nature.[43]

43. Cf. B. Kanitscheider, *Das Weltbild Albert Einsteins* (Munich: Beck, 1988), 179f.: Einstein "hat uns eine Sichtweise der Dinge geliefert, die ich die *kosmische Perspektive* nennen möchte. . . . Philosophen, Naturforscher, Methodologen haben immer wieder zu begründen versucht, daß die Erklärungsrichtung in der das Verstehen der Natur erfolgen muß, bei den Wahrnehmungen, Vorstellungen und Ideen der Menschen zu beginnen hat, daß wir uns in vielen konstruktiven Schritten, langsam die Welt des Menschen überschreitend, auf die Dinge zubewegen müssen, um sie in ihrer Objektivität zu approximieren. Einsteins Werk und seine eigenen Reflexionen darüber legen eine weitere Erklärungsrichtung nahe, die, ebenso wichtig, die erste ergänzen muß. Sie geht nicht von den anthropischen Gegebenheiten aus, sondern versucht, die Objektivität der Naturdinge antizipierend, vom umfassendsten System und seiner Geschichte auszugehen, und bemüht sich dann in kleinen Konstruktionsschritten zuletzt die Innenwelt des Menschen und sein Erkenntnisvermögen zu rekonstruieren. Hypothetisch wird dabei das fallible Wissen vorausgesetzt, daß der Kosmos, die großräumige Einbettung unserer lokalen Umgebung, der älteste Teil der Natur ist, der die notwendige Bedingung für die Existenz der späteren, komplexeren Entwicklungsstufen liefert. Einsteins kosmische Perspektive der Dinge scheint mir die

But the methods of physics can reveal, as we have shown above, only a fragment of reality, what Einstein called *einen kleinen Ausschnitt der Natur.*[44] Physical cosmology is only a restricted perspective on the universe.[45] The order of nature is much more than we can grasp by physical concepts. Therefore we need other methods and concepts to complete our knowledge about the universe and the position of man in the universe.

Nevertheless for Einstein the theory of physics reveals that nature is determined by an order independent from man.[46] It is constituted not only by the categories of human mind that give a form to the chaotic material of the sense perceptions, and it cannot be changed by human will. On the contrary, nature is a condition for the possibility of human existence. Therefore, the laws of physics are a sign that nature is governed by an *überlegene Vernunft* ("a superior intelligence")[47] and a *prästabilierte Harmonie* ("pre-established harmony"),[48] from which man can recognize only a *geringen Abglanz* ("pale reflection").[49]

By true scientific research man understands the limits of scientific concepts, and this insight opens him to a greater concept of reality. He is no longer locked into the narrow frame of his own methods, concepts, and interests. To be able to transcend oneself is traditionally a characteristic sign of religion. It thus follows that for Einstein the insight that there is an

---

unumgängliche Ergänzung zur anthropozentrischen Sehweise zu sein. Der Mensch wird nur dann ganz zu sich selbst finden, wenn er weiß, wo er in der Ordnung der Dinge steht."

44. Cf. A. Einstein, *Mein Weltbild*, ed. C. Seelig (Frankfurt am Main: Ullstein, 1981), 108: "Höchste Reinheit, Klarheit und Sicherheit auf Kosten der Vollständigkeit" (abridged ET: *The World as I See It*, trans. Alan Harris [New York: Philosophical Library, 1949]).

45. Cf. A. Einstein, *Aus meinen späten Jahren*, 2nd ed. (Stuttgart: Dt. Verl.-Anst., 1979), 107: "Ihr Bereich ist also durch die Methode gegeben, als der Inbegriff der Erfahrungsinhalte, die sich mathematisch erfassen lassen. Mit ihrem Fortschreiten hat sich der Bereich der Physik so erweitert, daß sie uns an jene Grenzen gebunden erscheint, die in ihrer Methode selbst liegen" (English original: *Out of My Later Years* [New York: Philosophical Library, 1950]). Therefore the progress in physics may complete the physical view of the world, but it cannot develop a complete worldview.

46. Albert Einstein, as cited in *Albert Einstein als Philosoph und Naturforscher*, ed. Paul Arthur Schilpp (Stuttgart: Kohlhammer, 1955), 2: "Da gab es draußen diese große Welt, die unabhängig von uns Menschen da ist und vor uns steht wie ein großes, ewiges Rätsel, wenigstens teilweise zugänglich unserem Schauen und Denken." Cf. also Albert Einstein, *Aus meinen späten Jahren*, 64–67, and Einstein, *Mein Weltbild*, 118.

47. Einstein, *Mein Weltbild*, 18.

48. Ibid., 109.

49. Ibid., 17.

order in nature *and* that nature is far more than physical concepts can reveal generates a deep feeling of respect and humility, a *kosmische Religiosität.*[50] The insight into the ontological foundation of physics opens man to transcendence. Though Einstein's concept of absolute being is inspired by Baruch de Spinoza and consequently differs from that of Cusanus, Einstein and Cusanus are in agreement that the order of the universe is a sign of an absolute being.

The concepts of truth in modern science and in religion are different, and scientific statements cannot be used for a cosmological proof of God; nevertheless, the motivation for science and religion is, as Einstein argues, the same. The real search for scientific insights is, as in antiquity, based on the search for truth, and the longing for truth is the condition for religion as well. The search for truth is the link between science and religion. Science cannot be understood without a reference to a human being that is searching for scientific insights. Though for scientific statements the reference to the perspective of the first person is, as we have seen, methodically excluded, the conditions of scientific insights cannot be understood without reflecting on man as a being who longs for truth. On the other hand, religion needs scientific insights about the order of nature to develop a cosmology and to explain the position of man in nature. Just in being different, science and religion complete one another because, as Einstein puts it: "Science without religion is lame, religion without science is blind."[51]

Conclusion: From Cusanus to Einstein

The starting point of the theory of relativity differs from the cosmology Cusanus developed, but the insight into the methodological and conceptual limits of a physical cosmology and into the ontological conditions of human life leads Einstein—as well as many other theoretical physicists of the twentieth century—to a view of the world that converges in a cer-

---

50. Ibid., 17f.

51. Albert Einstein, *Out of My Later Years,* 26. Cf. Einstein, *Aus meinen späten Jahren,* 37–47, and M. Jammer, *Einstein und die Religion* (Konstanz: Konstanz Universitätsverlag, 1995, revised ET: *Einstein and Religion: Physics and Theology* [Princeton: Princeton University Press, 1999]).

tain respect with that of Cusanus. Man seems to be a part in the order of nature that can be discovered only under restricted perspectives and that is founded in a timeless order of being in which physics, ethics, and religion converge.[52] This conclusion cannot be proven by the method of physics. Therefore this method has to be transcended by a speculative interpretation of physical insights *and* completed by regarding the whole complexity of human experience. *How* this transition to a more complete and complex view of the world can be made, taking into consideration the modern sciences as well, is still a task for future.

52. Cf. W. Heisenberg, "Das Naturbild Goethes und die technisch-naturwissenschaftliche Welt," in Heisenberg, *Schritte über Grenzen,* 5th ed. (Munich: Piper, 1984), 224, and A. N. Whitehead, *Process and Reality: An Essay in Cosmology,* ed. D. R. Griffin and D. W. Sherburne Whitehead (New York: Free Press, 1979), 342–51.

❧ Suggested Reading

Peter Casarella

There are many books and several bibliographies that introduce the study of Cusanus, and here I would like to make the reader aware of some of the more useful resources. The primer *Introducing Nicholas of Cusa: A Guide to a Renaissance Man,* ed. Christopher M. Bellitto, Gerald Christianson, and Thomas M. Izbicki (New York: Paulist Press, 2004) also contains helpful bibliographic tools.

Work on the modern critical edition began in Leipzig with the Heidelberg Academy of Sciences in 1931 and was completed in 2005. The edition bears the title *Nicolai de Cusa Opera omnia iussu et auctoritate Academiae Litterarum Heidelbergensis* (Leipzig-Hamburg: Meiner, 1932–2005). Each of these volumes includes textual variants, a copious apparatus of sources, and references to all parallel texts in Cusanus's works. The complete edition includes these volumes:

Felix Meiner Verlag is also publishing in its *Philosophische Bibliothek* the so-called *editio minor* of the speculative works. These handy volumes include the critical edition of the text, sparse notes, and a German translation. Scholarly essays containing invaluable research are sometimes appended to these volumes. There is one other modern edition that is sometimes cited by scholars: Nicholas of Cusa, *Philosophisch-Theologische Schriften,* ed. Leo Gabriel, trans. Wilhelm and Dietlind Dupré, 3 vols. (Vienna: Herder, 1982). These volumes have the advantage of including the works in just three volumes, together with a German translation.

The two major English translations of the philosophical and theological works are *Complete Philosophical and Theological Treatises of Nicholas of Cusa,* trans. Jasper Hopkins, 2 vols. (Minneapolis, Minn.: Banning Press, 2001), and *Nicholas of Cusa, Selected Spiritual Writings,* trans. H. Lawrence Bond (New York: Paulist Press, 1997). The former volumes include all of the speculative works and tend to adopt a more literal rendering of Cusanus's prose even in cases where the expressions involve neologisms or other such peculiarities. The latter focuses only on selected spiritual writings and employs a freer style of translation.

Neither of these works includes the political and ecclesiastical treatises. *De concordantia catholica* is available in *Nicholas of Cusa: The Catholic Concordance,* trans. Paul E. Sigmund (Cambridge: Cambridge University Press, 1991). A translation of *De auctoritate praesidendi* done by H. Lawrence Bond, Thomas M. Izbicki, and Gerald Christianson can be found in "Nicholas of Cusa: On Presidential Authority in a General Council," *Church History* 59 (1990): 19–34. Izbicki also published a translation of *Epistola ad Rodericum Sancium de Arevalo* in "The Church in the Light of Learned Ignorance," *Medieval Philosophy and Theology* 3 (1993): 186–214. Finally, the *Reformatio generalis* has been translated by Izbicki and Morimichi Watanabe in "Nicholas of Cusa, A General Reform of the Church," in *Nicholas of Cusa on Christ and the Church,* ed. G. Christianson and T. M. Izbicki (Leiden: Brill, 1996), 175–202. There is still no volume in English dedicated solely to the sermons, and only recently has this topic become a focus of research and even some translation projects by scholars writing in English. A good introduction to the sermons as a whole can be found in Klaus Reinhardt and Harald Schwaetzer, ed., *Nikolaus von Kues als Prediger* (Regensburg: S. Roderer-Verlag, 2004). Two issues of the MFCG (i.e., the proceedings of the 2004 and 2005 symposia respectively) are also dedicated to this theme.

In addition, several journals are dedicated to research on Cusanus. For example, the *Mitteilungen und Forschungsbeiträge der Cusanus-Gesellschaft* (MFCG) and *American Cusanus Society Newsletter* remain invaluable as guides for further research. In 2001 the Cusanus-Gesellschaft began issuing *Litterae Cusanae,* a newsletter about the Society and Cusanus-related publications. For online resources, one should consult, above all, the Web sites of the American Cusanus Society, the Institut für Cusanus-Forschung, and Jasper Hopkins (which includes all of his published translations as well as a supplement to the printed bibliographies listed below).

As of this writing, there is no single reliable database or published volume that includes all bibliographic information. The bibliography in the MFCG, for example, covers a period spanning six decades but ends at 1982:

1. Robert Danzer and Hans Kleinen, "Cusanus-Bibliographie (1920–1961)," MFCG 1 (Mainz: Matthias Grünewald Verlag, 1961), 95–126

2. Robert Danzer, "Cusanus-Bibliographie, Fortsetzung (1961–1964) und Nachträge," MFCG 3 (Mainz: Matthias Grünewald Verlag, 1963), 223–37

3. Mario Vasquez, "Cusanus-Bibliographie, 3. Fortsetzung (1967–1973) mit Ergänzungen," MFCG 10 (Mainz: Matthias Grünewald Verlag, 1973), 207–34

4. Alfred Kaiser, "Cusanus-Bibliographie, 4. Fortsetzung (1972–1982) mit Ergänzungen," MFCG 15 (Mainz: Matthias Grünewald Verlag, 1982), 111–47.

Hans Georg Senger wrote a supplement that was published as "Cusanus-Literatur der Jahre 1986–2001: Ein Forschungsbericht," Recherches de Théologie et Philosophie médiévales 69 (2002): 225–42.

Finally, Jasper Hopkins has compiled a substantial bibliography, which often includes recently completed dissertations. Unfortunately, this material is scattered throughout his many volumes: *A Concise Introduction to the Philosophy of Nicholas of Cusa* (Minneapolis, Minn.: University of Minnesota Press, 1978; 2nd ed., 1980; 3rd ed., 1986), 45–58; *Nicholas of Cusa on Learned Ignorance: A Translation and an Appraisal of De Docta Ignorantia* (Minneapolis, Minn.: Banning Press, 1981; 2nd ed., 1985), 163–69; *Nicholas of Cusa's Dialectical Mysticism: Text, Translation, and Interpretive Study of De Visione Dei* (Minneapolis, Minn.: Banning Press, 1985; 2nd ed., 1988), 275–80 (see also 281–84); *Nicholas of Cusa's De Pace Fidei and Cribratio Alkorani: Translation and Analysis* (Minneapolis, Minn.: Banning Press, 1990; 2nd ed., 1994), 245–50; *Nicholas of Cusa on Wisdom and Knowledge* (Minneapolis, Minn.: Banning Press, 1996), 521–34 (see also 535–40); and *Nicholas of Cusa: Metaphysical Speculations* [vol. 2] (Minneapolis, Minn.: Banning Press, 2000), 328–32.

All of these resources will be surpassed with the publication of Hans Gerhard Senger's comprehensive volume entitled *Verzeichnis der Schriften über Nikolaus von Kues. 1469–2001. Mit einem Nachtrag zu den Jahren 2002–2004.* It will appear in Schriften der Philosophisch-historischen Klasse der Heidelberger Akademie der Wissenschaften as *Cusanus-Studien*, vol. 12, and is scheduled to be published in 2006 by Universitätsverlag C. Winter in Heidelberg. Senger's bibliography includes over 4,400 titles and has two parts: (1) an alphabetical index of works about Nicholas of Cusa arranged according to author and (2) comprehensive indices that consider the subject matter from many points of view.

In addition, the website of the Institut für Cusanus-Forschung in Trier lists some bibliographic information starting in 1998. The *American Cusanus Society Newsletter* (as well as the society's Web page) is another useful means for learning about recent publications.

As already noted, the year 2001 marked the six-hundredth anniversary of the birth of Nicholas of Cusa and gave rise to congresses dedicated to his thought. These include *Nikolaus von Kues, 1401–2001*, ed. Klaus Kremer and Klaus Reinhardt, MFCG 28 (Trier: Paulinus, 2003); João Maria André and Mariano Álvarez Gómez, eds., *Concidencia Dos Opostos e Concordia: Caminhos do Pensamiento em Nicolau de Cusa* (Coimbra: Faculdade de Letras, 2002); João Maria André and Mariano Álvarez Gómez, eds., *Coincidentia de Opuestos y Concordia. Los caminos del Pensamiento en Nicolás de Cusa* (Salamanca: Universidad de Salamanca, 2002); Helmut Gestrich and Klaus Kremer, eds., *600 Jahre Nikolaus von Kues 1401–2001* (Trier: Paulinus 2003); Martin Thurner, ed., *Nicolaus Cusanus zwischen Deutschland und Italien. Beiträge eines deutsch-italienischen Symposiums in der Villa Vigoni* (Berlin: Akademie Verlag, 2002); Inigo Bocken, ed., *Conflict and Reconciliation: Perspectives on Nicholas of Cusa* (Leiden: Brill, 2004); and Kazuhiko Yamaki, ed., *Nicholas of Cusa. A Medieval Thinker for the Modern Age,* Waseda/Kurzon International Series, 2. (Richmond, Surrey: Curzon Press, 2002). The volume by Thurner has a bibliography of some forty-seven pages that covers Cusanus's dual German-Italian heritage. The 2001/2 issue of *Theologische Quartalschrift,* a journal published by the professors of Catholic theology at the University of Tübingen, was entitled *600 Jahre Nikolaus von Kues (1401–2001): Tradition und Aktualität Negativer Theologie* and includes essays that relate Cusanus's negative theology to aesthetics, Proclus, non-Christian religions, Eckhart, and the Kyoto School of Zen Buddhism.

❈ Contributors

Elizabeth Brient is an Associate Professor in the Department of Philosophy at the University of Georgia. She has published articles on the transition from the Middle Ages to modernity, dealing with Meister Eckhart, Nicholas of Cusa, Hans Blumenberg, and Hannah Arendt. She recently published with the Catholic University of America Press *The Immanence of the Infinite: Hans Blumenberg and the Threshold to Modernity.*

Peter Casarella is Associate Professor of Systematic Theology at the Catholic University of America and a Vice President of the American Cusanus Society. He has written articles on Nicholas of Cusa and contemporary theology. He coedited two books: *Christian Spirituality and the Culture of Modernity: The Thought of Louis Dupré* and *Cuerpo de Cristo: The Hispanic Presence in the U.S. Catholic Church.* His *Word as Bread: Language and Theology in Nicholas of Cusa* is forthcoming in the *Buchreihe der Cusanus-Gesellschaft.* In the academic year 2003–2004 he held the J. Houston Witherspoon Fellowship in Theology and Natural Science at the Center of Theological Inquiry in Princeton, N.J.

Louis Dupré was from 1973 until 1998 the T. Lawrason Riggs Professor in the Philosophy of Religion and is now Professor Emeritus in Religious Studies at Yale University. His numerous publications comprise fifteen books and some two hundred articles, including *The Philosophical Foundations of Marxism; The Other Dimension* (translated into six languages); *Transcendent Selfhood; A Dubious Heritage; The Deeper Life; Marx's Social Critique of Culture; The Common Life; Passage to Modernity: An Essay in the Hermeneutics of Nature and Culture,* and most recently *The Enlightenment and the Intellectual Development of Modern Culture.* He served as guest editor for the issue of the *American Catholic Philosophical Quarterly* dedicated to Nicholas of Cusa and coedited *Light from Light: An Anthology of Christian Mysticism.* He has been President of both the American Catholic Philosophical Association and the Hegel Society of America and is a member of the American Academy of Arts and Sciences as well as a foreign member of the Royal Academy of Arts, Sciences, and Letters of Belgium.

Wilhelm Dupré is professor emeritus of the Philosophy of Religion from the University of Nijmegen. He and his wife, Dietlind, produced the three-volume translation of Cusanus's works into German *Philosophisch-theologische Schriften*. He has written an introduction to the philosophy of religion, explored the encounter of Christian faith with Islam, and edited a volume in the series of the Cusanus Study Centre, Nijmegen, *The Persistent Challenge: Religion, Truth, and Scholarship*. In English his books include *Patterns in Meaning: Reflections on Meaning and Truth in Cultural Reality, Religious Traditions, and Dialogical Encounters* and *Religion in Primitive Cultures: A Study in Ethnophilosophy*. His essays on Cusanus have treated many topics, including the idea of a new logic, the controversy concerning his conception of the knowledge of God, man as microcosm, being human and the human being as truth in becoming, the image and the truth, and love as the form or life of all the virtues. During the jubilee year 2001 he published a short anthology of Cusanus's teachings entitled *In jedem Namen wird genannt was unnennbar bleibt: Wegmarken im Denken des Nikolaus von Kues 1401–1464*. In 2002 a Festschrift edited by Inigo Bocken, Donald Duclow, Stephan van Erp, and Frans Jespers was published in his honor: *On Cultural Ontology: Religion, Philosophy and Culture: Essays in Honor of Wilhelm Dupré*.

Walter Andreas Euler has been since 2001 Ordinary Professor for Fundamental and Ecumenical Theology at the Theological Faculty of Trier. He co-edited h XIX, Fasc. I: Sermones CCIV–CCXVI, and h XIX, Fasc. 3, Sermones CCXXXII–CCXLV, and remains an official collaborator *(freier Mitarbeiter)* on the Heidelberg Academy's *Cusanus-Edition*. His books include *Unitas et Pax: Religionsvergleich bei Raimundus Lullus und Nikolaus von Kues; Cusanus und die Reform der Kirche heute; "Pia philosophia" et "docta religio": Theologie und Religion bei Marsilio Ficino und Giovanni Pico della Mirandola*, and an edition of some Latin works of Ramón Llull *(Raimundi Lulli Opera Latina, Tomus XXIII)*. His publications in English include "Does Nicholas Cusanus Have a Theology of the Cross?" *(Journal of Religion* 80 [2000]: 405–20); "Proclamation of Christ in Selected Sermons from Cusanus' Brixen Period" in *Nicholas of Cusa and His Age*, edited by Thomas M. Izbicki and Christopher M. Bellitto; and "Christ and the Knowledge of God" in *Introducing Nicholas of Cusa*, edited by Christopher M. Bellitto, Thomas M. Izbicki, and Gerald Christianson. He is currently working in the area of the theology of religions and the relationship of Christianity and Islam.

Karsten Harries is professor, former chair, and director of graduate studies in the Department of Philosophy at Yale University. He has authored more than 140 articles and reviews, and his books include *The Meaning of Modern Art; The Bavarian Rococo Church: Between Faith and Aestheticism; The Meaning of Modern Art: A Philosophical Interpretation; The Broken Frame: Three*

Lectures; The Ethical Function of Architecture, which won the American Institute of Architects' 8th Annual International Architecture Book Award for Criticism; and, most recently, *Infinity and Perspective.* With Christoph Jamme, he edited *Martin Heidegger: Kunst, Politik, Technik,* which appeared in English as *Martin Heidegger: Politics, Art, and Technology.*

Jasper Hopkins is Professor of Philosophy at the University of Minnesota at Minneapolis. He has also been a visiting professor at the University of Munich and the University of Graz (Austria) and held fellowships from National Humanities Center, John Simon Guggenheim Memorial Foundation, National Endowment for the Humanities, and the American Council of Learned Societies. His areas of interest include ancient, medieval, and Renaissance philosophy, philosophy of religion, existentialism, philosophy of history, nineteenth-century German philosophy, Kantian studies, hermeneutics, and medical ethics. He has translated and written about the philosophy and theology of Anselm of Canterbury, Nicholas of Cusa, and most recently Hugh of Balma. He has published more than twenty books of essays, translations, and editions, including *Hugh of Balma on Mystical Theology: A Translation and an Overview of His* De Theologia Mystica; *A Concise Introduction to the Philosophy of Nicholas of Cusa; Complete Philosophical and Theological Treatises of Nicholas of Cusa,* 2 vols.; *Glaube und Vernunft im Denken des Nikolaus von Kues. Prolegomena zu einem Umriß seiner Auffassung* (Trierer Cusanus Lecture, 3); *Nicholas of Cusa: Metaphysical Speculations,* 2 vols.; *Complete Philosophical and Theological Treatises of Anselm of Canterbury;* and *Philosophical Criticism: Essays and Reviews.*

Nancy Hudson completed her Ph.D. at Yale in 1999 with a doctoral thesis on "Theosis in Nicholas of Cusa: Origin, Goal, and Realized Destiny of Creation." She coauthored "Nicholas of Cusa" in *A Companion to Philosophy in the Middle Ages.* She was a Visiting Assistant Professor and a member of the Graduate Faculty in the Department of Philosophy at the University of Toledo. In the academic year 2003–2004 she was a fellow at the Center for the Study of Religion at Princeton University, pursuing research on Cusanus and environmental ethics.

Regine Kather is Professor at the Philosophisches Institut of the University of Freiburg and Visiting Professor at the University of Cluj-Napoca (Romania). Her fields of specialization include philosophy of science, philosophy of nature, philosophical anthropology (in collaboration with biological anthropology), and intercultural philosophy. She has written articles on animal ethics, Spinoza, Whitehead, Einstein, Bergson, and Hildegard of Bingen. Her books include *Die Bestimmungen von "Leben". Eine Einführung unter naturphilosophischer und anthropologischer Perspektive; "Über Sprache überhaupt und über die Sprache des Menschen." Die Sprachphilosophie Walter Benjamins; Zeit und Ewigkeit. Die Vieldimensionalität menschlichen Erlebens; Der Mensch—Kind der Natur oder des Geistes? Wege zu einer ganzheitlichen Sicht der Natur; Ordnungen der Wirklichkeit. Die Kritik der philosophischen Kosmologie am mechanistischen* Paradigma; and *Gotteshauch oder künstliche Seele? Der Geist im Visier verschiedener Disziplinen.*

Il Kim is an architect and Ph.D. candidate in architectural history at Columbia University. His dissertation is entitled "The Cult of Light in Fifteenth-Century Italian Renaissance Architecture." His publications include studies of Italian Renaissance architecture and translations into Japanese of architectural books and articles. He has also coauthored several books on contemporary architecture: *New American Additions and Renovations; The New American House 3; Studio Apartments;* and *The New American Cottage.*

Bernard McGinn is professor emeritus of the Divinity School at the University of Chicago and until May 2003 held the Naomi Shenstone Donnelley Professorship of Historical Theology and the History of Christianity there. He has written extensively in the area of the history of apocalyptic thought, which includes books such as *Antichrist: Two Thousand Years of the Human Fascination with Evil; Apocalyptic Spirituality; Apocalypticism in the Western Tradition; The Calabrian Abbot: Joachim of Fiore in the History of Western Thought; Visions of the End: Apocalyptic Traditions in the Middle Ages;* and the coedited three-volume work, *The Encyclopedia of Apocalypticism.* He has also published and edited several works on Isaac of Stella, John Scottus Eriugena, the Beguines, and Meister Eckhart, including most recently *The Mystical Thought of Meister Eckhart: The Man from Whom God Hid Nothing.* His current long-range project is a six-volume history of Christian mysticism in the West under the general title *The Presence of God,* three volumes of which have appeared: *The Origins of Mysticism; The Growth of Mysticism;* and *The Flowering of Mysticism.* In 2003 he collaborated with Patricia Ferris McGinn on *Early Christian Mystics: The Divine Vision of the Spiritual Masters.*

Cary J. Nederman is Professor and Director of Graduate Studies in the department of Political Science at Texas A&M University. His most recent book, published on 2005, is *John of Salisbury,* which complements his partial translation of Salisbury's *Policraticus* (Cambridge: Cambridge University Press, 1st ed., 1990; rev. ed., 1992). He is also the author or editor of more than a dozen books, including *Worlds of Difference: European Discourses of Religious Toleration, c. 1100–c.1550; Medieval Aristotelianism and its Limits: Classical Traditions in Moral and Political Philosophy, 12th–15th Centuries; Marsiglio of Padua: Writings on the Empire;* and *Community and Consent: The Secular Political*

Theory of Marsiglio of Padua's Defensor Pacis. He coedited *Beyond the Persecuting Society: Religious Toleration before the Enlightenment* and *Three Tracts on Empire: Engelbert of Admont, Aeneas Silvius Piccolomini and Juan de Torquemada.* His other works include the coedited volumes *Speculum Sermonis: Interdisciplinary Reflections on the Medieval Sermon* and *Rhetoric and Renewal in the Latin West 1100–1500: Essays Presented to John O. Ward.* He is also the cofounder of Politicas: Society for the Study of Medieval Political Ideas.

Thomas Prügl received his Dr. Theol. in 1994 from the Ludwigs-Maximilians-Universität in Munich and is now the Tisch Family Associate Professor of Theology at the University of Notre Dame. His main areas of research are medieval ecclesiology and the history of scriptural interpretation in the Middle Ages. He has authored *Die Ekklesiologie Heinrich Kalteisens OP in der Auseinandersetzung mit dem Basler Konziliarismus.* He also edited Antonio da Cannara's *De potestate pape supra Concilium Generale contra errores Basiliensium* as well as a volume of essays to commemorate the fiftieth anniversary of Martin Grabmann's death, *Credo ut intelligam.* His current research project focuses on the interpretation of the Book of Job in the Latin Middle Ages.

Paul E. Sigmund, professor of Politics at Princeton University, is the author of numerous books and translations on the history of Western political thought, political theory, and Latin American politics. He has been a fellow at the Woodrow Wilson Center for Scholars and the Institute for Advanced Study, and has received fellowships from the National Endowment for the Humanities and the Harry Frank Guggenheim Foundation. His translation of Cusanus's *Catholic Concordance,* which was published in the "Cambridge Texts in the History of Political Thought," has become a standard reference work. His other books include *Religious Freedom and Evangelization in Latin America: The Challenge of Religious Pluralism; The United States and Democracy in Chile; Liberation Theology at the Crossroads: Democracy or Revolution? St. Thomas Aquinas on Ethics and Politics; Natural Law in Political Thought;* and *Nicholas of Cusa and Medieval Political Thought.* His most recent book is a Norton Critical Edition of *The Selected Political Writings of John Locke.*

Frank Tobin is Professor Emeritus of German at the University of Nevada, Reno. His writings cover the history of German literature and especially the medieval period. He coedited a two-volume *Survey of German Literature* and published three studies on medieval German figures: *Gregorius and Der arme Heinrich: Hartmann's Dualistic and Gradualistic Views of Reality; Meister Eckhart: Thought and Language;* and *Mechtild von Magdeburg: A Medieval Mystic in Modern Eyes.* In addition, he translated and edited both Mechtild of Magdeburg's *Flowing Light of the Godhead* and Henry Suso's *The Exemplar* (with two

German sermons) and was cotranslator of *Meister Eckhart: Teacher and Preacher.* All three of these volumes were published by Paulist Press in the series "The Classics of Western Spirituality." He was also cotranslator of the complete works of the Middle High German epic poet and minnesinger Hartmann von Aue.

Morimichi Watanabe is President of the American Cusanus Society and editor of *American Cusanus Society Newsletter* since 1984. His publications include *The Political Ideas of Nicholas of Cusa with Special Reference to His* De Concordantia Catholica (Geneva, 1963), and numerous articles on Renaissance thought, political and legal theory, and Nicholas of Cusa, some of which can be found in the Variorum reprint *Concord and Reform: Nicholas of Cusa and Legal and Political Thought in the Fifteenth Century* (Aldershot, 2001), which was edited by Thomas M. Izbicki and Gerald Christianson. There is also a volume of essays, also edited by Christianson and Izbicki, published in his honor in 1991: *Nicholas of Cusa in Search of God and Wisdom.*

⚮ Index of Names

Index of Subjects

absolute maximum. *See* maximum, absolute

act of existing *(actus existendi)*. *See* actuality, God's

action, xvii, 22, 35, 99, 101, 102n, 119; causal, 77; conciliar, 177, 199; contemplation and, 31 governmental, 196; liturgical, 39–40. *See also* life: daily

actuality: God's, 76, 104, 232; of human intellect, 223–24; perfect, 223

ad infinitum, 212, 220. *See also* infinite / infinity; *nulla proportio finiti ad infinitum*

administration: decentralized, 201; fiscal, 187; *gubernatio*, 197; of justice, 190; of sacraments, 159; powers of, 205–6

aesthetics, xxiv, xxviii, 102, 106, 144, 254. *See also* beauty

affection, xv

agnosticism. *See* unknowability

alterity, xxvii. *See also* otherness

Alles–Sehende. *See* omnivoyance

amazement. *See* wonder

American Cusanus Society, ix, x, xi

analogy, 59, 69; of the sun, 230; of the word *(see* naming, theology of*)*

angels / angelic, 8, 13, 202

apophaticism. *See* God, as invisible or unknowable; *via negativa*

archbishop. *See* bishop

arithmetic, 107, 214n14

art. *See* craft / artisanry; history: of art

Art amativa (Ramón Llull), 69

ascent: numerical, 211, 215, 216, 217, 221; soul's, 30

assimilation, xv, xxvii, 91, 96–98, 104; active, 99; to wisdom, 97. *See also* likeness

atheism, 74

atonement, theory of, 61–67, 71

audience, as addressee of a sermon, 1, 2

authority, ecclesiastical, xiv, 152–77; imperial, 178–95, 197–208; of Cicero, 122–23; of God, 154, 163; of Pope, xvii, xxv, 152–77; of Scripture, 154; universal, 191; *See also* name index, Nicholas of Cusa: works of: *De auctoritate praesidendi*

autopoetic process, xv, 101

autonomy: of nation-state, 180, 186, 190–91; of will, 62 *(see also* will, free*)*

Basel, Council of. *See under* Council / s

beatitude. *See* vision, beatific

beauty, xv, xxviii, xxix; absolute, 126; and call of the beloved, 126; defined by proportion and resplendence, 124; enables vision, 124; of human body, 126; God's, 102n; principle of human activity and culture, 102; splendor of form, 125; unity of, 102; two kinds of, 125; Virgin Mary's, 63; of the visible, 116. *See also* aesthetics

being, 6n7, 77; absolute, 75, 226–31, 238, 249; of being, xiv; of Christ, 17; conceptual, 115; creature's *esse* as identical to God's, 76; dependent *(esse ab alio)*, 75–76; finite, 81, 223n40, 227, 229–33; God as, xiv, xx, 2, 3, 8–9, 10, 71–88, 118, 227–28, 232, 234; hierarchy of, 239; beyond immanence and transcendence, 77; infinite, 229, 231, 234; scholastic account of, xxii *(see also* scholasticism); spiritual, 14, 85; uncreated, 77; well-, 89, 200, 208

belief. *See* faith

Bernkastel-Kues, xi, xii, xx, xxii

beyond opposites, 230. *See also* God, beyond coincidence of opposites

bible. *See* Scripture

bishop / s, xx, 1, 41, 75–76, 107n6, 156–58, 160n20, 168n37, 169, 202, 203, 204. *See also* conciliarism; Rome, bishop of

body: animal life, 95n12; beauty of, 126; and corporeal elements, 3, 13; human, 124; man's as measure, 120; and perception, 18; and soul, 16–17. *See also* name index, Christ, body of; sensibility / sensation / sense perception

Bonum est diffusivum sui, 86

bread: Christ as, xiii, 3–4, 18; necessary for both heavenly and earthly natures, 15; our daily, 3–4, 15–20. *See also* food

Brixen-Bressanone, xii, xx–xxiii

Buenos Aires, xii

Cusanus was designed and composed in Dante by Kachergis Book Design of Pittsboro, North
Carolina. It was printed on 60-pound Natures Natural and bound by Thomson-Shore, of Dexter,
Michigan.